Sorolla
THE MASTERWORKS

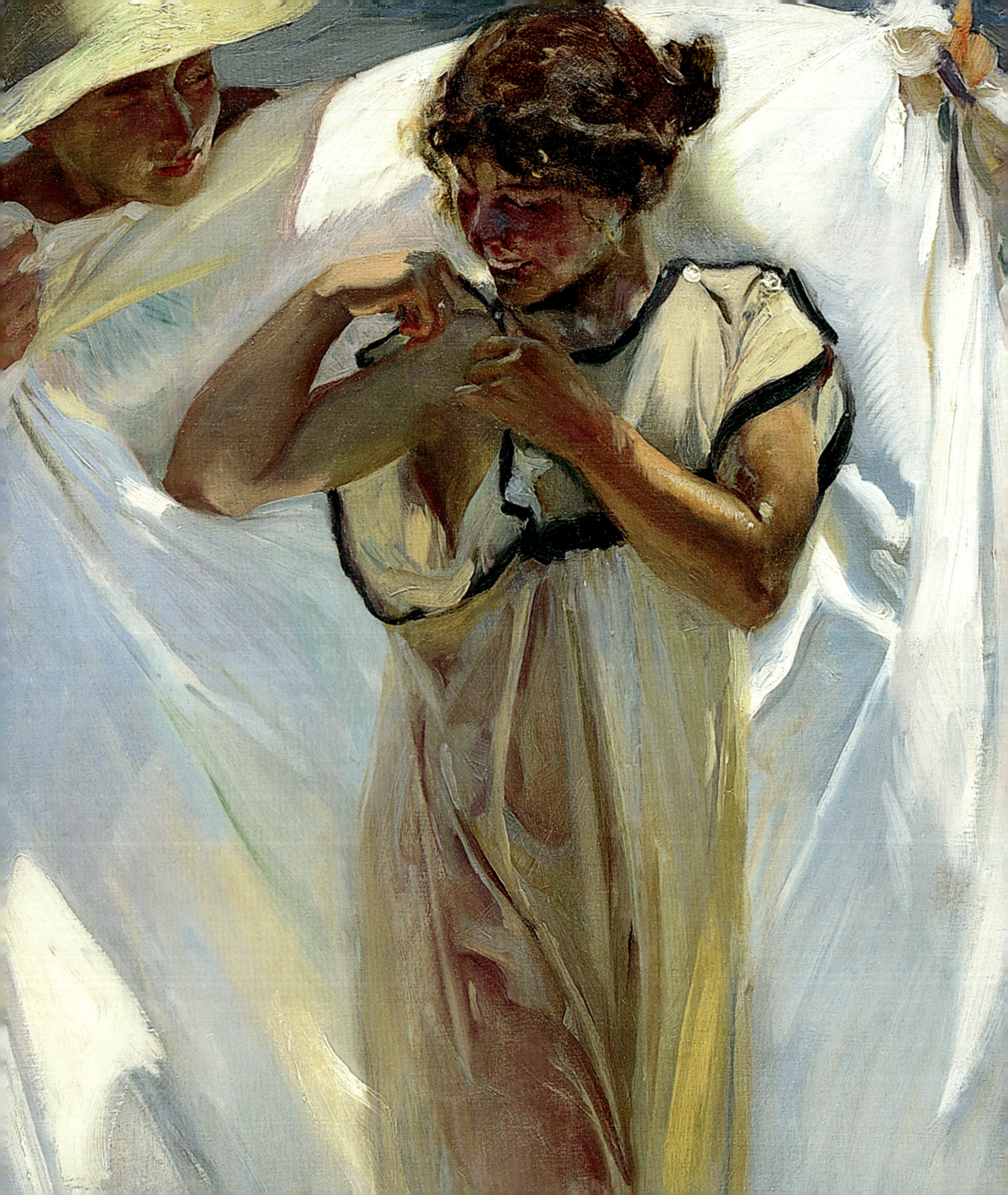

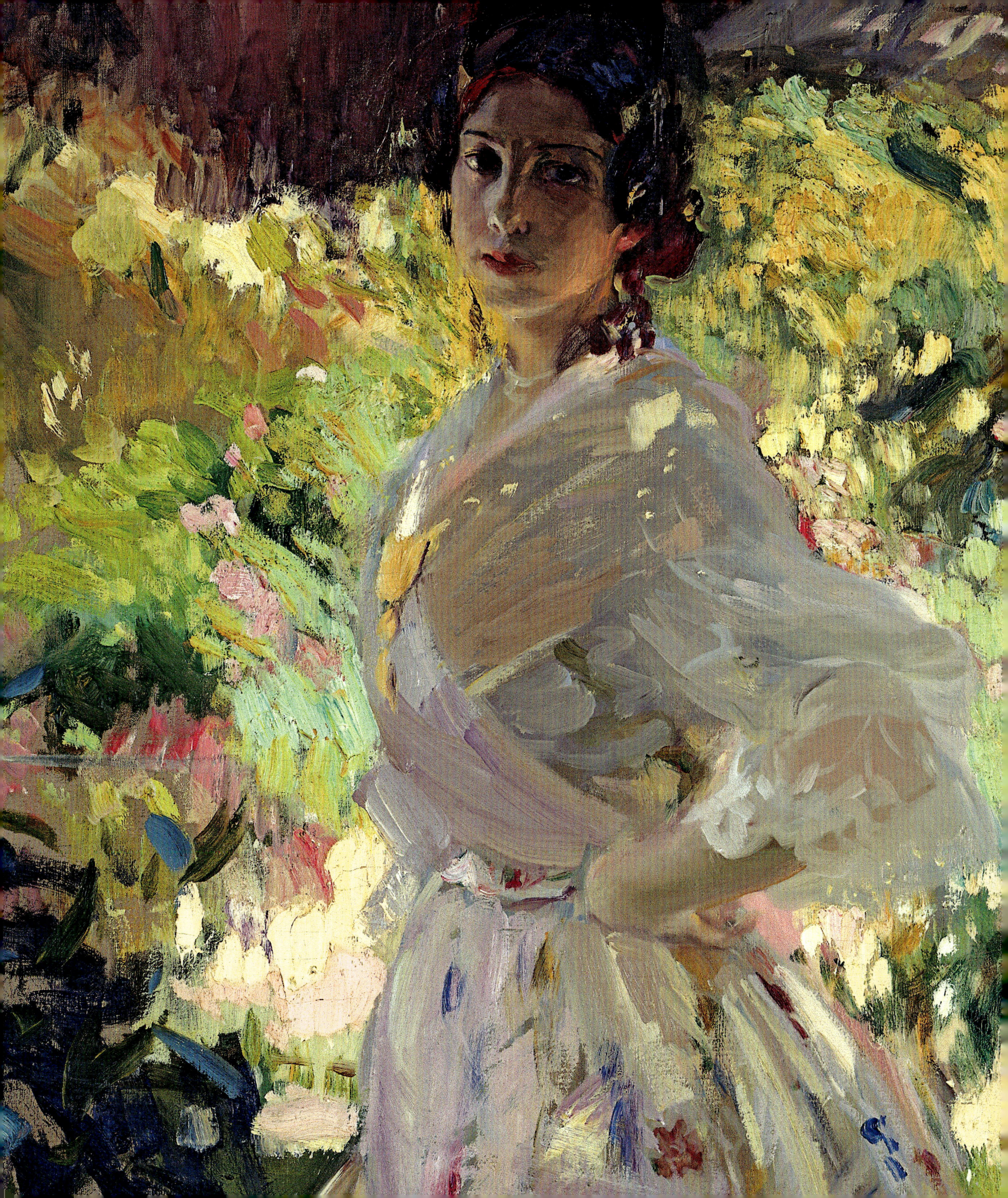

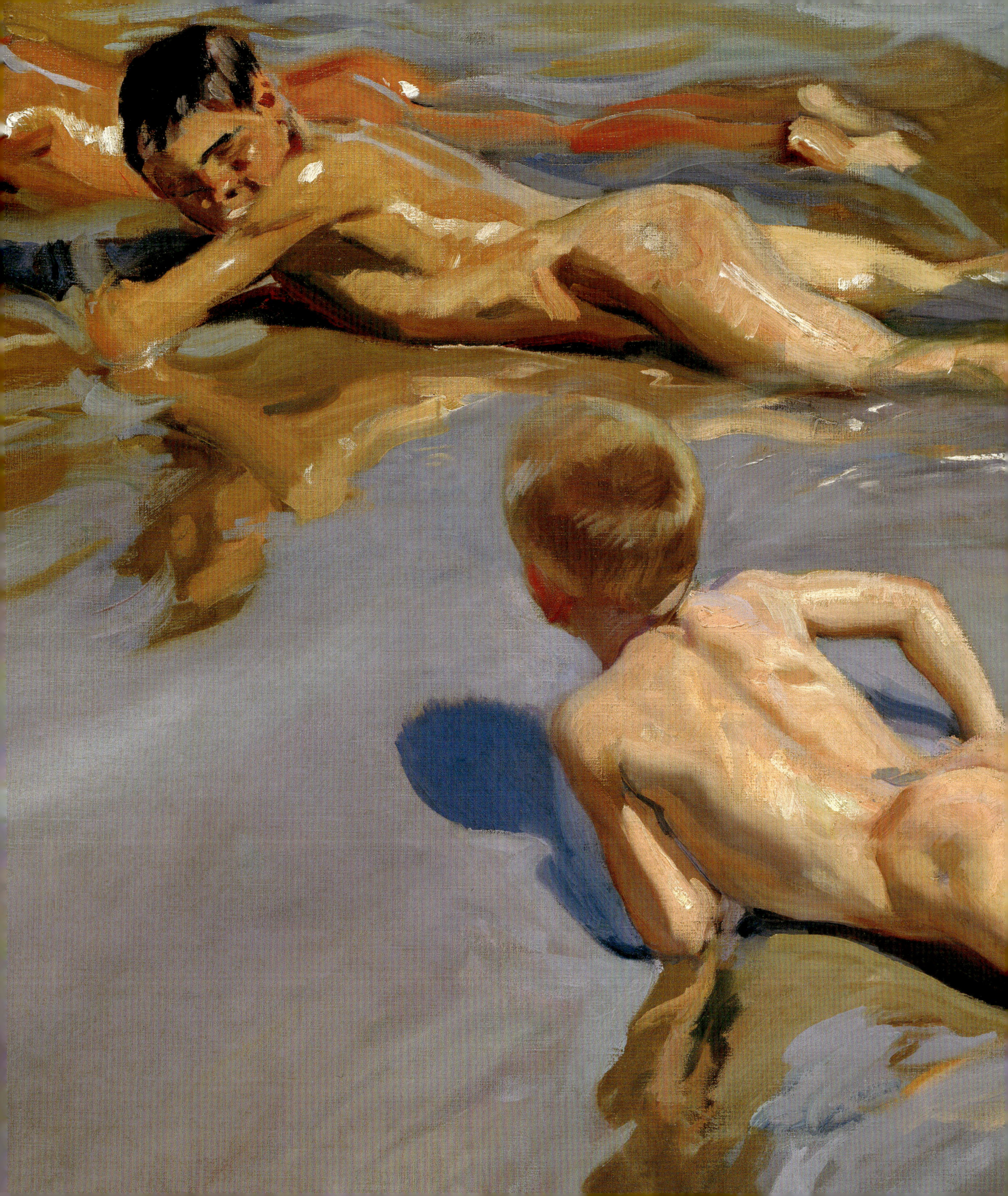

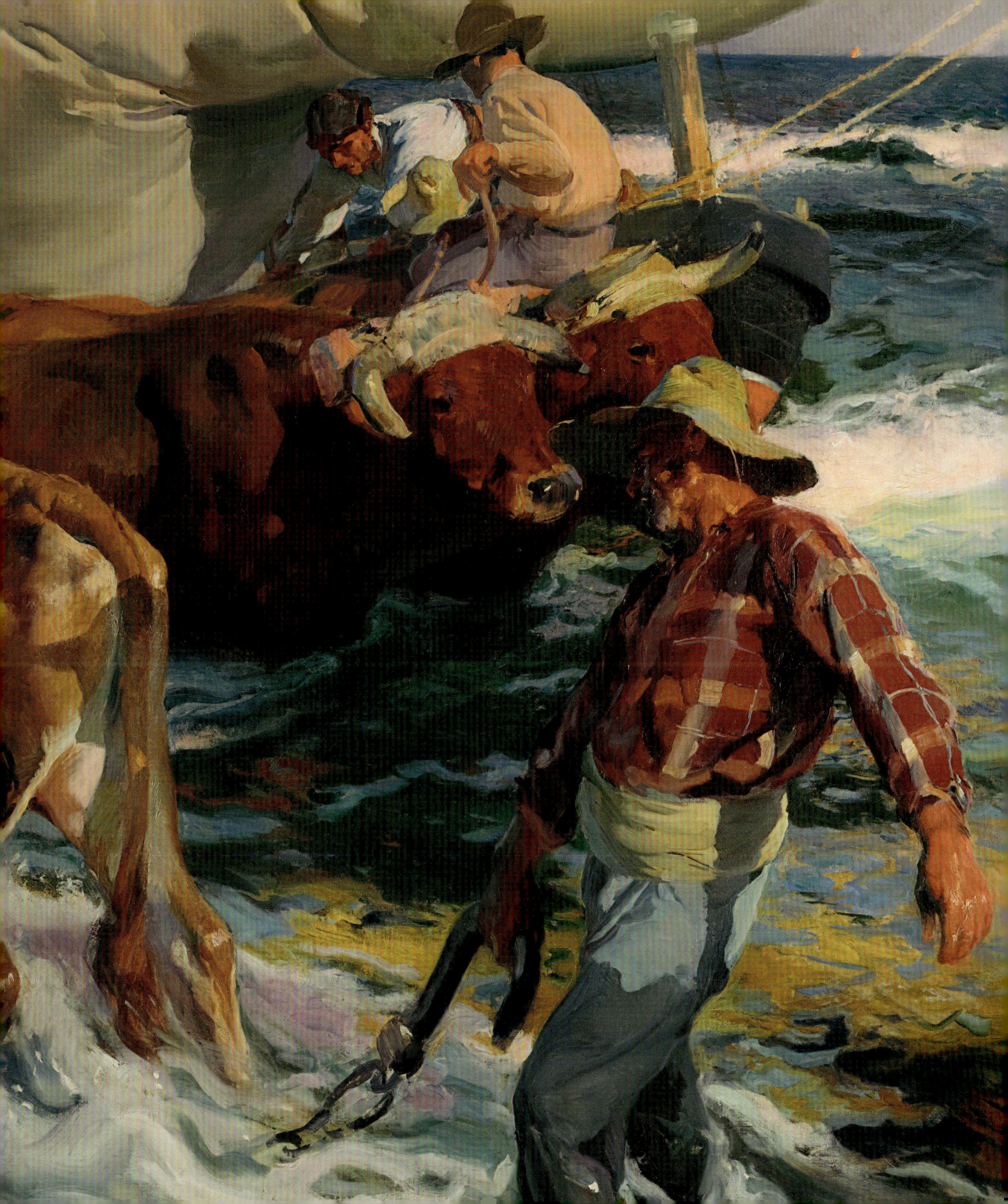

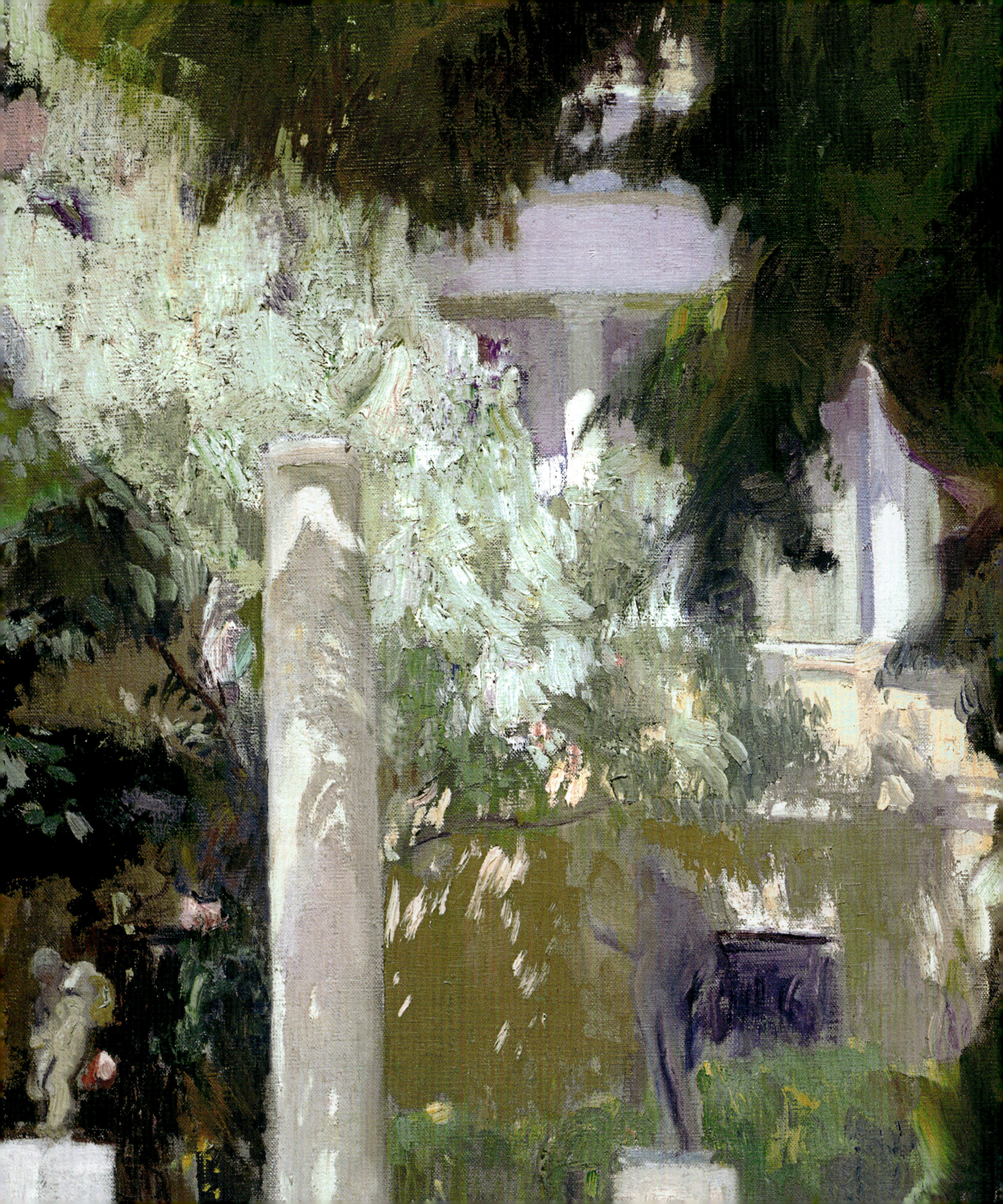

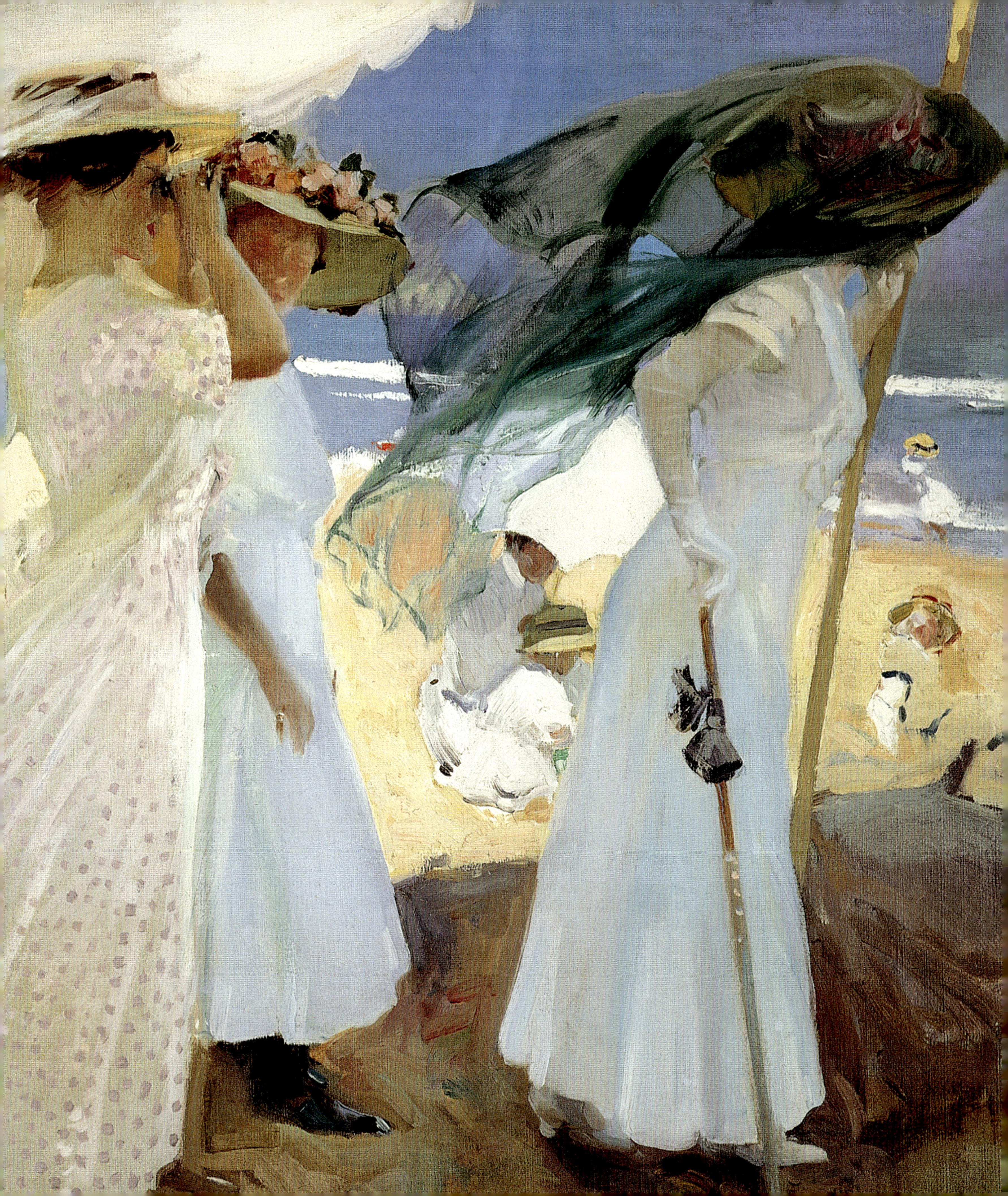

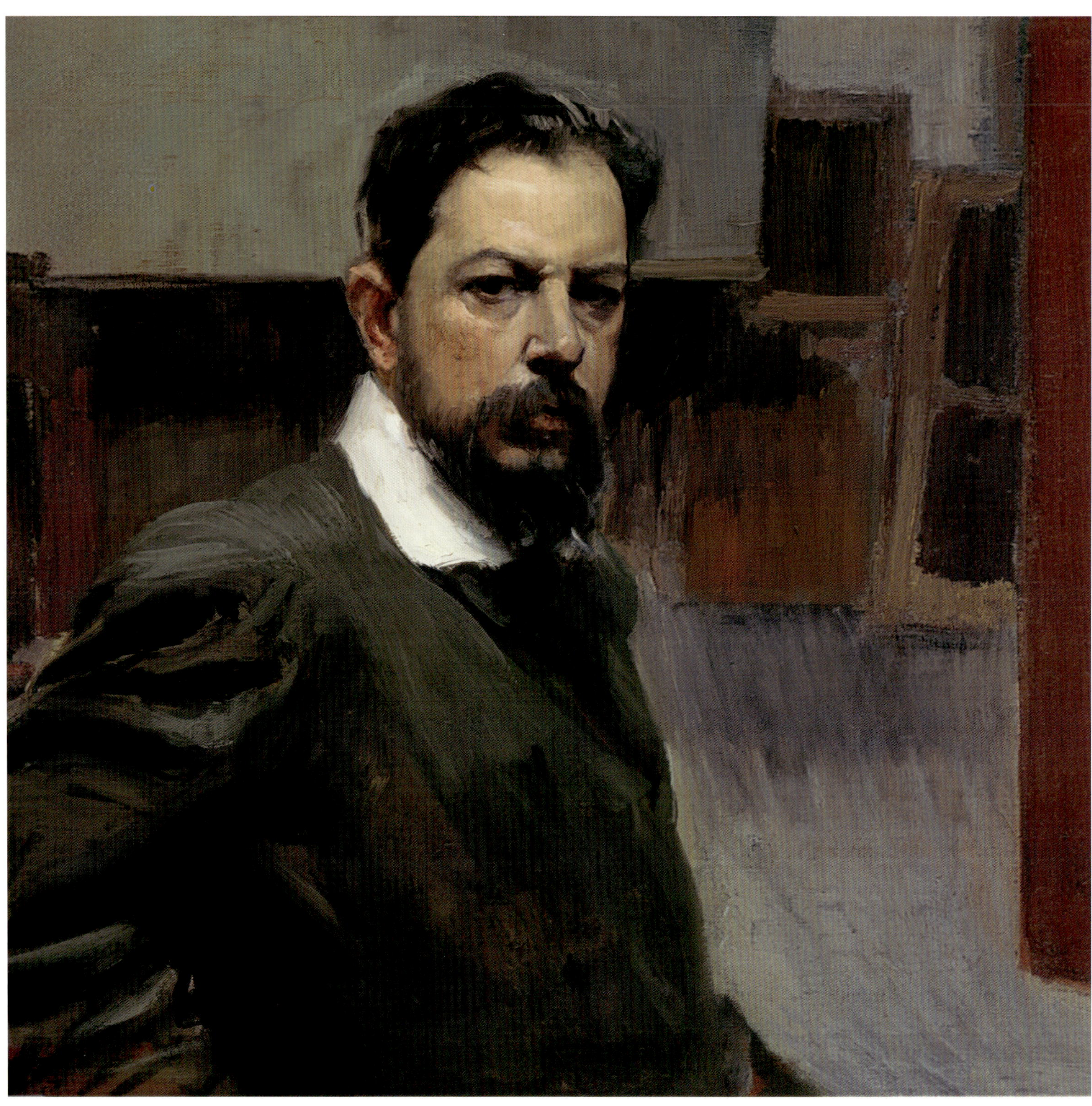

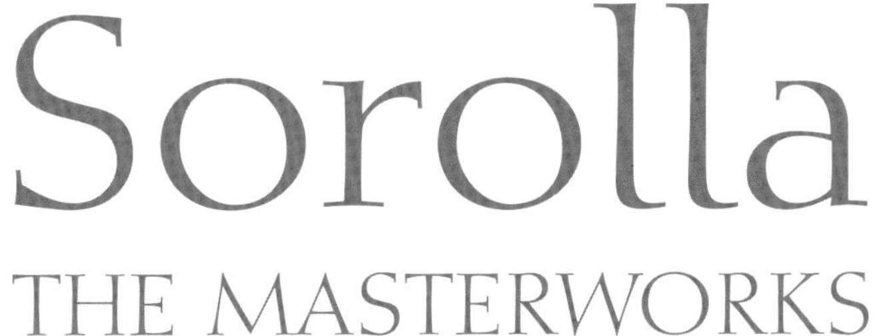

Sorolla
THE MASTERWORKS

BLANCA PONS-SOROLLA

Rizzoli Electa

Joaquín Sorolla painting *Grandmother and Granddaughter, Types from Ansó* in his studio on Paseo del Obelisco, 1911. Photograph by Ricardo del Rivero. Madrid, Museo Sorolla [80.123]

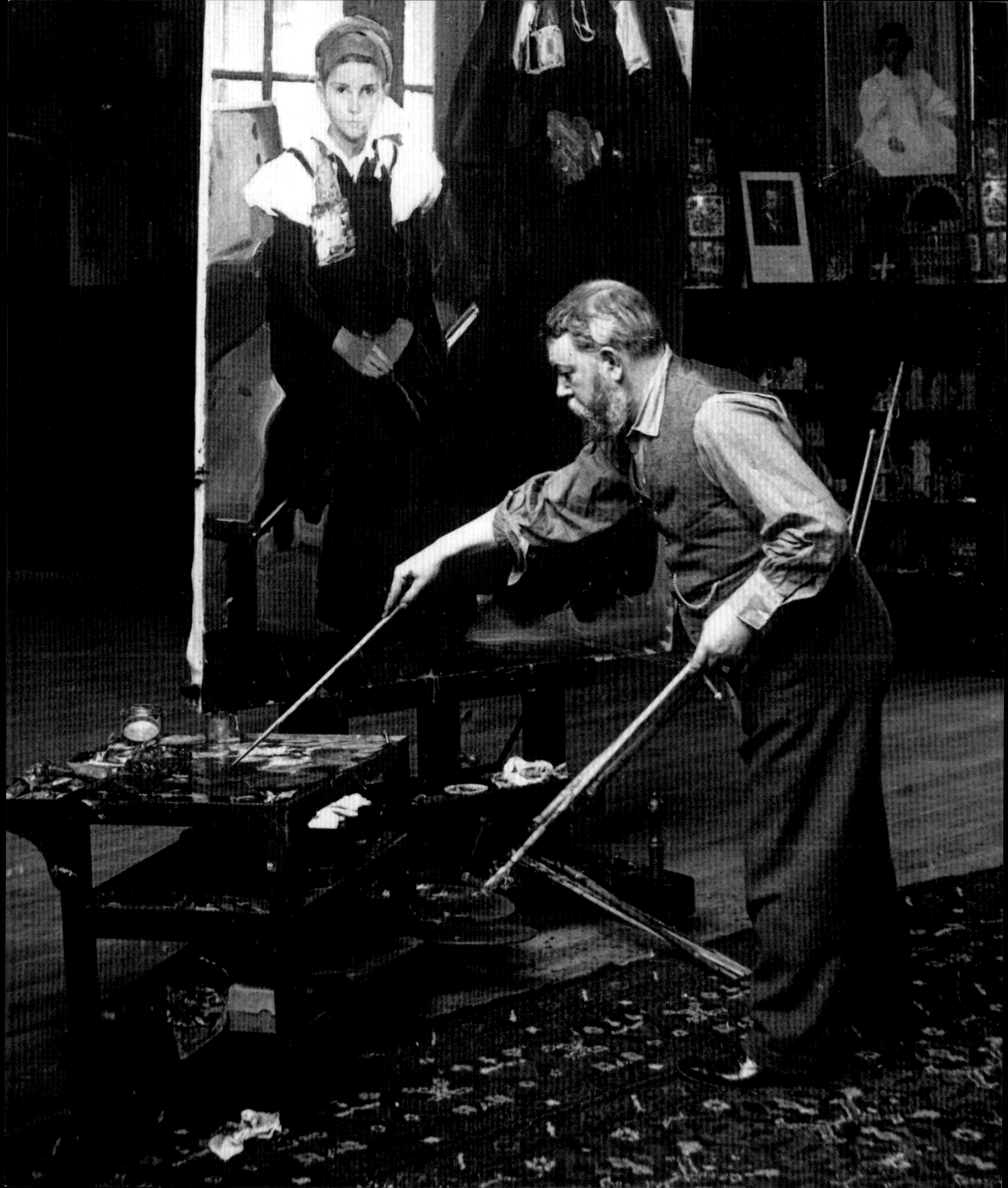

Contents

INTRODUCTION

On March 8, 1909, at the Hispanic Society of America in New York, an exhibition dedicated to the Spanish painter Joaquín Sorolla (1863–1923) came to a close. It was deemed "the most emphatic popular success ever known in the history of art in New York."[1] Since its inauguration on February 4, and despite the bad weather, the exhibit had received 159,831 visitors.[2] On Sunday, March 7, the day before the exhibit's closure, and again despite the prevailing terrible weather, 29,461 visitors came to see it. The American media, which had introduced Sorolla as "one of the leaders of the modern Spanish school,"[3] "one of the great modern masters,"[4] and "one of the half dozen (are there so many?) great living painters,"[5] said of the exhibition: "What might have been in some circumstances a mere ripple of artistic interest has risen to a tidal wave of enthusiasm."[6]

The exhibition's success was preceded by its acquisition of an outstanding reputation in Europe, where it had received various awards and triumphed at the Georges Petit Gallery in Paris in 1906 with 497 works on display. It is true that some of his other exhibits had less impact, but perhaps this was because the artist was not in attendance, as was the case during the shows in Germany in 1907 and at the Grafton Galleries in London in 1908. However, this last event precipitated an encounter with Archer Milton Huntington, who presented Sorolla with the opportunity to exhibit his works in the newly founded Hispanic Society.

This moment was the culminating point of Sorolla's artistic career. Sorolla started his artistic development in Spain with a strong academic aesthetic, which led him to create great historical paintings. However, he was later guided by teachers such as Gonzaló Salvá (1845–1923), a follower of Barbizon's landscapes, and Ignacio Pinazo Camarlench (1849–1916), who had been influenced by the works of the

Italian *macchiaioli*, toward the use of a looser technique on works in the outdoors. This technique was also developed through observation of Diego Velázquez's (1599–1660) works in the Prado Museum.

In 1885 Sorolla traveled from Rome—where he had been studying with the financial help of the Provincial Council of Valencia—to Paris, where he discovered the works of Jules Bastien-Lepage (1848–1884) and Adolf von Menzel (1815–1905), two naturalist painters. They inspired Sorolla to develop a simple, naturalistic style that was very different from the strong eclecticism then current in Italy. After several experiments, Sorolla started to produce works with themes grounded in social realism, in which he gave great importance to color and with which he triumphed in nationwide competitions. This led to more *costumbrista* paintings; those with sailors and fishermen as subjects show Sorolla's attention to the sun's reflection on the sea's surface and the white sails and cloths. This is when Sorolla began to develop his name as a portrait painter and accumulate a considerable clientele.

His participation at the Spanish Pavilion of the Universal Exposition of Paris in 1900 won him the Grand Prix, but more importantly, it gave him the opportunity to observe works by painters who were influenced by Velázquez, Delacroix, and photography,[7] such as the Nordic painters Anders Zorn (1860–1920) and Peder Severin Krøyer (1851–1909), and the American painters James Abbott McNeill Whistler (1834–1903), John Singer Sargent (1856–1925), William Merritt Chase (1849–1916), Alexander Harrison (1853–1930), Cecilia Beaux (1855–1942), and Gari Melchers (1860–1932). All of these painters can be placed within the naturalist movement, although they each developed their own personal style within naturalism. This was also the case with Sorolla, who, seeing the support of his critics and public, dedicated himself freely to themes that he truly liked to paint: *costumbrismo* (everyday life) and beach landscapes. And paint he did: his works reach four thousand in number, in addition to around eight thousand drawings.[8]

At times he was criticized for painting too swiftly, thereby not paying sufficient attention to the minute details. To this Sorolla would retort: "Even if I wanted to, it would be impossible for me to paint slowly outdoors…none of what surrounds us is static.… But even if everything was fixed and stagnant, it would just take the sun's movement, which is continuous, to change the scene being observed…."[9]

His emphasis on capturing the light's effects caused him to be viewed as an impressionist painter, even though his style does not fit neatly within that definition. Impressionist painters attempted to express light through the application of small brushstrokes with pure colors, and they left the representation of forms and volumes on the back burner, while Sorolla never stopped being a naturalist painter, attaching importance to the effect light had on different surfaces. His skill in capturing light came from his mastery in handling shadows, for which he lightened earthy, opaque colors and avoided the "chocolate brown" used by former masters. From the impressionists, he valued what he considered the greatest development in painting since Velázquez: the color violet.[10]

It is difficult to find a definition that encompasses Sorolla's pictorial style. He even said himself that an artist's job should be to "express his internal ego," and worrying about tradition served only to create mistrust in oneself, imitate others, and doubt one's abilities. The absence of a pictorial tradition in the United States was, in his opinion, beneficial to American artists in letting them avoid preconceived notions on art, which propelled them to search for truth and steered them directly toward nature.[11]

One of the best examples of his fruitful career was the Hispanic Society exhibition in 1909. Among the 356 works on display, of which 195 were sold, were beach, countryside and garden scenes, as well as portraits and sketches for future great works.

The works that show scenes of Mediterranean beaches, painted entirely outdoors, had the greatest success and gave Sorolla his fame. The intense light is clearly the main protagonist in the paintings that depict the arrival and departure of boats, life by the sea, and children swimming. In these works the brushstrokes are loose and energized, and he uses bright colors such as cobalt and navy blue, greens, and yellows. In later years, these hues would decrease in intensity and the color white, reinforced with violet shadows, would become more important.

Sorolla also painted northern beaches and countrysides later on in his artistic career, although in these works the palette was dimmed to reproduce a softer light, much like the works of the Swedish painter Zorn. These later paintings resemble sketches and are of simple subjects, with a predominance of light colors and lighting effects such as chiaroscuro.

From 1907, gardens were common subjects in Sorolla's artistic output. In the New York exhibition, there were several works that depicted the gardens of La Granja and the Alcázar in Seville. Later on, he worked in the Alhambra and the Generalife in Granada, again in Seville, and, most importantly, in the garden of his own home in Madrid. In all of these gardens he looks for photographic framing and daring angles, and he works with a sketch technique, with loose brushstrokes in rich colors, capturing the way shadows and light interact and showing a great interest in reflections.

Sorolla's portraits represent a very important section of his artistic output. Declaring on several occasions that he felt particularly proud of other types of work, such as his *Return from Fishing* (1894), *Afternoon Sun, Beaching the Boat* (1903), or *Leonese Peasants* (1907), the artist did not, however, consider himself a specialist in portraits. He believed he would never be one, because he was unwilling to lose his freedom and his prime interest was to paint the sun.[12] However, portraits were his foremost source of income. Sargent himself encouraged Sorolla to stay in London and make a business out of this genre.[13] In fact, many of the portraits he painted of his family served as a portfolio for future clients. At the 1909 exhibit, Sorolla's goal was reached and indeed surpassed: the painter received a great number of commissions, more than he could handle.[14] He even traveled to Washington, D.C., to paint a portrait for President William Howard Taft at the White House. He decided to stay in New York through June to finish up several portraits, among which were those of Mrs. Morgan and Mrs. Huntington. He must have enjoyed working in New York, because on several occasions he stated that the light in the American city was identical to that of Madrid, with the same sun and the same blue sky.[15] This contrasts greatly with his view of Paris and especially of London, where the sky was "gray, gray, gray, always gray."[16]

Sorolla's portraits progressed from a naturalist style that used dark colors from which the more important elements of a work emerged, such as the face or the hands, toward a more personal style that used less meticulous and looser brushstrokes. He continued using a dark palette but increased his precision in capturing light. His illustration of the effects of light, which filters through foliage to the ground, through the environment and the subjects, is the real protagonist of his outdoor portraits. In the United States, he adapted to the refined tastes of his more elegant clientele, working in a style similar to the great portrait painter John Singer Sargent, although he made sure to keep present his mastery of light.[17]

After the exhibition in New York, a few of his works were presented at the Fine Arts Academy in Buffalo and at the Copley Society in Boston. In 1911 Sorolla repeated his previous success with exhibitions at the Art Institute in Chicago and the City Art Museum in Saint Louis. In November of that same year, Sorolla signed a contract in Paris with Archer Milton Huntington to create monumental works that would represent motifs in the life of Spain and would serve to decorate the library at the Hispanic Society. This project would keep him busy for the last years of his life, although it did not prevent him from creating other works.

Exactly one hundred years after the successful exhibition in 1909, the Prado Museum in Madrid held a retrospective on the artist that drew 459,267 visitors, the largest number for any exhibit over the past decade.[18] The public has kept its loyalty to Sorolla, who was the Spanish painter with the greatest international impact of his time,[19] and whose fame provided him with an economic and social status that had previously been unthinkable for a painter. His works, of a realist nature, did not need to depend on complex codes for iconographic interpretation, although in the case of the portraits from the Belle Époque, the code is a universal and timeless one. His way of capturing light, the resonance of his brushstrokes, and the way he framed his paintings in a photographic style have all maintained a distance from transient trends.

Sorolla, referring to his exhibition at the 1895 Salon, lamented that the luminosity of his work seemed depleted by the cold light of Paris.[20] However, even in the current gray times, Sorolla's great works shine as brightly as ever.

NOTES

1. "As Sorolla Sees Art in Europe and America," *The New York Times* (March 14, 1909).
2. Thomas R. Ybarra, "The American Success of a Great Spanish Painter," *The World's Work*, XVIII, 1 (1909), p. 1556.
3. "Sorolla and Others," *New-York Daily Tribune* (February 7, 1909).
4. "Art at Home and Abroad. The Paintings of Senor Sorolla y Bastida, Now on Exhibition at the Hispanic Society Museum, Show Him to be One of the Great Modern Masters," *The New York Times* (February 14, 1909).
5. "Sorolla y Bastida," *The Sun* (February 14, 1909).
6. Henry Tyrrell, "Sorolla's 300 Sunny Spanish Pictures," *The Evening World* (February 27, 1909).
7. Tomàs Llorens, "Sargent, Sorolla y el arte moderno," in *Sargent/Sorolla* [exhibition catalog], Madrid, Museo Thyssen-Bornemisza, 2006, p. 5.
8. Blanca Pons-Sorolla, "La personalidad artística de Sorolla," in José Luis Díez and Javier Barón (eds.), *Joaquín Sorolla, 1863–1923* [exhibition catalog], Madrid, Museo Nacional del Prado, 2009, p. 177.
9. Bernardino de Pantorba, *La vida y la obra de Joaquín Sorolla. Estudio biográfico y crítico*, Madrid, Extensa, 1970, p. 60.
10. William E. B. Starkweather, "Joaquín Sorolla. The Man and His Work," in *Eight Essays on Joaquín Sorolla y Bastida*, New York, Hispanic Society of America, 1909, Vol. II, pp. 40 and 45.
11. "As Sorolla Sees Art in Europe and America," *The New York Times* (March 14, 1909).
12. "Sorolla Prolongs His Visit Here," *The New York Times* (March 15, 1909).
13. Blanca Pons-Sorolla, "Retrato de María Lorente, señora de Rodríguez," in Tomàs Llorens and Boye Llorens (dirs.), *Retratos de la Belle Époque* [exhibition catalog], Madrid, Consorcio de Museos de la Comunidad Valenciana, Fundación "La Caixa" and Ediciones El Viso, 2011, p. 110.
14. Ybarra 1909, p. 1555.
15. "As Sorolla Sees Art in Europe and America," *The New York Times* (March 14, 1909).
16. "Sorolla Prolongs His Visit Here," *The New York Times* (March 15, 1909).
17. José Luis Díez and Javier Barón, "Joaquín Sorolla, pintor," in José Luis Díez and Javier Barón (eds.), *Joaquín Sorolla, 1863–1923* [exhibition catalog], Madrid, Museo Nacional del Prado, 2009, p. 92.
18. Isabel Lafont, "La exposición de Sorolla en el Prado se convierte en la más vista de la década," *El País* (September 15, 2009).
19. Díez and Barón 2009, p. 20
20. Javier Barón Thaidigsmann, "La vuelta de la pesca," in José Luis Díez and Javier Barón (eds.), *Joaquín Sorolla, 1863–1923* [exhibition catalog], Madrid, Museo Nacional del Prado, 2009, p. 240.

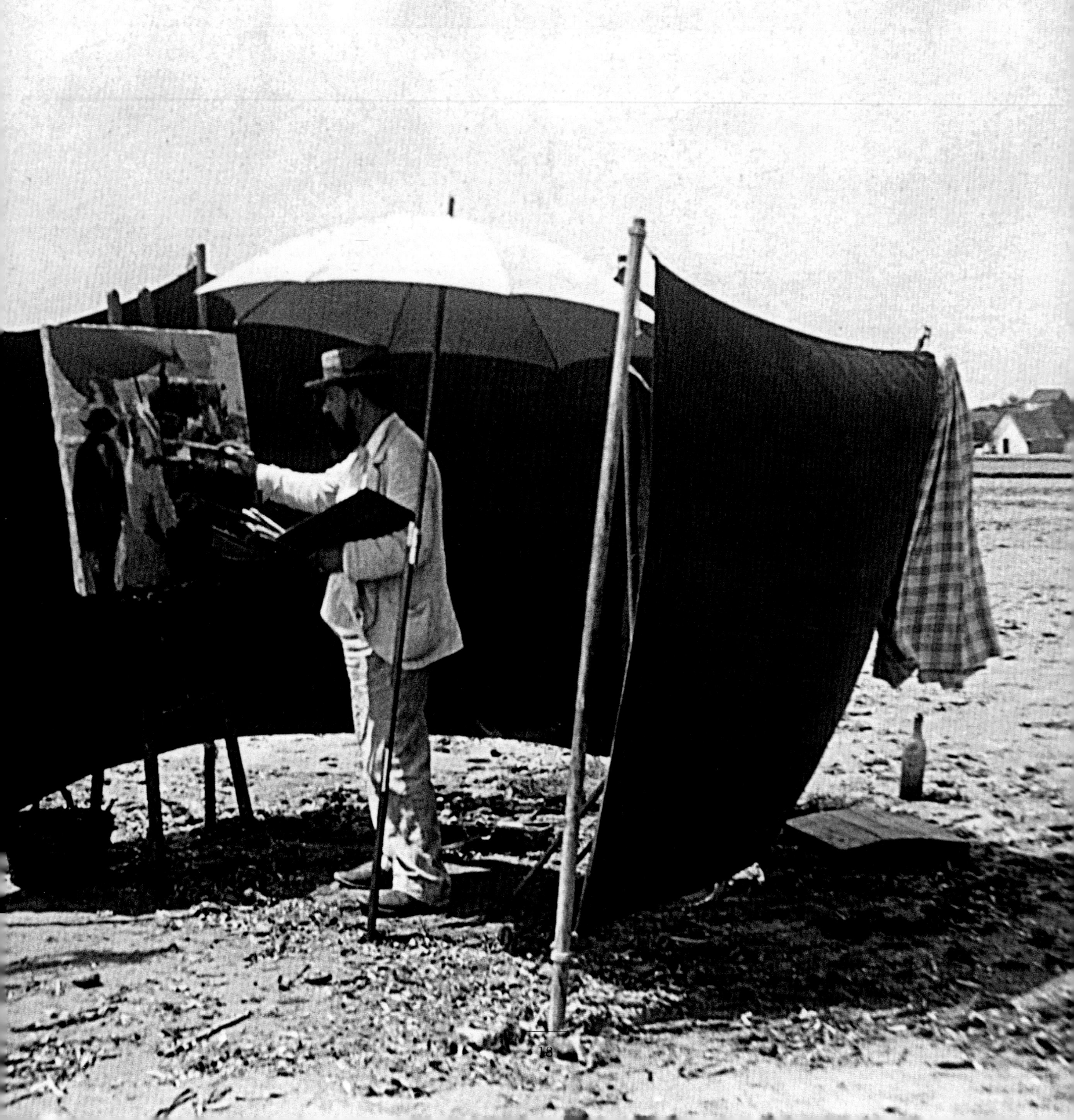

TRAINING AND DEVELOPMENT (1880–1903)

Joaquín Sorolla painting *Valencia Beach, Afternoon Sun*, 1901. Madrid, Museo Sorolla [80.022]

Joaquín Sorolla was born in Valencia in 1863 and died in Cercedilla, a town in the Sierra de Guadarrama near Madrid, in 1923. His artistic career lasted from 1880 to 1920, when he suffered a brain hemorrhage that permanently retired him from painting. The forty years he spent painting were incredibly productive and left an extensive pictorial legacy comprising four thousand works. During these years he did nothing but paint, as he said to his wife in a letter: "I have already told you about my day, … I always tell you the same thing, I paint and I love you, and that's it: isn't that enough??"[1]

His fulfillment as a painter went hand in hand with his fulfillment as a person, and we have the possibility of verifying this through the daily correspondence he maintained with his wife when they could not be together. The biographical information given here is mainly based on this interesting correspondence.[2]

Joaquín Sorolla's father was a simple textile merchant who had established his business in Valencia years before marrying. In 1865, and with a difference of only three days, Sorolla's parents became victims of the cholera epidemic that devastated Valencia. Sorolla was orphaned at the age of only two. He was taken in and cared for with great affection by his childless aunt and uncle. She was his mother's sister, he a locksmith.

His first years in Valencia were spent either at school or at the shop of his uncle, José Piqueres, who merits our gratitude, for he noticed the child's abilities and his passion for drawing and encouraged him to take night classes and study painting at the School for Artisans.

This moment was the beginning of his training, which went from his first steps as a painter until the year 1903. This apprenticeship, he would later say, was what he used to reach and secure his ideal. During this phase he discovered his two great loves, which were to accompany him through the rest of his life: his painting and his family. This period of formation can be divided into two stages, one consisting of his academic training, which lasted until the year 1889, and the other of his creative growth from 1890 to 1903, which leads up to his full development as a painter.

His academic training started at the age of fifteen at the Fine Arts Academy of San Carlos in Valencia. Here the young Sorolla met his future father-in-law, Antonio García, a well-known Valencian photographer who was very interested in painting. Upon finding out about young Sorolla's precarious financial situation, he offered to pay for his studies in exchange for Sorolla doing small jobs as an illuminator at his photography studio. At García's house, Sorolla met and fell in love with Clotilde, the third of his five children, who in time would become Sorolla's wife.

In 1881, he traveled for the first time to Madrid and discovered Velázquez, whom he studied in great depth at the Prado Museum. From this point on, Velázquez was his "great master," and his influence was consistently apparent throughout Sorolla's work.

In 1883, at the age of twenty, he received his first gold medal at the Regional Exposition of Valencia with a painting influenced by Francisco Domingo. The next year, he received a second medal at the National Exhibition of Fine Arts in Madrid with a picture of a historical subject that he painted in the corrals of Valencia's bullring, and in which he used fireworks in order to create the artillery smoke. He evidently had an innate tendency toward realism and painting in the outdoors.

In 1884, after submitting a picture on a Valencian historical theme, Sorolla was awarded a grant to study painting in Rome by the Council of Valencia. He traveled to Rome in January 1885, briefly interrupting his stay there to visit Paris for some months with Pedro Gil Moreno de Mora,[3] who was to become a great friend in the future. He hoped to find the winds of change and renovation that de Mora assured him were there. He visited museums, that year's Salon, and Jules Bastien-Lepage's and Adolf von Menzel's exhibitions.[4] This trip was decisive in his evolution toward painting light. There he became conscious that his painting was linked to realization in the outdoors, which was currently popular in Paris and at the same time very much against the aesthetic traditions of the period.

Upon his return to Rome, and following the school's and his director's suggestions, Sorolla began work on a religious painting, *The Burial of Christ*,[5] which he hoped to send to the National Exhibition the following year, and which took him more than a year to complete. The unfavorable criticism and lack of recognition from the judges led him to seclude himself in Assisi, away from the bustle of Rome, where he submerged himself in a state of reflection. Here he painted his last piece for submission to the Council of Valencia, which allowed his grant to be extended for one more year.

In September 1888, one year before his definitive return to Spain, Sorolla married Clotilde in Valencia, immediately returning to Italy with his new wife and once again establishing himself in Assisi. There he lived a happy and tranquil life, dedicating his time to painting while enjoying his wife's company and care. From this point on, Clotilde was his companion, his children's mother, and his model. She always looked after her husband and was ever willing to fix any problem that might arise, thereby giving him the tranquillity he needed to paint. The way in which she fully accepted what the painter considered his life can be seen in a letter from 1908: "I understand that for a man like you, one who puts being a painter ahead of being

Joaquín Sorolla painting *Messalina in the Arms of the Gladiator* in the studio of Pedro Gil Moreno de Mora in Rome. On the back wall, *The Burial of Christ*, 1886. Madrid, Museo Sorolla [80.009]

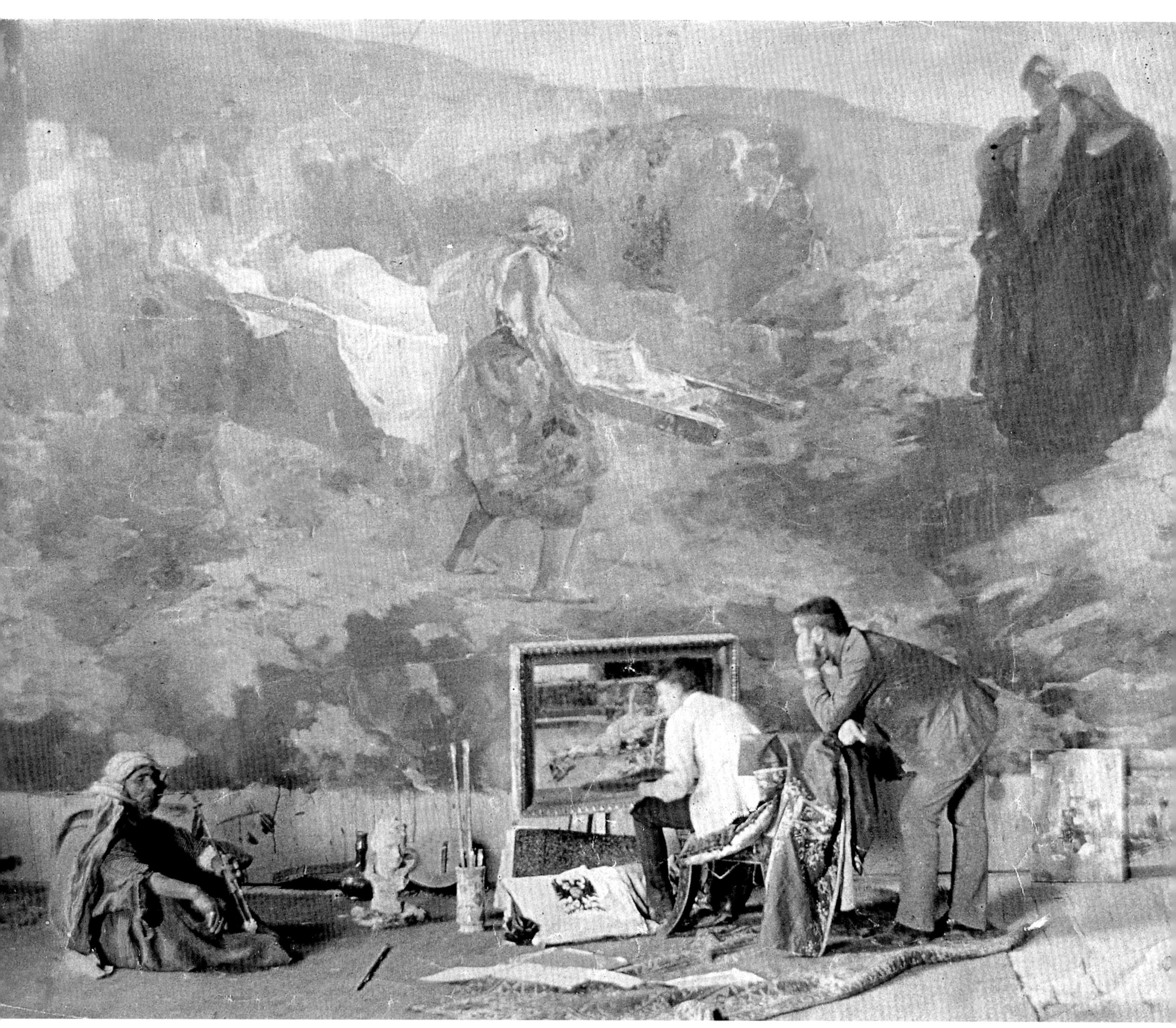

husband and father, you would prefer to paint everything else."[6] *Clotilde Contemplating the Venus de Milo* [fig. 9], a portrait painted as a gift for his in-laws, and one of the many he would paint of her, categorizes her as a model among the classical canons of beauty.

When he returned to Spain, it was with his future artistic career in mind that they decided to move to Madrid, where in a few months his first daughter, María, was born.

Settling in Madrid was the commencement of the second stage of his period of apprenticeship: his autodidactic creative development, leading to his establishment as a painter. This was the stage of his official painting career, and he sent paintings to all the important competitions and expositions, both national and international, where he procured recognition for his work. His attendance at the Salon in Paris would be constant from 1893 on.

José Jiménez Aranda and Aureliano de Beruete, two great painters, each helped him in his moments of triumph in their particular ways. Aranda advised him on the subjects to take to the expositions, while Beruete presented him as a portrait painter to Madrid's high society.

During the first three years of this period, Sorolla had three children: María in 1890, Joaquín in 1892, and Elena in 1895. Before his last daughter, Elena, was born, in 1893, the family moved to a larger and more luminous home.

The next ten years were full of innumerable exhibitions, works, and awards.

At the National Exhibition in Madrid in 1890, Sorolla came in first place with *Paris Boulevard*,[7] a work with a certain air of grandiosity painted in his study with the help of sketches he drew during visits to Paris in 1885 and 1889.

In 1892, at the International Exposition in Madrid, Sorolla presented two works that were very successful: *After the Bath* [fig. 1] and *Another Marguerite!*[8] The latter, which won first prize, was painted in a low-class carriage on a siding at Valencia's train station. Sorolla comments: "A studio in itself, except to paint a certain type of portrait, is something artificial, almost like a trick. I admit, I don't like to paint in the studio; I hate it with all my soul."[9] In 1893, with this painting, he was to win a medal of honor in Chicago.

Also in 1893, at the Salon in Paris, Sorolla was awarded the gold medal for *Kissing the Relic*,[10] which would moreover be honored with the first prize at the International Exposition in Vienna in 1894.

From the year 1894, with *The Return from Fishing* [fig. 4], Sorolla consciously found his pictorial ideal. Thereafter, he started to create works that were more personal and without constraints, the majority painted outdoors. At the same time he worked on academic paintings, which were meant for expositions, and with these he continued to win all of the top awards. He presented the painting *The Return from Fishing* at the Salon in 1895, where he was awarded the gold medal and the painting was acquired by the French State for the Musée du Luxembourg for 6,000 francs. One of the toughest art critics of that time, Charles Yriarte, anticipated the success of this painting, describing it as the most striking picture in the Salon: "C'est encore un étranger, M. Joaquín Sorolla, de Valence, qui donne ici la note retentissante et produit la grande impression." ("It is a stranger, Joaquín Sorolla of Valencia, who set the score and created the biggest impression.")[11]

When Sorolla traveled to Paris to receive his award, numerous artists and friends invited him to their homes. He writes about them to his wife:

> After lunch I went to Bonnat's house, where I had a wonderful time, for he has such a great studio with a collection of gorgeous paintings, such as Rembrandts, Grecos, Riberas, etc. that it seems to be a museum which I could never dream of having, what a life, my dear Clota…! It is a dream.

> Benjamin Constant also has a beautiful home; it has less lovely things, but, in exchange, antiquities and comfort are prominent, both of the men were very welcoming, and their compliments to my painting are unanimous.[12]

In 1894, Sorolla created his first important portrait: *Benito Pérez Galdós* [fig. 6].

At the National Exhibition in Madrid in 1895, he was awarded first prize for the painting *And They Still Say Fish Is Expensive!*,[13] [fig. 3] which was then bought by the Prado Museum.

From 1895 on, Sorolla began to really enjoy what he did for a living and to express his emotions on canvas. In 1896, upon the discovery of Jávea, a Mediterranean town close to Valencia, he sent a telegram to his wife saying: "Jávea, sublime, immense, the best place I know to paint. It inspires everything. I will stay here a few days; if you were here, it would be two months."[14] *The Cape of San Antonio, Jávea* [fig. 8], presented at the National Exhibition in Madrid the following year, particularly caught the press's attention.

At the International Exposition in Berlin in 1896, he was presented with the gold medal for *Valencian Fishermen* [fig. 5]. He would also receive a new prize at the Salon in Paris in 1897 for *Sewing the Sail* [fig. 7], a painting which was also given the Grand Prize of the Austrian State at the International Exposition in Vienna the following year.

In 1899, at the Venice Biennale, the Gallery of Modern Art in Udine acquired a fourth painting from 1892, *The Happy Day* [fig. 2].

For another painting with a social theme, *Sad Inheritance*,[15] Sorolla again received the highest accolades: the Grand Prix at the Universal Exposition in Paris in 1900 and a medal of honor at the National Exhibition in Madrid in 1901. The French State granted him the Cross of the Legion of Honor.

Despite his great success in Paris in 1900, when he traveled there to collect his award, he wrote to his wife:

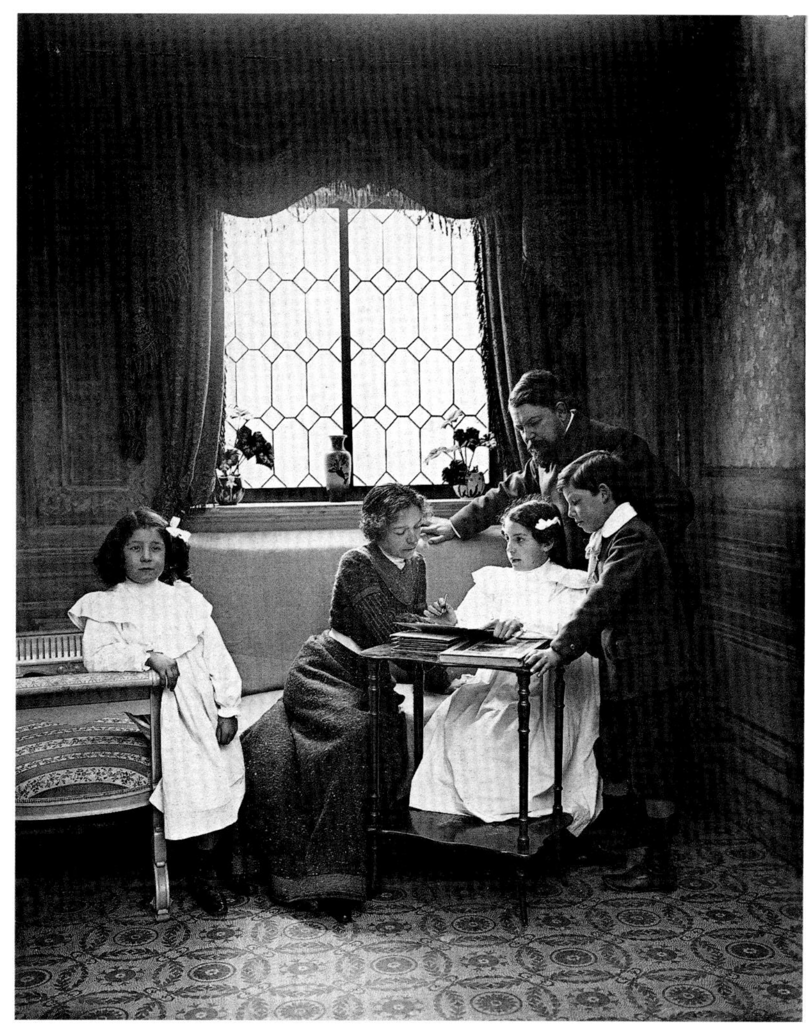

Joaquín Sorolla with his wife and children. Photograph by Antonio García Peris

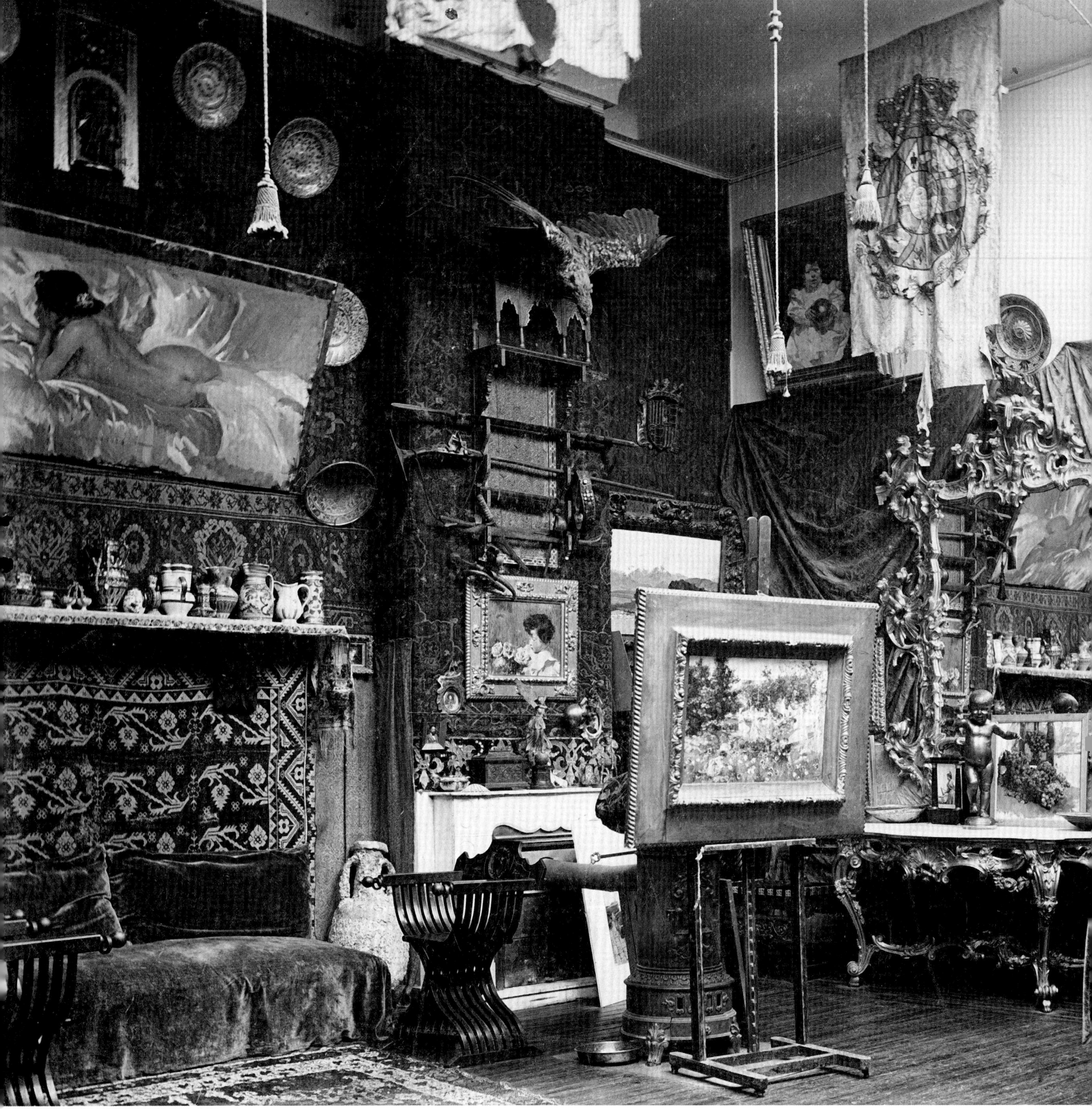

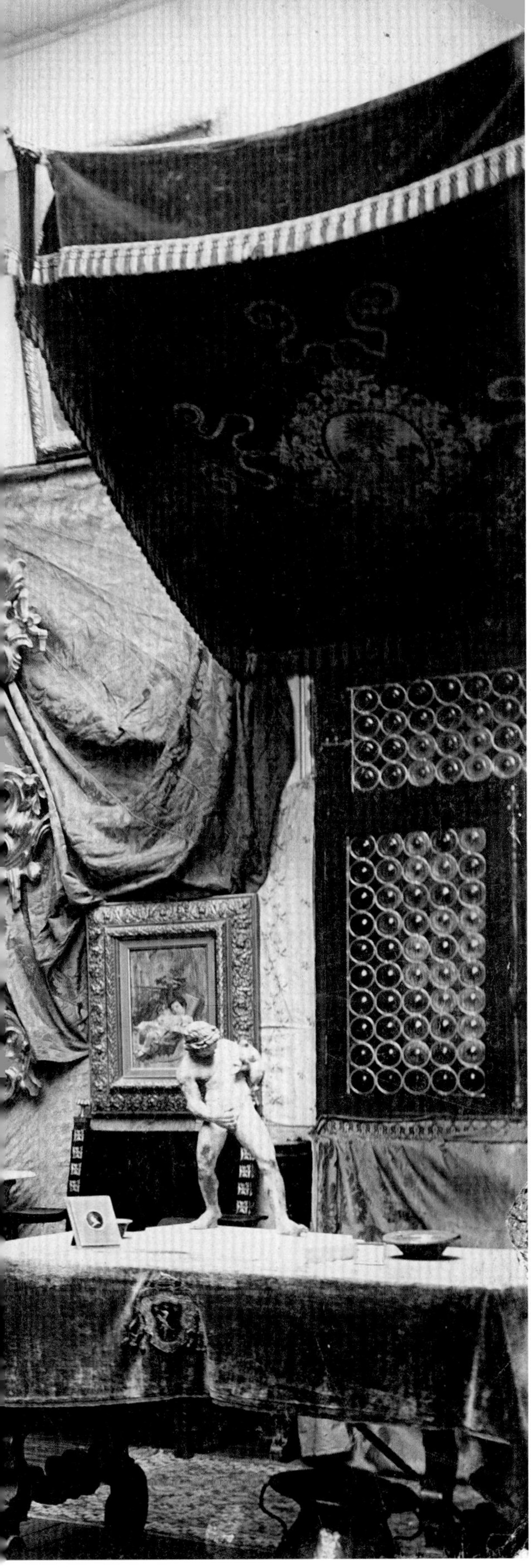

Sorolla's studio in Pasaje de la Alhambra, *c.* 1902

> Our section is dreadful in its content and its decoration; there is a great legend about the goodness of the painting, which all in all we do in the poorest and most backward-minded ways. I go more with the stream than most people, but I can and should do something more, and I will; my blood already boils from not having started already.[16]

We know by the correspondence he sent his wife that during the six days he stayed in Paris, he visited the exhibition assiduously and met the painters Sargent, Boldini, Krøyer, and Zorn, striking up friendships with some of them, and that Francisco Domingo, Carolus-Duran, Léon Bonnat, Benjamin Constant, and Jean-Léon Gérôme invited him to celebrate his triumph.

From this point on, Sorolla decided to end his career as an official painter of salons and grand national and international expositions, a genre to which he would not return.

It is during this time that he finished a very special painting he had started in 1895. Related to Sorolla's family situation at that time, *The Mother* [fig. 11] is a depiction of his wife with their newborn daughter Elena and was presented at the National Exhibition in 1901. From 1900 comes *María Clotilde* [fig. 12], one of the many portraits he painted of his daughter, which stands out among those painted of his family at that time.

In the first years of the twentieth century, Sorolla went back to Velázquez for inspiration and painted some works related to masterpieces by the famous painter: *My Family*[17] in 1901 [fig. 19], indebted to *Las Meninas*, and *Female Nude* in 1902 [fig. 20], inspired by *The Rokeby Venus*. These tendencies to return to Velázquez, his "great master," were always to appear after a major success.

In 1903, Sorolla painted *Afternoon Sun, Beaching the Boat*[18] [fig. 25], which he believed to embody the achievement of the ideal he strove for. He had now reached maturity.

Says Sorolla:

> Ever since I started to paint, my obsession was to destroy all conventionality, how difficult it has been to achieve this at times! …
>
> Solid on my foundation, I began to form without an ounce of fear my way of creating, good or bad, I don't know, but true, sincere, a real reflection of what I see with my eyes and feel with my heart…the exact manifestation of what I believe should be art!
>
> How many years have I taken to delimit this art? Twenty years! Until the painting I have in the Luxembourg [he is referring to *The Return from Fishing*], I didn't see the ideal I was searching for was presenting itself to me. It was a laborious process, but methodical and well-reasoned; my hesitations came to find the norm, but not suddenly, not without progressions. It started in Assisi, took form in the work I realized there, appeared clearly in *Paris Boulevard*, I found it almost completely defined in *Another Marguerite!*, and it presented itself to me fully, real, touchable, resolved, in the bulls pulling the boat ashore in *Afternoon Sun.*[19]

Now that Sorolla had reached his ideal, and now that he interpreted the world just as he saw it, he painted everything the world had to offer him with a feverish activity: gardens, landscapes, beaches, figures…. And in doing so, he tried to capture the fleeting moments of light.

For Sorolla, nature was thenceforth a succession of instants, and the truth, as he said, was an ever-changing concept that was best represented in his "sketches in oil paints." Said Sorolla: "I paint because I love painting. For me, painting is an immense pleasure."[20]

His enjoyment of painting was already starting to be revealed in his works of that time, which had subjects as different as the portraits *Amelia Romea, Señora de Laiglesia* [fig. 10], *The Painter Aureliano de Beruete* [fig. 22] or *The Photographer Christian Franzen* [fig. 23]; the maritime studies *Transporting Grapes, Jávea* [fig. 14], *End of the Day, Jávea* [fig. 15], *Mending the Nets* [fig. 16] and *Valencia Beach, Morning Sun* [fig. 17]; works depicting what Pérez de Ayala refers to as "summer leisure,"[21] like *Children on the Seashore* [fig. 24] (a constant in his work from then on); and landscapes, such as *Asturian Landscape* [fig. 21].

Encouraged by his successes of the year 1903, and thinking of the need of his wife and his daughter María for an outdoor life, Sorolla transferred his home and his studio to a house with a garden in a residential area of Madrid, on Calle de Miguel Ángel.

NOTES

1. Letter from Sorolla (Seville) to his wife Clotilde (Madrid), February 23 and 24, 1908. *Epistolarios de Joaquín Sorolla III. Correspondencia con Clotilde García del Castillo (1891–1911)*, eds. Blanca Pons-Sorolla and Víctor Lorente, Barcelona, Anthropos, 2009, letter no. 258, pp. 223 and 224.
2. Preserved in the family archive of correspondence at the Museo Sorolla are 988 letters from Sorolla to Clotilde García del Castillo and their children, which have been published in *Epistolarios de Joaquín Sorolla, II. Correspondencia con Clotilde García del Castillo (1912–1919)*, eds. Víctor Lorente, Blanca Pons-Sorolla, and Marina Moya, Barcelona, Anthropos, 2008; and *Epistolarios de Joaquín Sorolla, III. Correspondencia con Clotilde García del Castillo (1891–1911)*, eds. Blanca Pons-Sorolla and Víctor Lorente, Barcelona, Anthropos, 2009.
3. On the close relationship between Joaquín Sorolla and Pedro Gil Moreno de Mora, see *Epistolarios de Joaquín Sorolla, I. Correspondencia con Pedro Gil Moreno de Mora*, eds. Facundo Tomás, Felipe Garín, Isabel Justo, and Sofía Barrón, Barcelona, Anthropos, 2007.
4. The retrospective exhibition in homage to Jules Bastien-Lepage, a French artist who had recently died at the age of only thirty-six, took place in Paris in April 1885, and that of Adolf von Menzel, a German painter who was by then over seventy, was held in May.
5. Abandoned by Sorolla, this painting was rolled up and left in the basement of his house, the current Museo Sorolla, and was eventually almost completely destroyed by humidity and time. Four fragments were retrieved and donated by Francisco Pons-Sorolla to the Museo Sorolla on February 8, 1980, inv. nos. 158, 159, 160, and 161 [BPS 132, 133, 134 and 135].
6. Letter from Clotilde (Madrid) to Sorolla (Valencia), 13 December 1907. *Epistolarios de Joaquín Sorolla III*, note 495, p. 186.
7. Whereabouts unknown [BPS 206].
8. Saint Louis (Missouri), Mildred Lane Kemper Art Museum, Washington University in St. Louis, donated by Charles Nagel in 1894, inv. WU 2930 [BPS 841].
9. Leonard Williams, "El pintor Sorolla juzgado en el extranjero," *El País*, Madrid (May 22, 1904).
10. This painting is preserved in the Museo de Bellas Artes de Bilbao as a contribution of the Council of Bilbao, 1913, inv. 69/228 [BPS-763].
11. Charles Yriarte, "Le Salon des Champs Elysées. La Peinture," *Le Figaro*, Paris (April 30, 1895)
12. Sorolla (Paris) to Clotilde (Valencia), June 1895. *Epistolarios de Joaquín Sorolla III*, letter no. 96, pp. 86 and 87.
13. Acquisition by Royal Decree from Joaquín Sorolla for 4,000 pesetas on July 12, 1895 for the Museo del Prado (inv. N.A. 1198); Madrid, Museo de Arte Moderno, August 10, 1896 (reg. nos. 30-S and 59-S). Currently at the Museo del Prado, inv. P-4649 [BPS 848].
14. Sorolla (Jávea) to Clotilde (Valencia), October 7, 1896. *Epistolarios de Joaquín Sorolla III*, letter no. 110, p. 95.
15. Now belonging to the art collection of the Caja de Ahorros de Valencia, Castellón y Alicante, "Bancaja" [BPS 807].
16. Letter from Sorolla (Paris) to Clotilde (Valencia), July 16, 1900. *Epistolarios de Joaquín Sorolla III*, letter no. 128, p. 109.
17. Gift from the artist to the Ayuntamiento de Valencia, inv. 55. [BPS 1710].
18. New York, The Hispanic Society of America, 1909. Acquired at Sorolla's personal exhibition in New York in 1909 for $10,000 [BPS 1449].
19. Rodolfo Gil, *Sorolla*, Madrid, Sáenz de Juberá-Hermanos (*Monografías de Arte Universal*, 7), 1913, pp. 25–30.
20. Francisco Martín Caballero, "Sorolla en su estudio." Also published in *Vidas Ajenas*, Madrid, Imprenta Hispano-Alemana, 1914.
21. Eduardo Quesada, "Ramón Pérez de Ayala y las artes plásticas," in *Ramón Pérez de Ayala y las artes plásticas*, Granada, Fundación Rodríguez-Acosta, 1991, p. 31.

1 *After the Bath*

1892
Oil on canvas, 50½ x 76 in.
Signed: "J. Sorolla"
Private collection
(BPS 866)

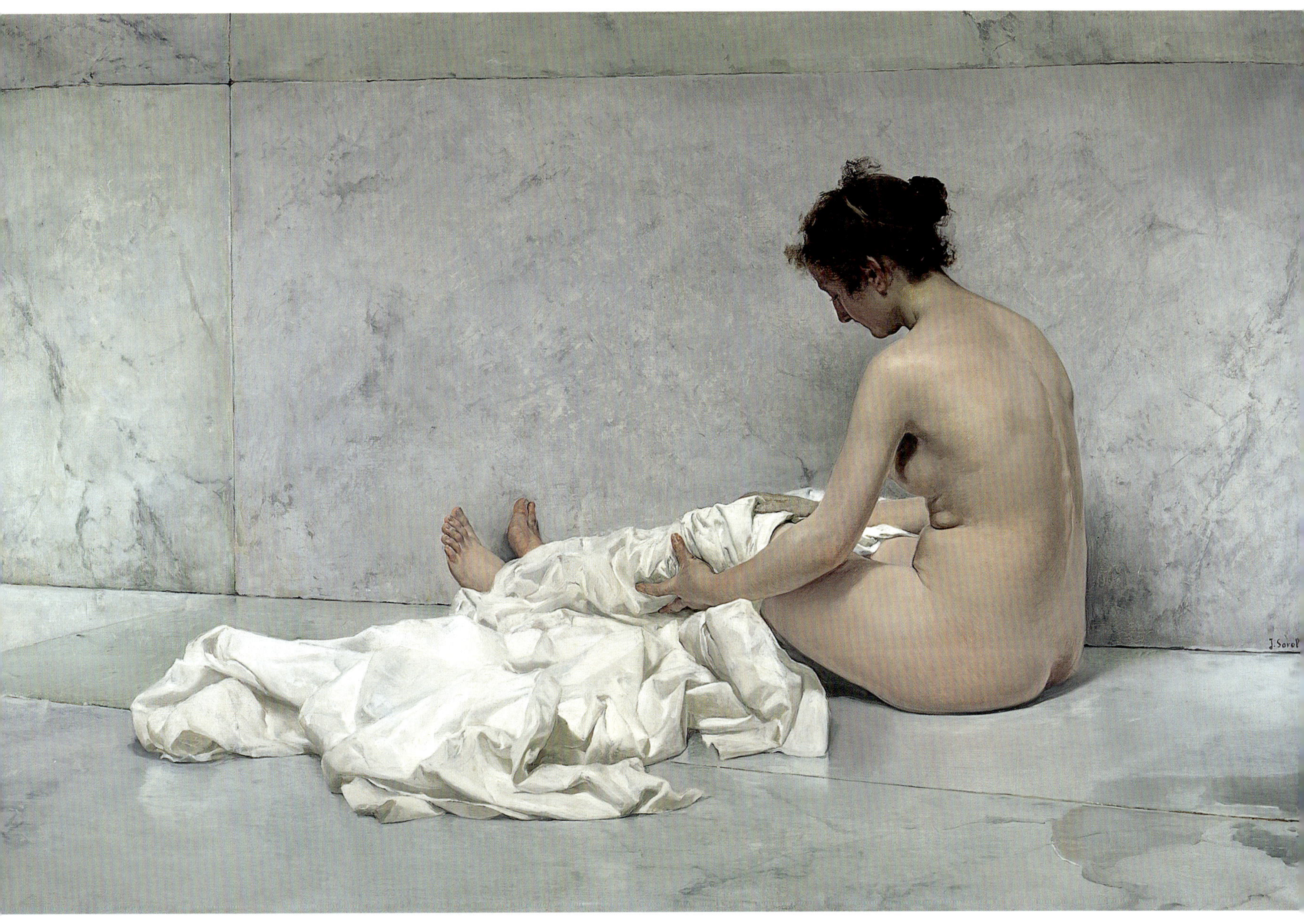

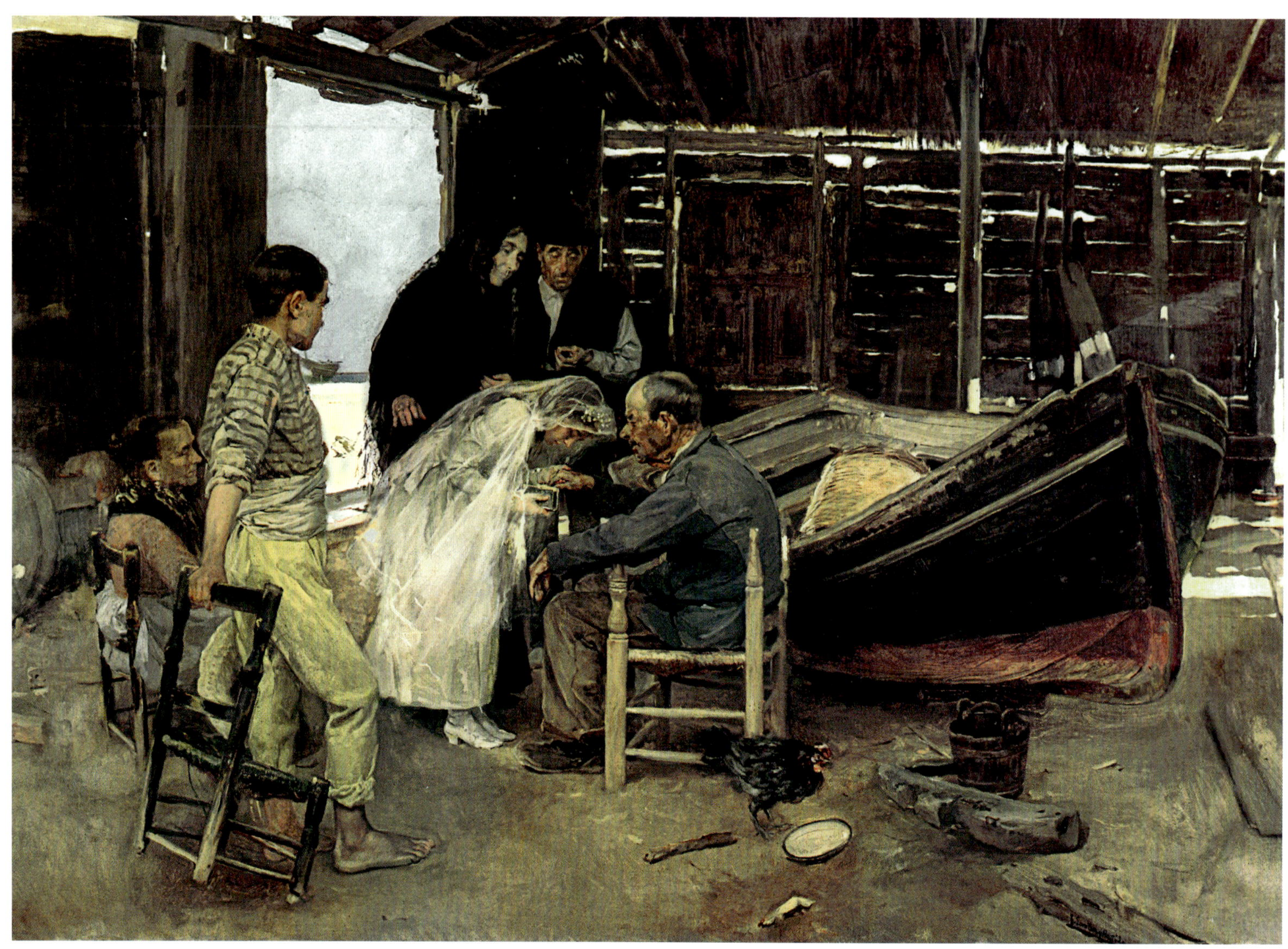

2 *The Happy Day*

1892
Oil on canvas, 32¾ x 45¾ in.
Signed: "J. Sorolla y Bastida 1892"
Udine, Civici Musei e Gallerie di Storia e Arte
(BPS 847)

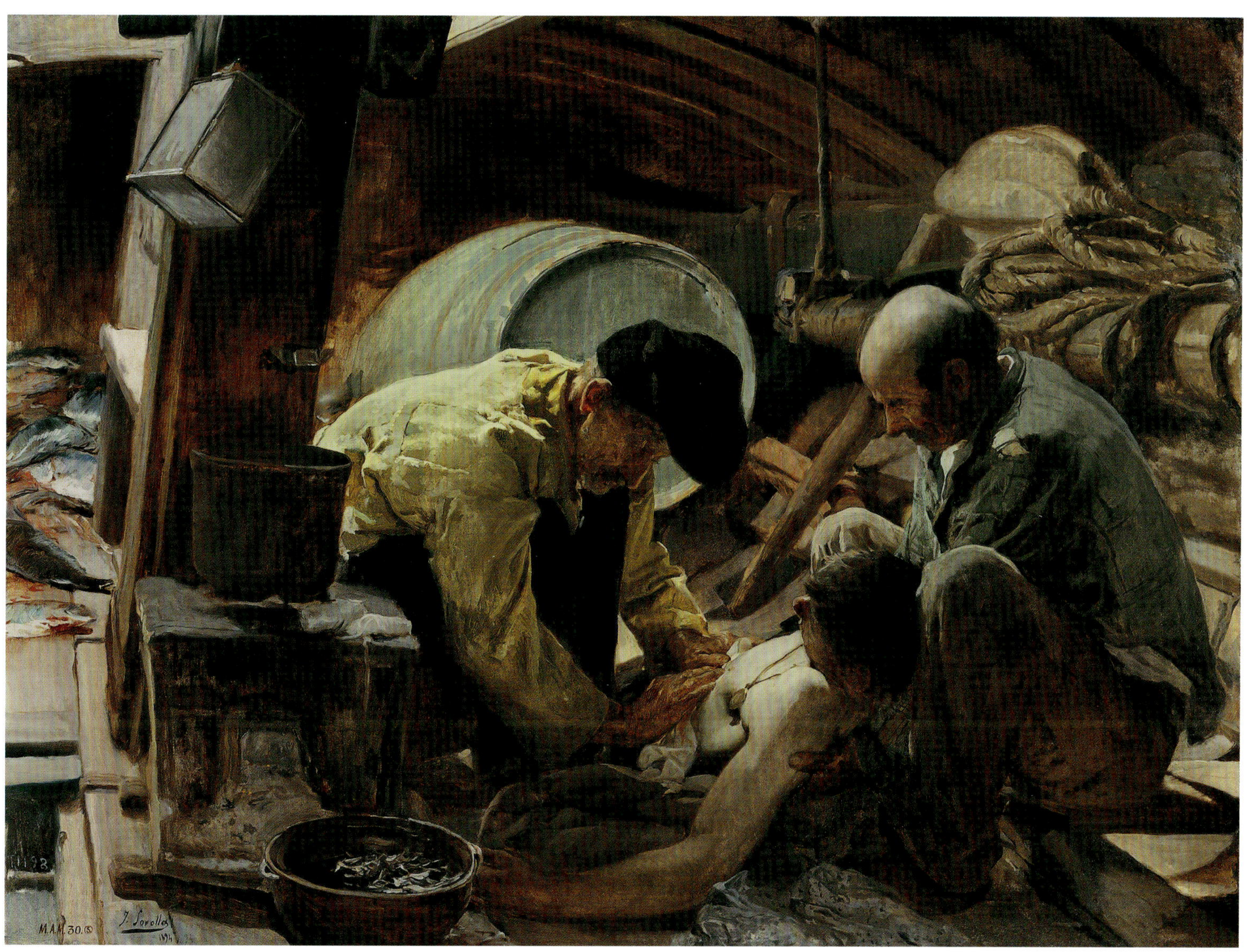

3 *And They Still Say Fish Is Expensive!*

1894
Oil on canvas, 59¾ x 80¼ in.
Signed: "J. Sorolla / 1894"
Inventory inscription: "T. 1198", "M.A.M. 30. (S.)"
Madrid, Museo Nacional del Prado [P–4649]
(BPS 848)

NEXT DOUBLE PAGE

4 *The Return from Fishing*

1894
Oil on canvas, 8 ft. 8½ in. x 10 ft. 8 in.
Signed: "J Sorolla 1894 / Valencia"
Paris, Musée d'Orsay [inv. R.F. 948]
(BPS 729)

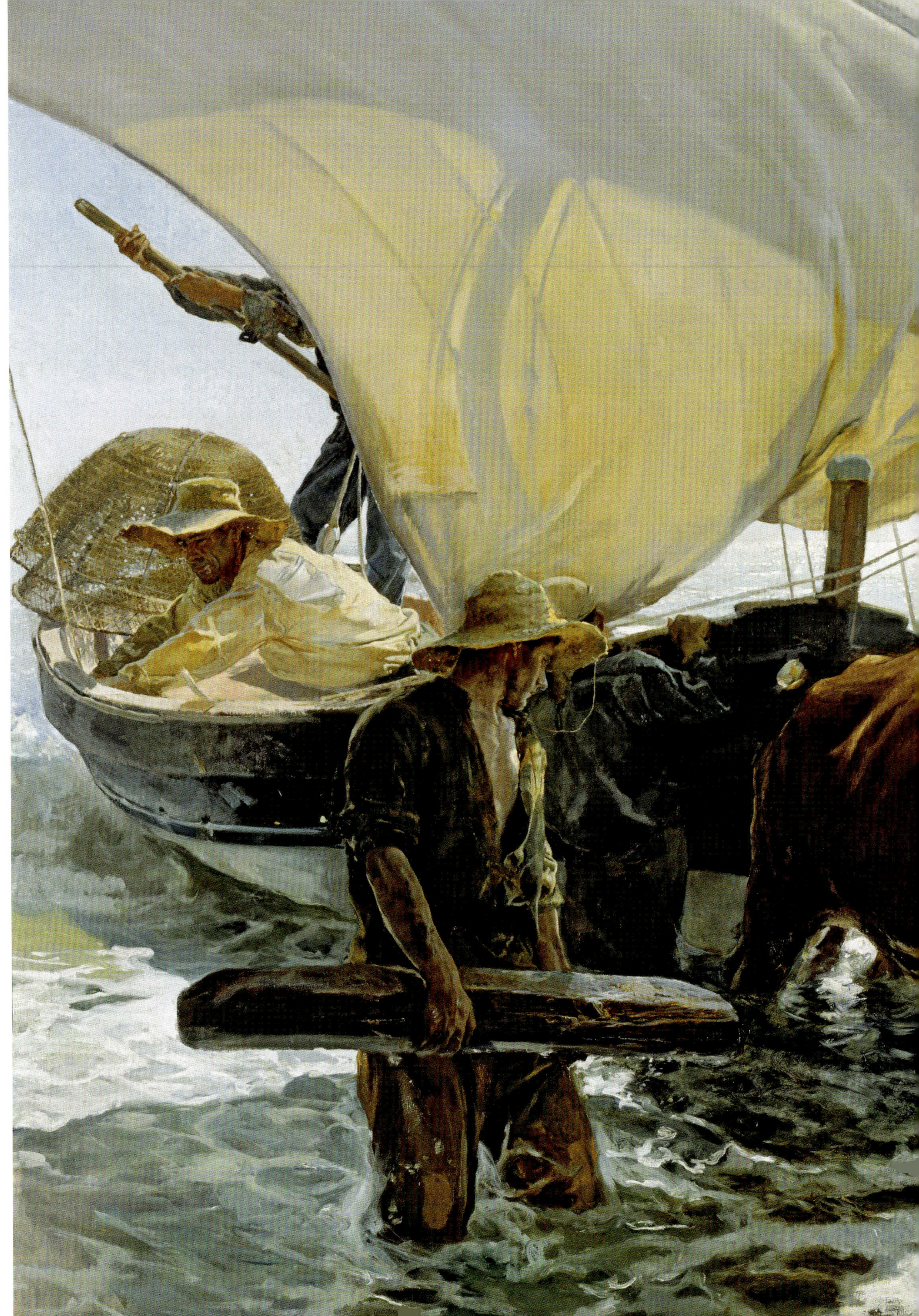

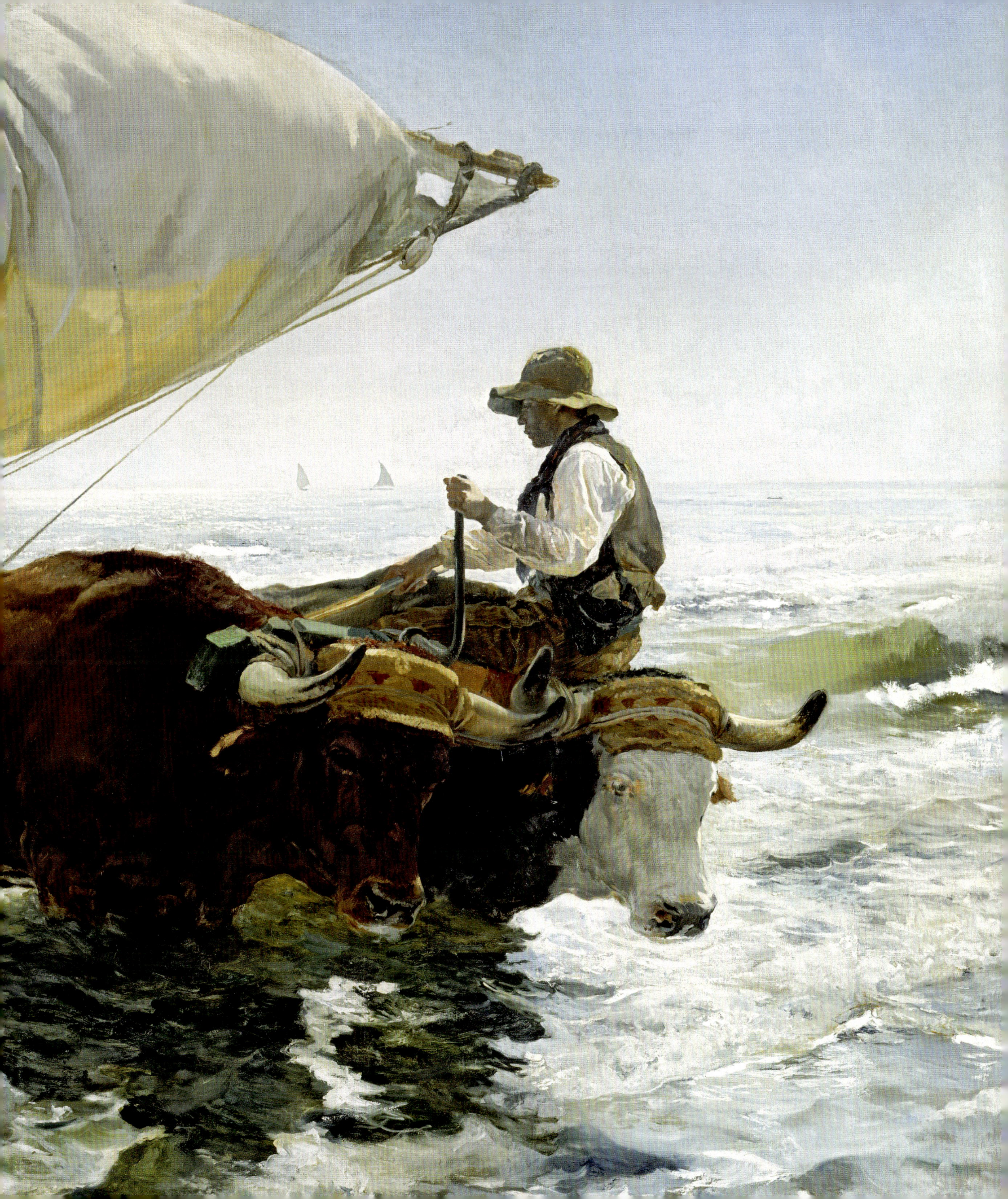

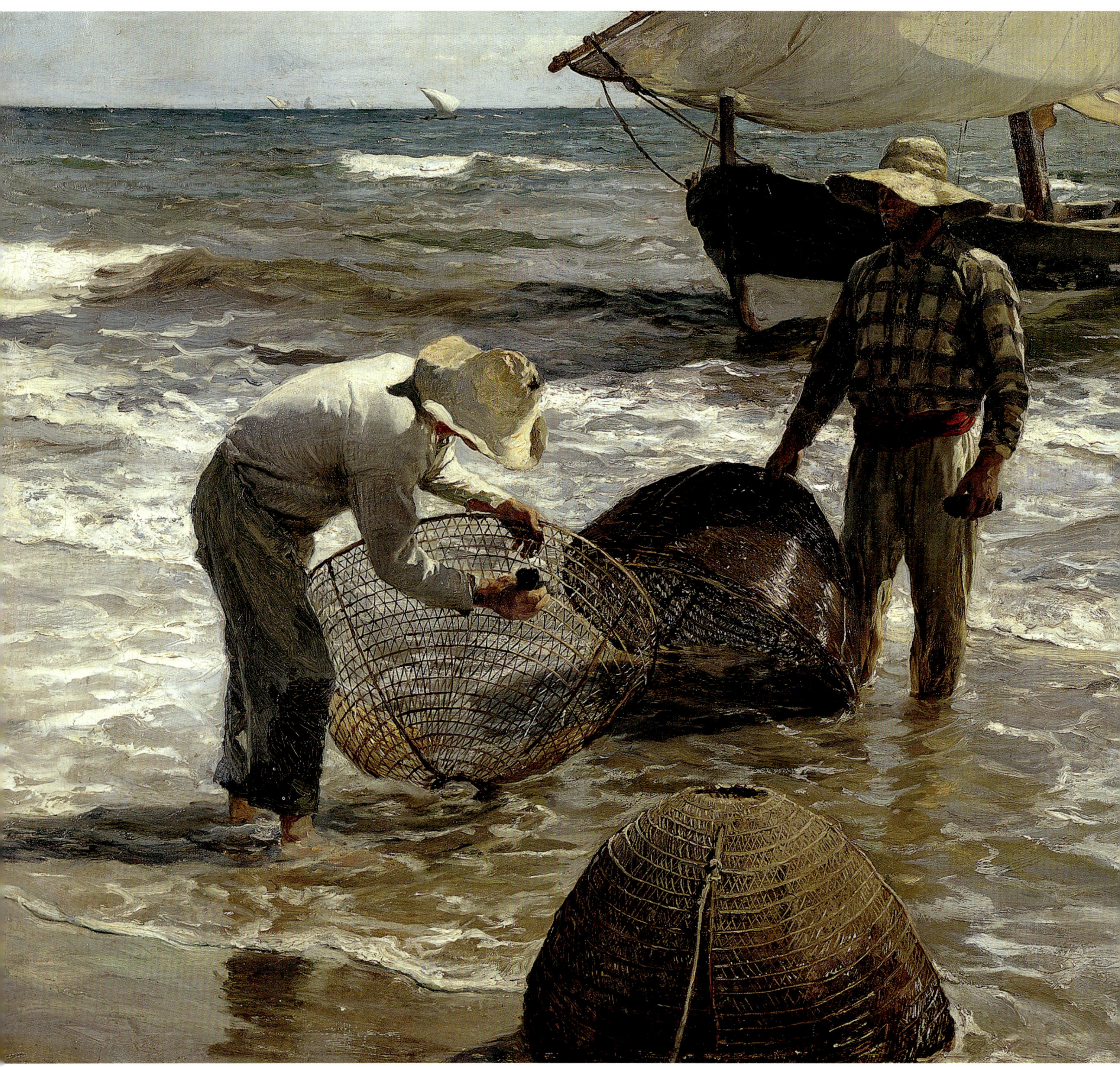

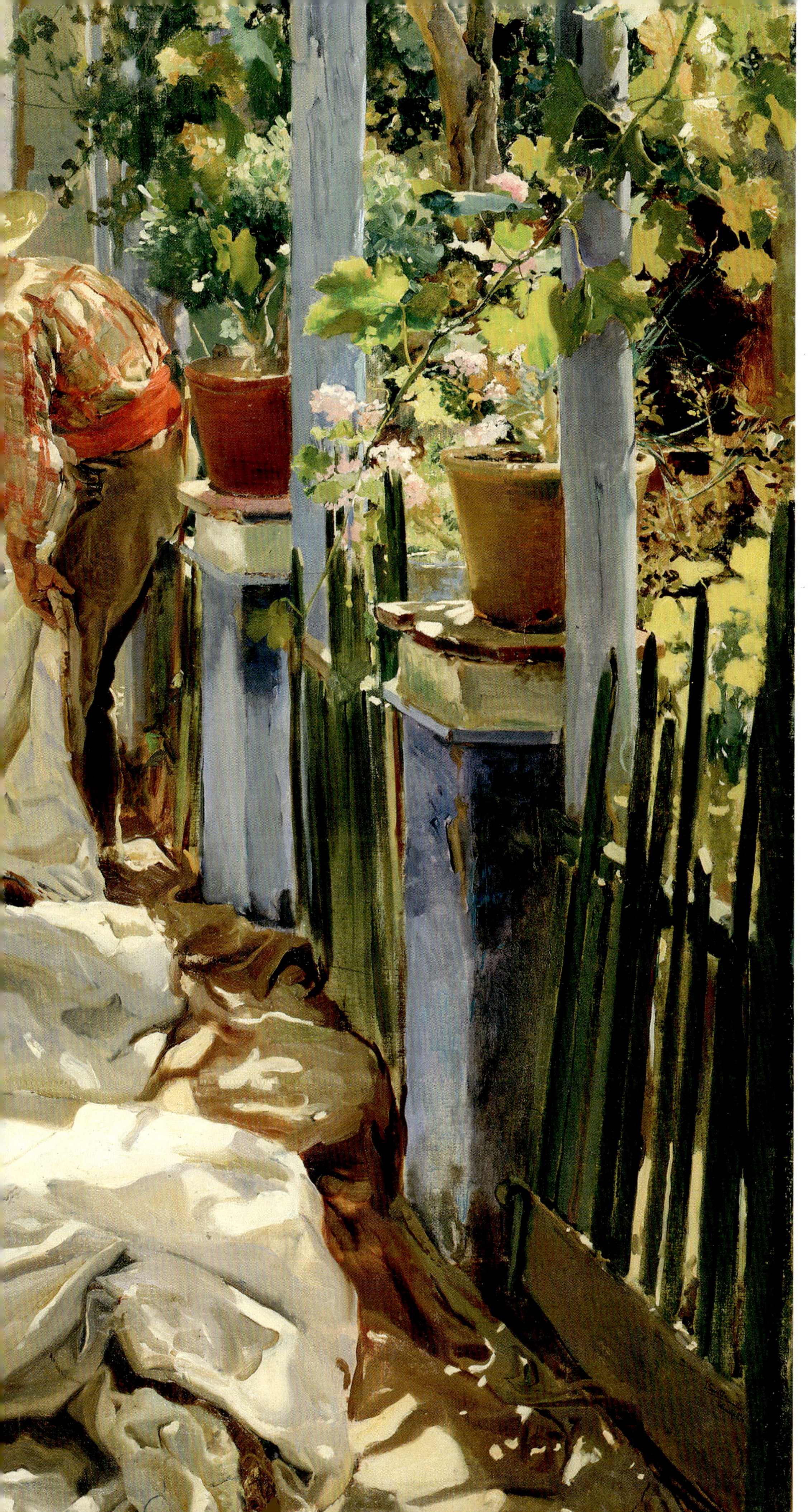

7 *Sewing the Sail*

1896
Oil on canvas, 87½ x 118 in.
Signed: "J. Sorolla / Valencia 1896"
Venice, Museo d'Arte Moderna Ca' Pesaro
(BPS 745)

8 *The Cape of San Antonio, Jávea*

1896
Oil on canvas, 19 x 28¼ in.
Signed: "J. Sorolla Bastida / 1896"
Private collection
(BPS 1071)

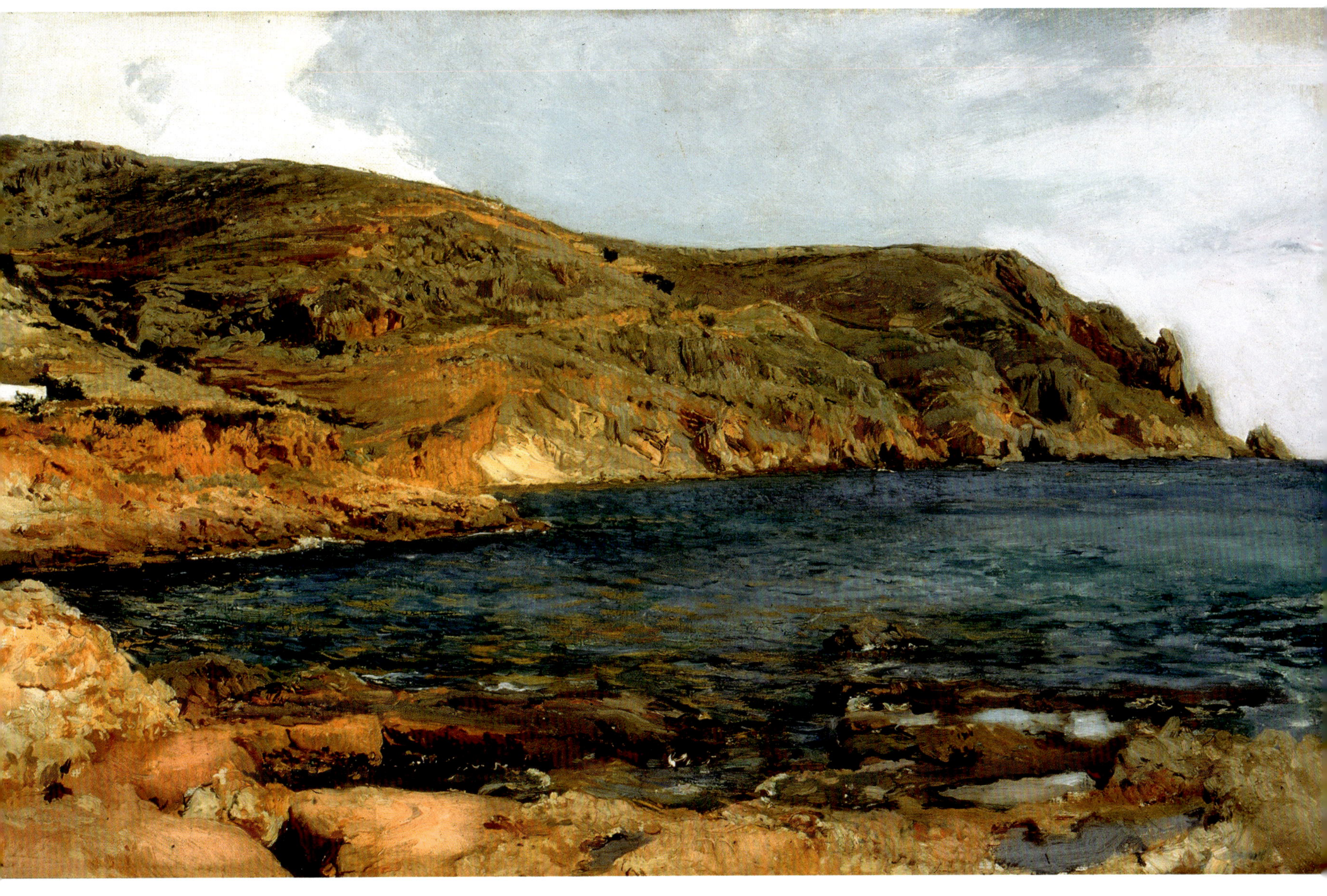

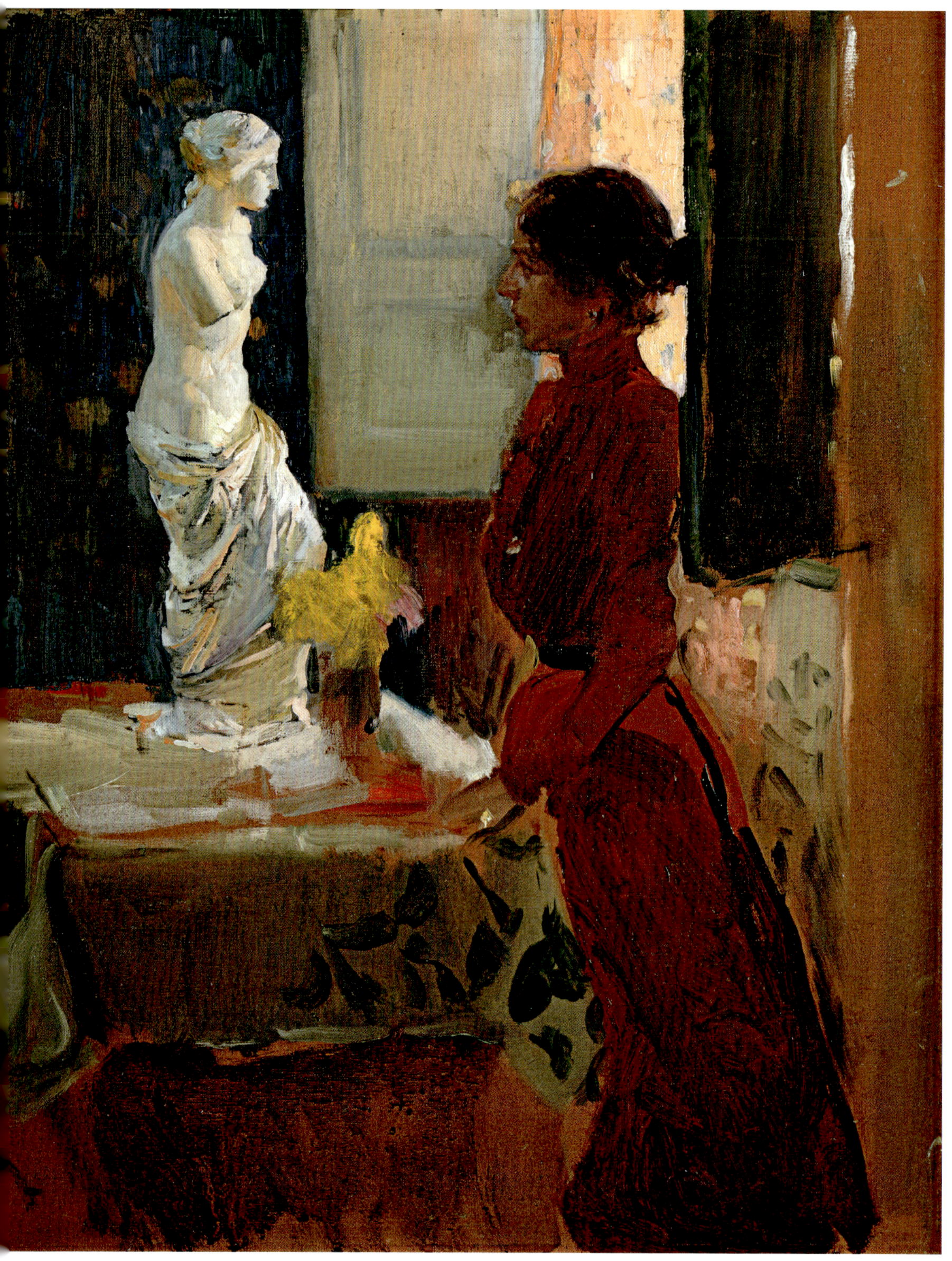

9 *Clotilde Contemplating the Venus de Milo*

c. 1897–98
Oil on canvas, 28¼ x 18¾ in.
Valencia, Museo de Bellas Artes de Valencia [inv. 894]
(BPS 221)

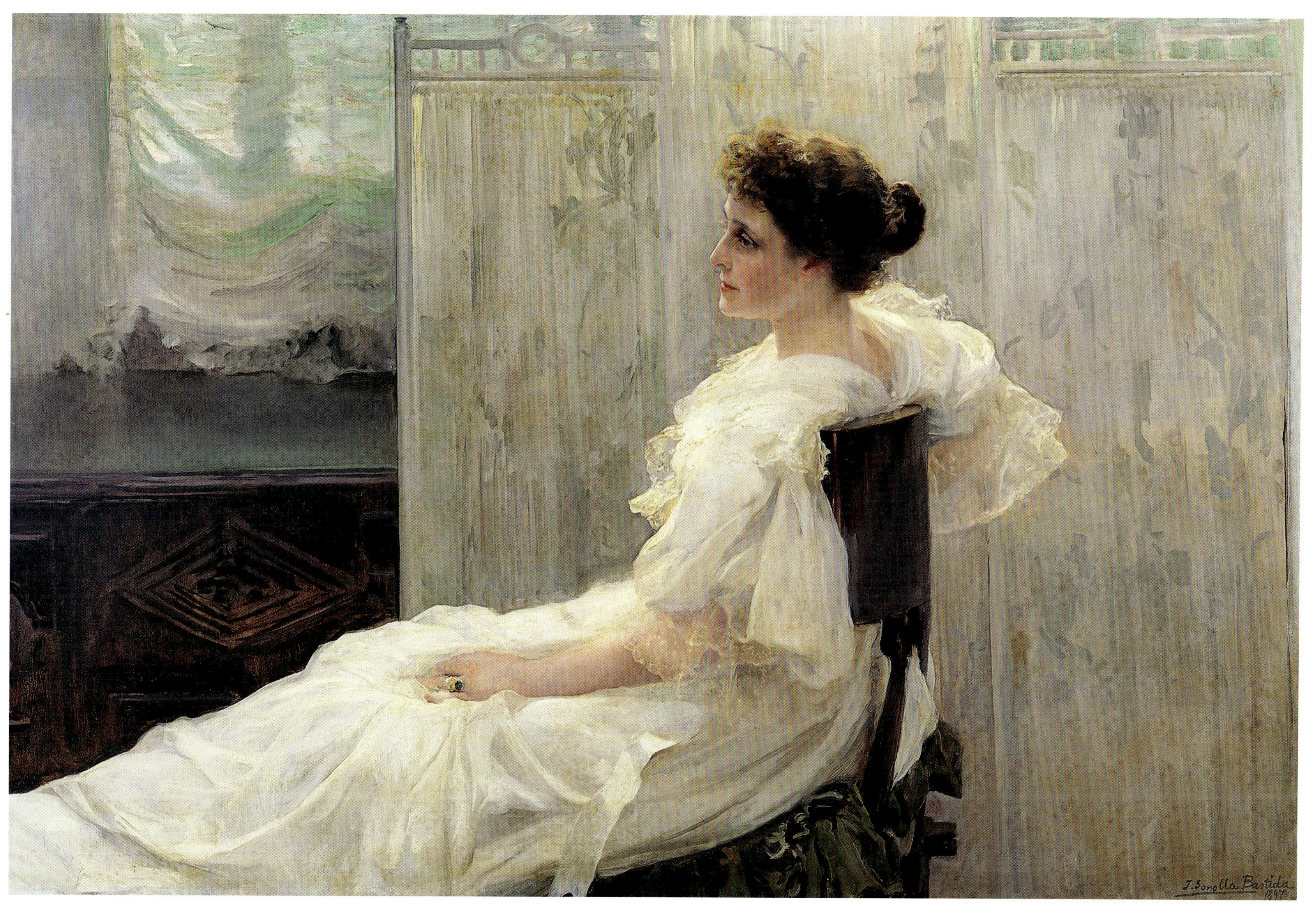

10 *Amelia Romea, Señora de Laiglesia*

1897
Oil on canvas, 42¼ x 59¼ in.
Signed: "J. Sorolla Bastida / 1897"
Private collection
(BPS 853)

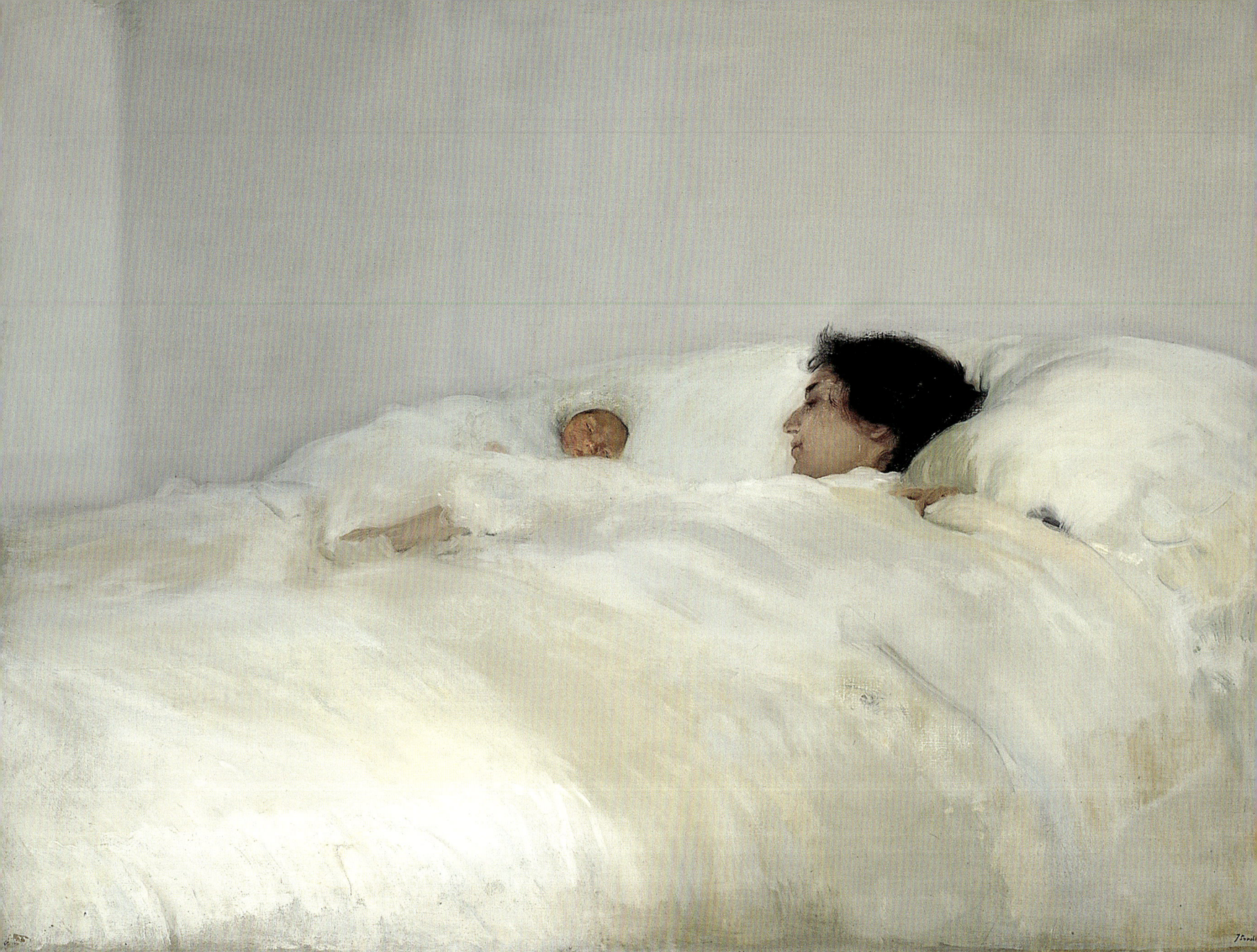

11 *The Mother*

1895–1900
Oil on canvas, 49¼ x 66½ in.
Signed: “J Sorolla y Bastida”
Madrid, Museo Sorolla [inv. 324]
(BPS 1131)

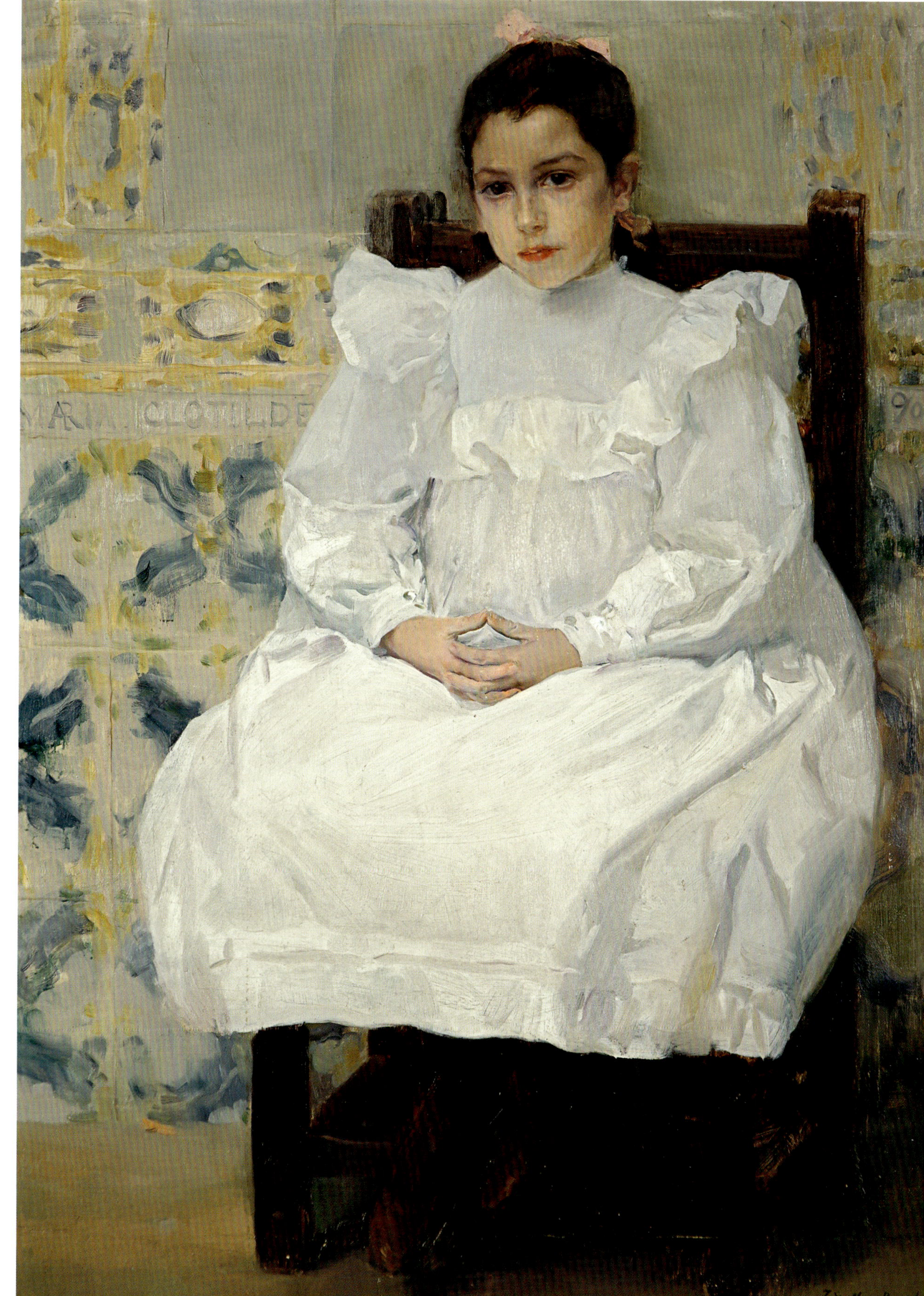

12 *María Clotilde*

1900
Oil on canvas, 43¼ x 31½ in.
Signed: "J. Sorolla y Bastida / 1900"
Inscriptions: "MARÍA CLOTILDE";
"1900"
Private collection
(BPS 1053)

13 *Eating in the Boat*

1898
Oil on canvas, 71 x 98½ in.
Signed: "J. Sorolla B / 1898"
Madrid, Museo de la Real Academia de Bellas Artes de San Fernando [inv. 804]
(BPS 783)

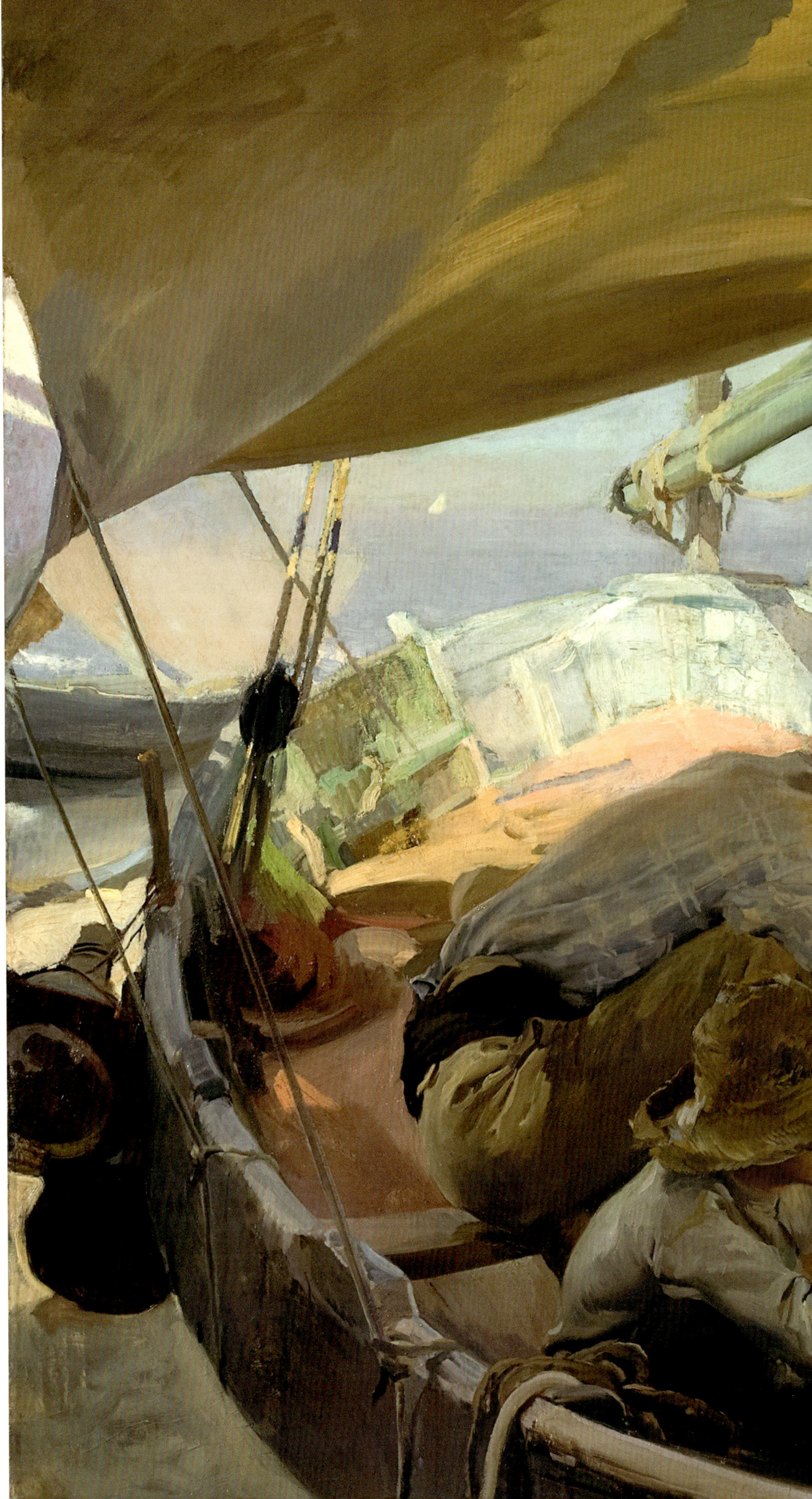

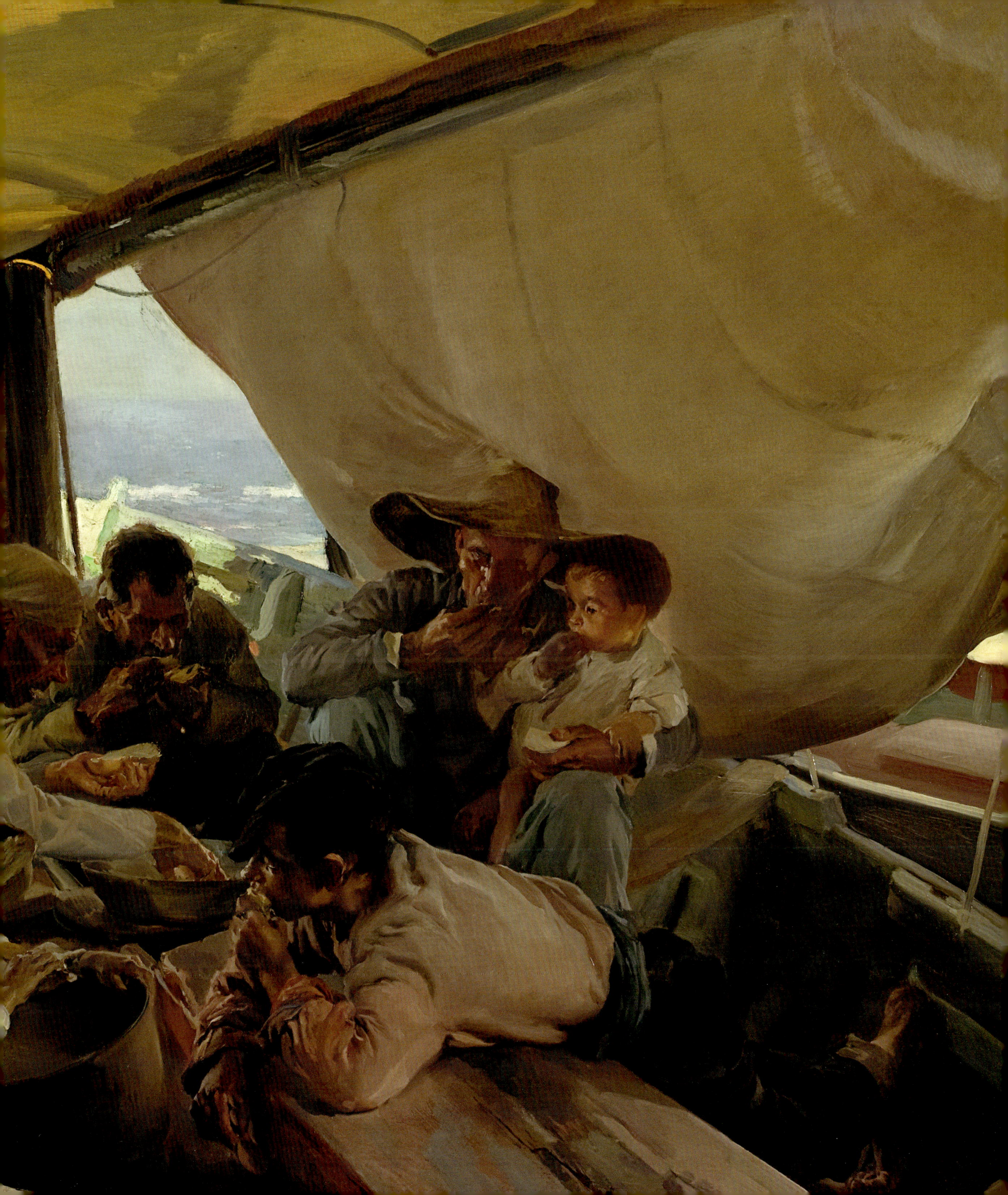

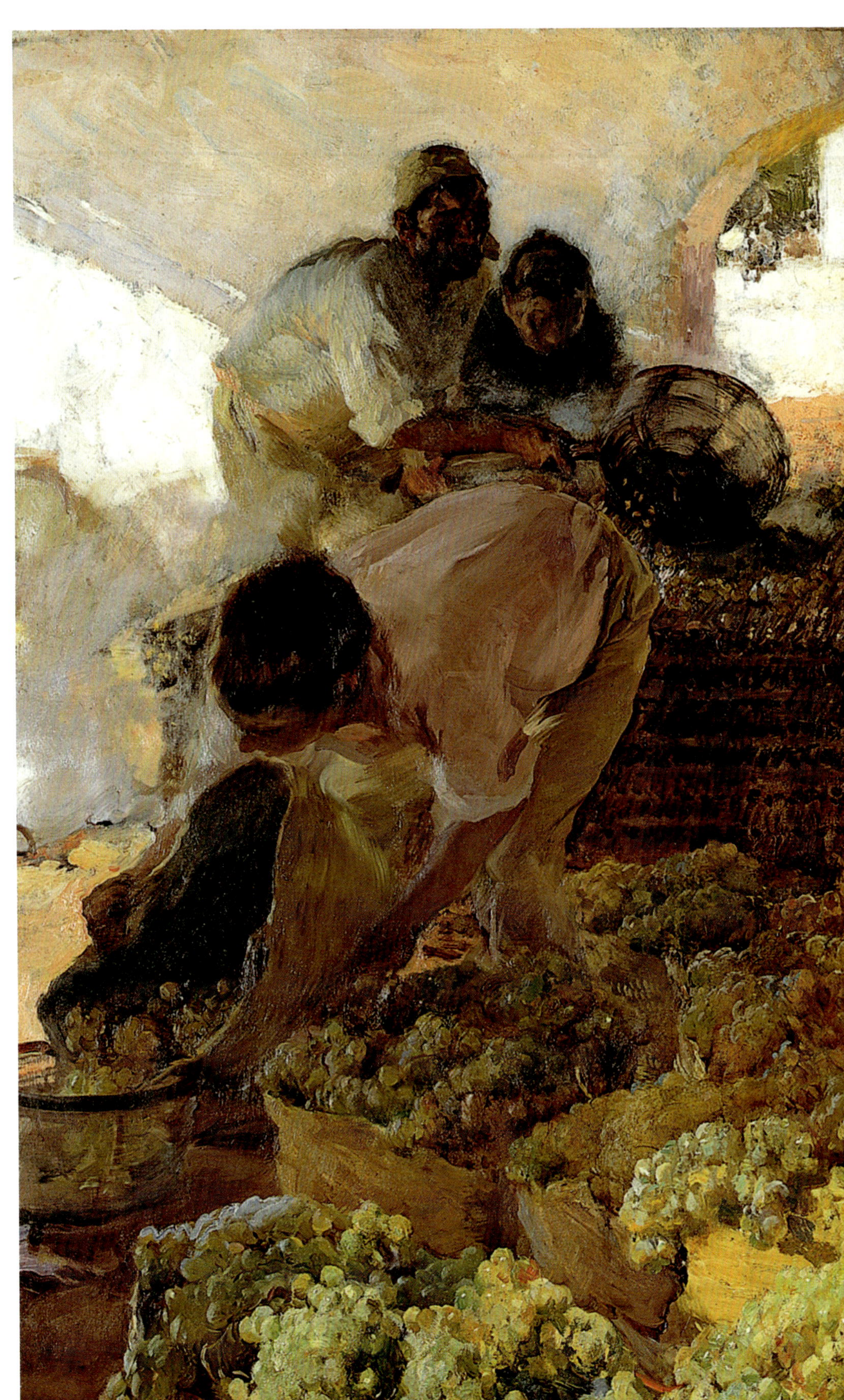

14 *Transporting Grapes, Jávea*

1900
Oil on canvas, 49¼ x 78¼ in.
Signed: "J. Sorolla y Bastida / 1900"
Oviedo, Museo de Bellas Artes de Asturias,
Pedro Masaveu Collection [inv. 1812]
(BPS 976)

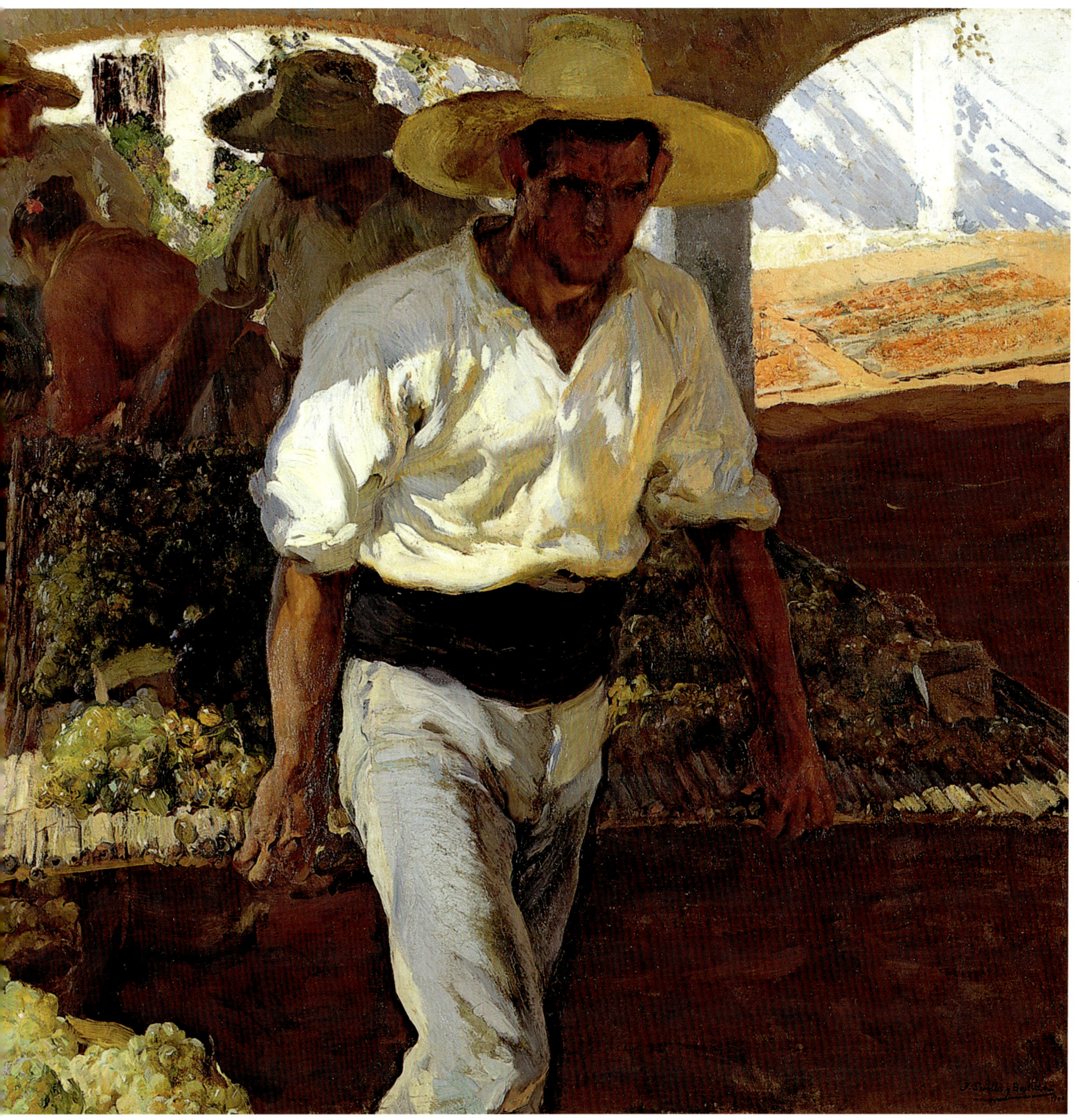

16 *Mending the Nets*

1901
Oil on canvas, 64 x 51½ in.
Signed: "J Sorolla y Bastida / 1901"
Mexico City, Museo Nacional
de San Carlos Collection,
CONACULTA-INBA
(BPS 1713)

15 *End of the Day, Jávea*

1900
Oil on canvas, 34¾ x 50½ in.
Signed: "J. Sorolla y Bastida / 1900"
Private collection
(BPS 982)

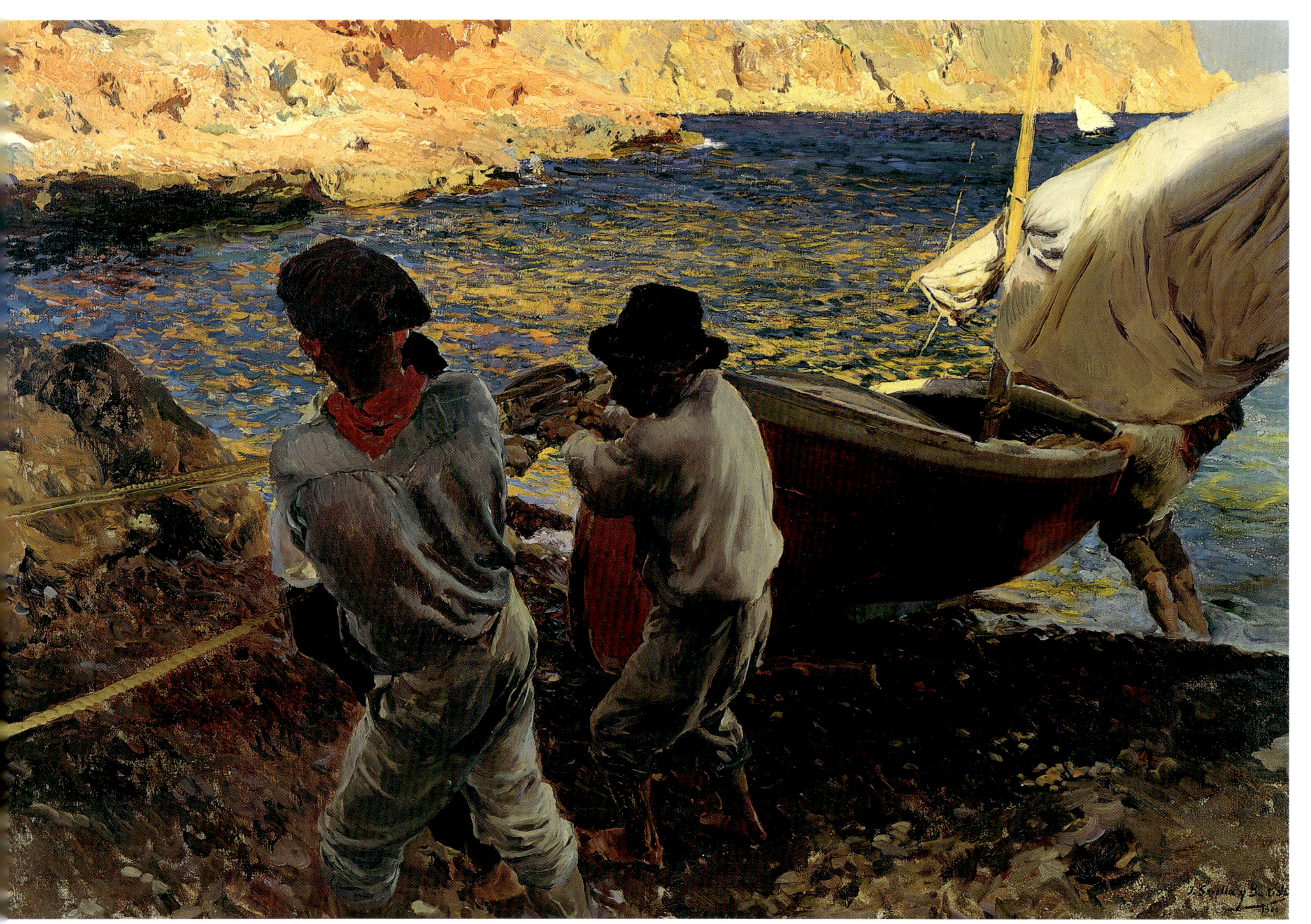

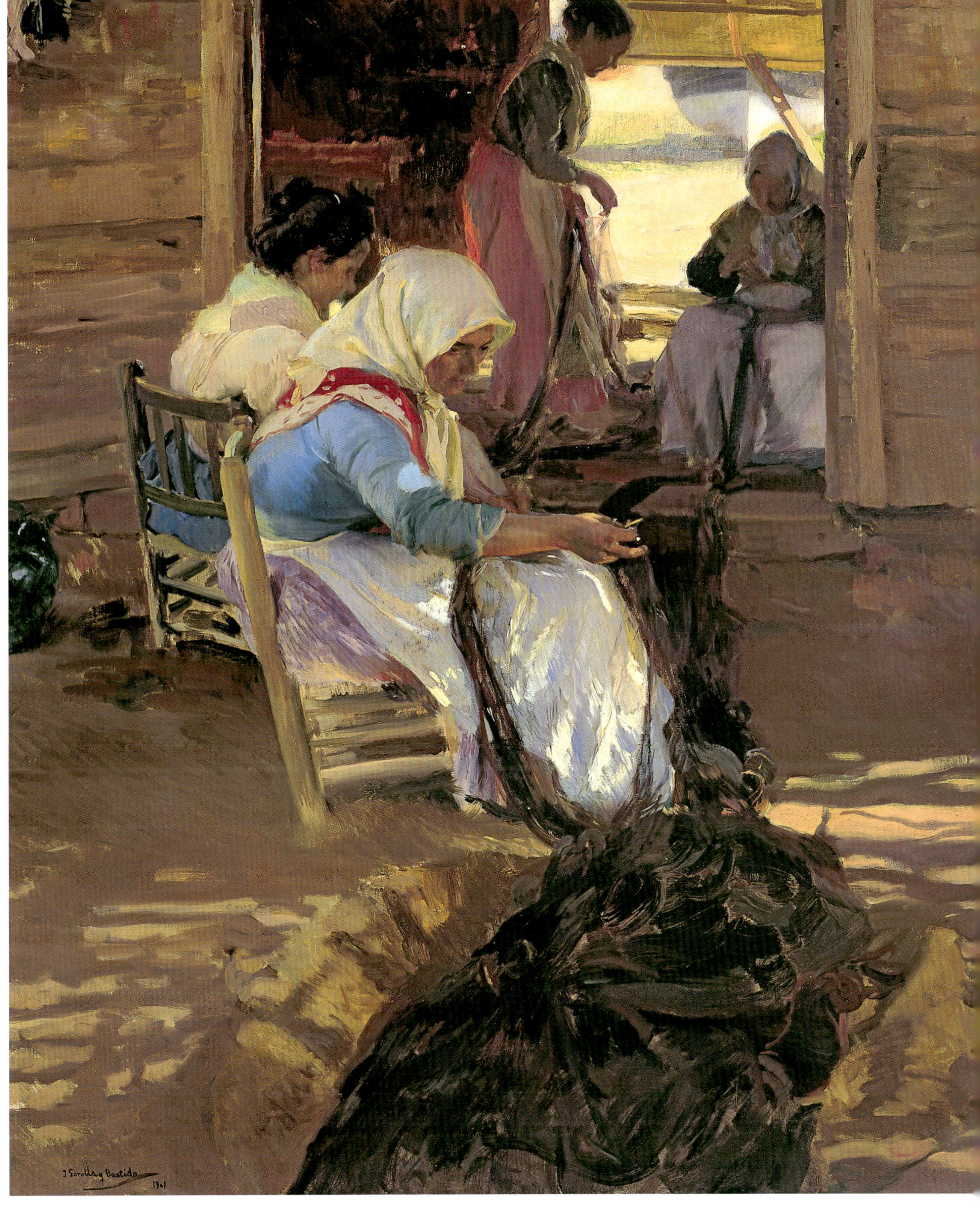
J Sorolla y Bastida
1901

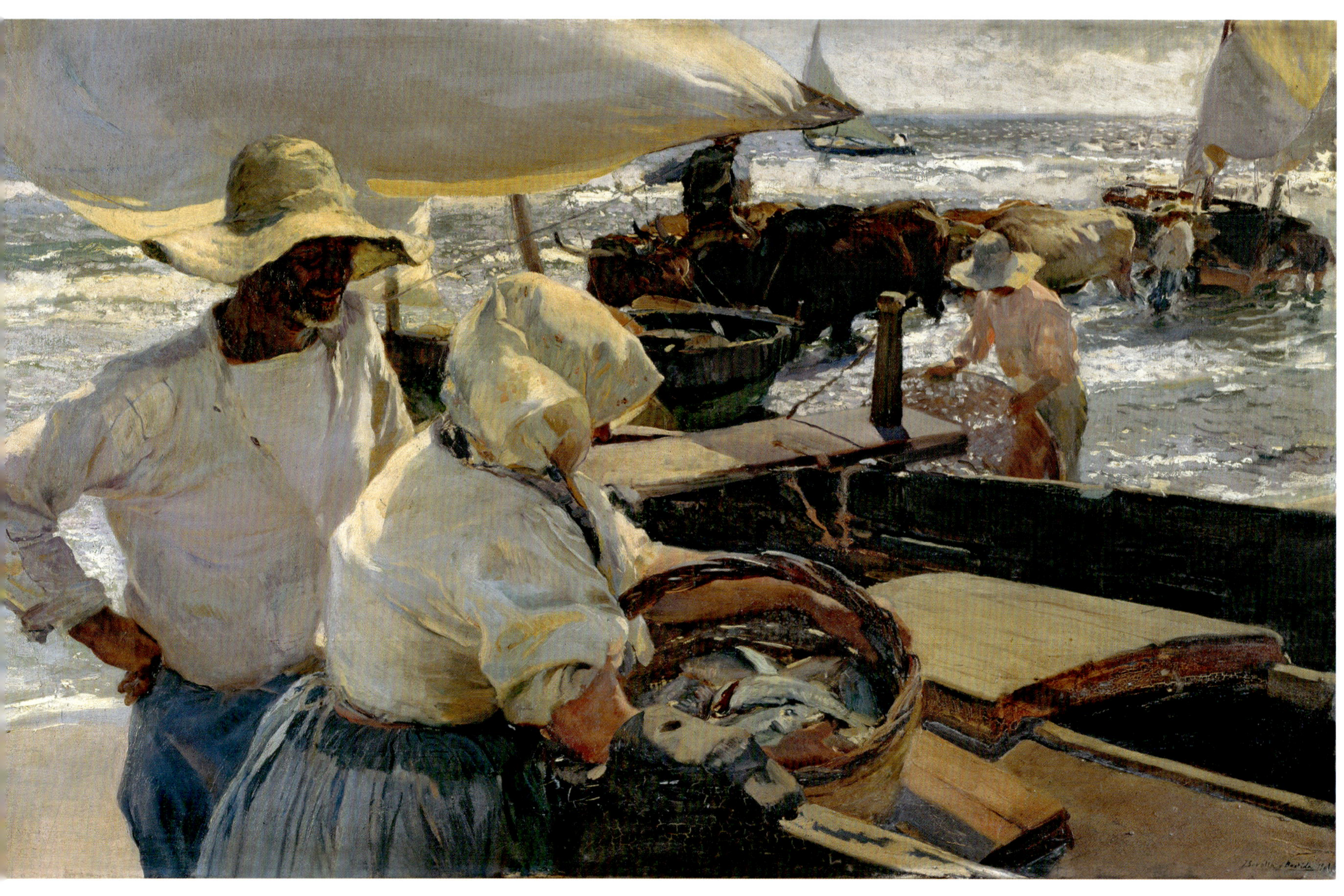

17 *Valencia Beach, Morning Sun*

1901
Oil on canvas, 32 x 50½ in.
Signed: "J Sorolla y Bastida / 1901"
Mexico, Pérez Simón Collection
(BPS 1811)

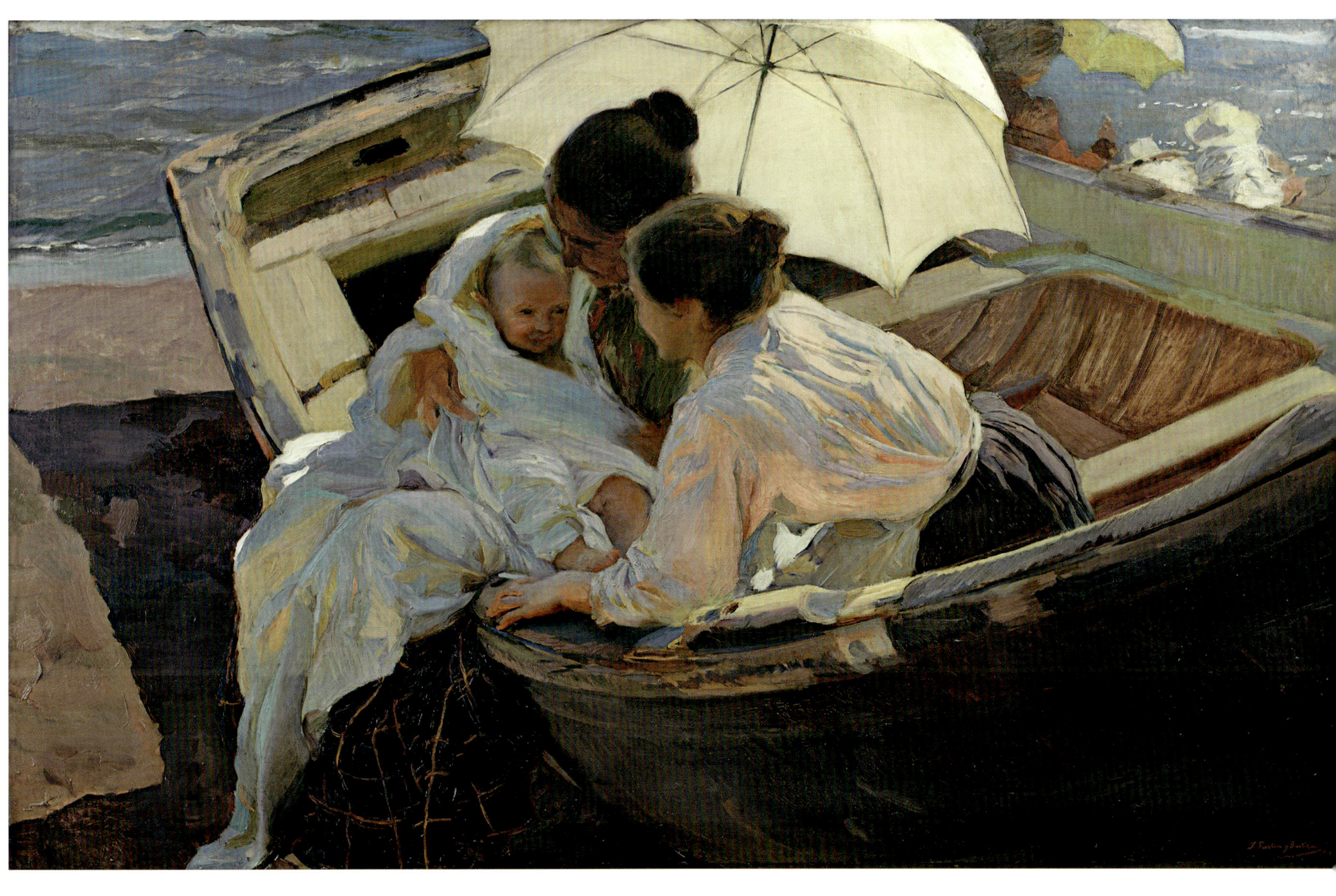

18 *After the Bath*

1902
Oil on canvas, 40½ x 64¼ in.
Signed: "J. Sorolla y Bastida / 1902"
Private collection
(BPS 1814)

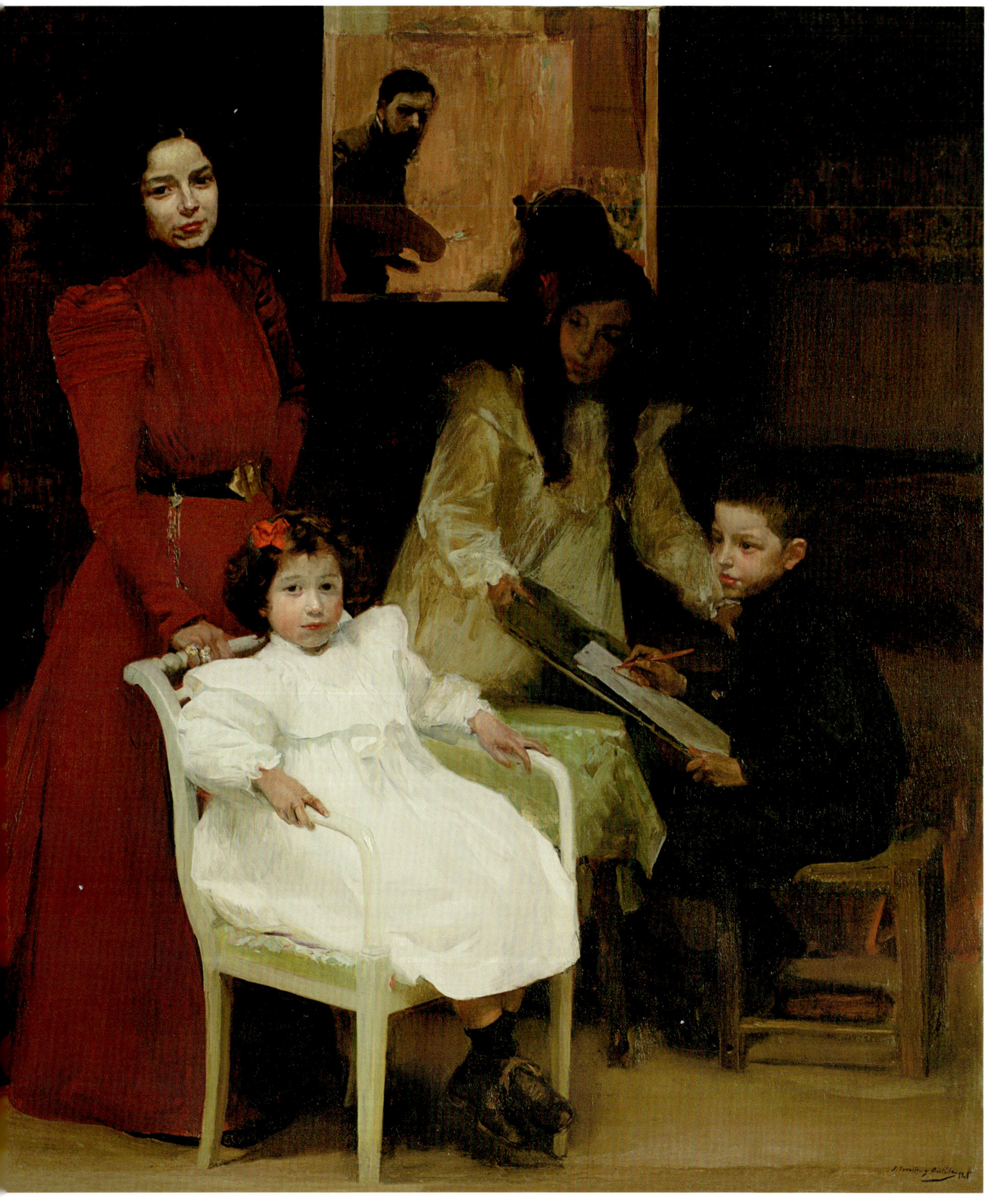

19 *My Family*

1901
Oil on canvas, 74¾ x 62½ in.
Signed: "J. Sorolla y Bastida / 1901"
Valencia, Ayuntamiento [inv. 55]
(BPS 1710)

20 *Female Nude*

1902
Oil on canvas, 41¾ x 73¼ in.
Signed: "J. Sorolla y Bastida / 1902"
Private collection
(BPS 2138)

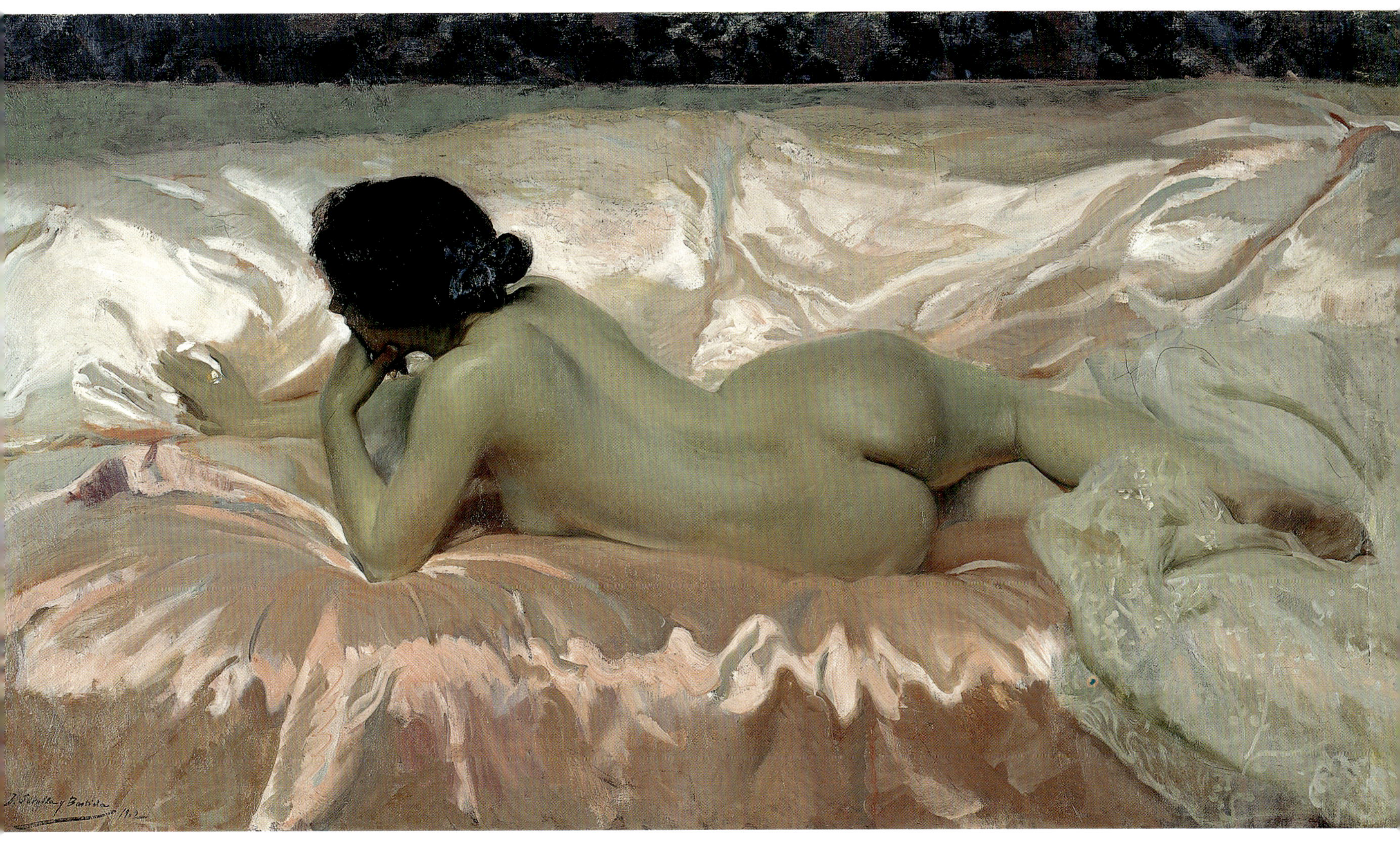

21 *Asturian Landscape*

1903–4
Oil on canvas, 24½ x 37 in.
Signed: "J. Sorolla y Bastida / 1904"
New York, Brooklyn Museum,
Caroline H. Polhemus Fund [14.559]
(BPS 3457)

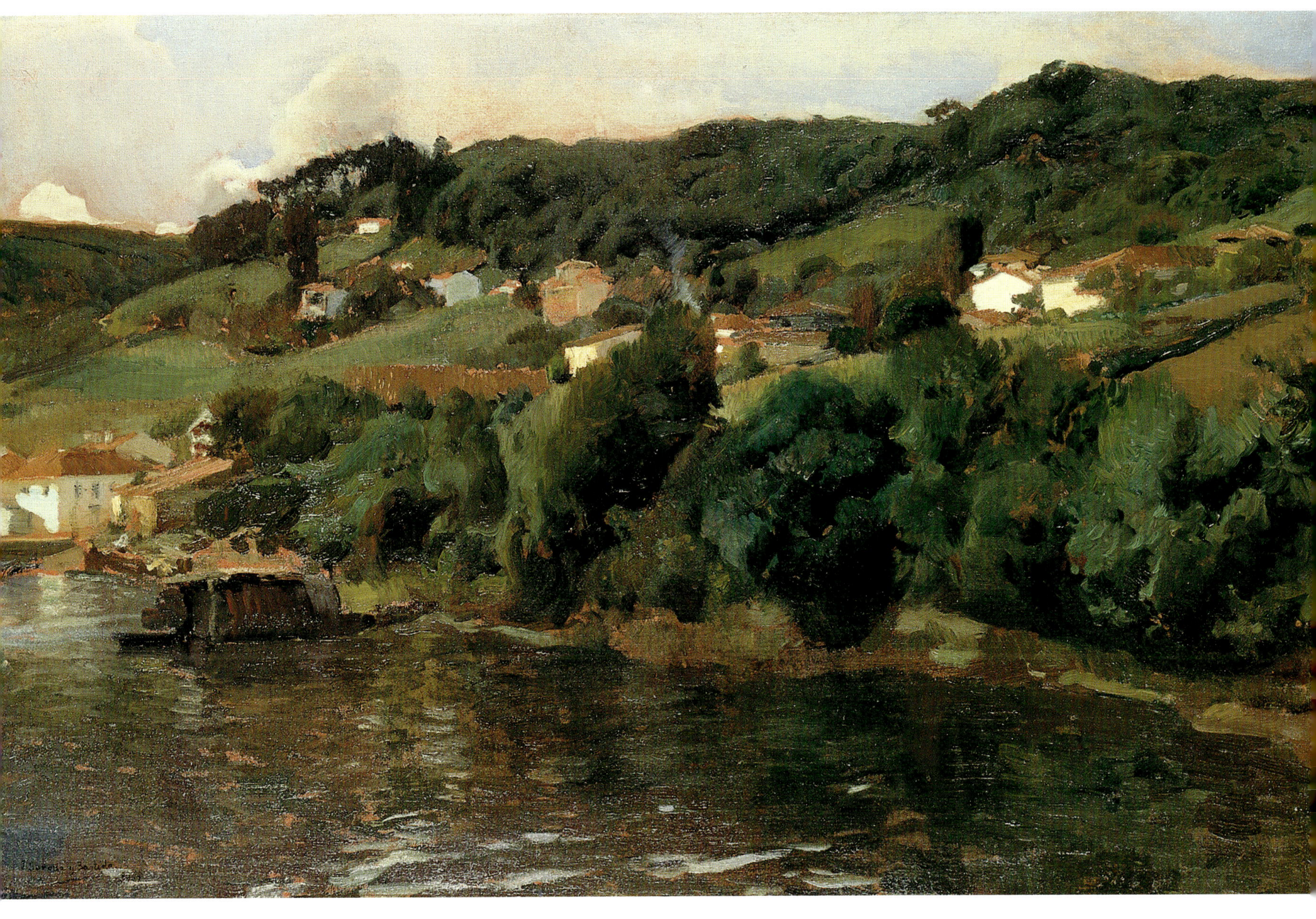

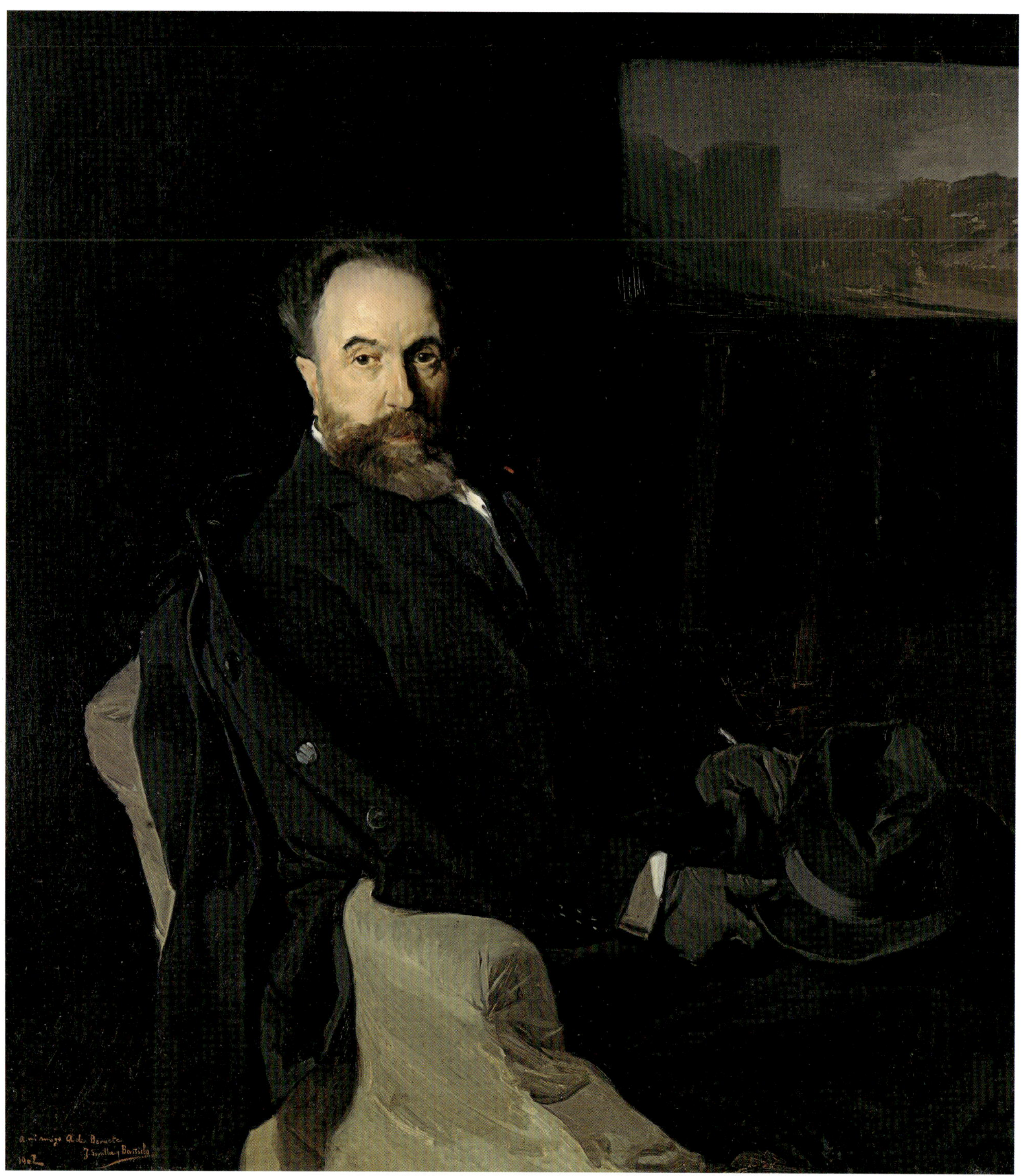

22 *The Painter Aureliano de Beruete*

1902
Oil on canvas, 45½ x 43½ in.
Signed: "A mi amigo A. de Beruete /
J. Sorolla y Bastida / 1902"
Madrid, Museo Nacional del Prado [P–4646]
(BPS 1715)

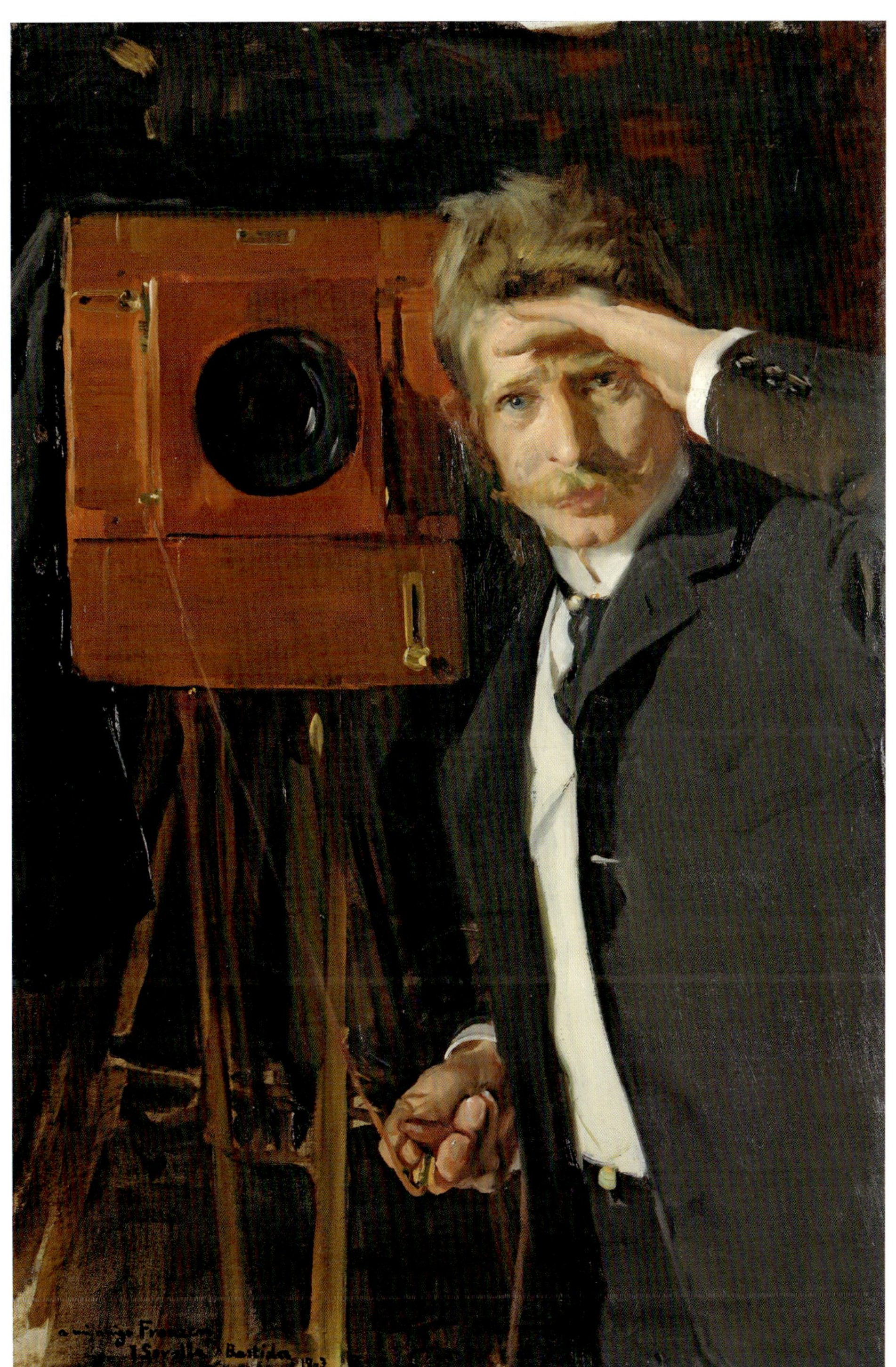

23 *The Photographer Christian Franzen*

1903
Oil on canvas, 39½ x 26 in.
Signed: "a mi amigo Franzen /
J. Sorolla y Bastida / 1903"
Private collection
(BPS 1986)

24 *Children on the Seashore*

1903
Oil on canvas, 38 x 51½ in.
Signed: "J. Sorolla y Bastida / 1903 / Valencia"
Philadelphia, Pennsylvania, Philadelphia Museum of Art, purchased with the W. P. Wilstach Fund, 1904 [W1904–1–55]
(BPS 1718)

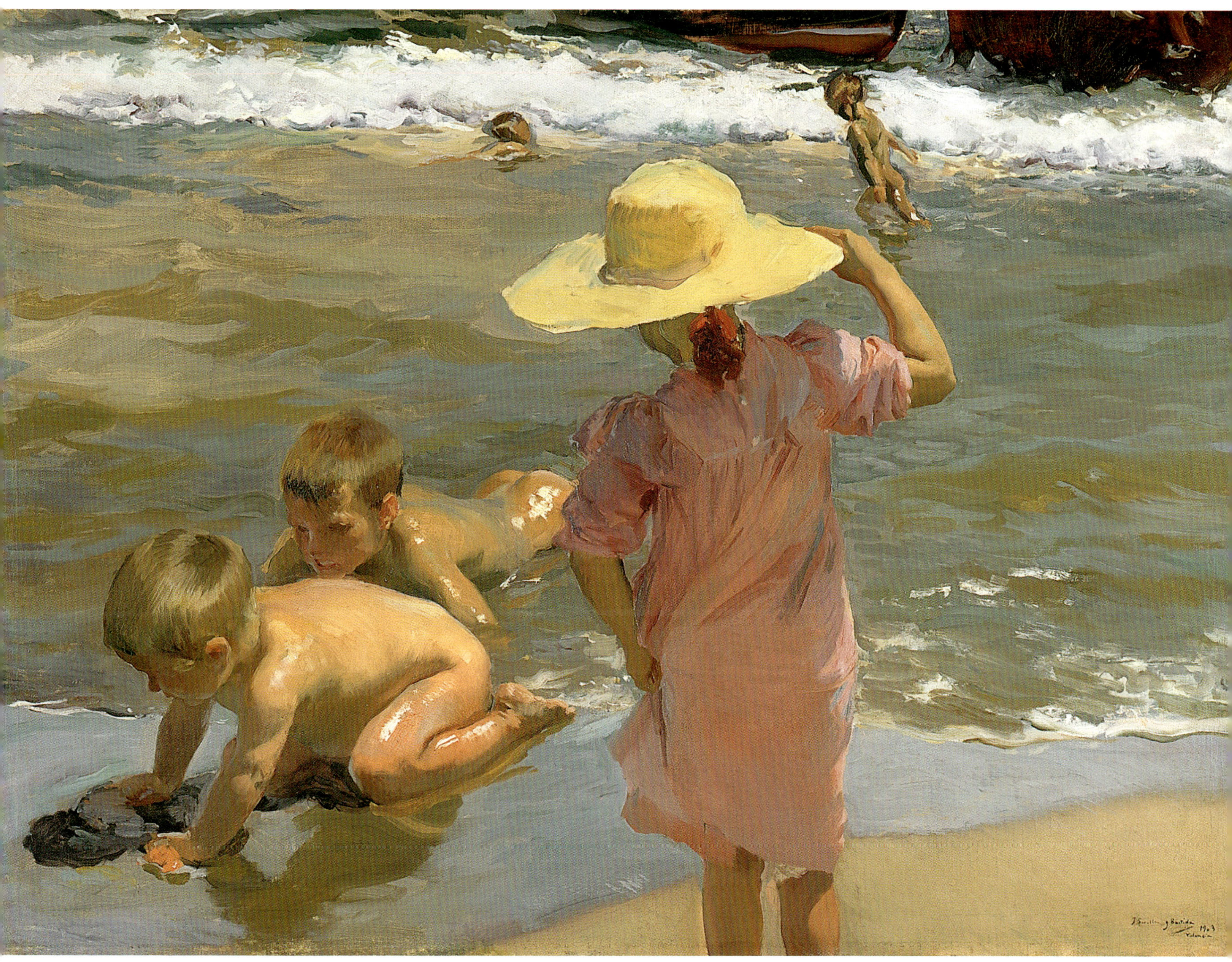

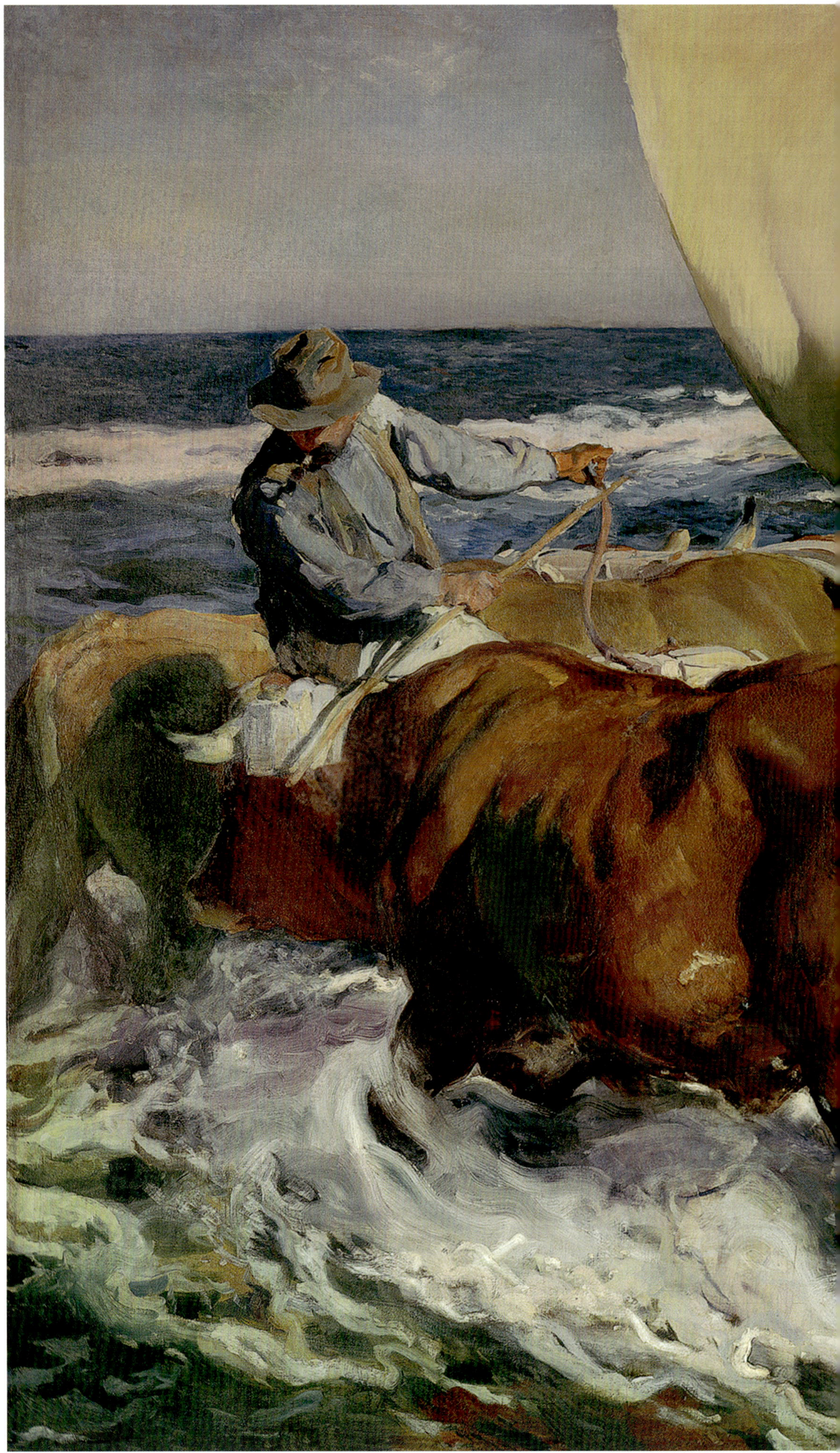

25 *Afternoon Sun, Beaching the Boat*

1903
Oil on canvas,
9 ft. 9¾ in. x 14 ft. 5½ in.
Signed: "J. Sorolla y Bastida / 1903 / Valencia"
New York, The Hispanic Society of America [inv. A 58]
(BPS 1449)

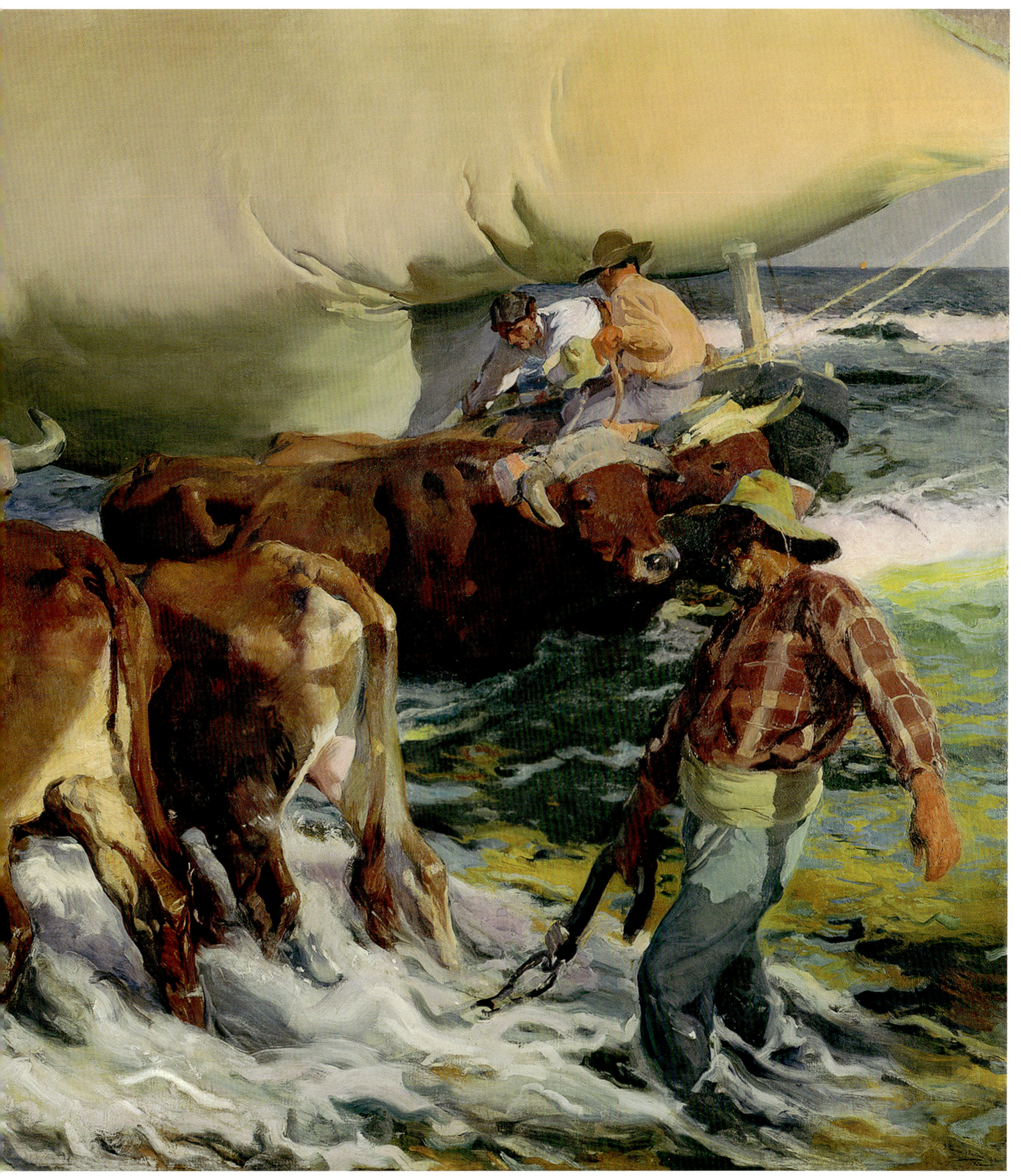

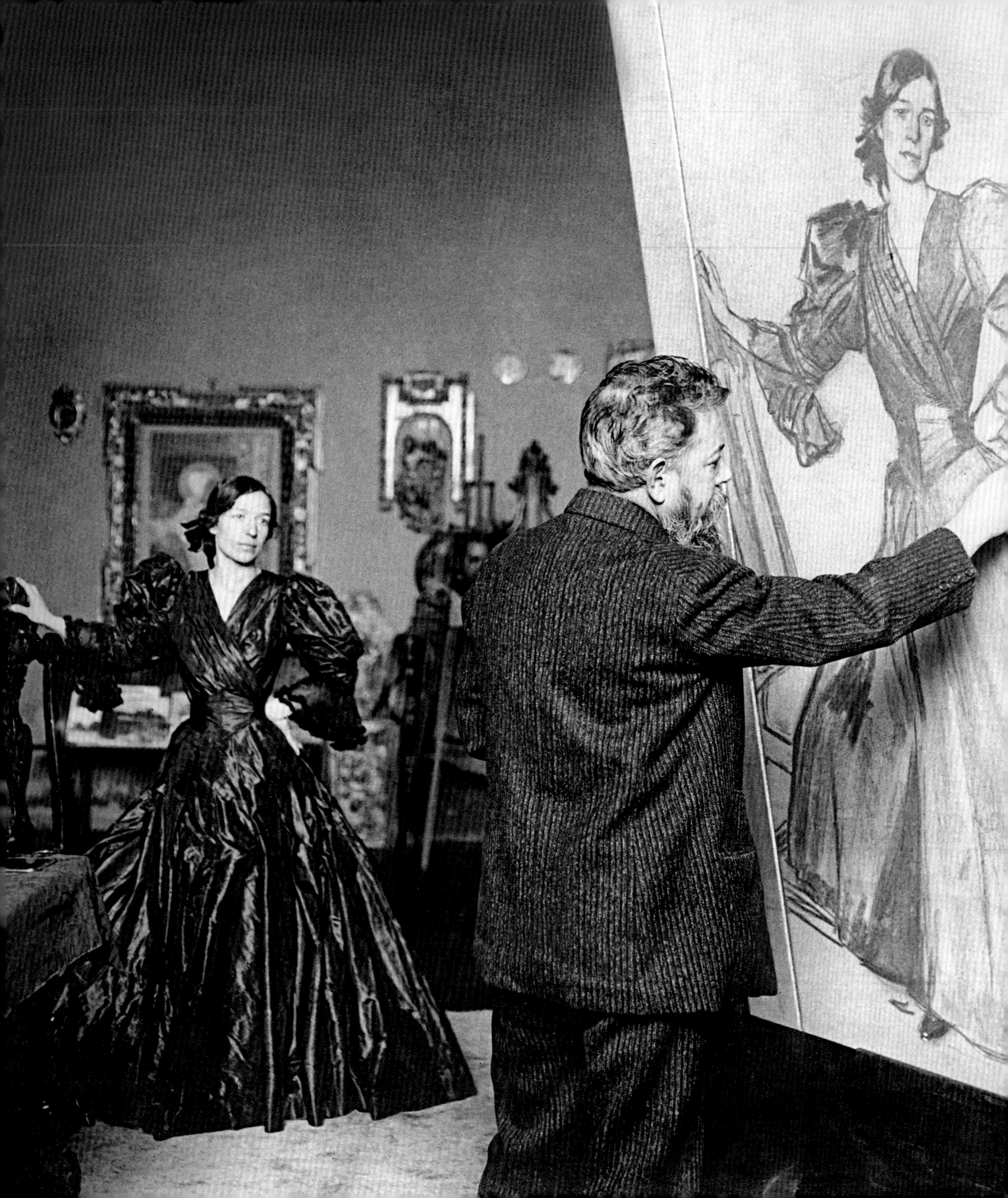

ARTISTIC PROSPERITY (1904–11)

The second stage of Sorolla's life as a painter spans the period from 1904 to 1911. It is during this time that Sorolla's painting style became clearly defined. Thus, he decided to show the world what he was capable of doing by personally taking his works to individual exhibitions in major cities of Europe and the United States. Although this period is relatively short, within it is a whirlwind of activity and productivity.

The beginning of this period is marked by the predominance of beach themes. A great number of paintings, such as *Summer* [fig. 28], *Midday at Valencia Beach* [fig. 29] and *Bath-Time*, are of maritime scenes. The 1905 paintings of swimmers and children bathing in Jávea—*The White Boat, Jávea* [fig. 31], *The Bath, Jávea* [fig. 32]—are the most representative of that time. The mastery he shows in representing light and movement is undeniable.

Sorolla also painted high-quality multiple and individual portraits, which he presented in his personal exhibitions. Outstanding works in the first group include *My Children* [fig. 27], *The Family of Rafael Errázuriz* [fig. 33], and *The Benlliure Arana Family,* or *Lucrecia Arana with Her Son* [fig. 35], while the second includes such striking pictures as *José Echegaray* [fig. 34], *Señora de Sorolla in Black* [fig. 36], and his first great portrait in the open air, *María Dressed as a Valencian Farmworker* [fig. 38].

In 1906, Sorolla exhibited 497 works at the Georges Petit Gallery with great success among the critics and public and with numerous sales. The French State granted him the Cross of Officer of the National Order of the Legion of Honor. French artists were delighted by his paintings and attended painting sessions for Raimundo de Madrazo y Garreta's portrait held in his garden in Paris that summer [fig. 37].

Sorolla's outstanding success in France was described as mad, huge, hectic, and surpassing all predictions. The politician and writer Henri Rochefort, known for his personal criterion and for being opposed to impressionists, reacts to his visit to the exhibition:

Joaquín Sorolla painting *Señora de Sorolla in Black*, 1906. Photograph by Christian Franzen y Nissen. Madrid, Museo Sorolla [80.037]

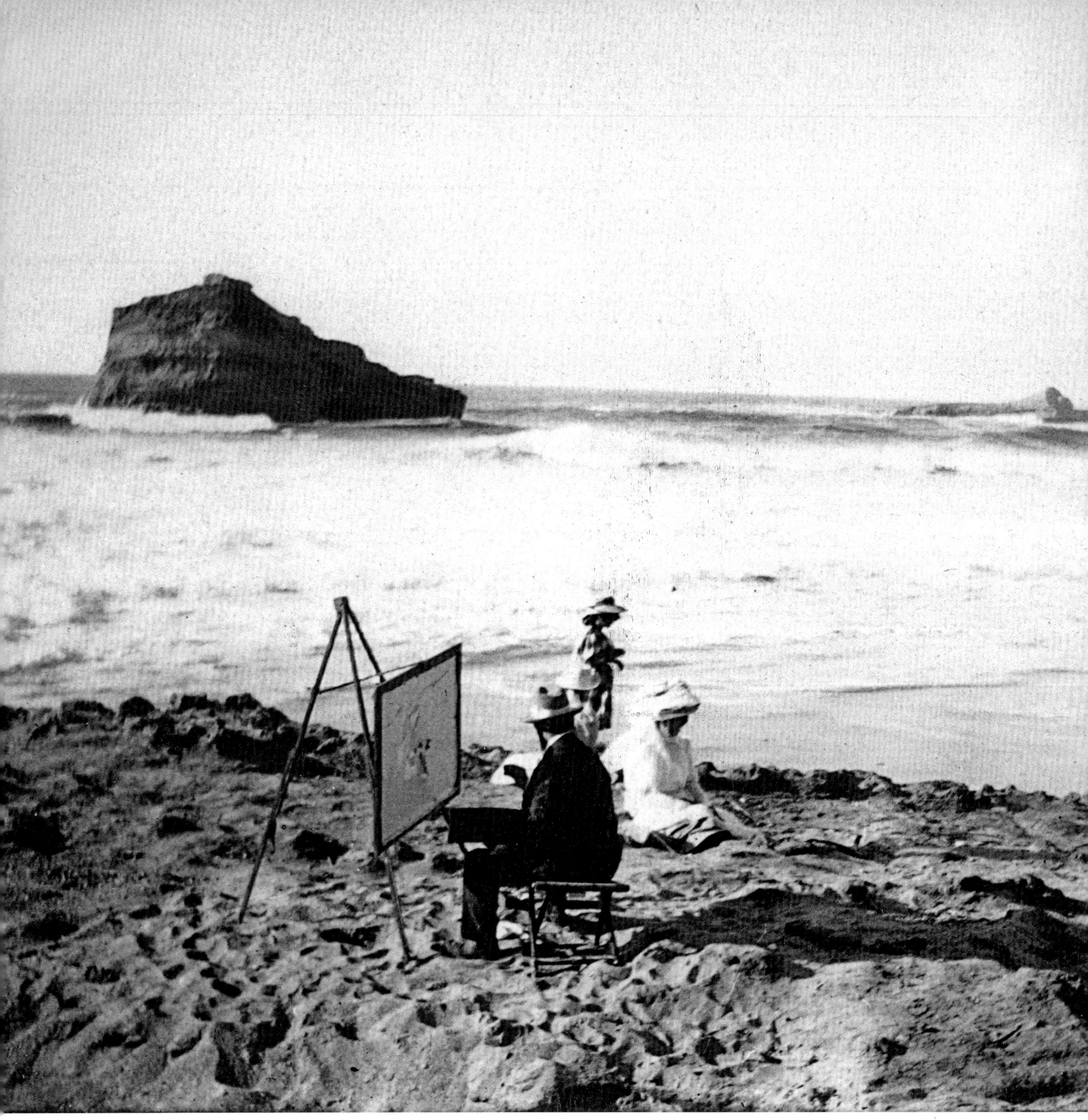

> A great painter has been born. Unfortunately, he is not from France.... I do not know of any brush that contains as much sun.... This artist paints in a way that has nothing to do with impressionism, but is incredibly impressionable. What science in the composition! What truth in the figures' movements! What poetry in the atmosphere! Sorolla has in his eyes all the flames of the Orient, and in his hand all of the confident draftsmanship of the most disciplined masters.... This painter, who is a great painter and who will be the glory of his country, does not follow any formal rules, and paints what he sees with incredible talent—that of a genius, I am tempted to say—making him one of the greatest additions to the fantastic collection of marvels at the Petit Gallery.[1]

Sorolla, who during his first stay in Paris had grasped the great discovery of the impressionists, which is nothing more than the alteration produced in a color when it finds itself close to others and an intense light surrounds them, combines this knowledge with Velázquez's great Spanish tradition, thereby achieving a very individual and highly captivating style of painting. This stay in Paris was focused on his personal exhibition, and Sorolla now felt that because his works were exhibited in dimly lit galleries, and especially because of the lack of Valencia's golden sunshine, they did not have the effect he desired. From this point on, Sorolla varied his palette substantially, lowering the intensity and making mauves and pinks more prominent to contrast with the yellows. This change is evident in the paintings completed that summer in Biarritz—*Low Tide, Elena in Biarritz* [fig. 39], *Snapshot, Biarritz* [fig. 40], *Lighthouse Walk at Biarritz* [fig. 41]—and that autumn in both Toledo— *The Shadow of Alcántara Bridge* [fig. 42], *The Blind Man of Toledo* [fig. 43]—and Segovia.

Joaquín Sorolla painting
Snapshot, Biarritz, 1906.
Madrid, Museo Sorolla [80.059]

In 1907, Sorolla sent 280 paintings to Berlin, Düsseldorf, and Cologne. Although commercially the exhibitions were a disappointment, there was no doubt they were an exceptional artistic success. Schulte, the owner of the galleries in which Sorolla showed his works, said that he had seen the exhibitions "filled with artists who studied his works with exclamations of admiration."[2] The lack of economic success was probably due to the fact that Sorolla was not present. His daughter María was ill with tuberculosis at El Pardo—represented in *María Convalescing in El Pardo* [fig. 44]—and he did not want to leave her side. In addition to this, because his wife was also attending to María, she could not organize the works or shipping lists. When his daughter began to recuperate, they moved to La Granja de San Ildefonso, a holiday retreat for the Royal Family of Spain, where Sorolla painted numerous landscapes and gardens while at the same time creating marvelous outdoor portraits of his family—*María at La Granja* [fig. 47], *Clotilde Strolling in the Gardens of La Granja* [fig. 48]—and applying the same concept to his portraits of Spain's royalty, such as *King Alfonso XIII in Hussar's Uniform* [fig. 46].

María, trained by her father and encouraged by her mother, painted incessantly, as we can see in *María Painting in El Pardo* [fig. 45], which gave Sorolla great joy. For him, "one can only be truly happy by being a painter."

With María completely restored to good health, Sorolla traveled to Seville at the beginning of 1908 to paint a portrait for the queen. This was to be the front-runner in his next personal exhibition in London. Sorolla took advantage of this trip to paint the gardens of the Alcázar in *Gardens of the Alcázar of Seville in Winter* [fig. 50], *Reflections in a Fountain* [fig. 51], and *Fountain of the Moorish King, Alcázar of Seville* [fig. 52]. The exhibit opened in June at the Grafton Galleries and was a great success with the public. As with the previous exhibit, Sorolla won praise from other artists, who presented him with a magnificent banquet at the Royal Academy presided over by the Prince of Wales.

The exhibition did not have as much economic success as Sorolla had hoped, and the money obtained from the sales was half of what he had earned in Paris. During this trip, however, there occurred a significant event that was to have a great effect on the success of Sorolla's career. It was precisely in Paris that the great American Hispanist Archer Milton Huntington discovered and was enthused by Sorolla's work and offered him the chance to take it to the Hispanic Society of America in New York. Sorolla wrote a letter to Clotilde about the experience, saying: "Today I have decided something that I believe will be of great importance for our artistic success in New York, with such admirable advantages that Paris will be incomparable. I think I have found God in human form."[3]

That summer, already thinking about his exhibit in New York, Sorolla painted on Valencia's beach with a frenetic intensity. In these works his interest in movement is even more evident. There are numerous scenes of children running along the beach and wonderful paintings of girls and women leaving the water wrapped in wet, semi-transparent robes that cling to the curves of their bodies. These paintings are created with a virtuosity and a gentleness found in Greek sculptures, as can be seen in *Going for a Bath, Valencia* [fig. 53], *Running along the Beach* [fig. 54], *After the Bath* [fig. 55] and, *Sea Idyll* [fig. 56]. The Greek influences that are now more prominent in his works originated in the friezes from the Parthenon he had seen in London, and, as he says to his wife in a letter, "[they] have provided me with a sublime afternoon."

In January of 1909, the couple moved to New York with their two oldest children, María and Joaquín, and in February, the exhibition opened at the gallery of the Hispanic Society of America with 356 paintings.

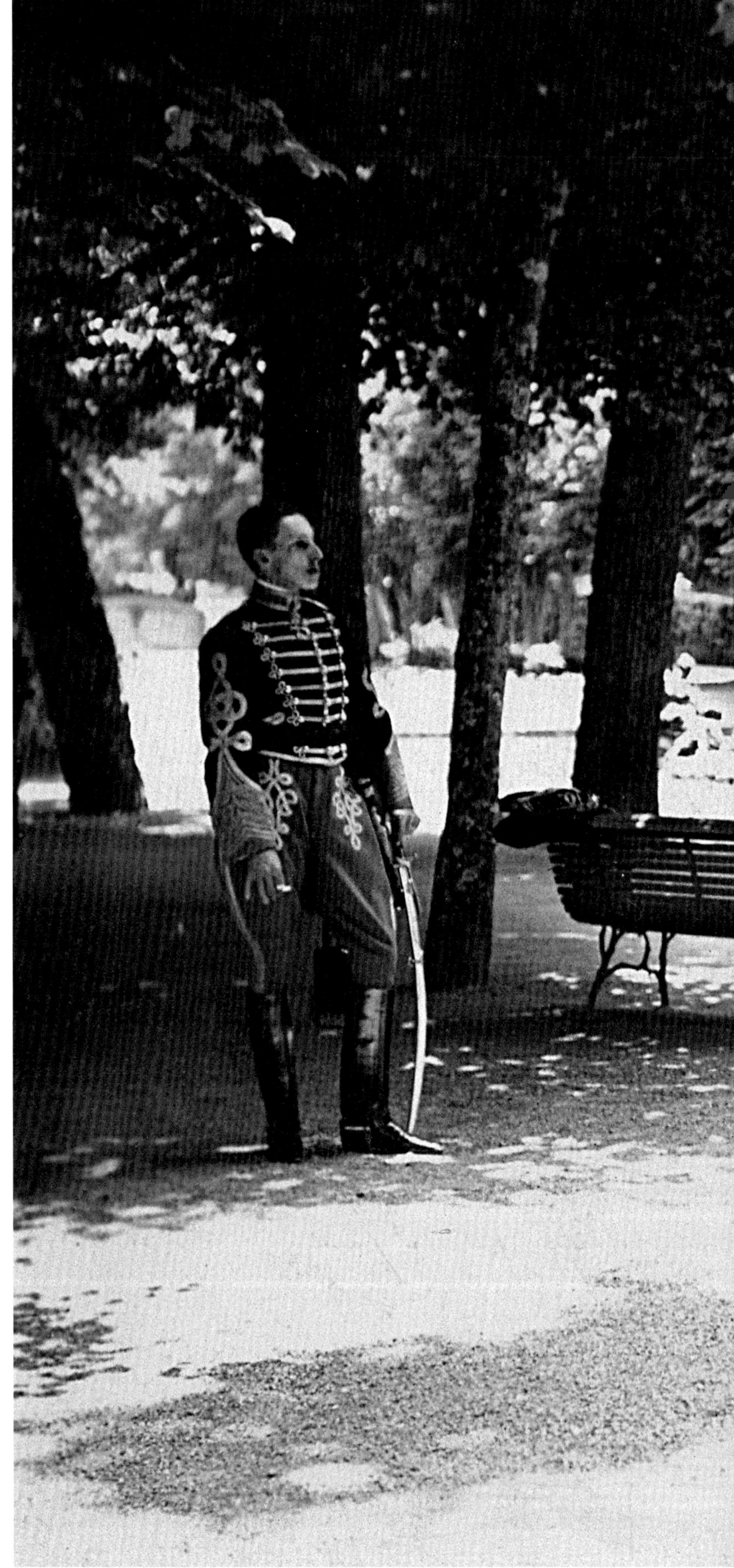

Joaquín Sorolla painting the portrait of *King Alfonso XIII in Hussar's Uniform* at La Granja, 1907

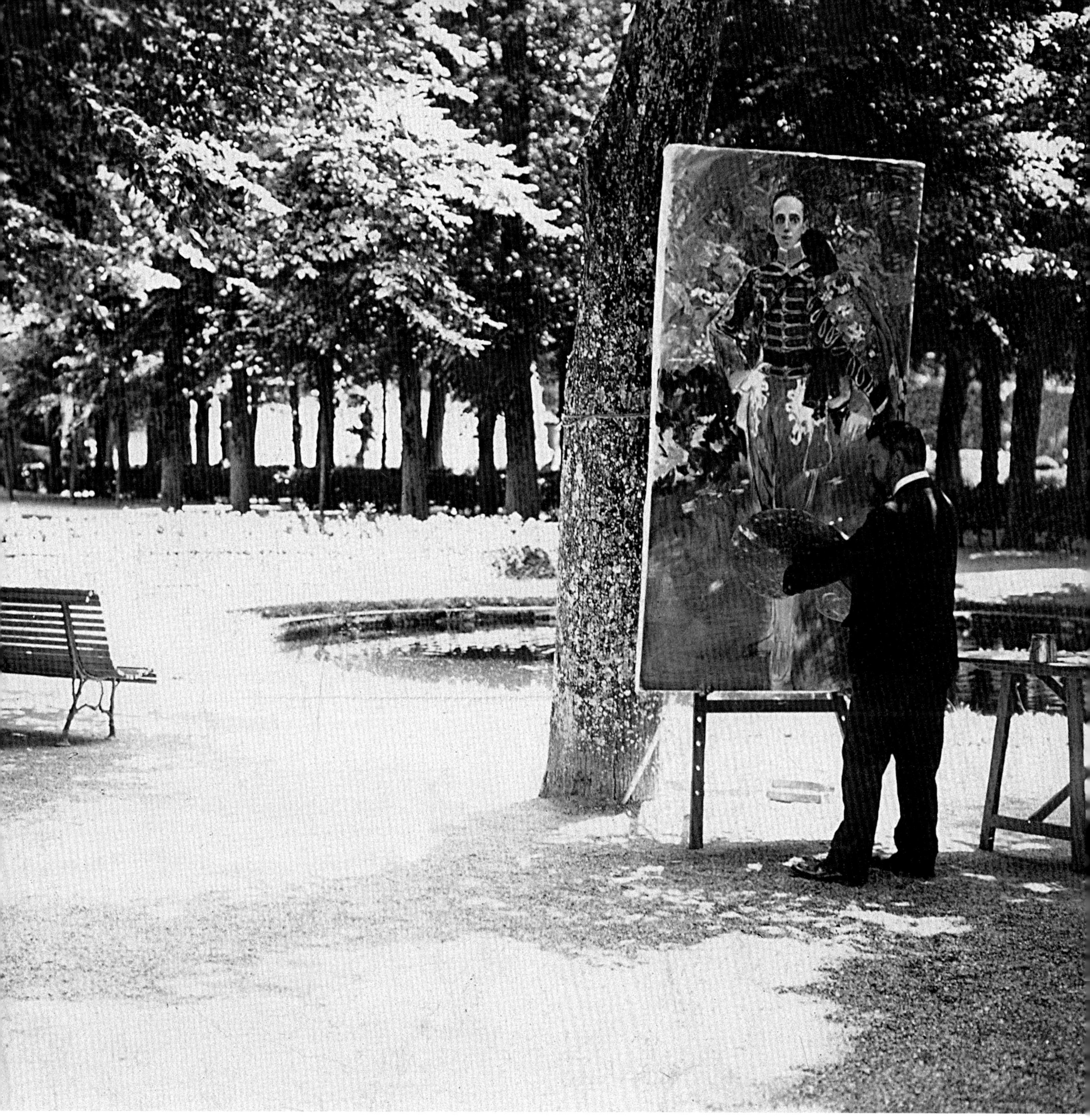

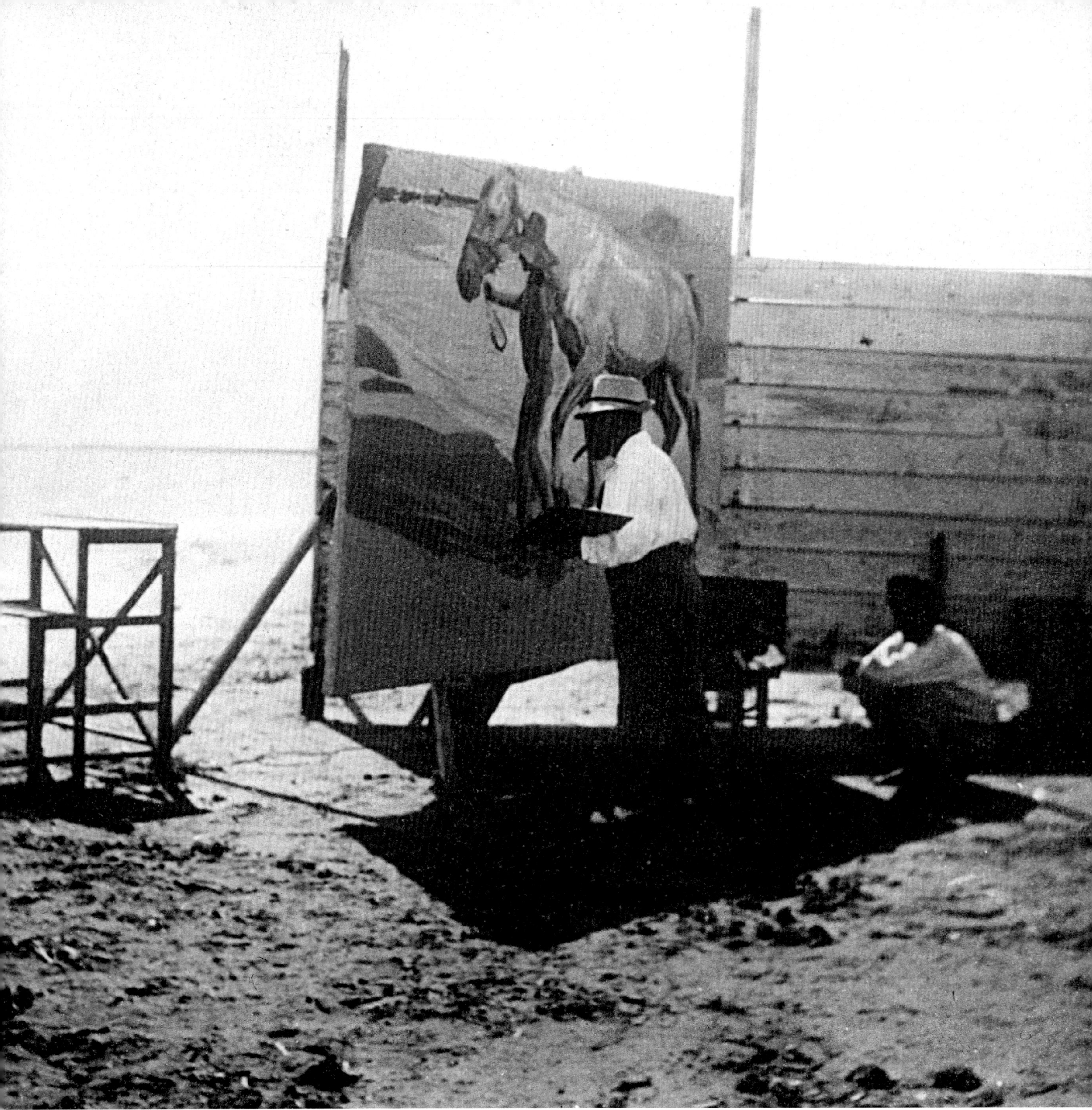

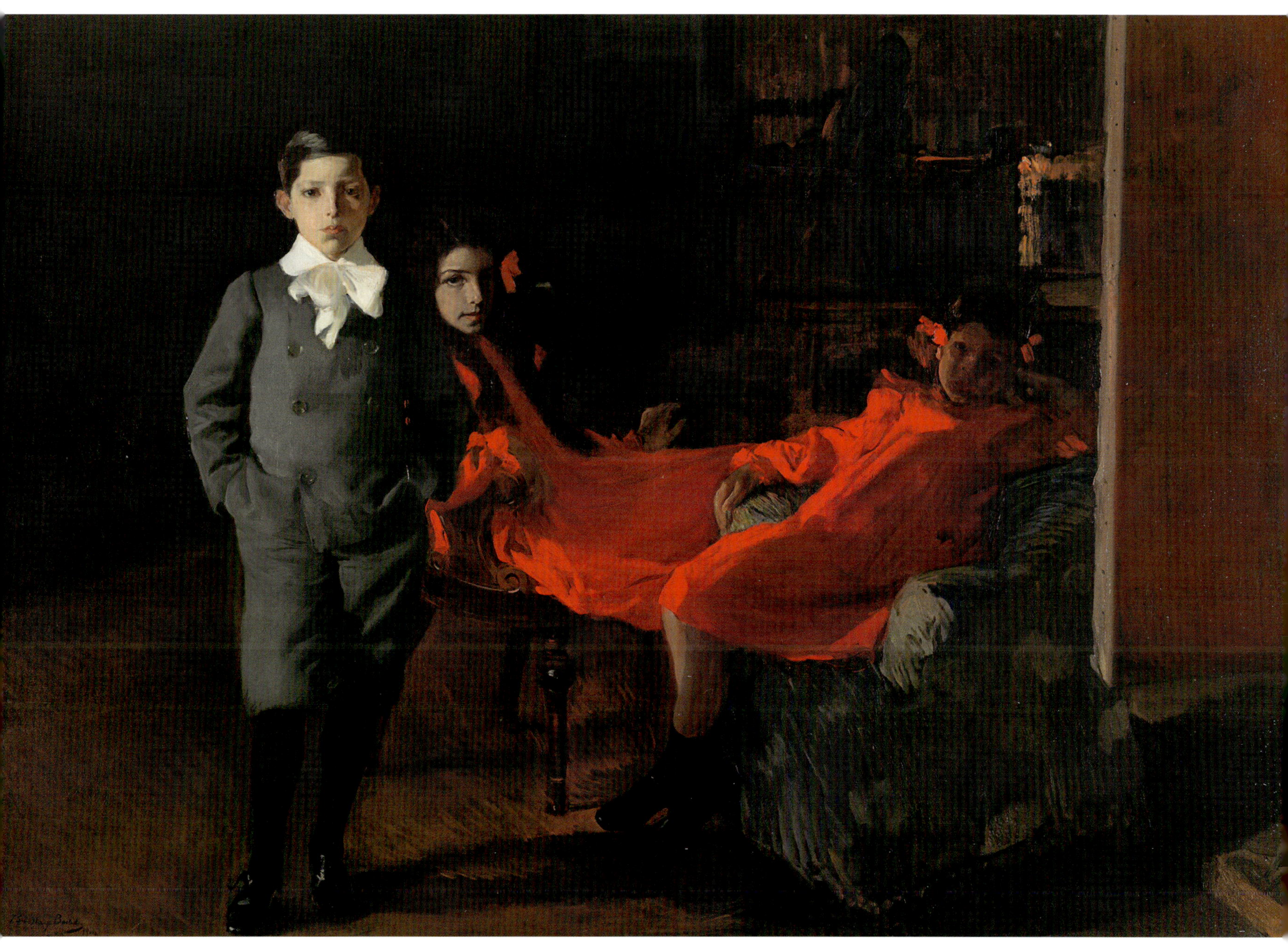

28 *Summer*

1904
Oil on canvas, 58¾ x 99¼ in.
Signed: "J. Sorolla Bastida / 1904"
Havana, Museo Nacional de Bellas Artes de Cuba [inv. R /79 /370 /93–145]
(BPS 1771)

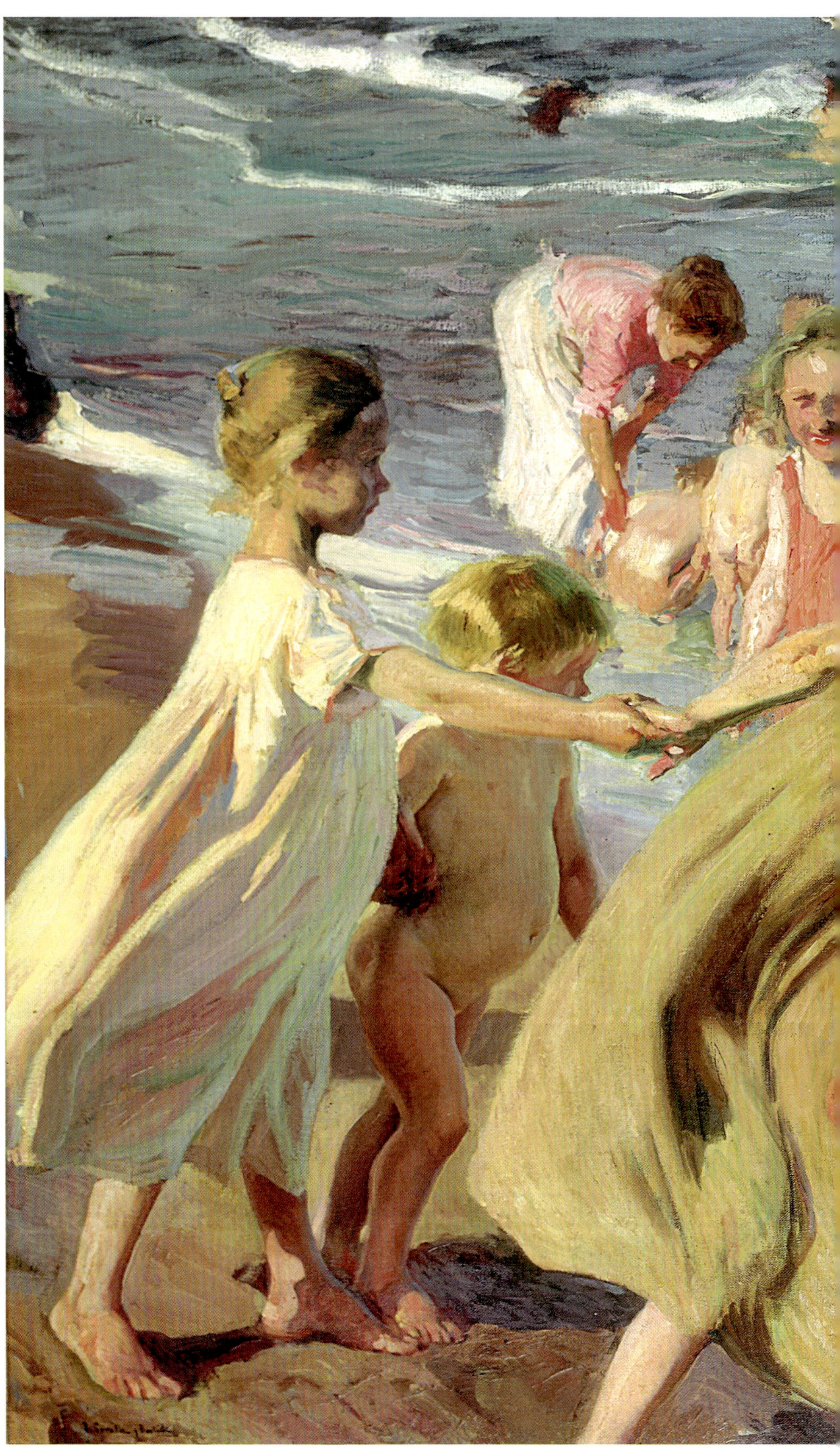

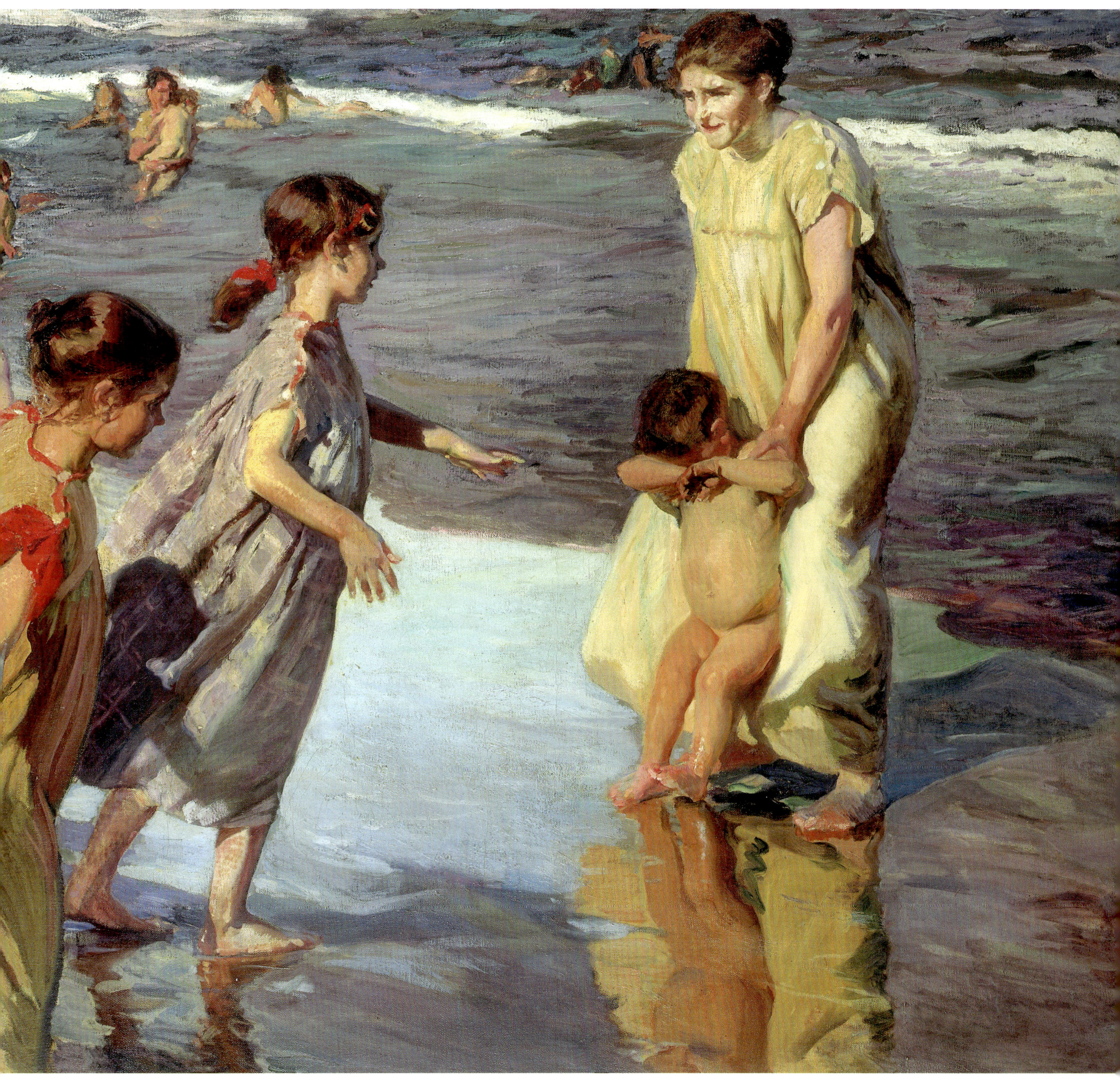

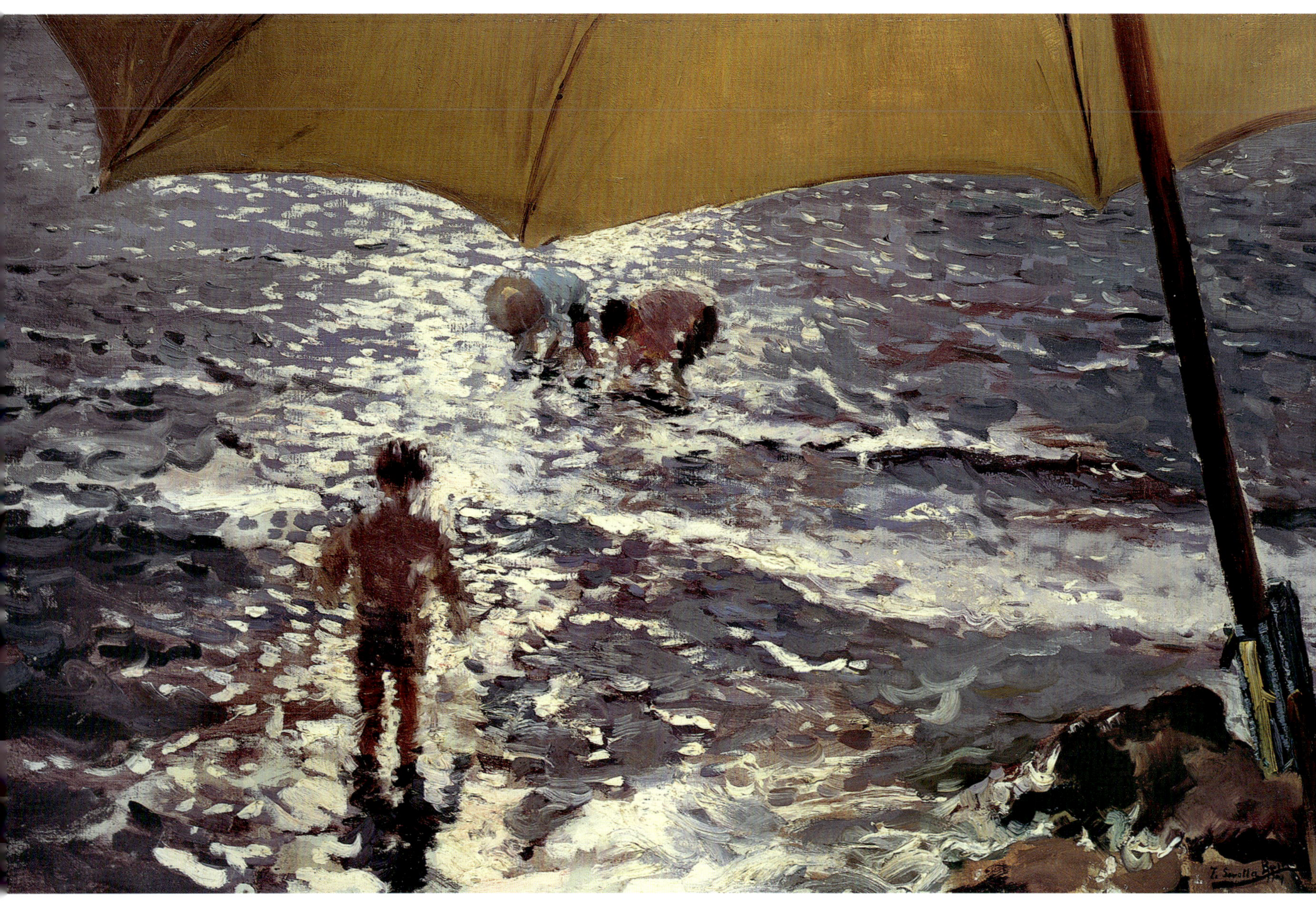

29 *Midday at Valencia Beach*

1904
Oil on canvas, 25¼ x 38¼ in.
Signed: "J Sorolla Bastida / 1904"
Arango Collection
(BPS 1829)

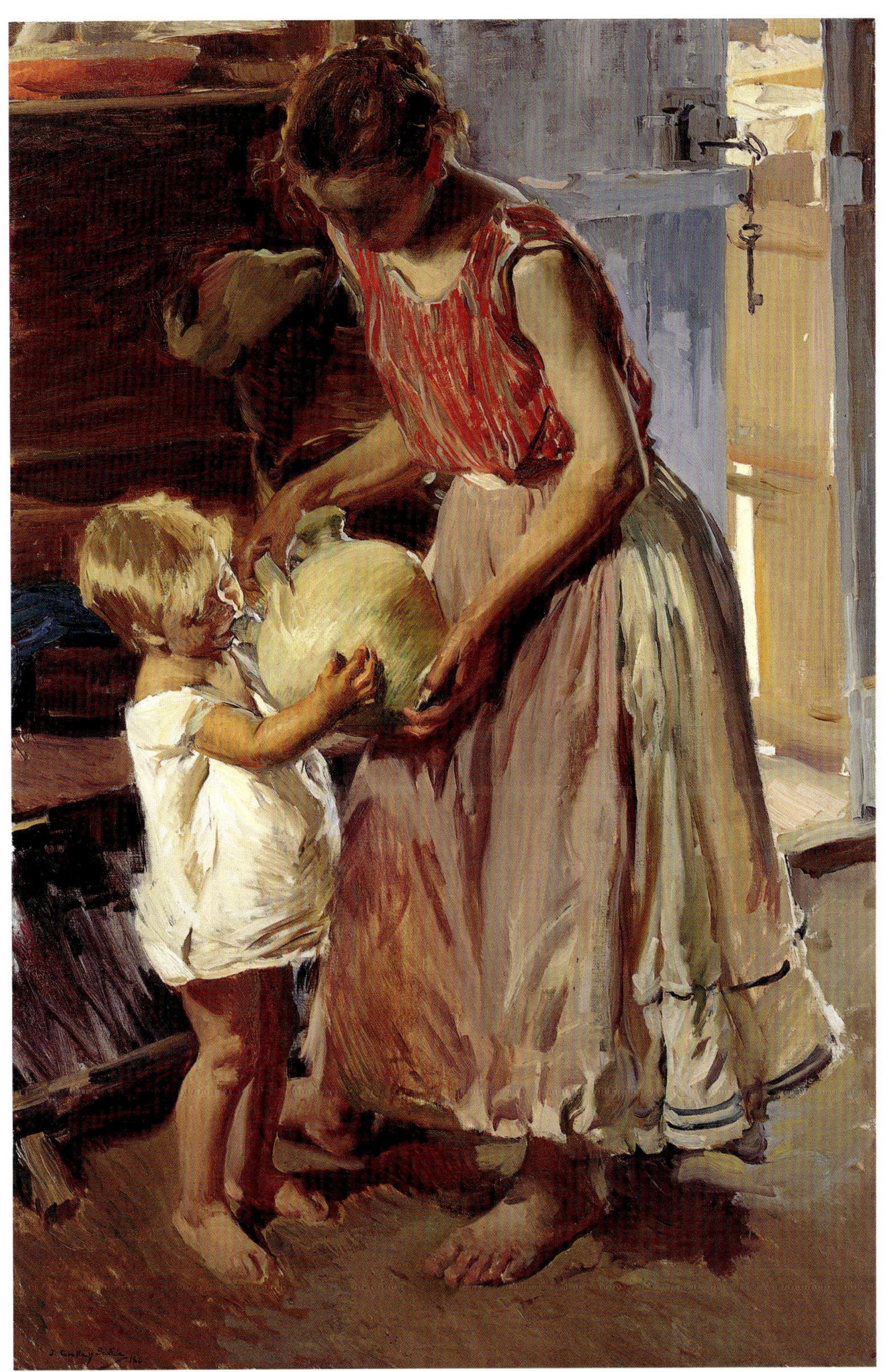

30 *The Drinking Jug*

1904
Oil on canvas, 59½ x 38½ in.
Signed: "J. Sorolla y Bastida / 1904"
Private collection
(BPS 1839)

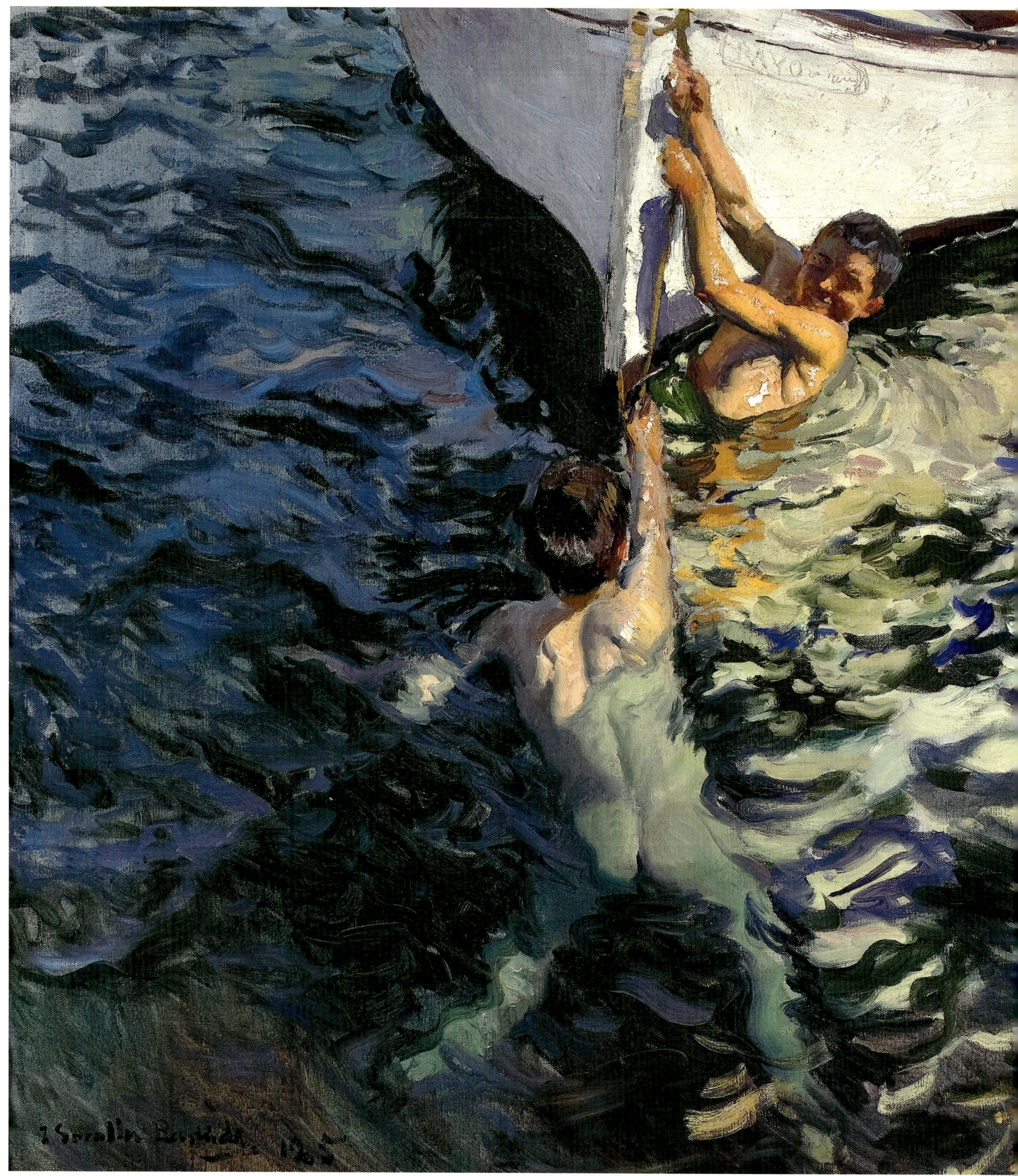
RAYO

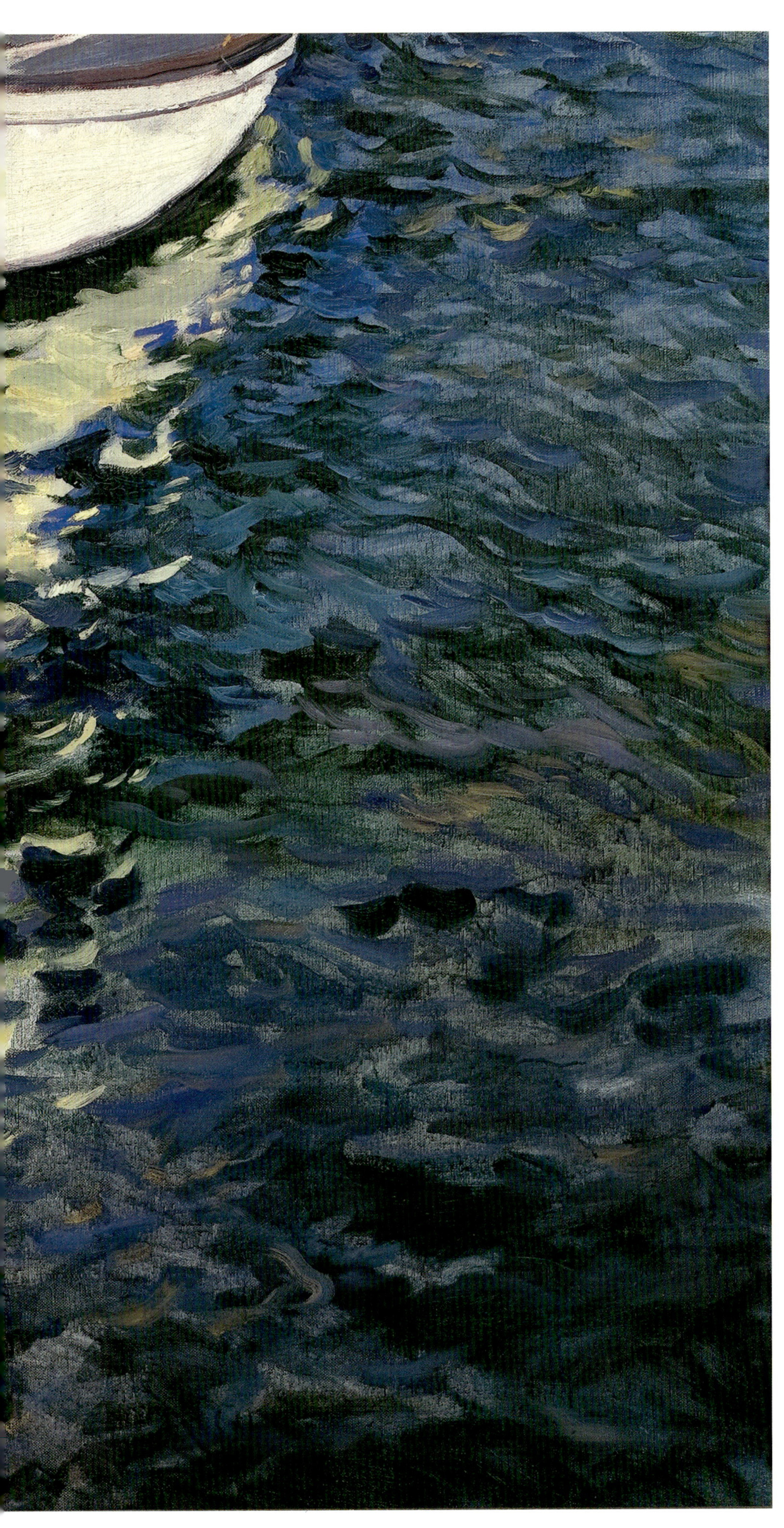

31 *The White Boat, Jávea*

1905
Oil on canvas, 41¼ x 59 in.
Signed: "J Sorolla Bastida / 1905"
Private collection
(BPS 1846)

32 *The Bath, Jávea*

1905
Oil on canvas, 35½ x 50½ in.
Signed: "J. Sorolla Bastida / 1905"
New York, The Metropolitan Museum
of Art, Catharine Lorillard Wolfe Collection,
Wolfe Fund, 1909 [09.71.2]
(BPS 1731)

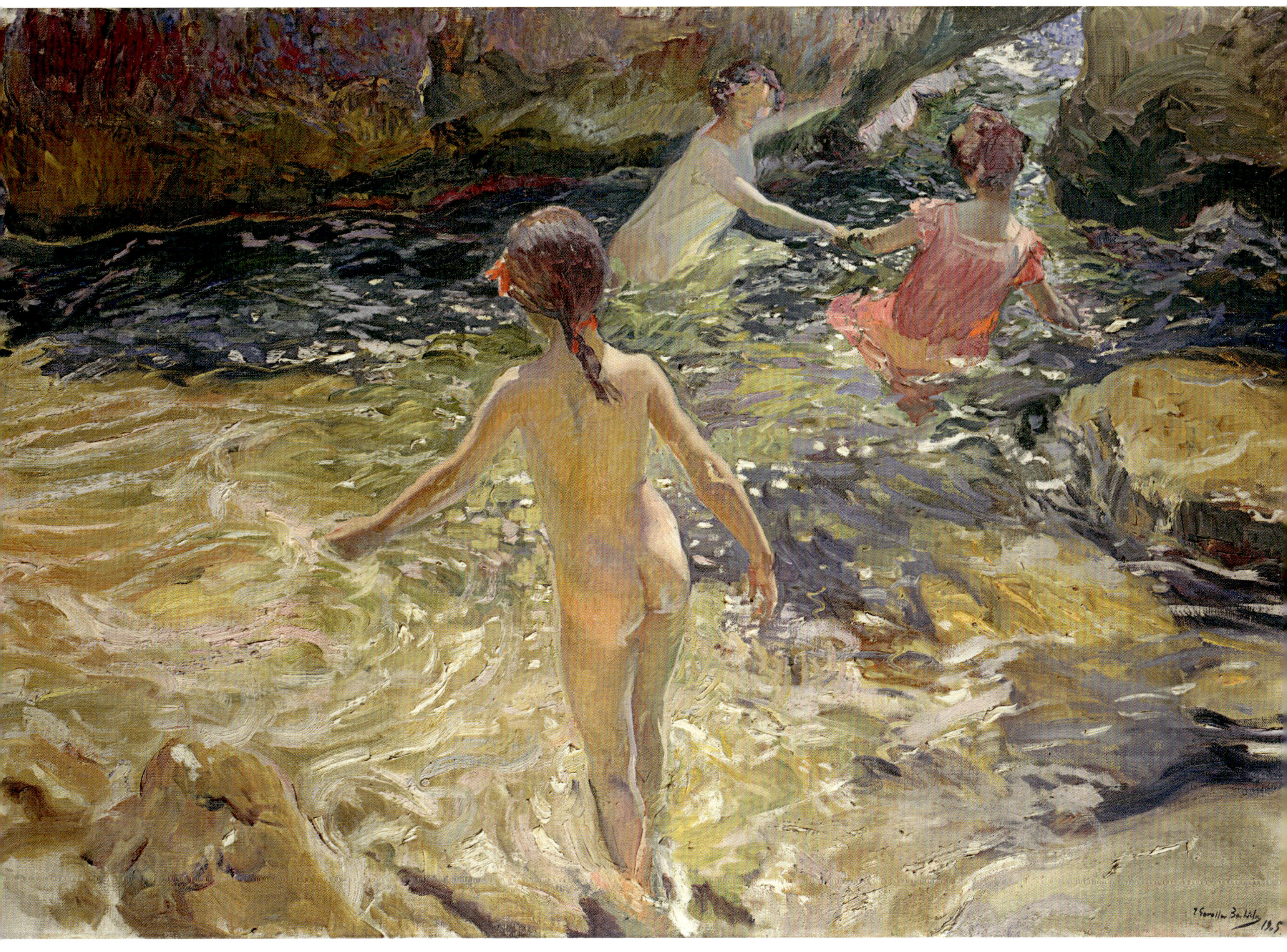

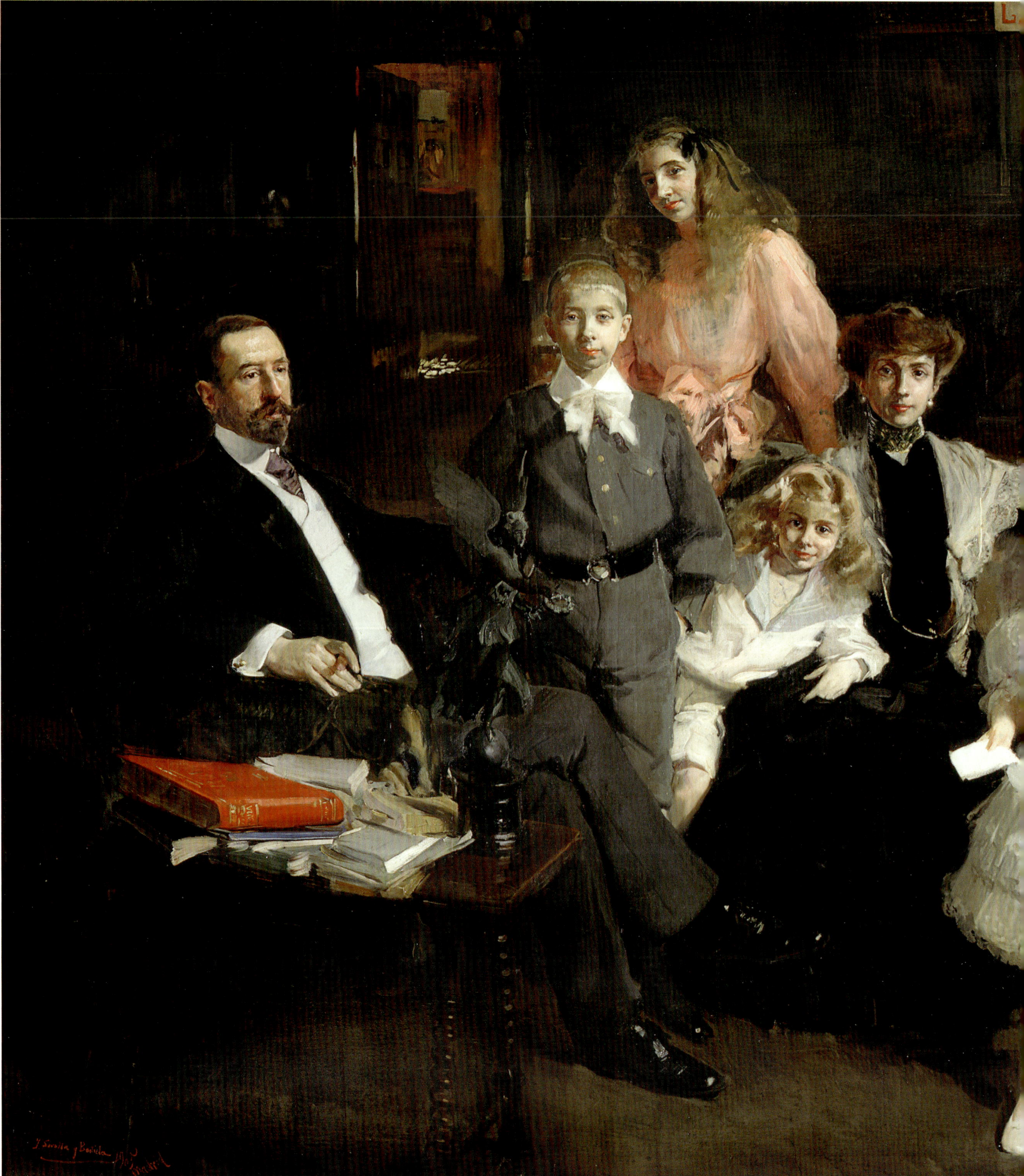

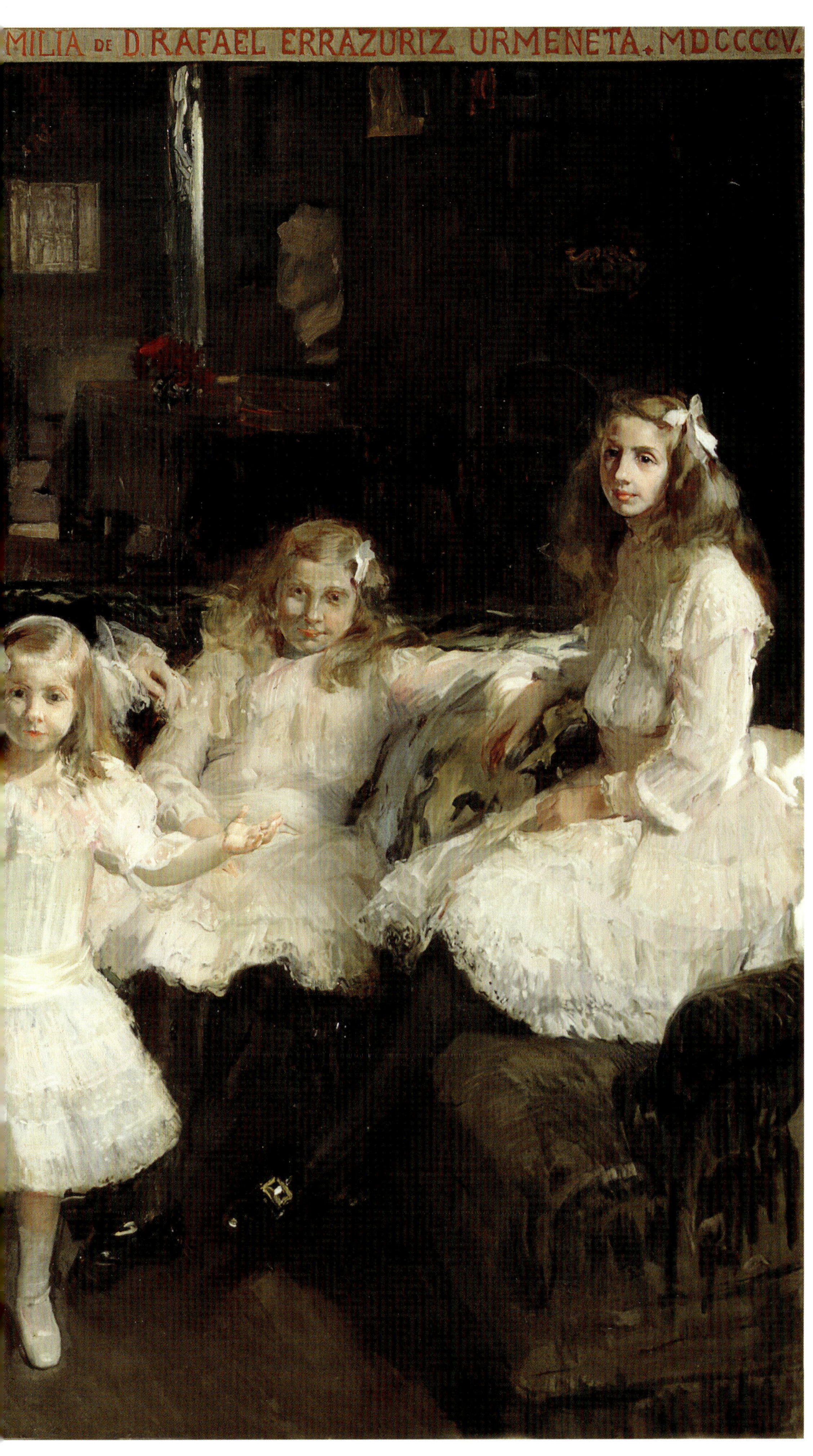

33 *The Family of Rafael Errázuriz*

1905
Oil on canvas, 89 x 131 in.
Signed: "J. Sorolla y Bastida / 1905 / Madrid"
Inscription: "LA FAMILIA DE D. RAFAEL ERRAZURIZ URMENETA. MDCCCCV."
Masaveu Collection
(BPS 1519)

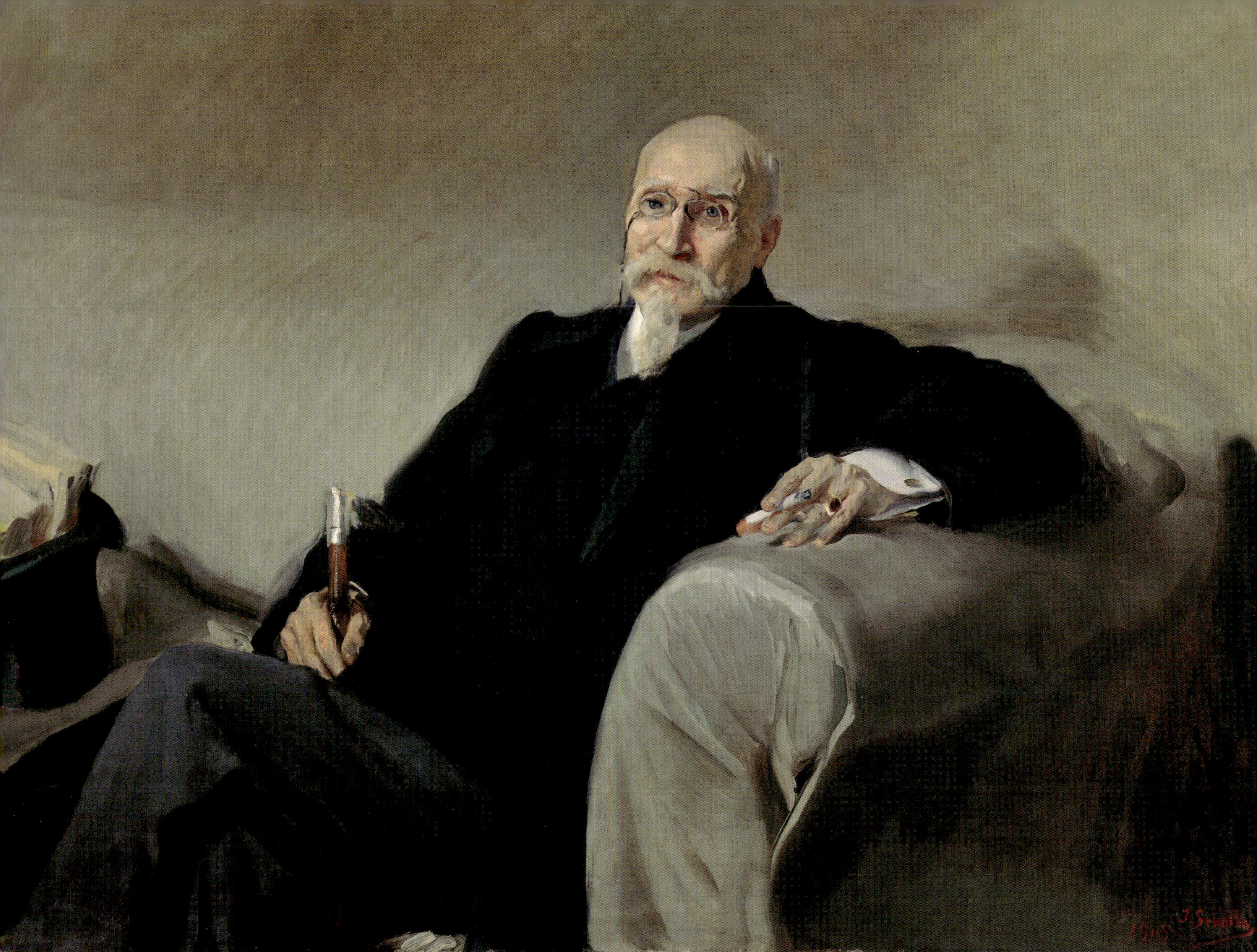

34 *José Echegaray*

1905
Oil on canvas, 39¼ x 52¼ in.
Signed: "J. Sorolla"
Madrid, Banco de España [inv. 295]
(BPS 2001)

38 *María Dressed as a Valencian Farmworker*

1906
Oil on canvas, 74½ x 37½ in.
Signed: "3. Junio. 1906 / J Sorolla Bastida"
Private collection
(BPS 1557)

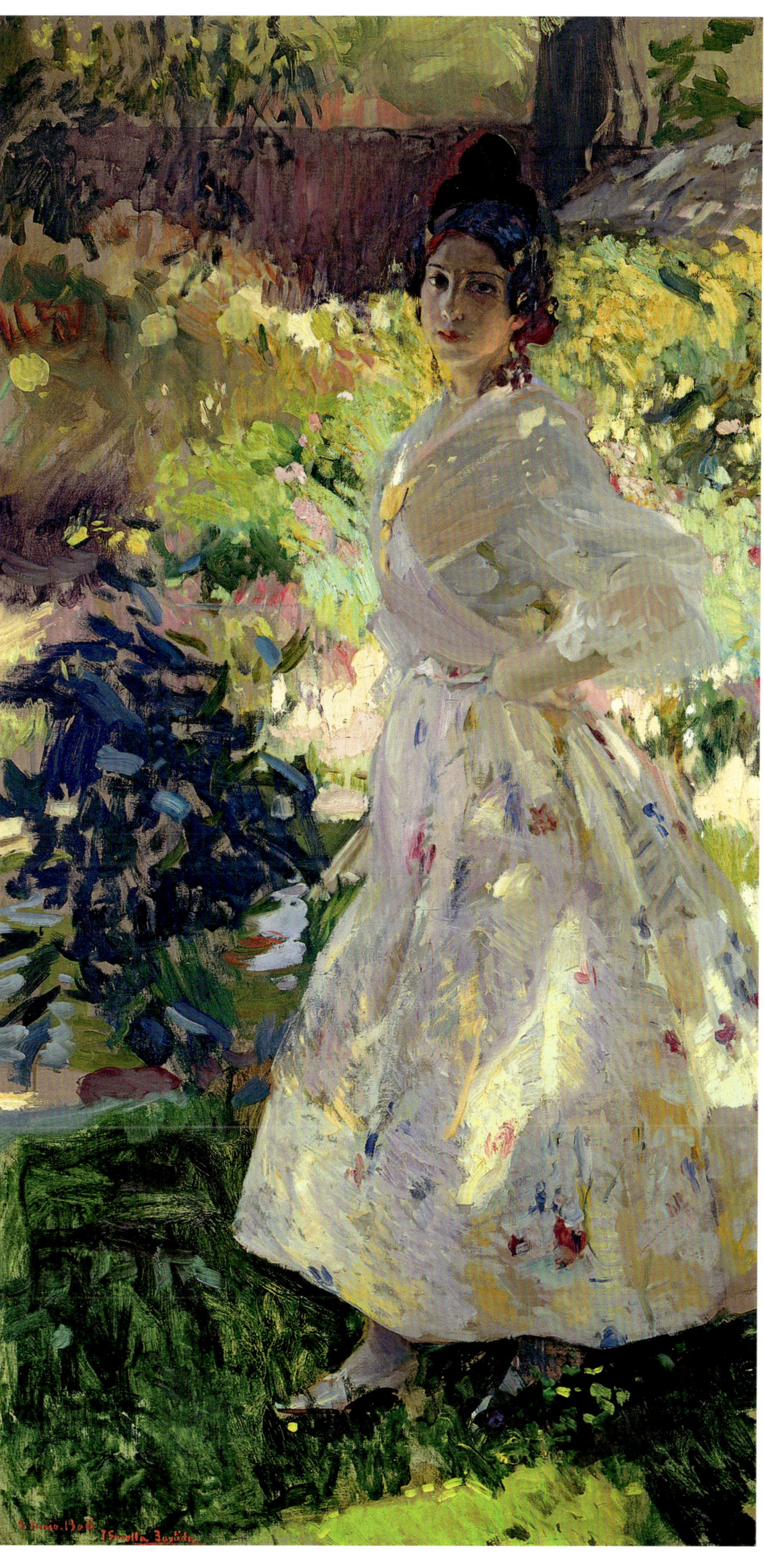

39 *Low Tide, Elena in Biarritz*

1906
Oil on canvas, 69 x 56 in.
Signed: "J. Sorolla y Bastida / 1906 / Biarritz"
Private collection
(BPS 1863)

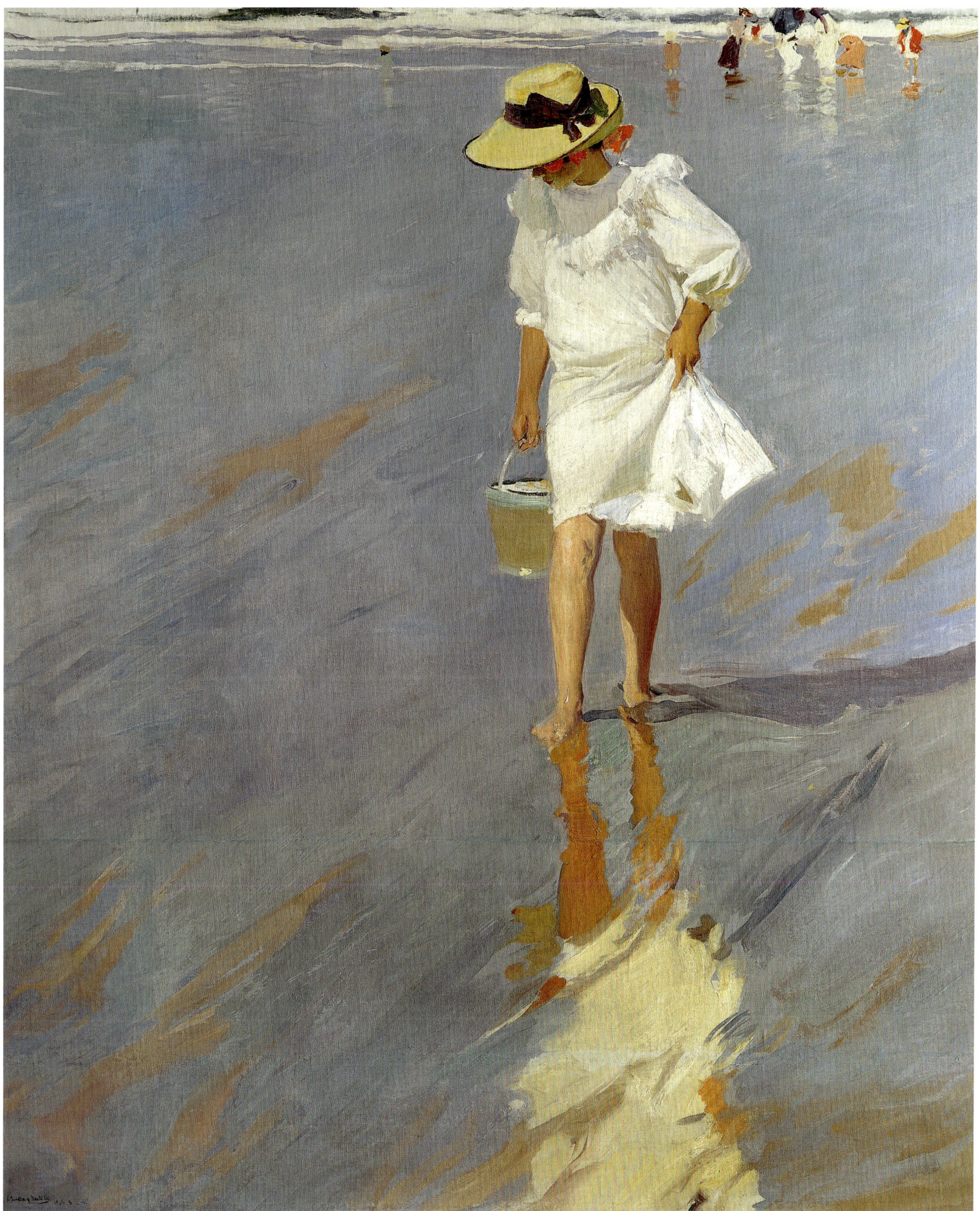

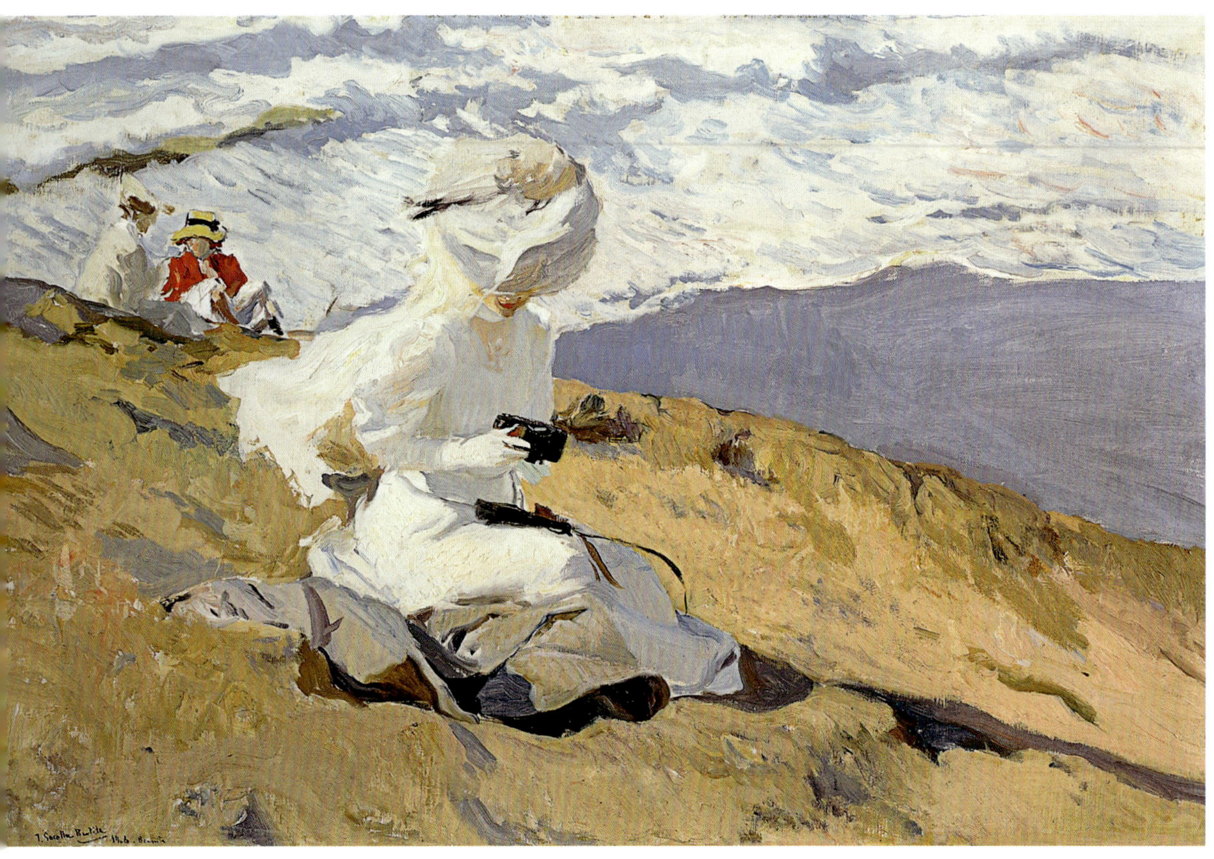

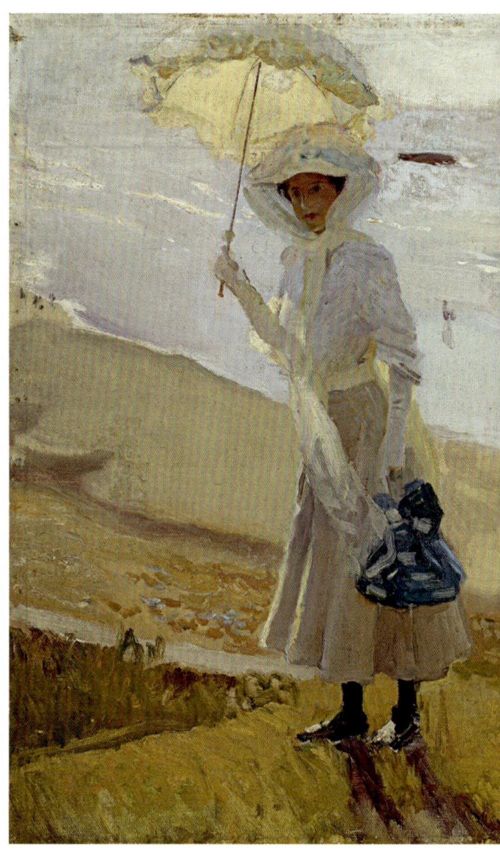

40 *Snapshot, Biarritz*

1906
Oil on canvas, 24½ x 36¾ in.
Signed: "J. Sorolla Bastida / 1906. Biarritz"
Madrid, Museo Sorolla [inv. 776]
(BPS 2466)

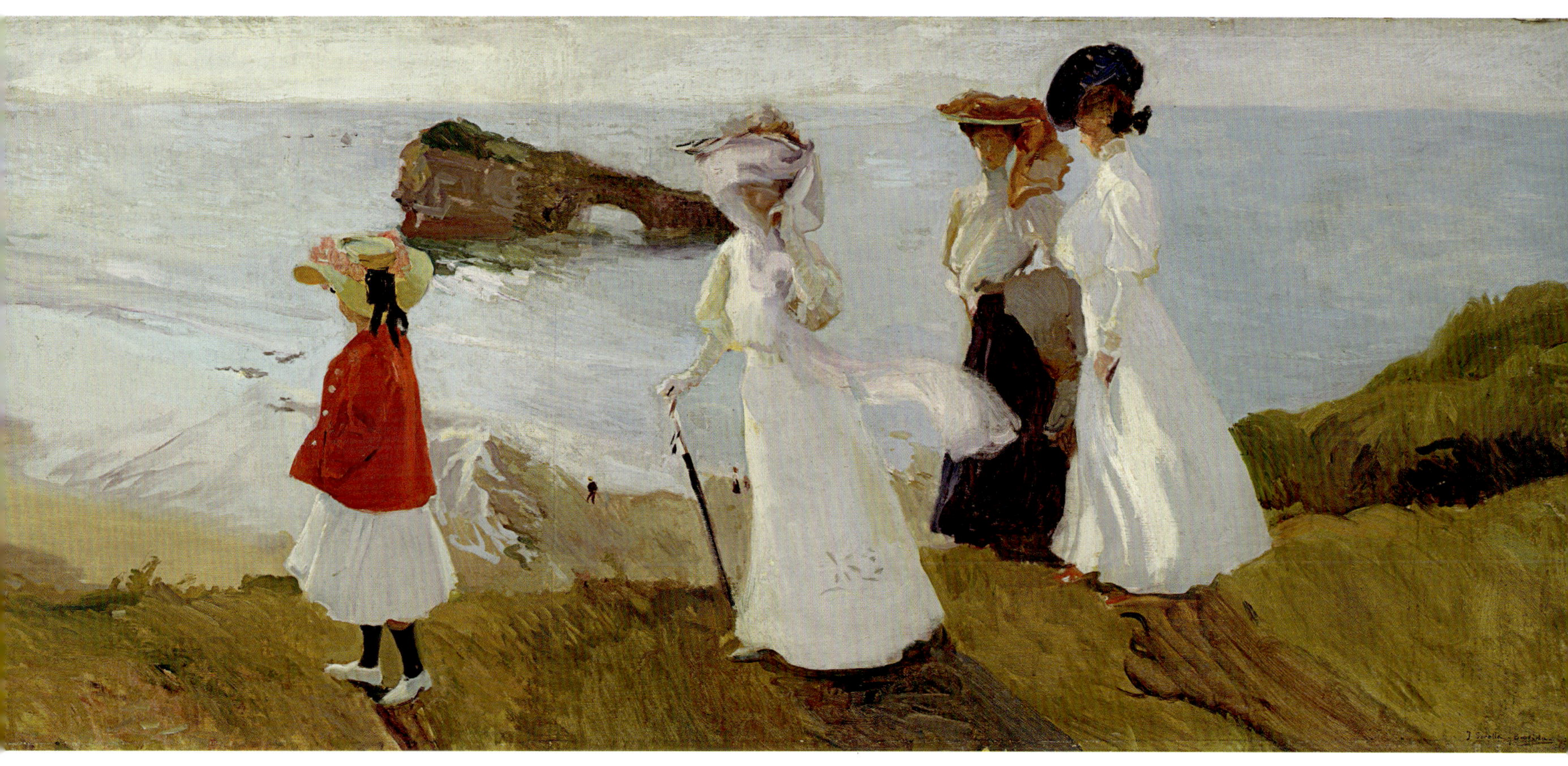

41 *Lighthouse Walk at Biarritz*

1906
Oil on canvas, 27 x 74¼ in.
Signed: "J Sorolla y Bastida / 1906"
Boston, Massachusetts, Museum of Fine Arts,
Peter Chardon Brooks Memorial Collection;
Gift of Mrs. Richard M. Saltonstall [inv. 22.691]
(BPS 1864)

42 *The Shadow of Alcántara Bridge*

1906
Oil on canvas, 26¼ x 36½ in.
Signed: "J. Sorolla y Bastida 1906"
Private collection
(BPS 1876)

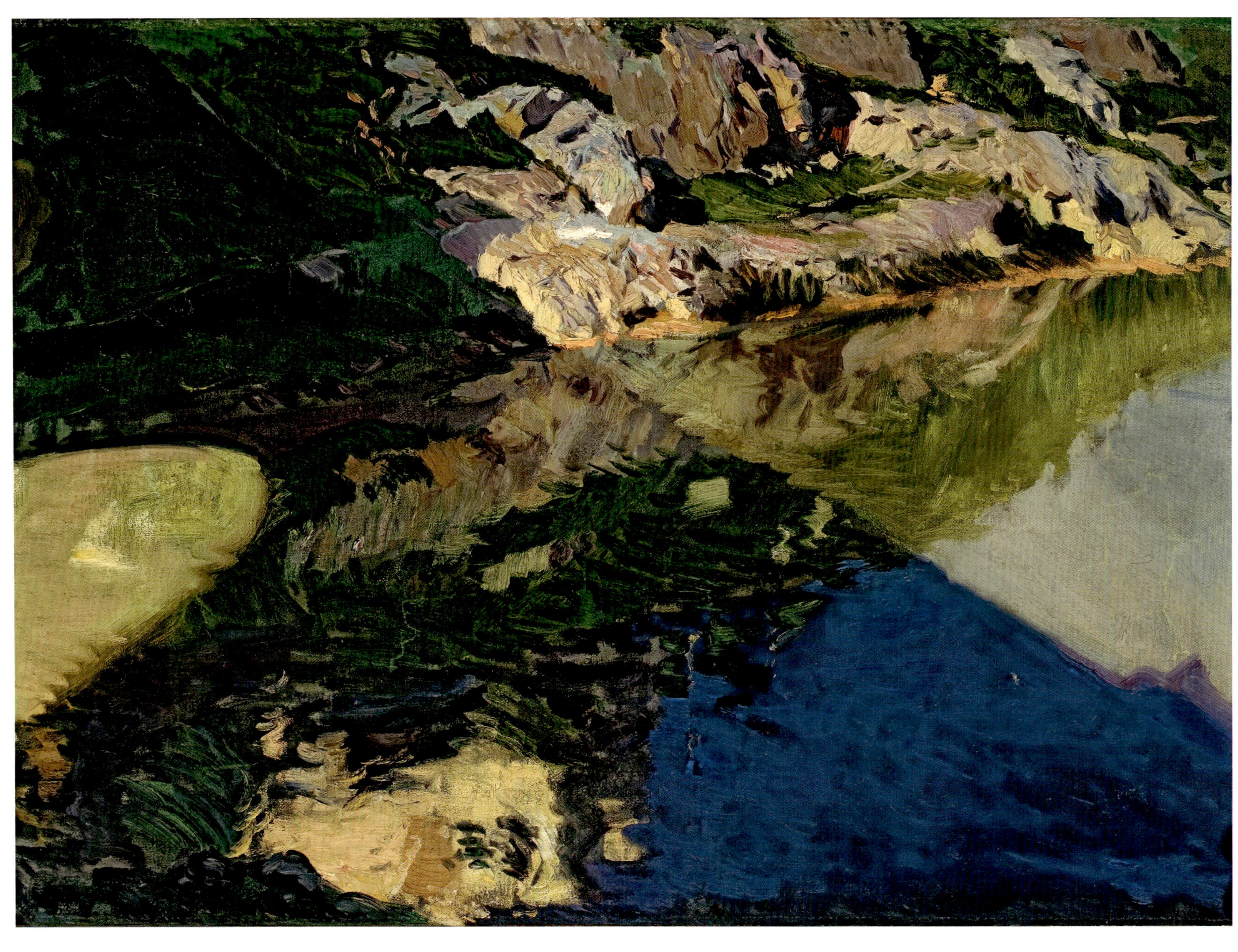

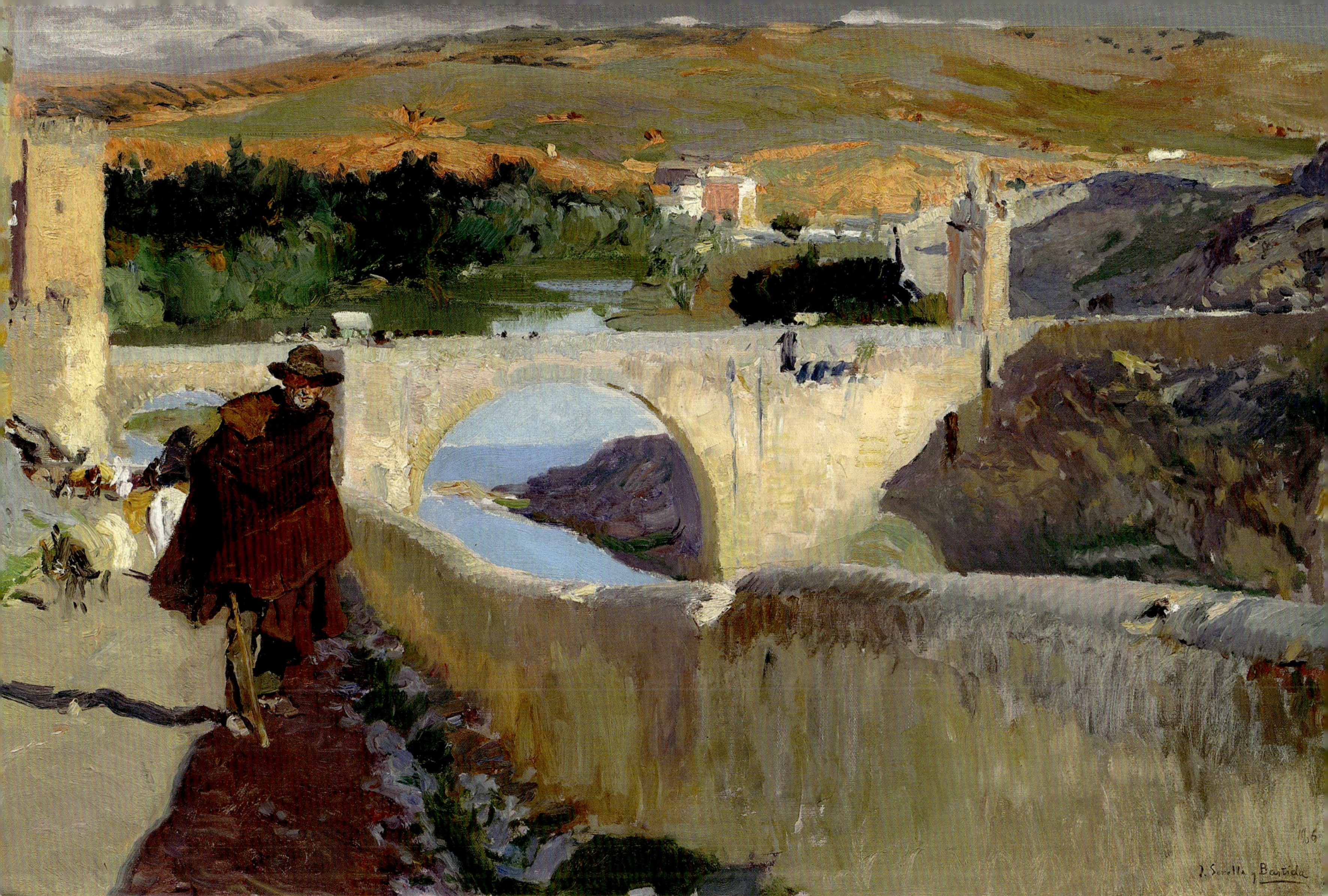

43 *The Blind Man of Toledo*

1906
Oil on canvas, 24½ x 36½ in.
Signed: "1906 / J. Sorolla y Bastida"
Dallas, Meadows Museum, Southern Methodist University, Museum Purchase; Meadows Foundation, Fund with private donations [MM.03.01]
(BPS 1879)

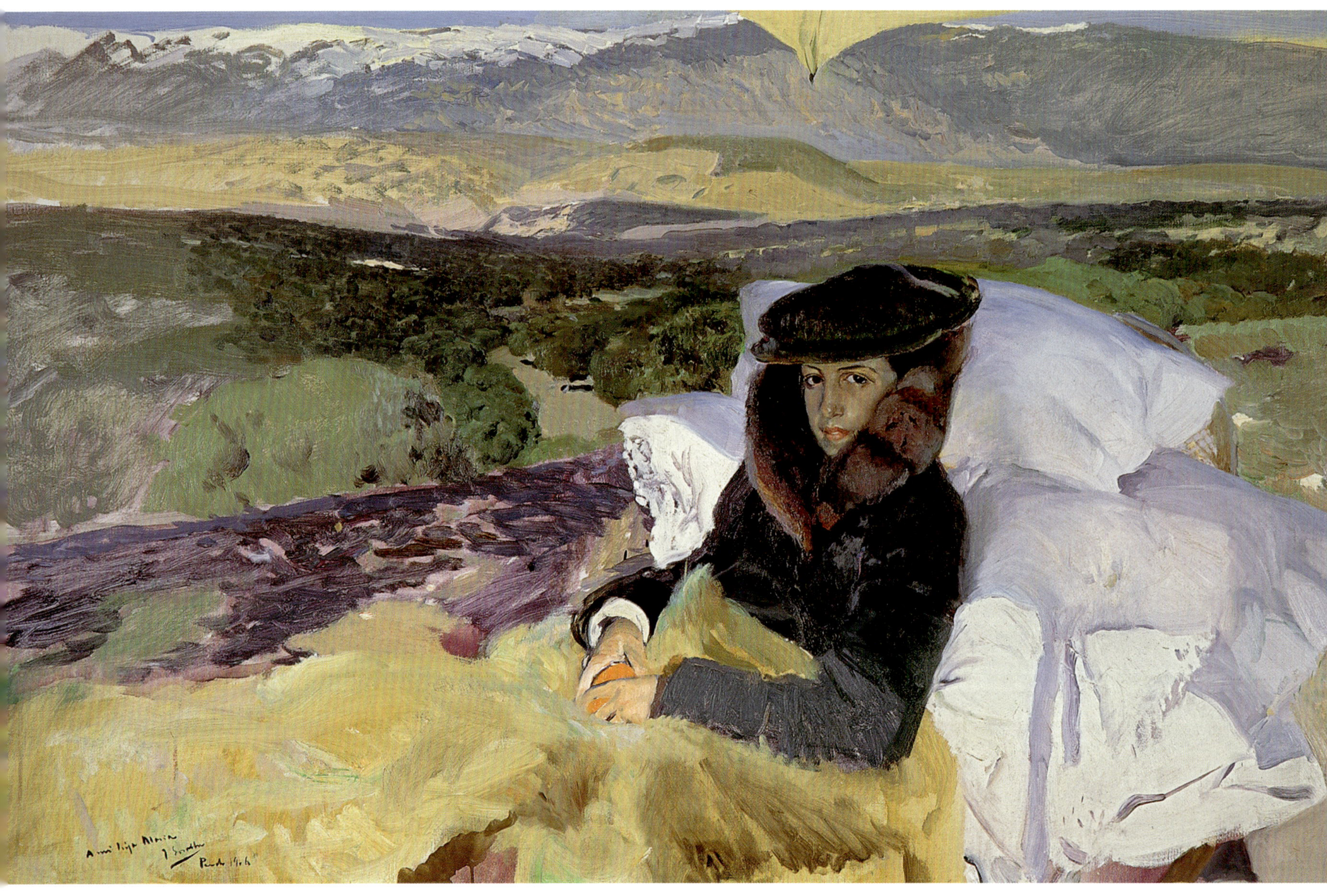

44 *María Convalescing in El Pardo*

1907
Oil on canvas, 29 x 45¼ in.
Signed: "A mi hija María /
J. Sorolla / Pardo 1906"
Private collection
(BPS 2174)

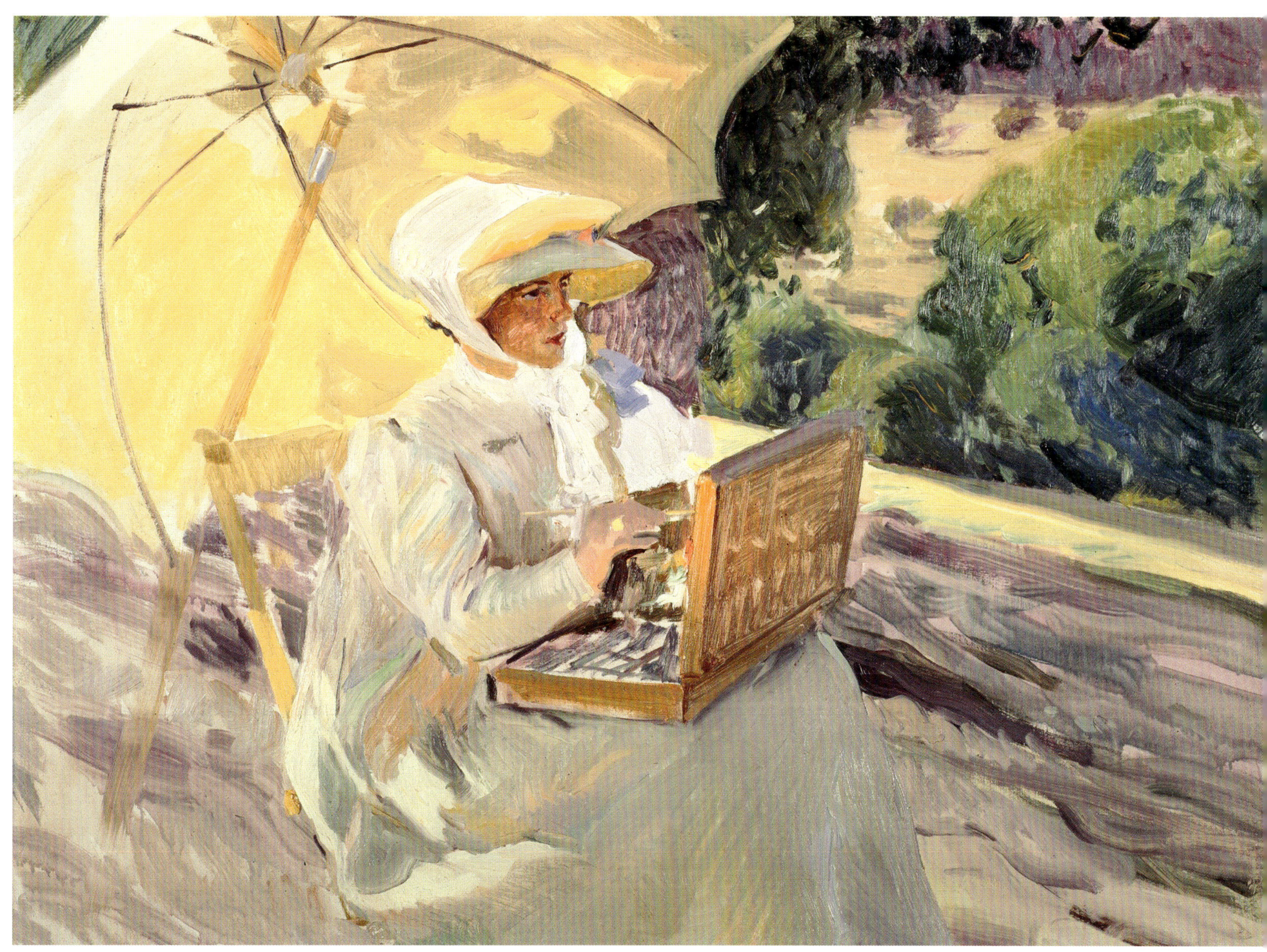

45 *María Painting in El Pardo*

1907
Oil on canvas, 31½ x 41¾ in.
Private collection
(BPS 2149)

46 *King Alfonso XIII in Hussar's Uniform*

1907
Oil on canvas, 82 x 42¾ in.
Signed: "J. Sorolla B. / 1907 / San Ildefonso"
Property of H. M. the King
(BPS 1741)

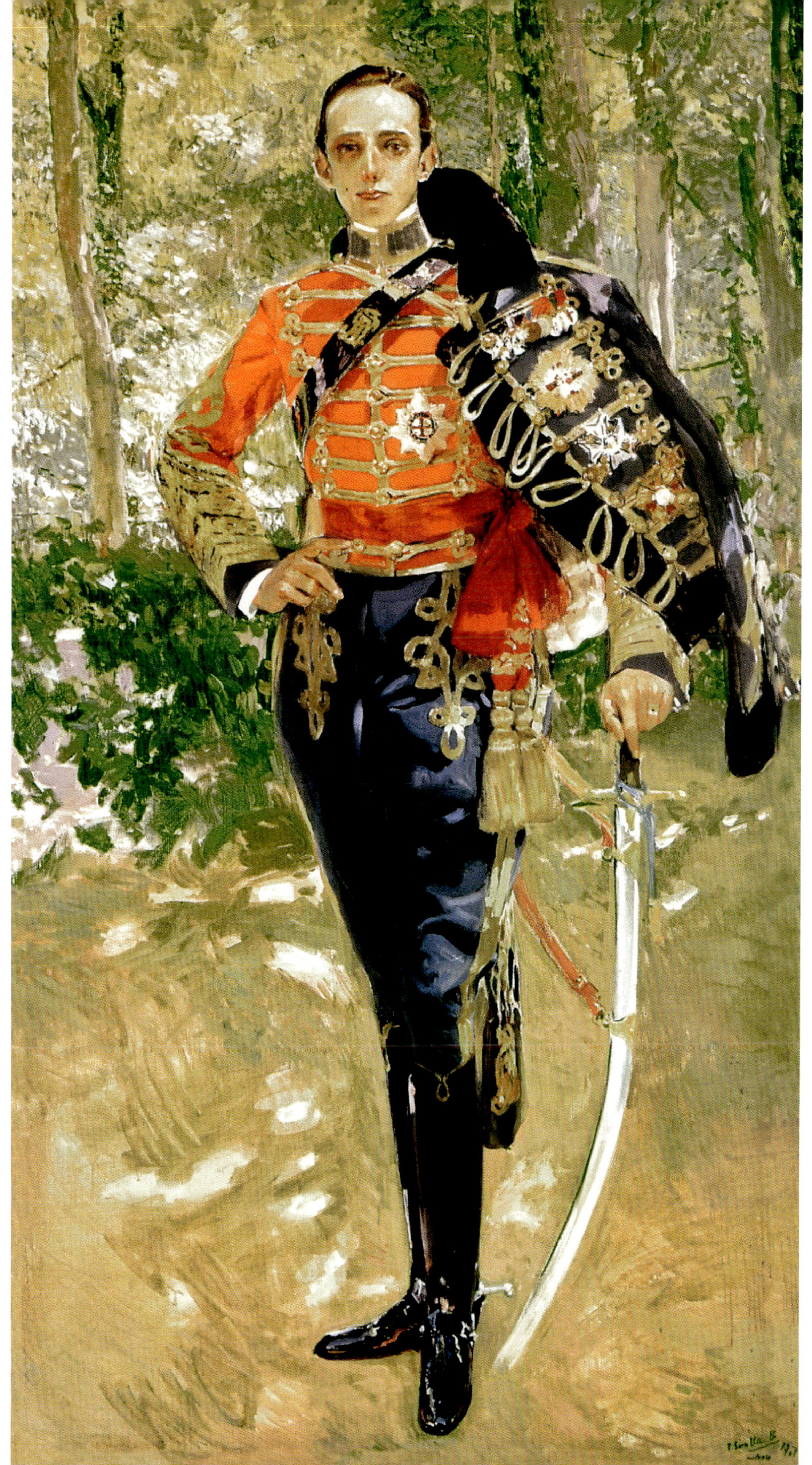

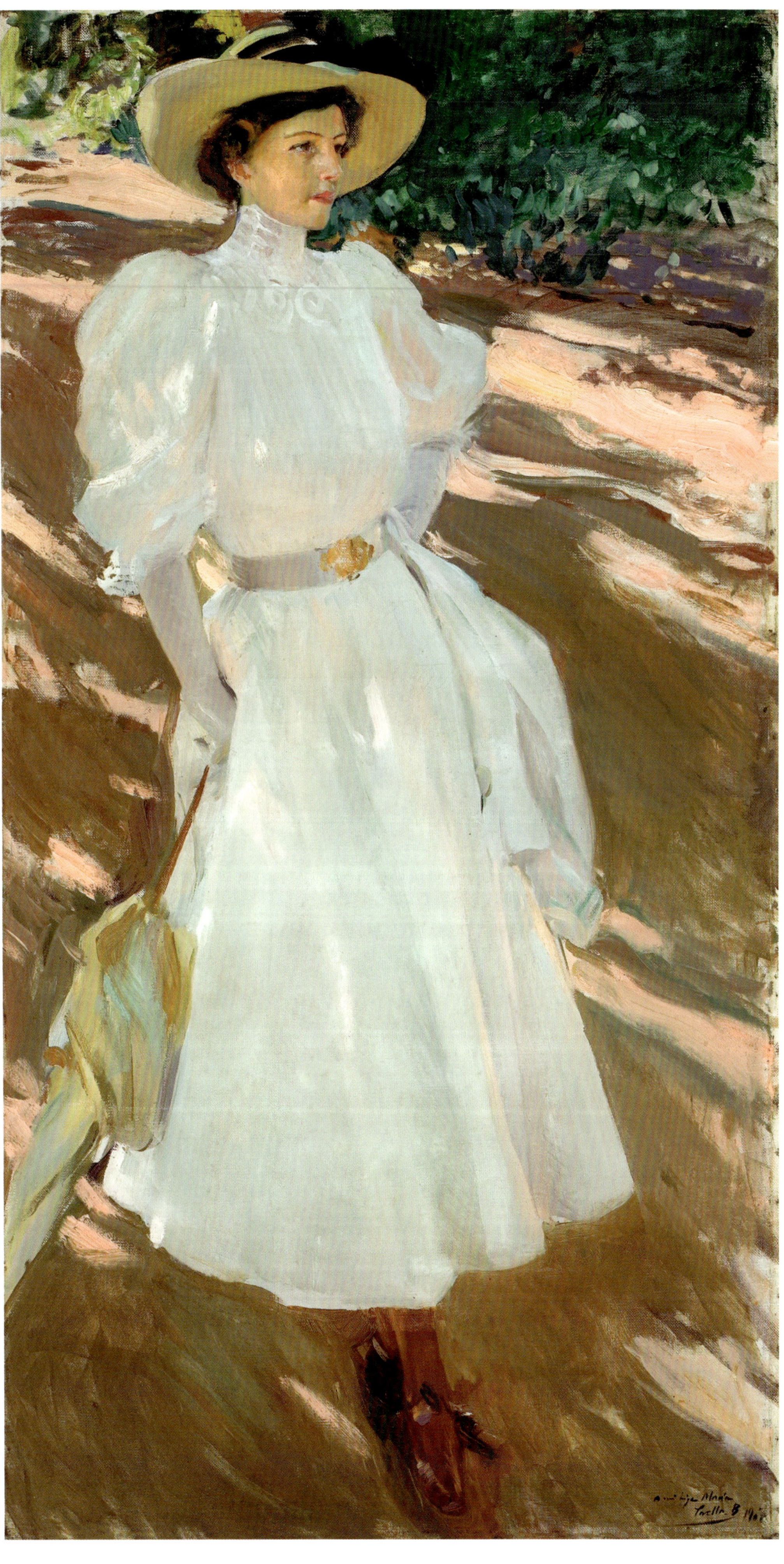

47 *María at La Granja*

1907
Oil on canvas, 67 x 33½ in.
Signed: "A mi hija María / Sorolla B. / 1907"
San Diego, California, San Diego Museum of Art, gift of Mr. Archer M. Huntington in memory of his mother, Arabella D. Huntington
[1925.001]
(BPS 1881)

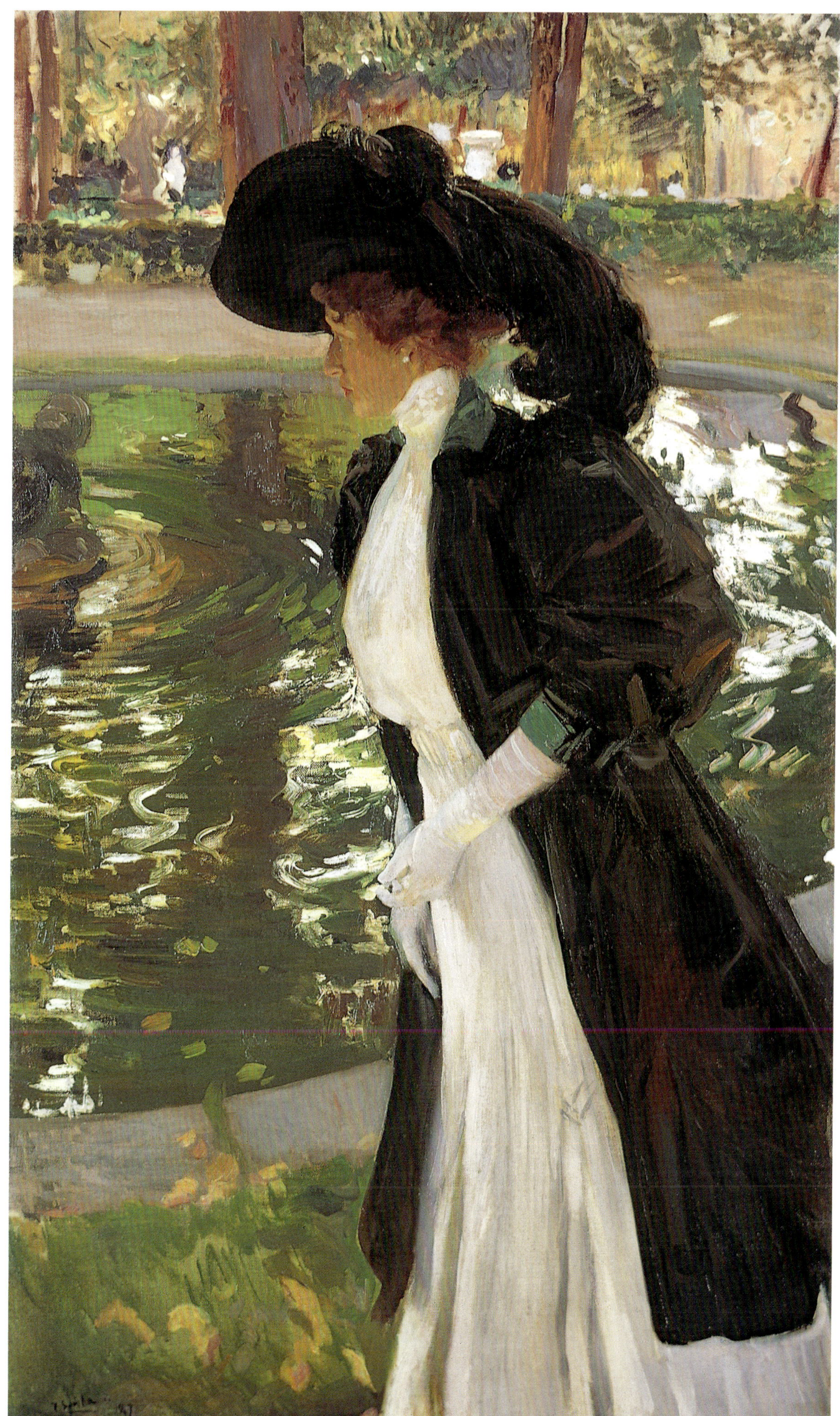

48 *Clotilde Strolling in the Gardens of La Granja*

1907
Oil on canvas, 67 x 39¼ in.
Signed: "J. Sorolla Bastida / 1907"
Havana, Museo Nacional de Bellas Artes de Cuba [inv. 5–330]
(BPS 1776)

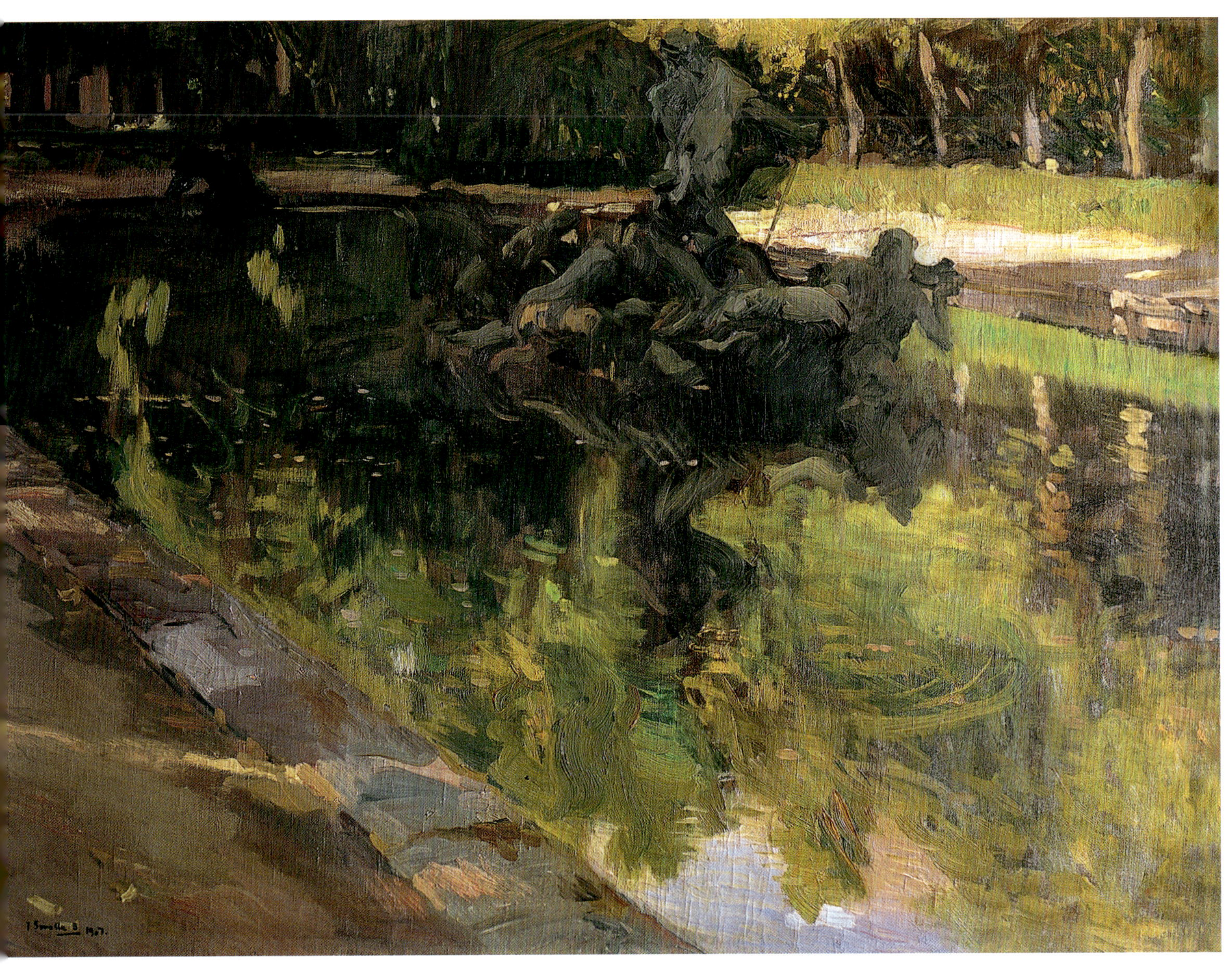

49 *Fountain of Neptune, La Granja*

1907
Oil on canvas, 32 x 41¾ in.
Signed: "J Sorolla B / 1907."
Valencia, Museo de Bellas Artes de Valencia,
Orts-Bosch Collection
(BPS 1574)

50 *Gardens of the Alcázar of Seville in Winter*

1908
Oil on canvas, 41 x 28¾ in.
Signed: "J. Sorolla Bastida / 1908"
Private collection
(BPS 2152)

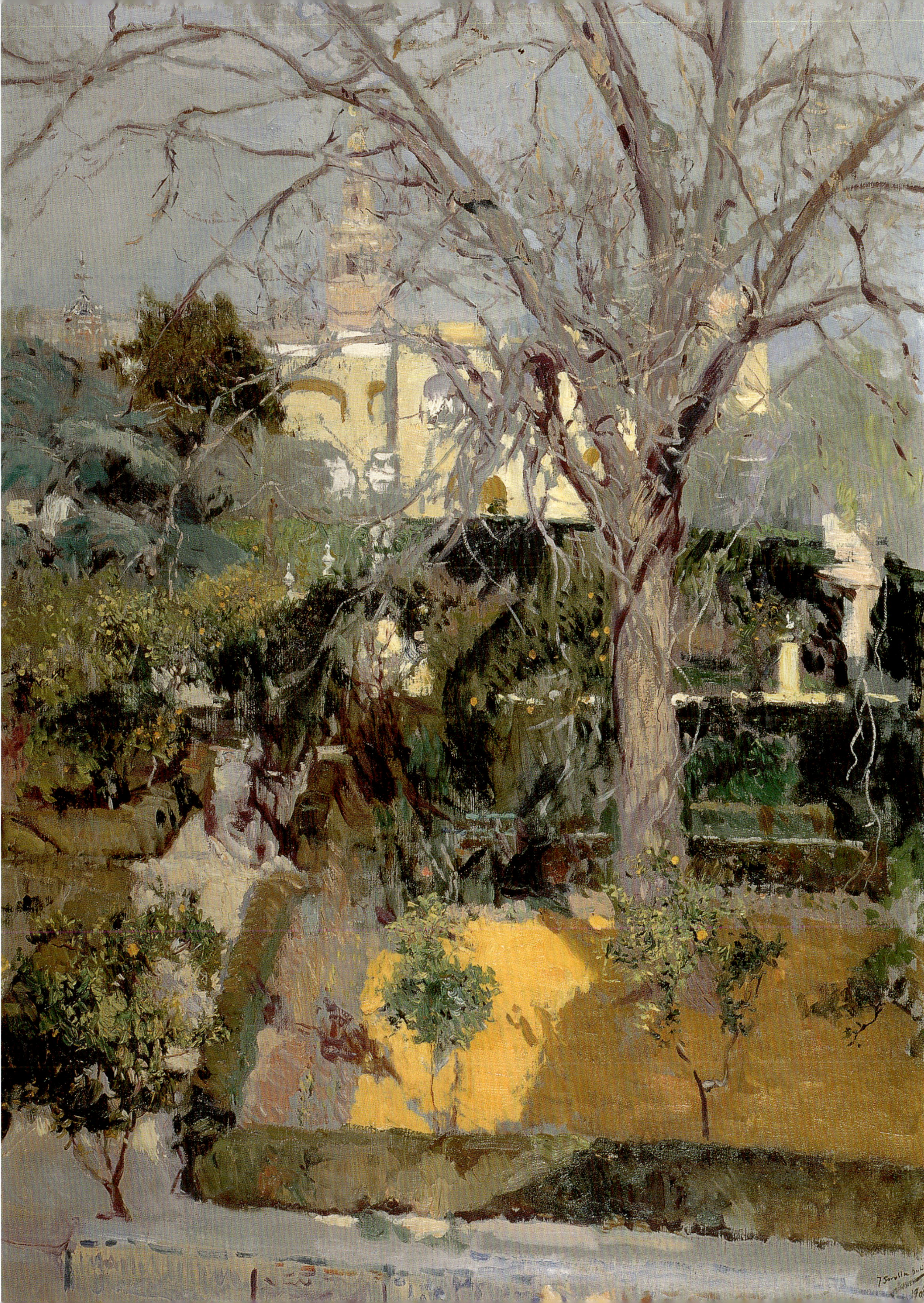

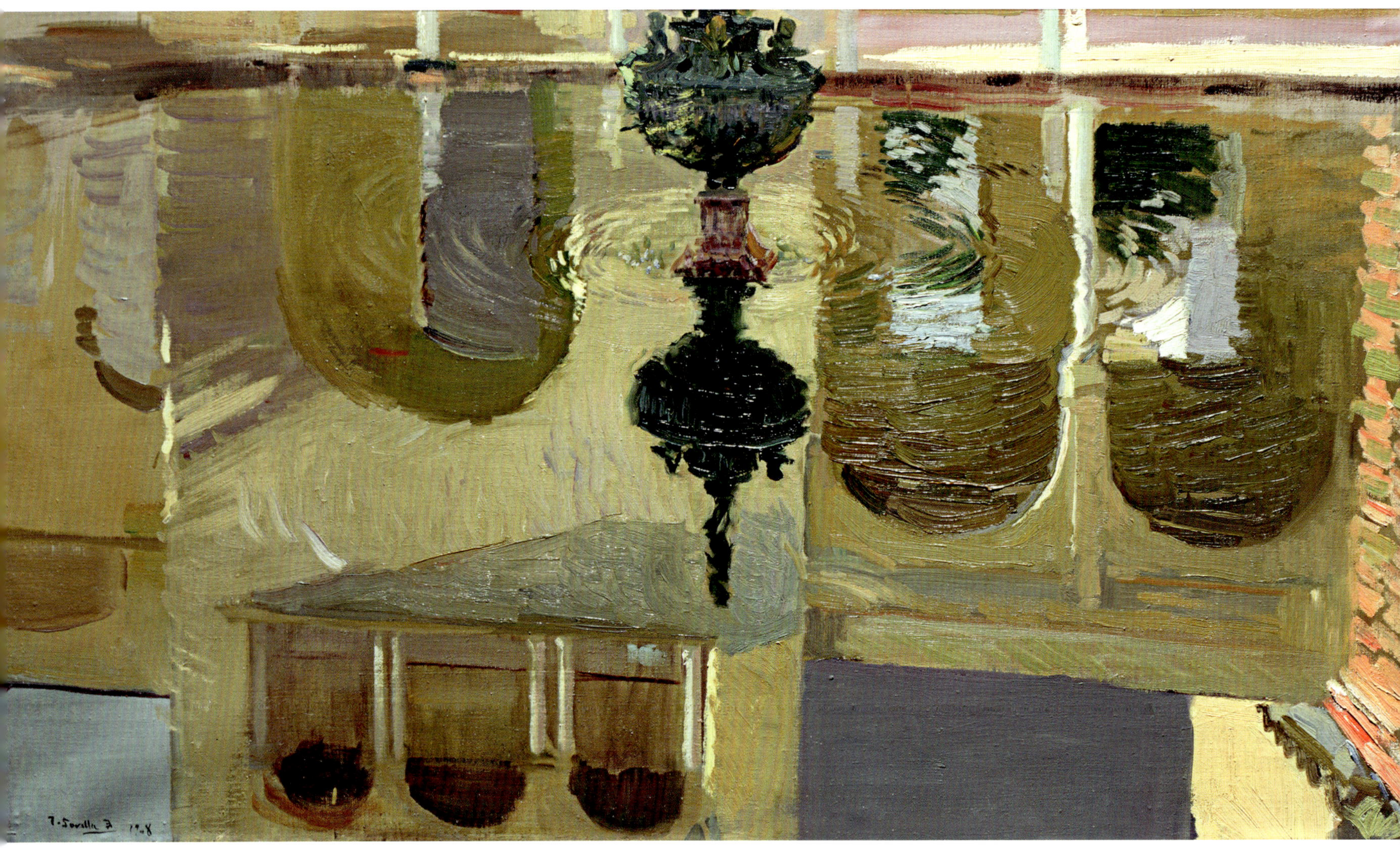

51 *Reflections in a Fountain*

1908
Oil on canvas, 23½ x 39 in.
Signed: "J. Sorolla B. / 1908"
Madrid, Fundación Museo Sorolla
[inv. FMS 810]
(BPS 2500)

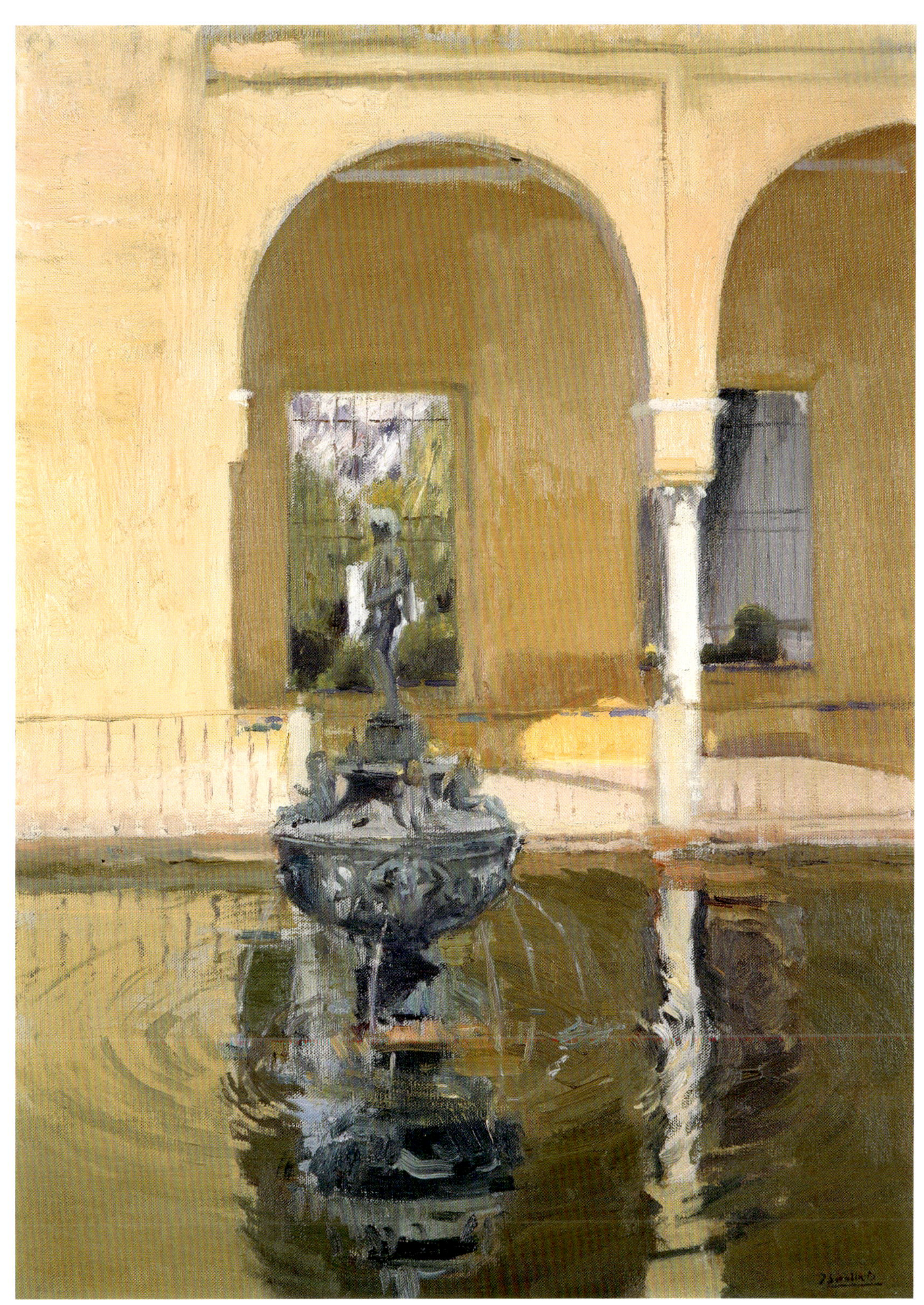

52 *Fountain of the Moorish King, Alcázar of Seville*

1908
Oil on canvas, 28¼ x 20½ in.
Signed: "J Sorolla B"
Private collection
(BPS 2154)

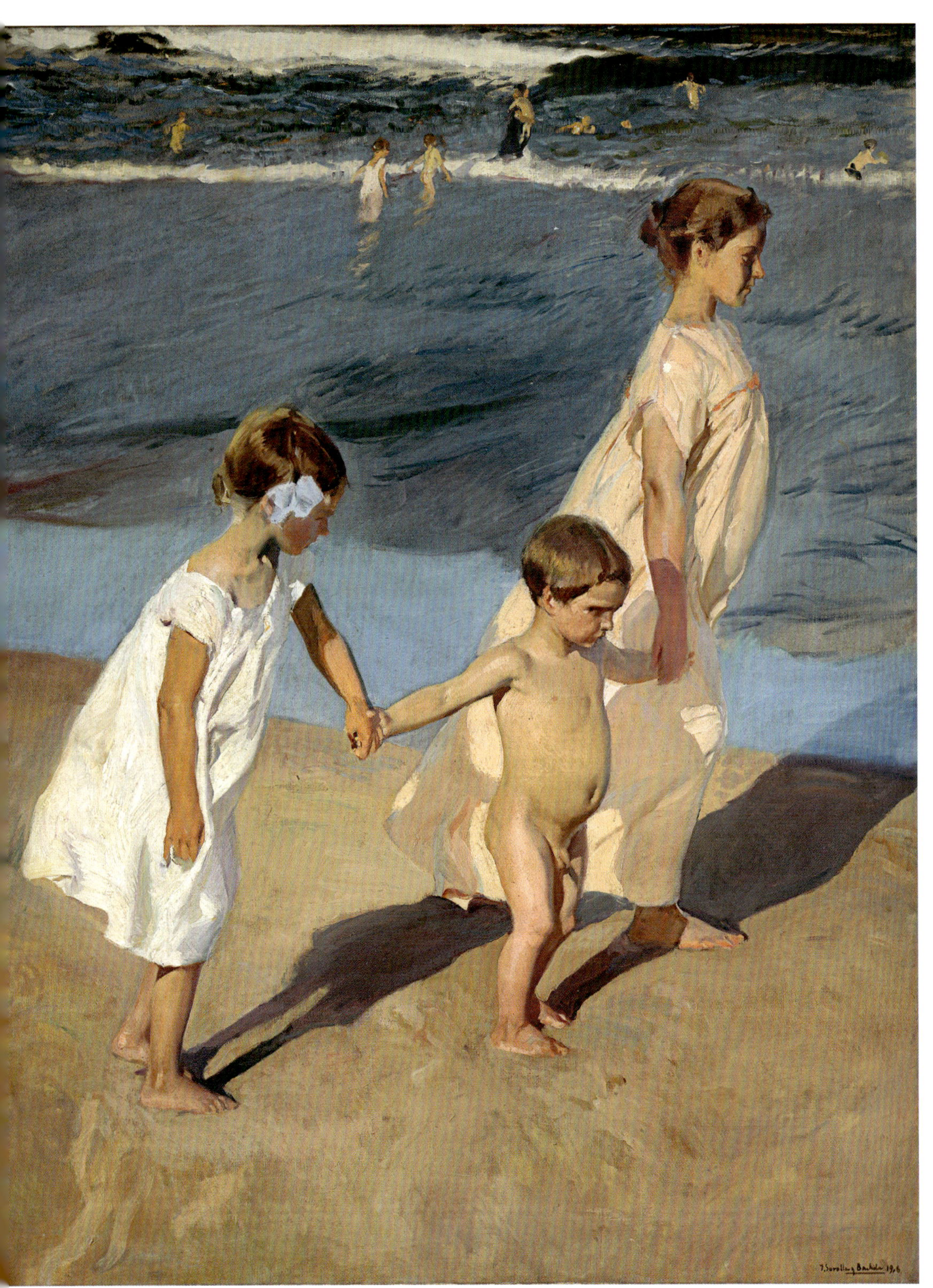

53 *Going for a Bath, Valencia*

1908
Oil on canvas, 78¾ x 59 in.
Signed: "J. Sorolla Bastida 1908"
Private collection
(BPS 1611)

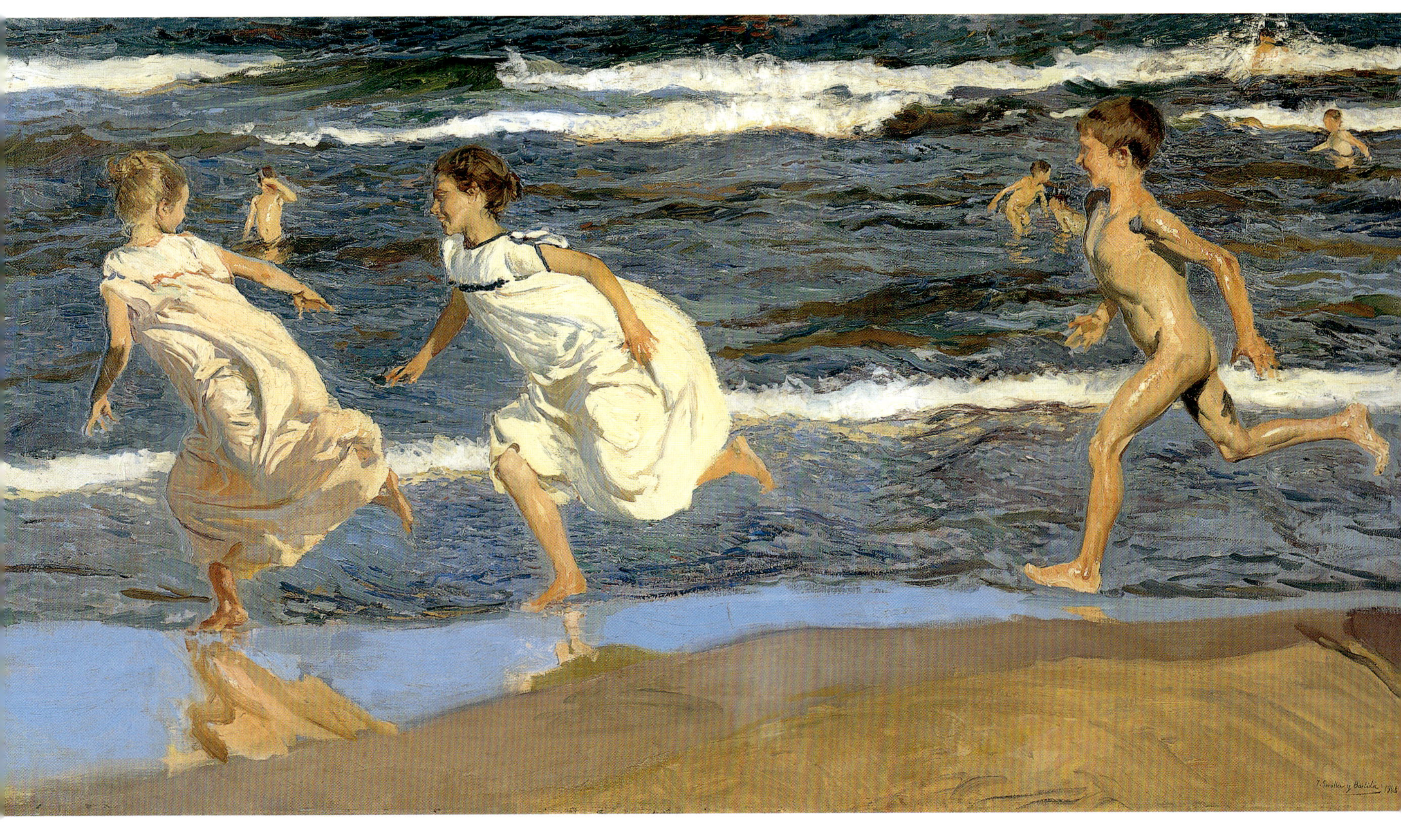

54 *Running along the Beach*

1908
Oil on canvas, 35½ x 65½ in.
Signed: "J. Sorolla y Bastida / 1908."
Oviedo, Museo de Bellas Artes de Asturias,
Pedro Masaveu Collection
(BPS 1613)

55 *After the Bath*

1908
Oil on canvas, 69¼ x 44 in.
Signed: "J Sorolla Bastida / 1908"
New York, The Hispanic Society of America [inv. A 296]
(BPS 1696)

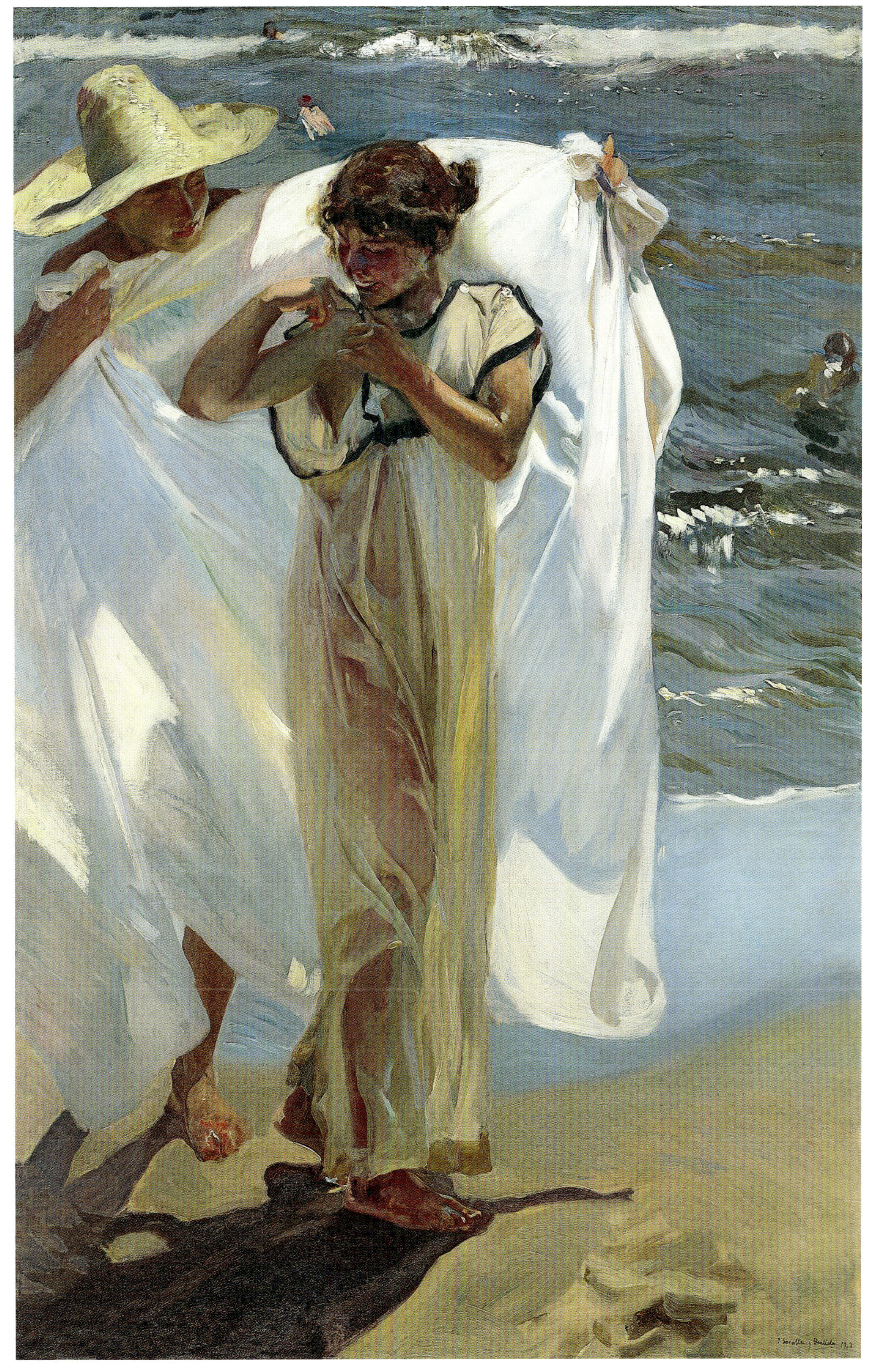

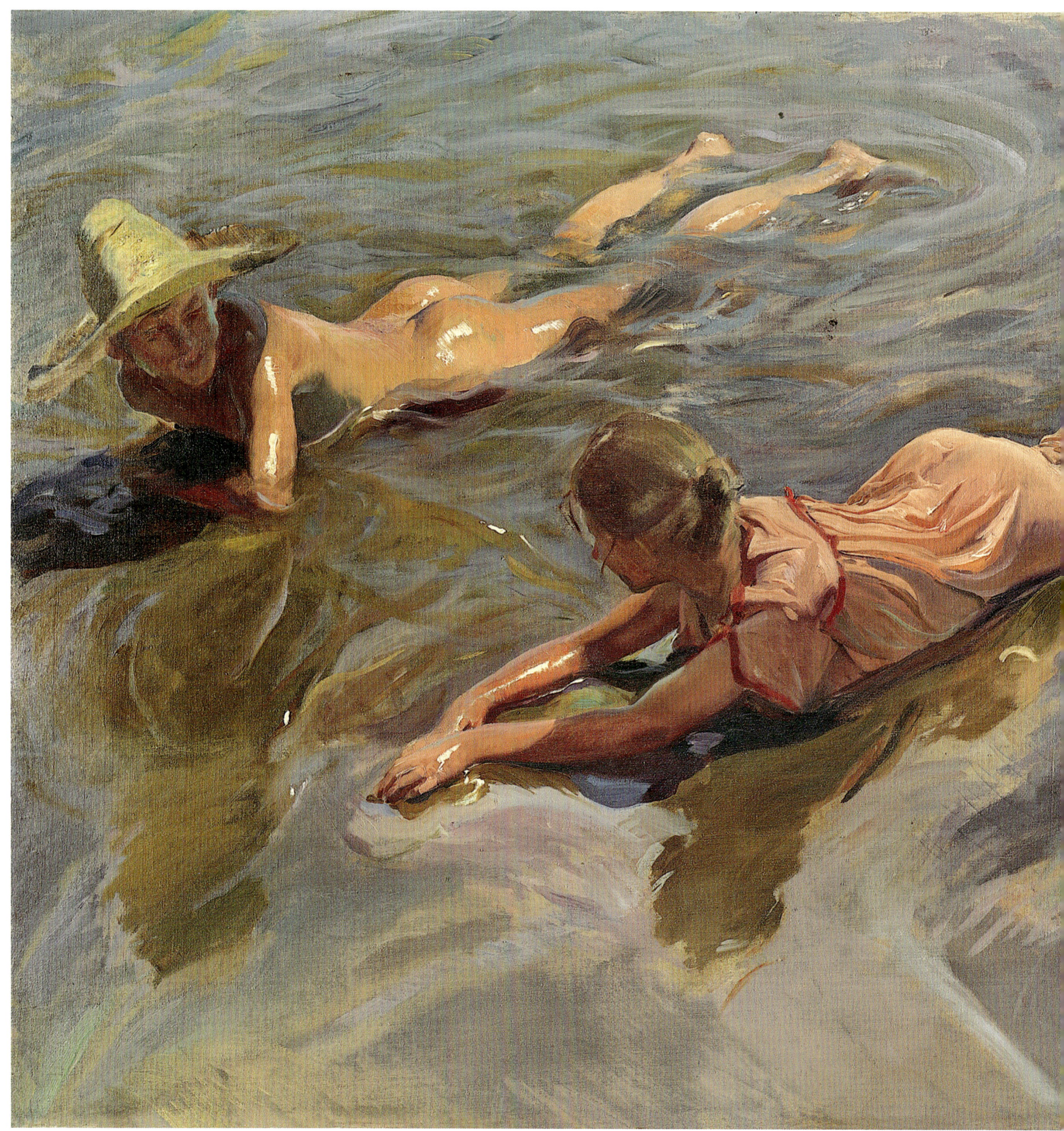

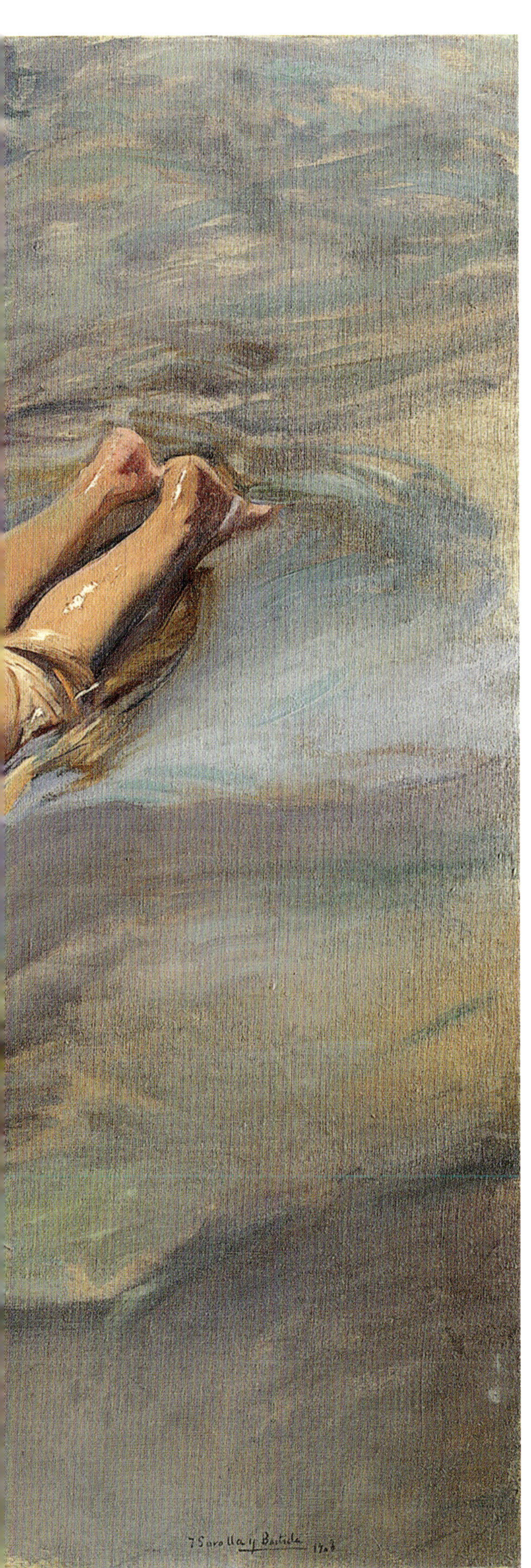

56 *Sea Idyll*

1908
Oil on canvas, 59½ x 78¼ in.
Signed: "J. Sorolla y Bastida / 1908"
New York, The Hispanic Society of America [inv. A 298]
(BPS 1697)

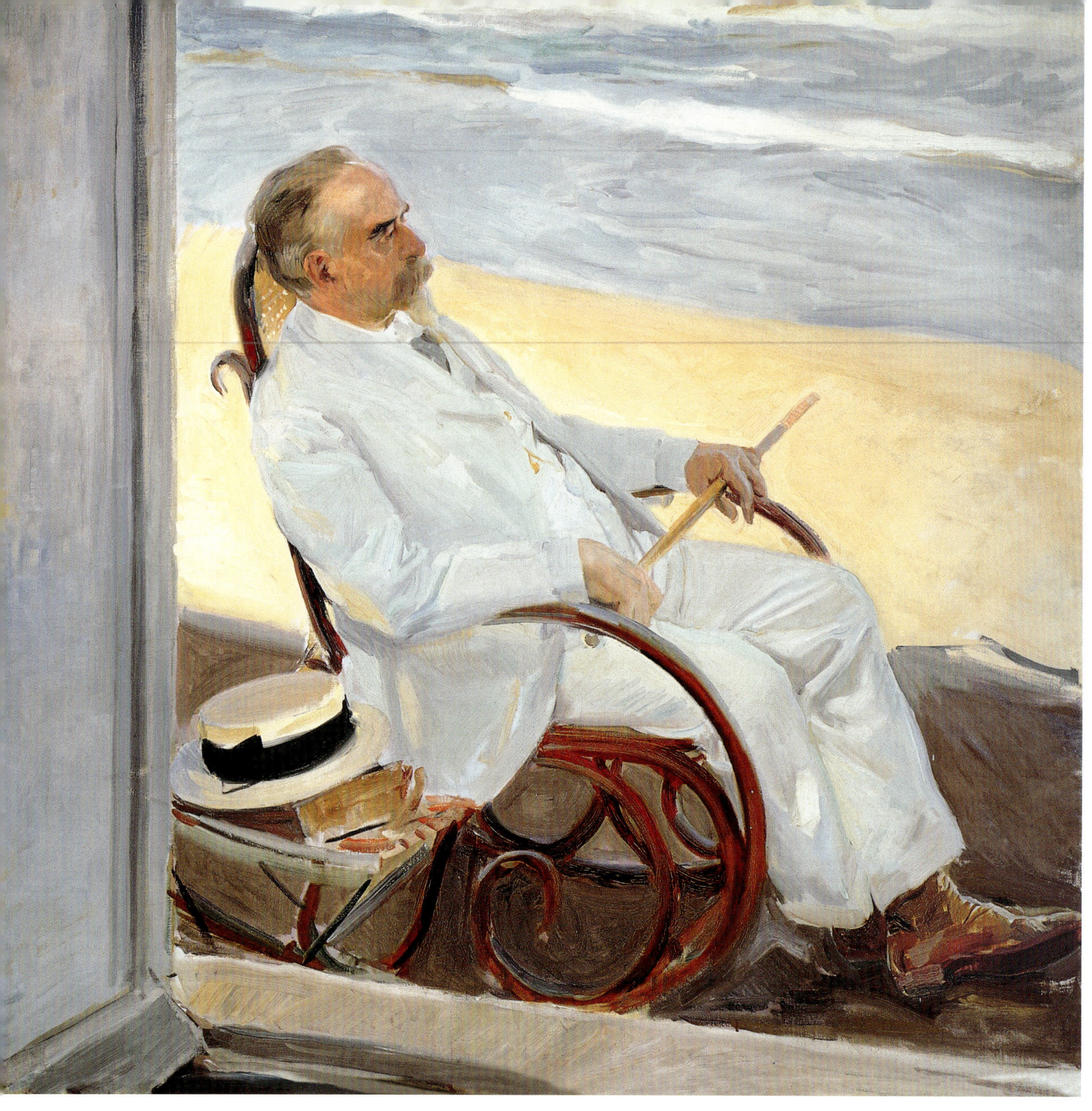

57 *Antonio García on the Beach*

1909
Oil on canvas, 59 x 59 in.
Madrid, Museo Sorolla [inv. 841]
(BPS 2531)

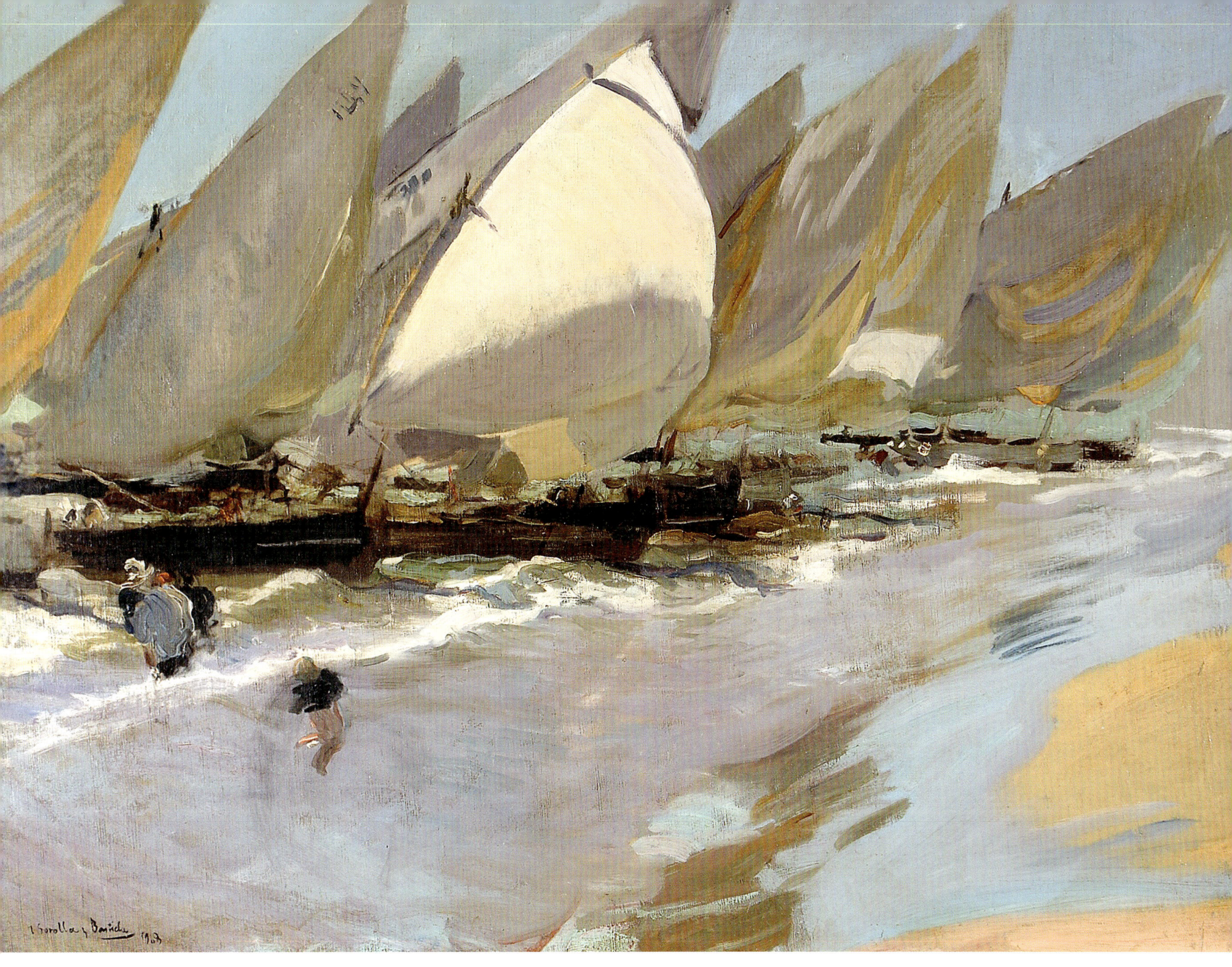

58 *Fishing Boats, Valencia*

1908
Oil on canvas, 31½ x 45¾ in.
Signed: "J. Sorolla y Bastida / 1908"
Private collection
(BPS 1927)

59 *Bath Time, Valencia*

1909
Oil on canvas, 59 x 59¼ in.
Inscription: "J Sorolla / 1909"
Madrid, Fundación Museo Sorolla [inv. 835]
(BPS 2525)

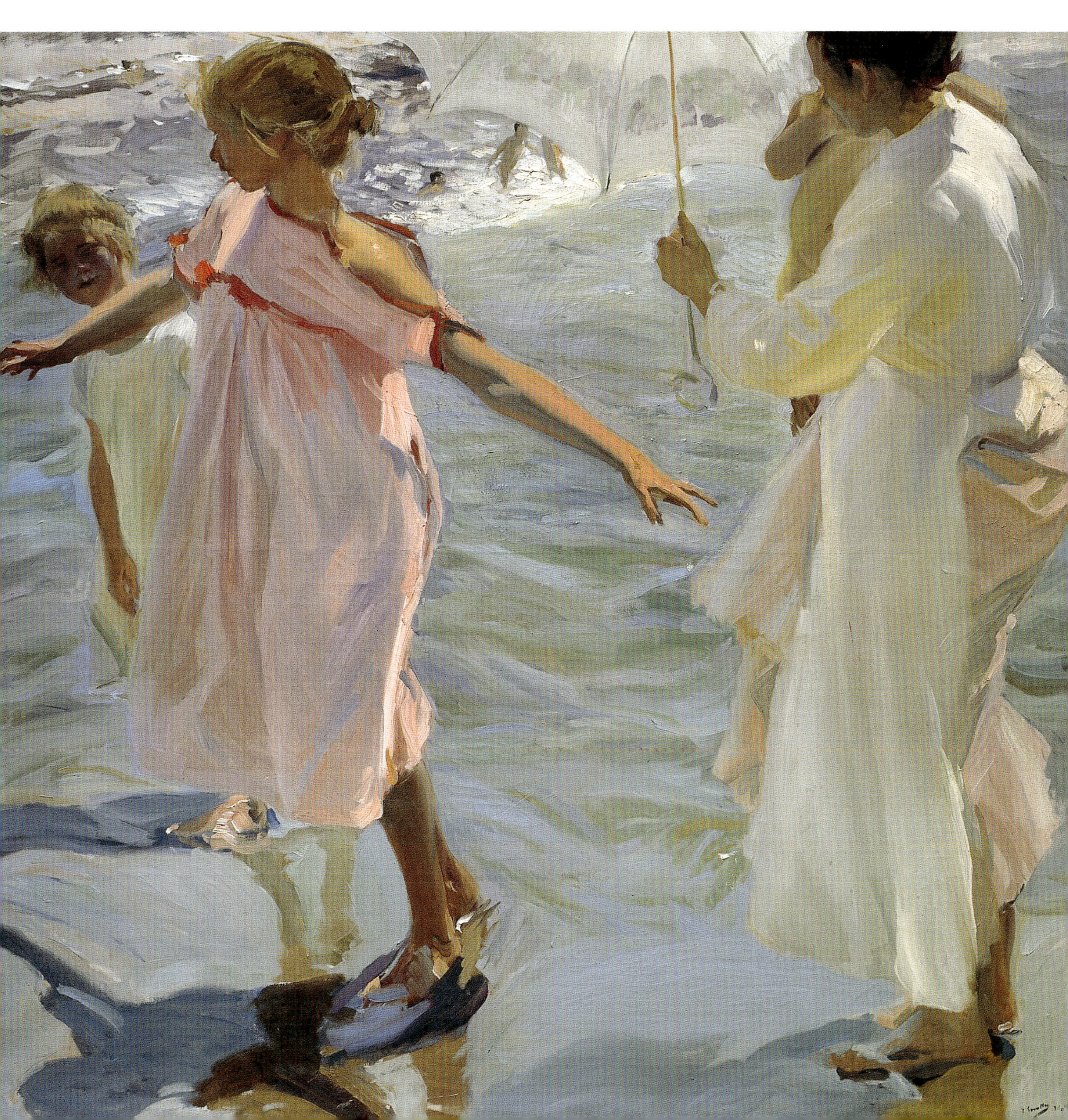

60 *The Two Sisters*

1909
Oil on canvas, 69½ x 43¼ in.
Signed: "J. Sorolla / 1909"
Chicago, Illinois, The Art Institute of Chicago, gift of Mrs. William Stanley North in memory of William Stanley North [1911.28]
(BPS 1752)

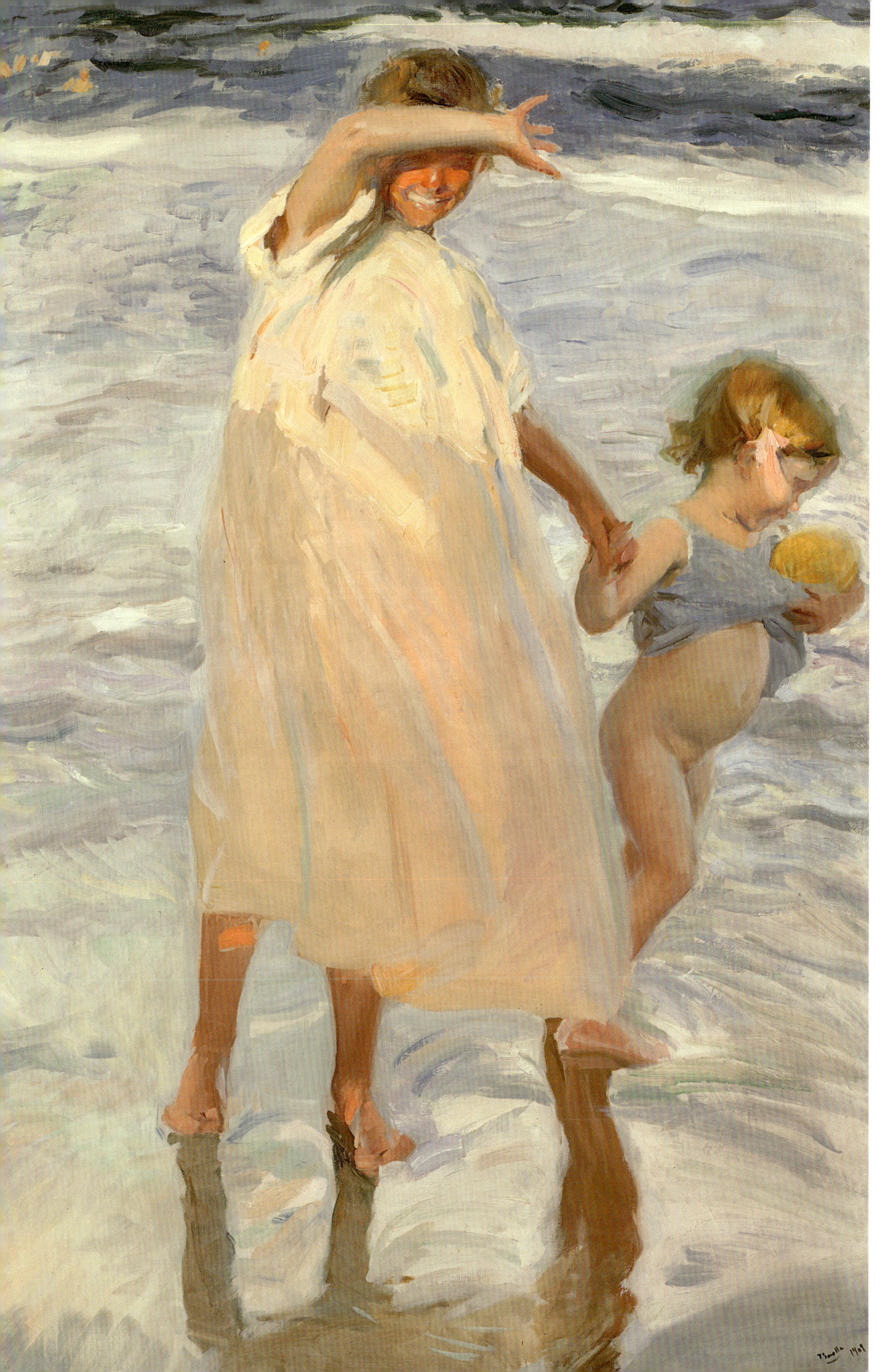

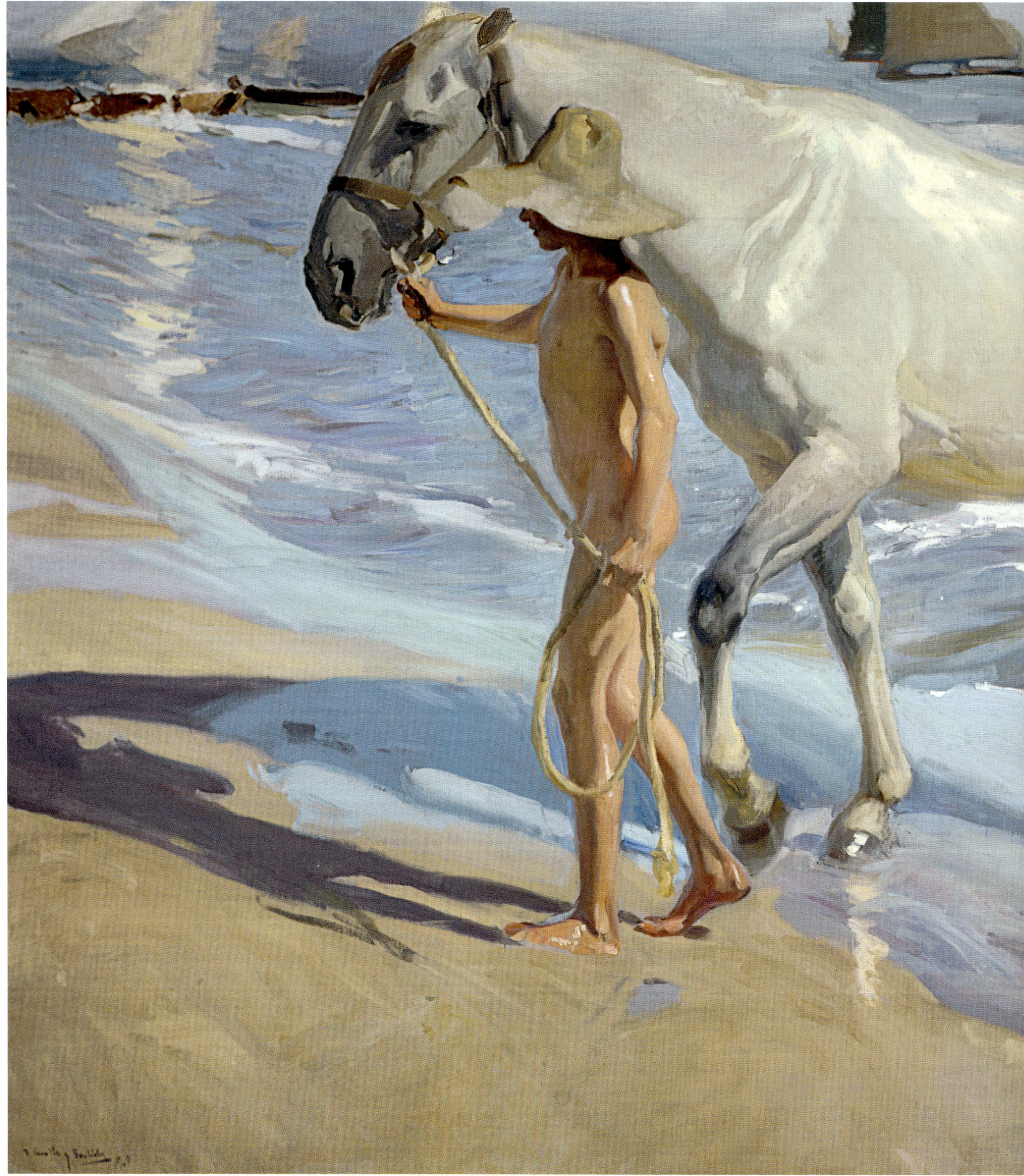

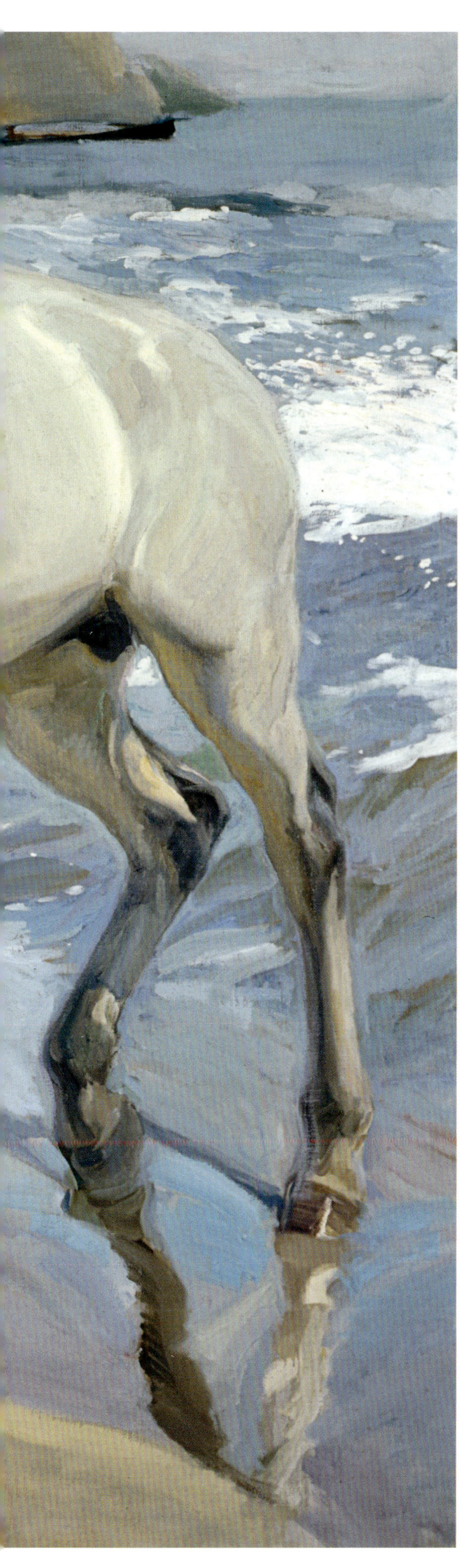

61 *The Horse's Bath*

1909
Oil on canvas, 80¾ x 98½ in.
Signed: "J Sorolla y Bastida / 1909"
Madrid, Museo Sorolla [inv. 839]
(BPS 2529)

62 *Boys on the Beach*

1910
Oil on canvas, 46½ x 72¾ in.
Signed: "J. Sorolla B. 1910"
Inscription: "M. A. M.–77
Madrid, Museo Nacional
del Prado [P–4648]
(BPS 1760)

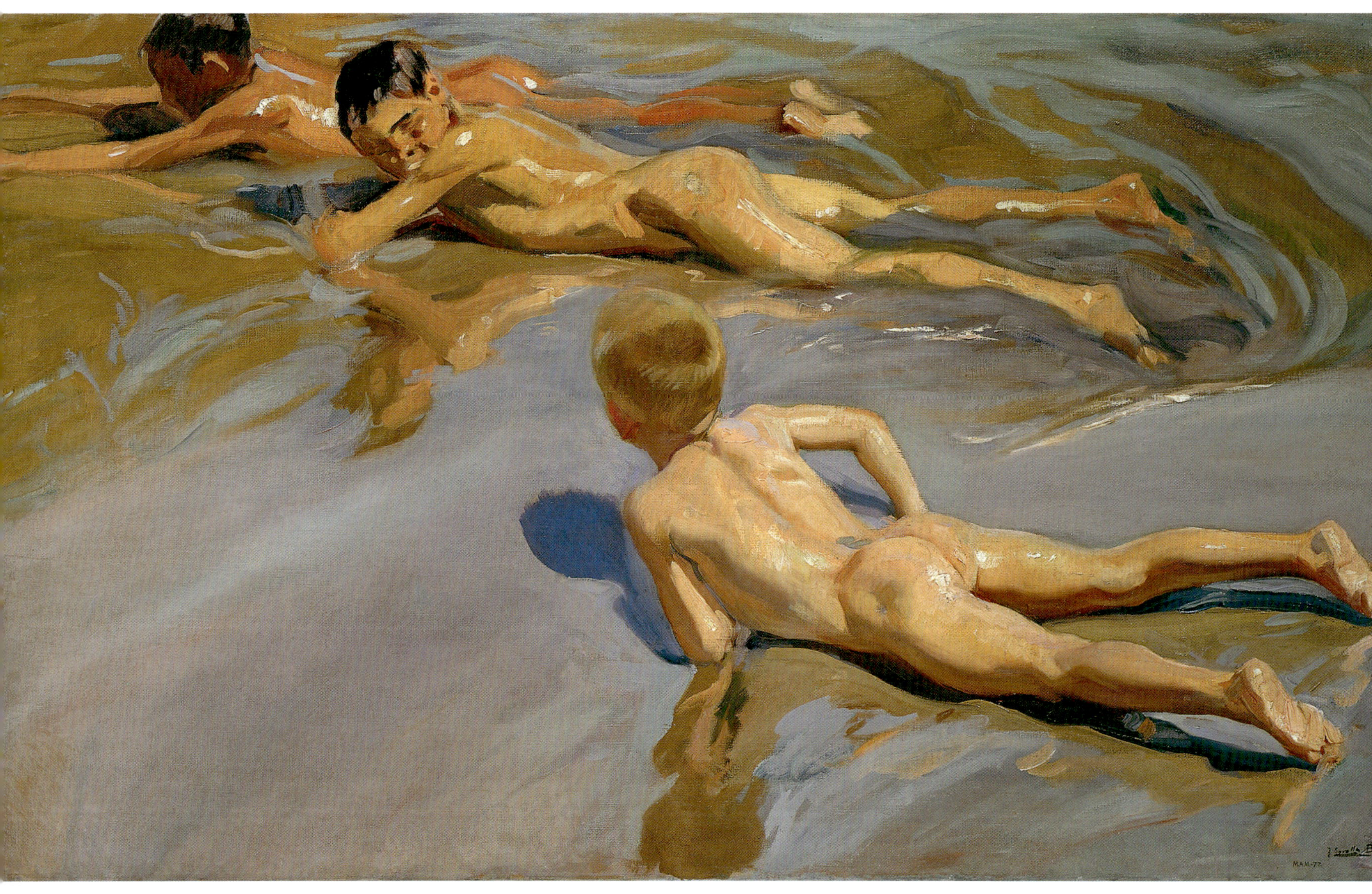

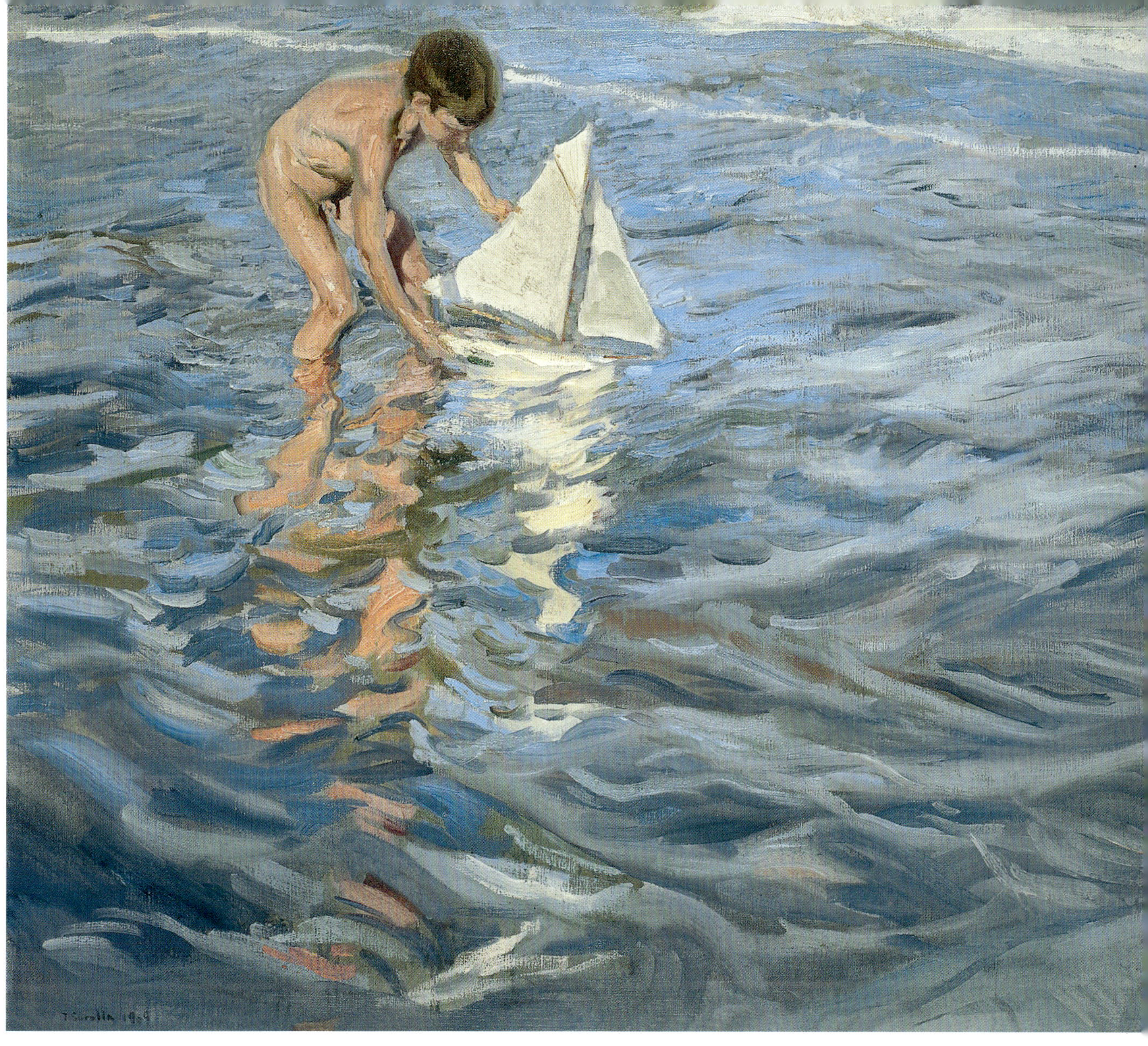

63 *The Little Sailing Boat*

1909
Oil on canvas, 39½ x 43¼ in.
Signed: "J. Sorolla / 1909"
Madrid, Museo Sorolla [inv. 838]
(BPS 2528)

64 *Strolling along the Seashore*

1909
Oil on canvas, 80¾ x 78¾ in.
Signed: "J. Sorolla B / 1909"
Madrid, Fundación Museo Sorolla [inv. FMS 834]
(BPS 2524)

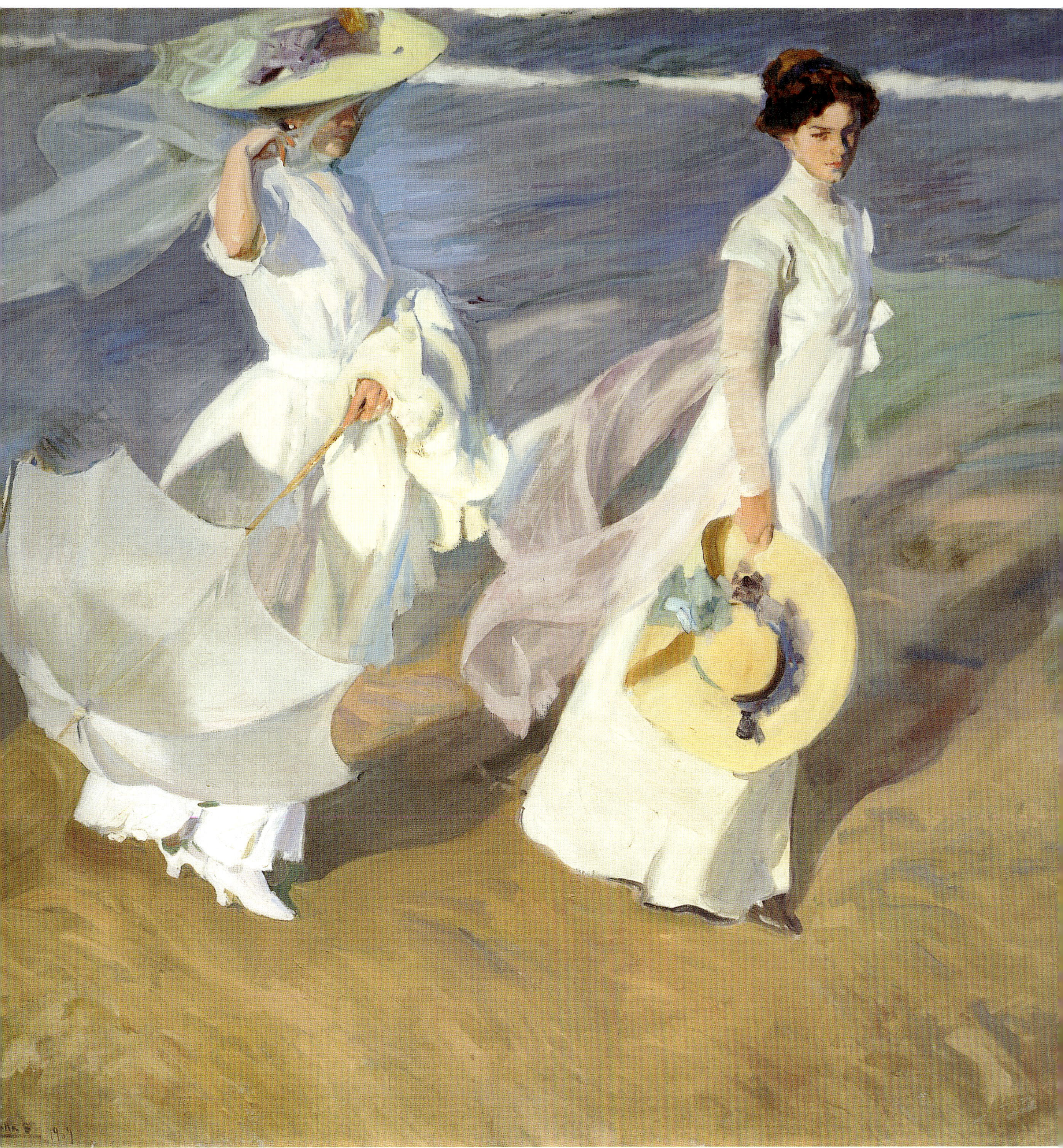

65 *Under the Awning, Beach at Zarautz*

1910
Oil on canvas, 39 x 45 in.
Signed: "J Sorolla / 1910"
St. Louis, Missouri, Saint Louis Art Museum,
purchase [acc. no. 20: 1911]
(BPS 1757)

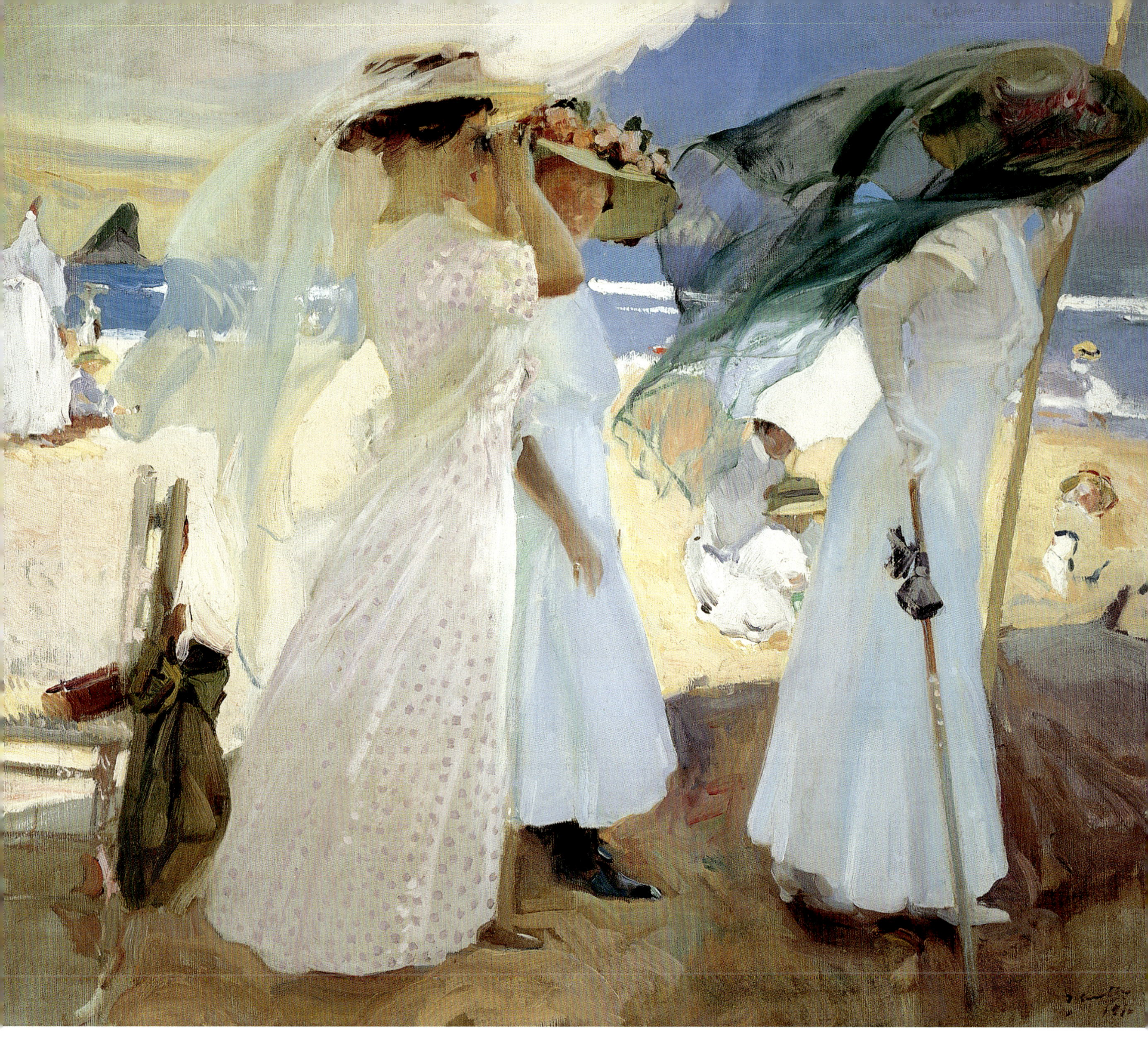

66 *Tower of the Seven Points, Alhambra, Granada*

1910
Oil on canvas, 32 x 41¾ in.
Signed: "J. Sorolla / 1910"
Madrid, Museo Sorolla [inv. 857]
(BPS 2547)

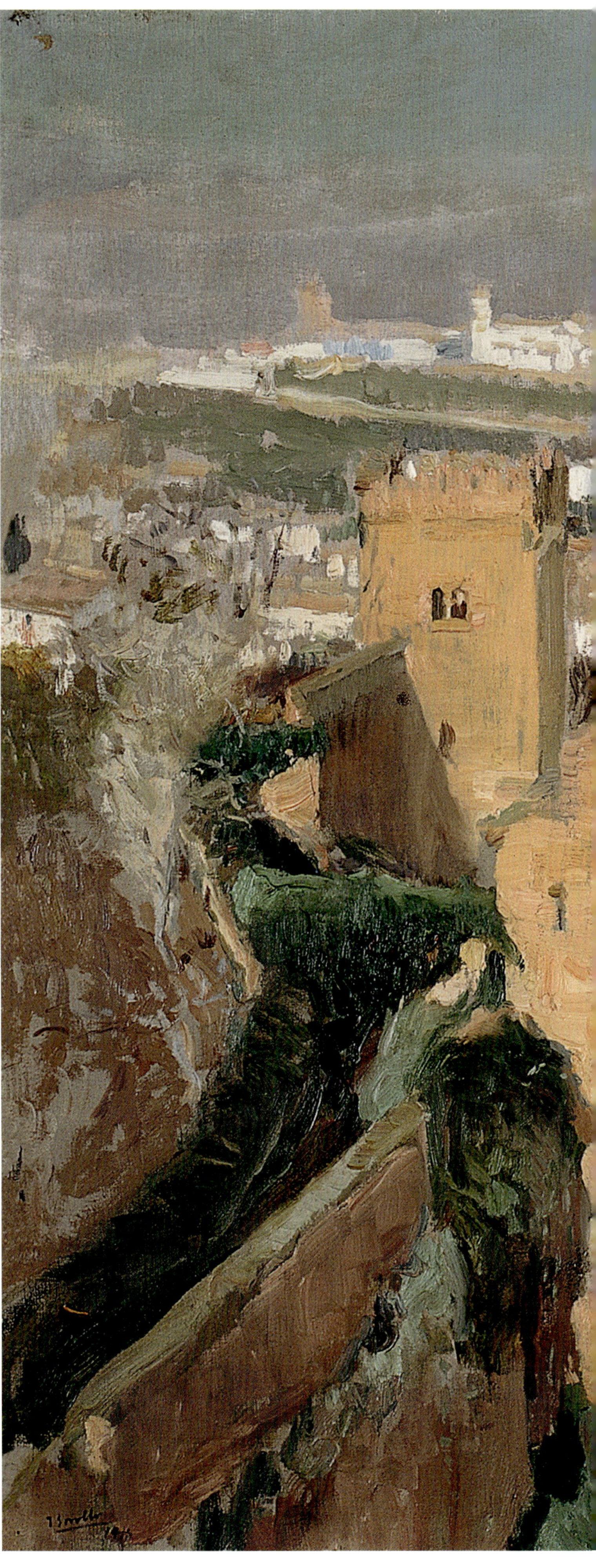

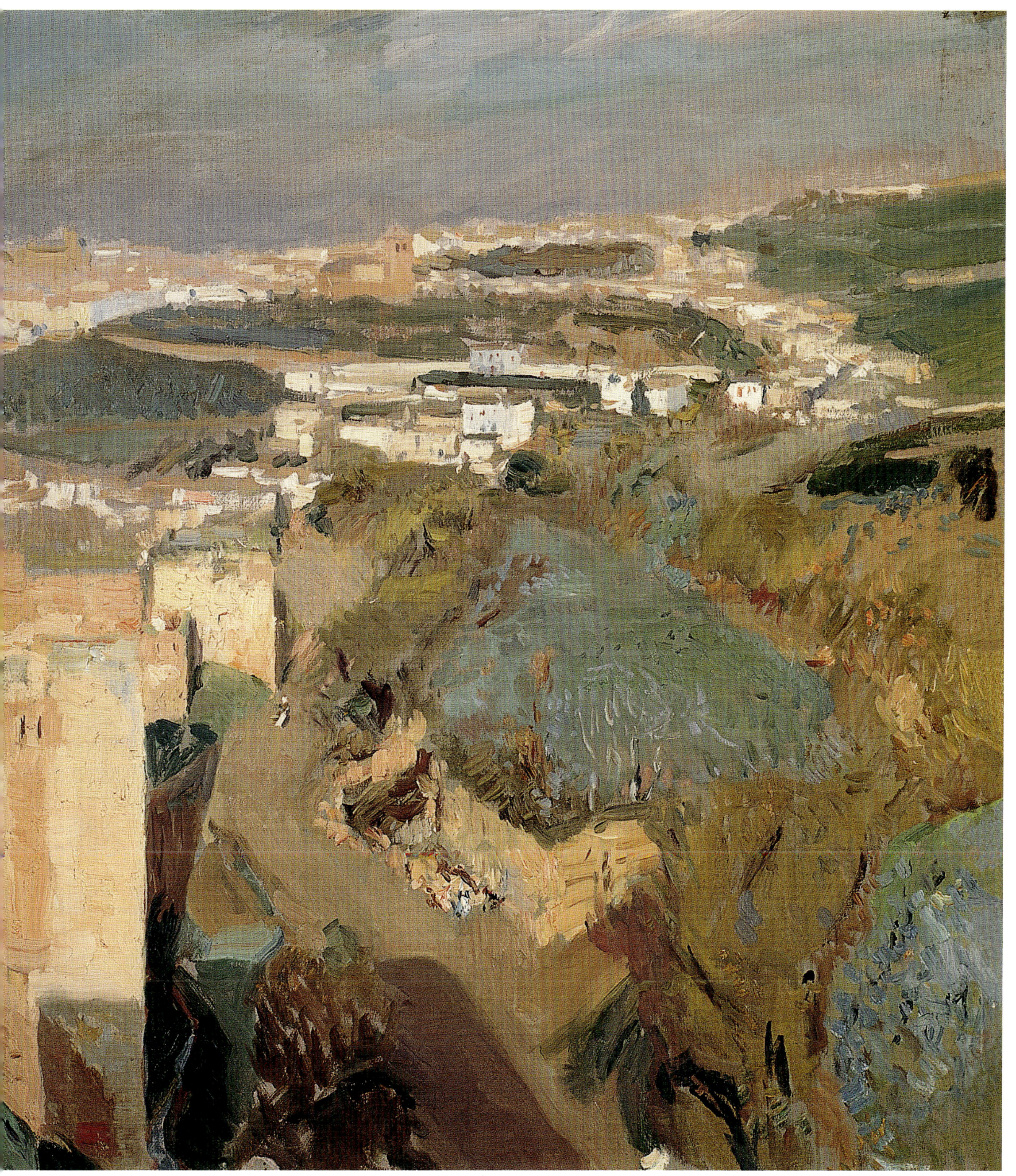

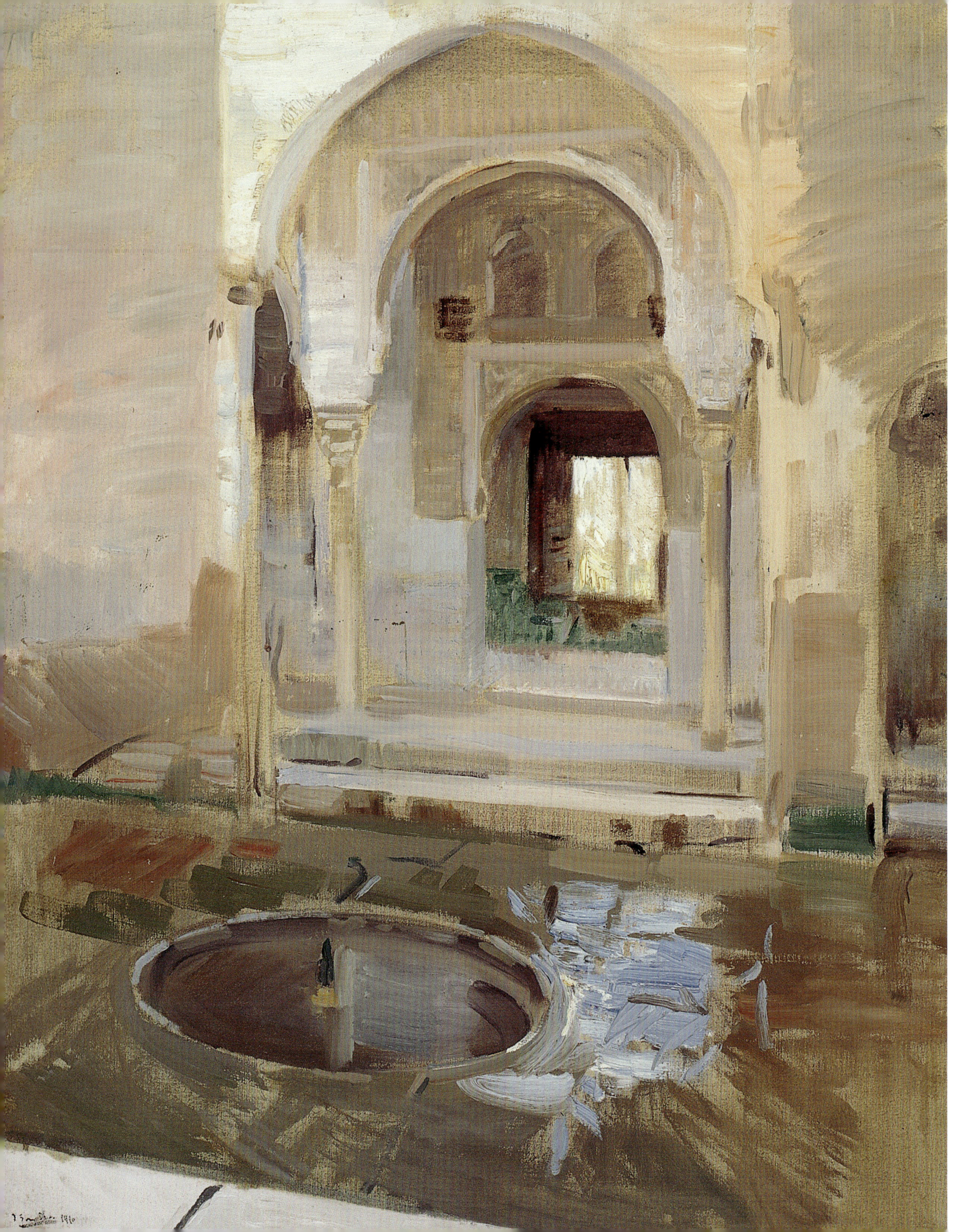

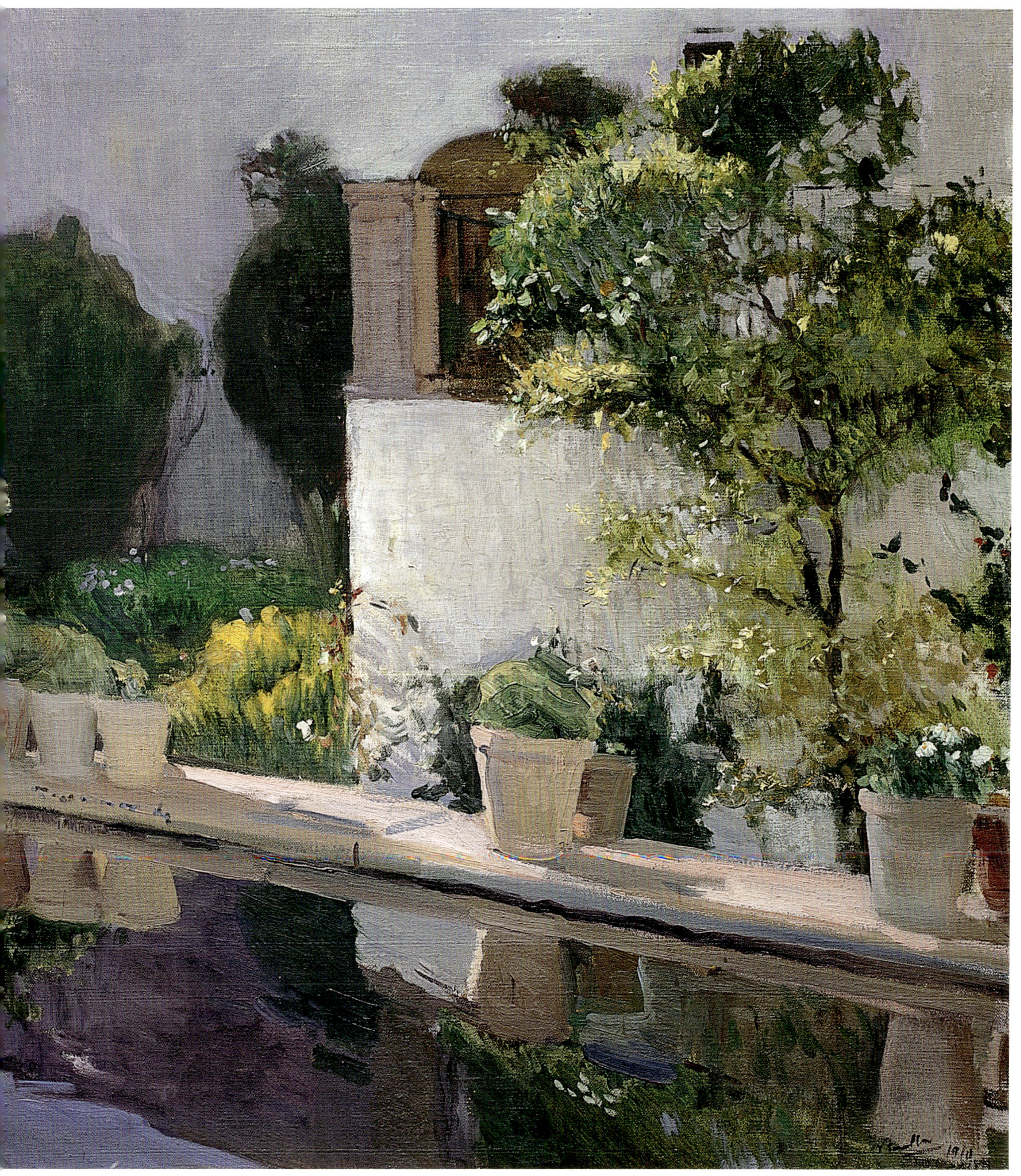

71 *Garden of the Sorolla Residence, Calle Miguel Ángel, Madrid*

1910
Oil on canvas, 39½ x 42 in.
Signed: "J. Sorolla Bastida"
Madrid, Museo Sorolla [inv. 932]
(BPS 2622)

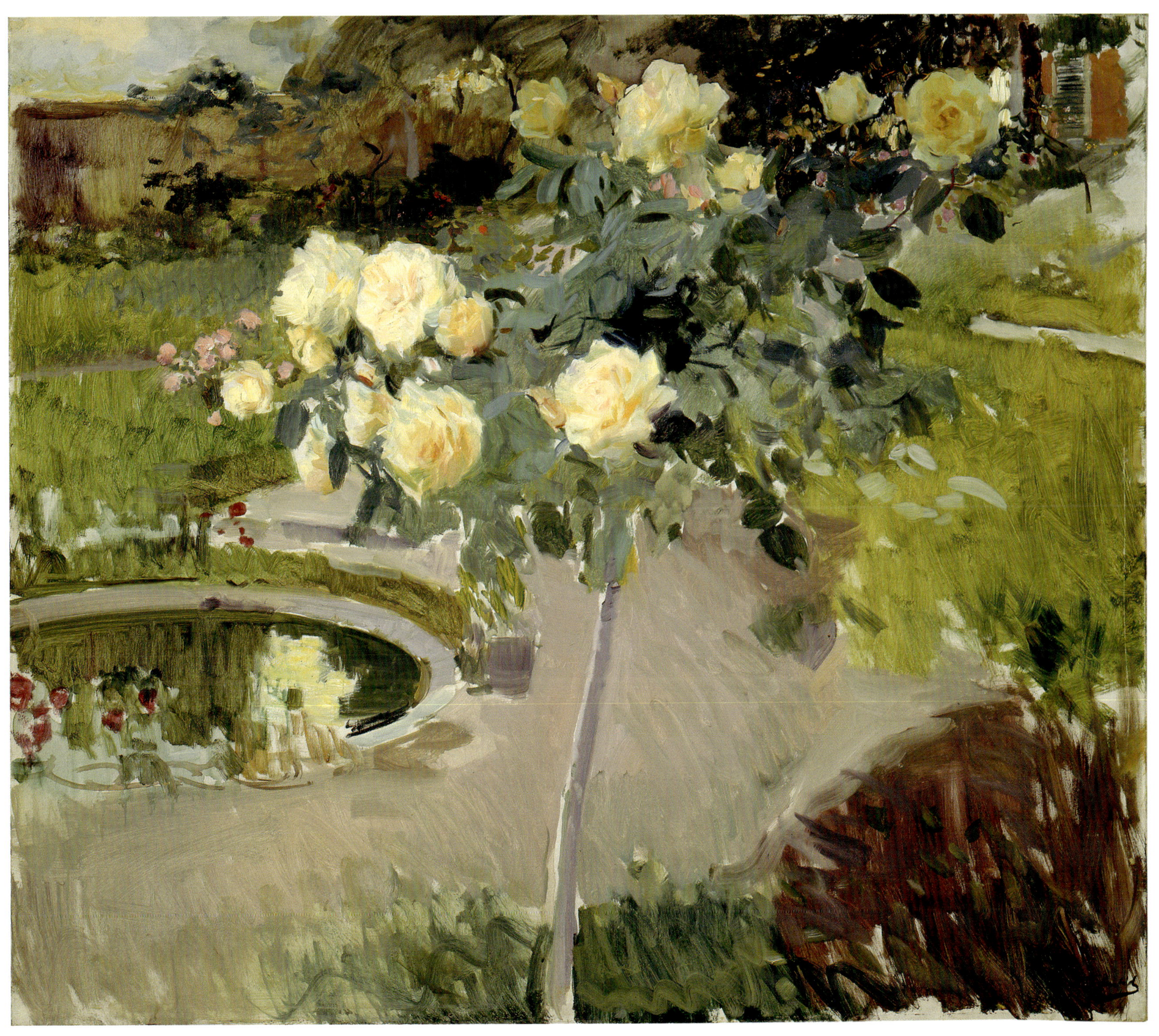

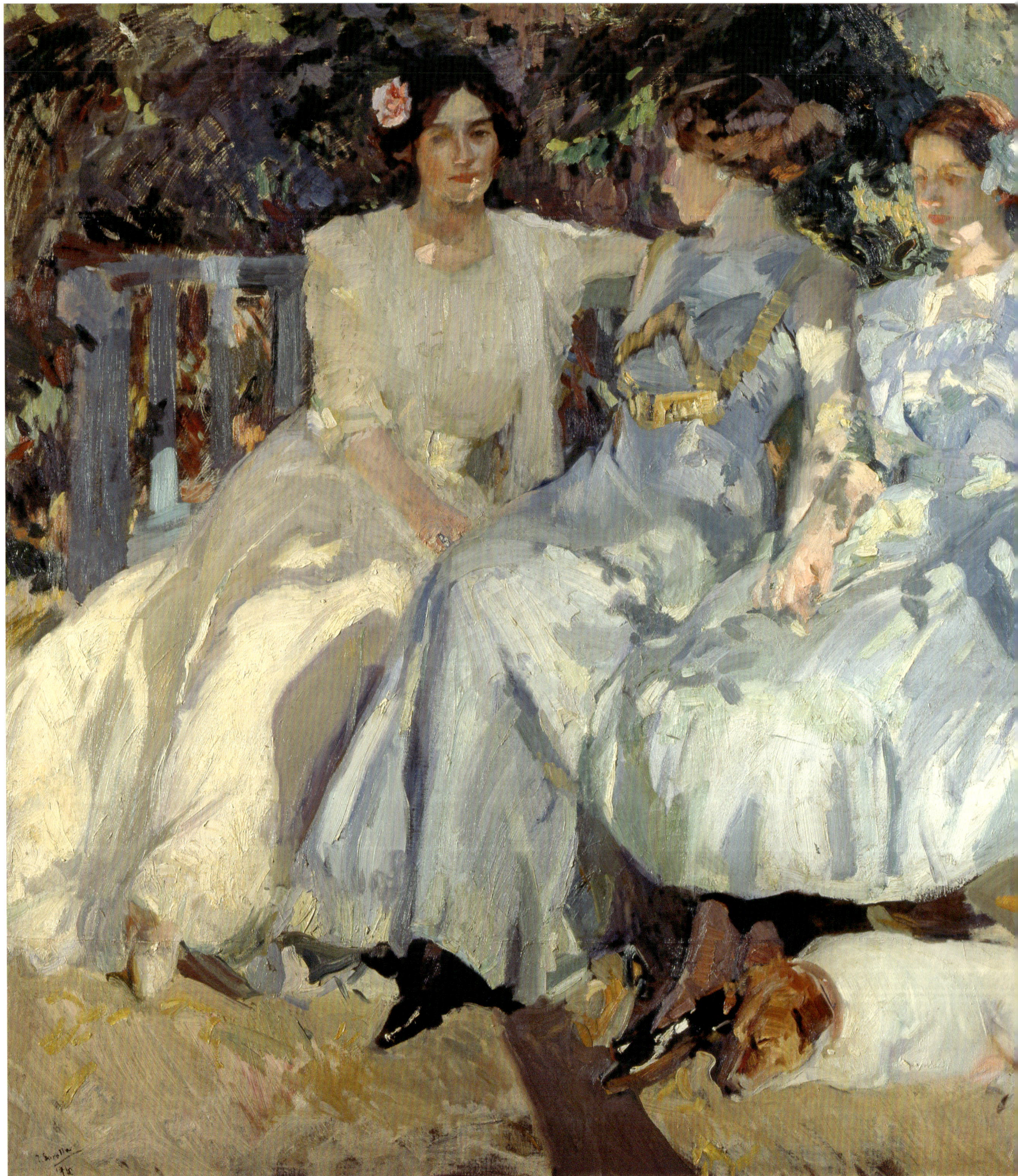

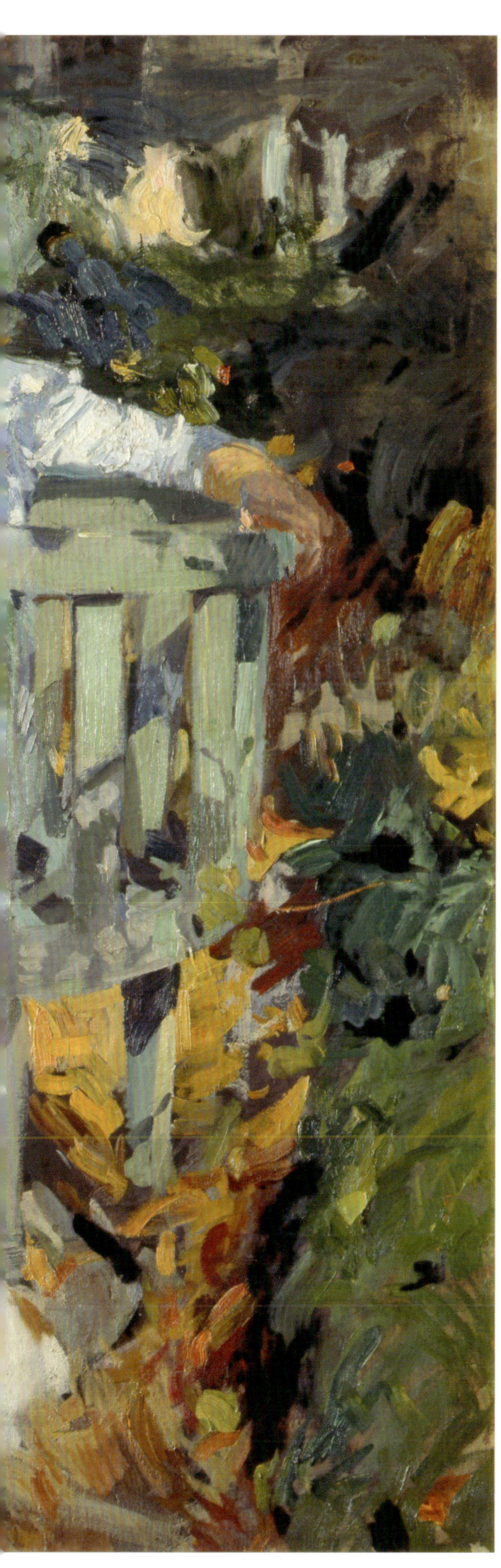

72 *My Wife and Daughters in the Garden*

1910
Oil on canvas, 65¼ x 81 in.
Signed: "J. Sorolla / 1910"
Masaveu Collection
(BPS 1970)

73 *Arched Gate of Santa María, Burgos*

1910
Oil on canvas, 41¼ x 32¼ in.
Signed: "J. Sorolla / 1910"
New York, The Hispanic Society of America [inv. A 276]
(BPS 1706)

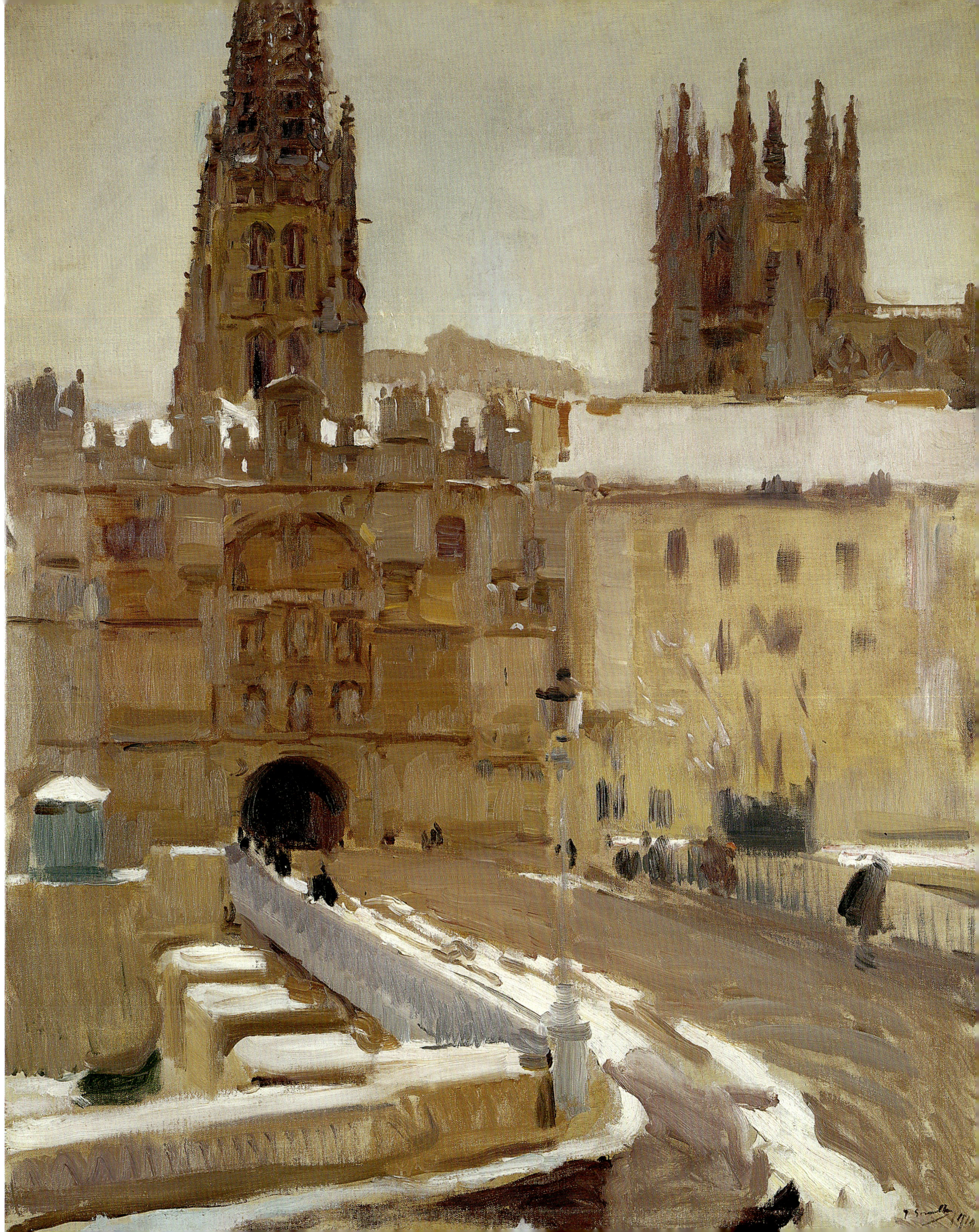

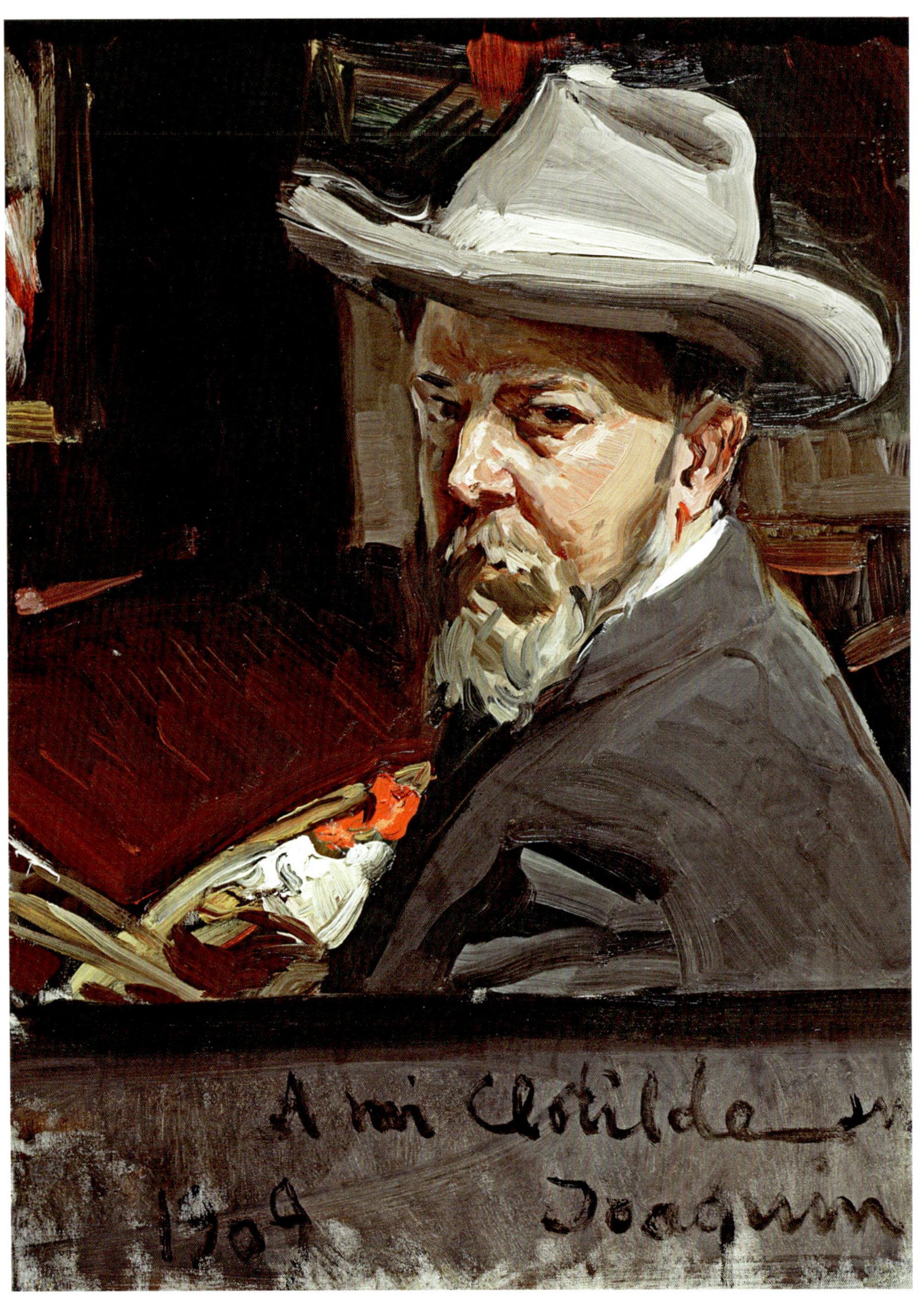

74 *Self-Portrait*

1909
Oil on canvas, 27¾ x 19¾ in.
Signed: "A mi Clotilde su / 1909 / Joaquín"
Madrid, Museo Sorolla [inv. 840]
(BPS 2530)

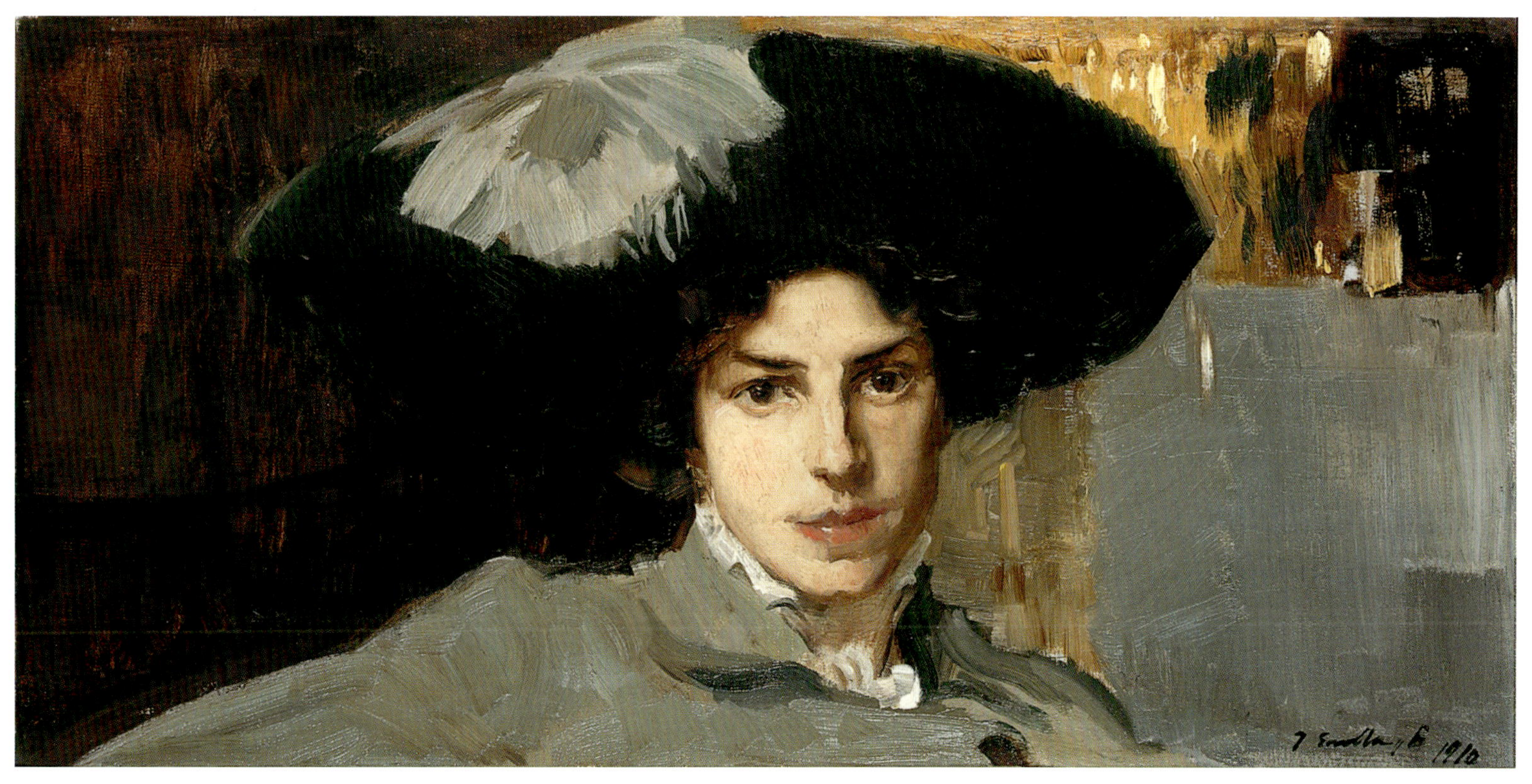

75 *María with Hat*

1910
Oil on canvas, 15¾ x 31½ in.
Signed: "J Sorolla y B / 1910"
Private collection
(BPS 2159)

76 *Mrs. Ira Nelson Morris and Her Children*

1911
Oil on canvas, 86½ x 66½ in.
Signed: "J. Sorolla y Bastida / 1911 / Chicago"
New York, The Hispanic Society of America.
Bequest of Constance Lily Rothschild Morris, 1954 [inv. A 3216]
(BPS 2926)

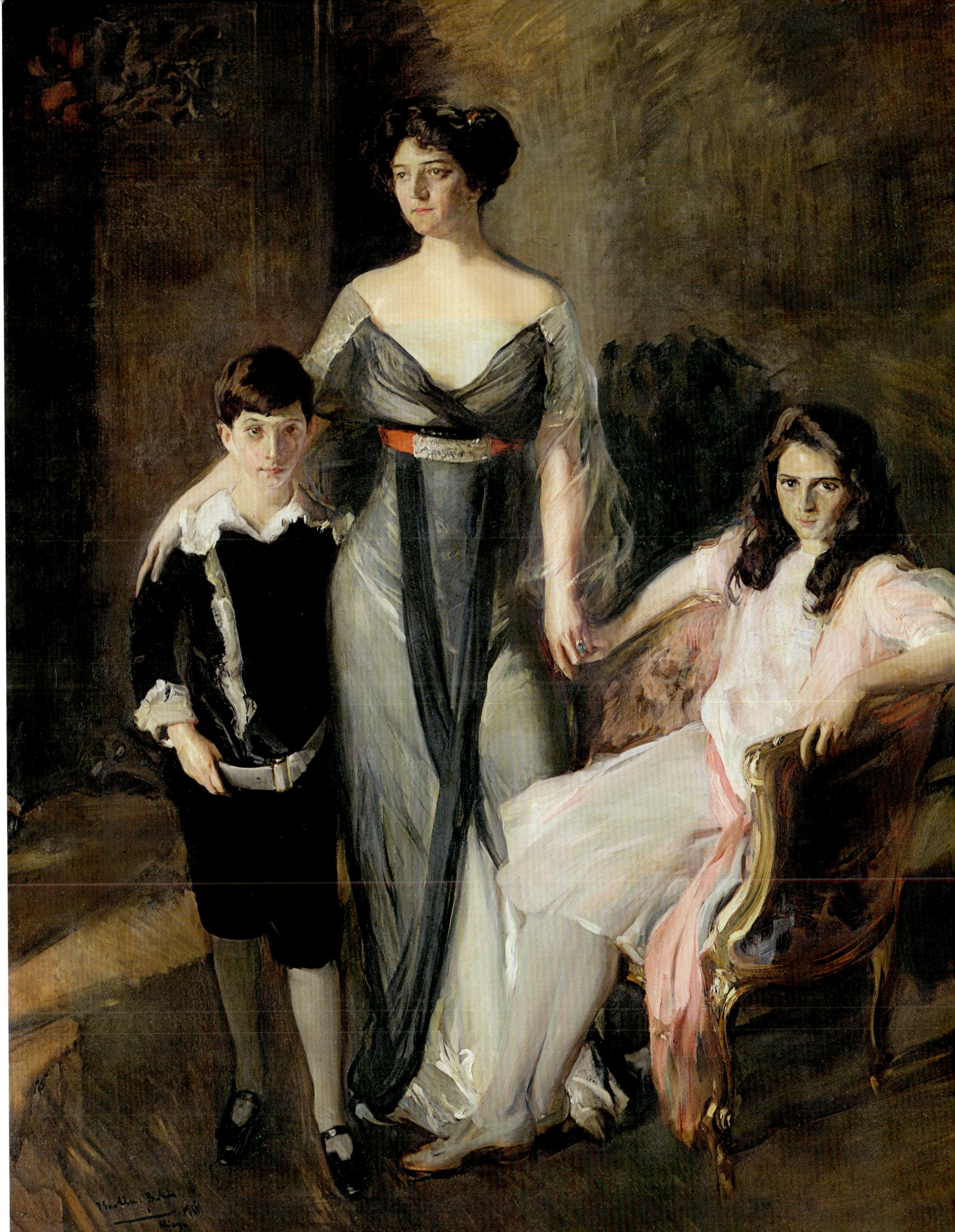

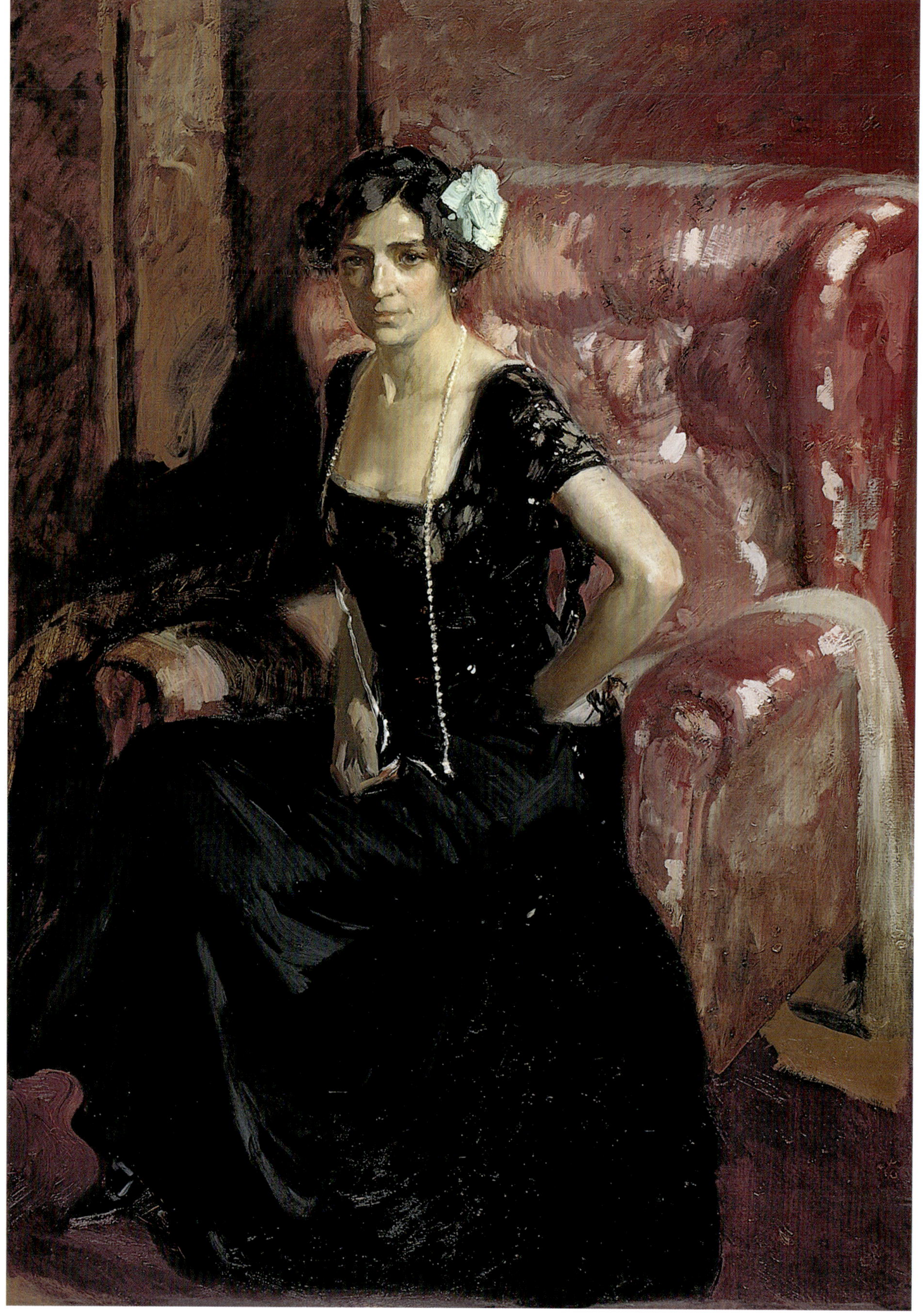

77 *Clotilde in Evening Dress*

c. 1910
Oil on canvas, 59 x 41¼ in.
Madrid, Museo Sorolla [inv. 949]
(BPS 3121)

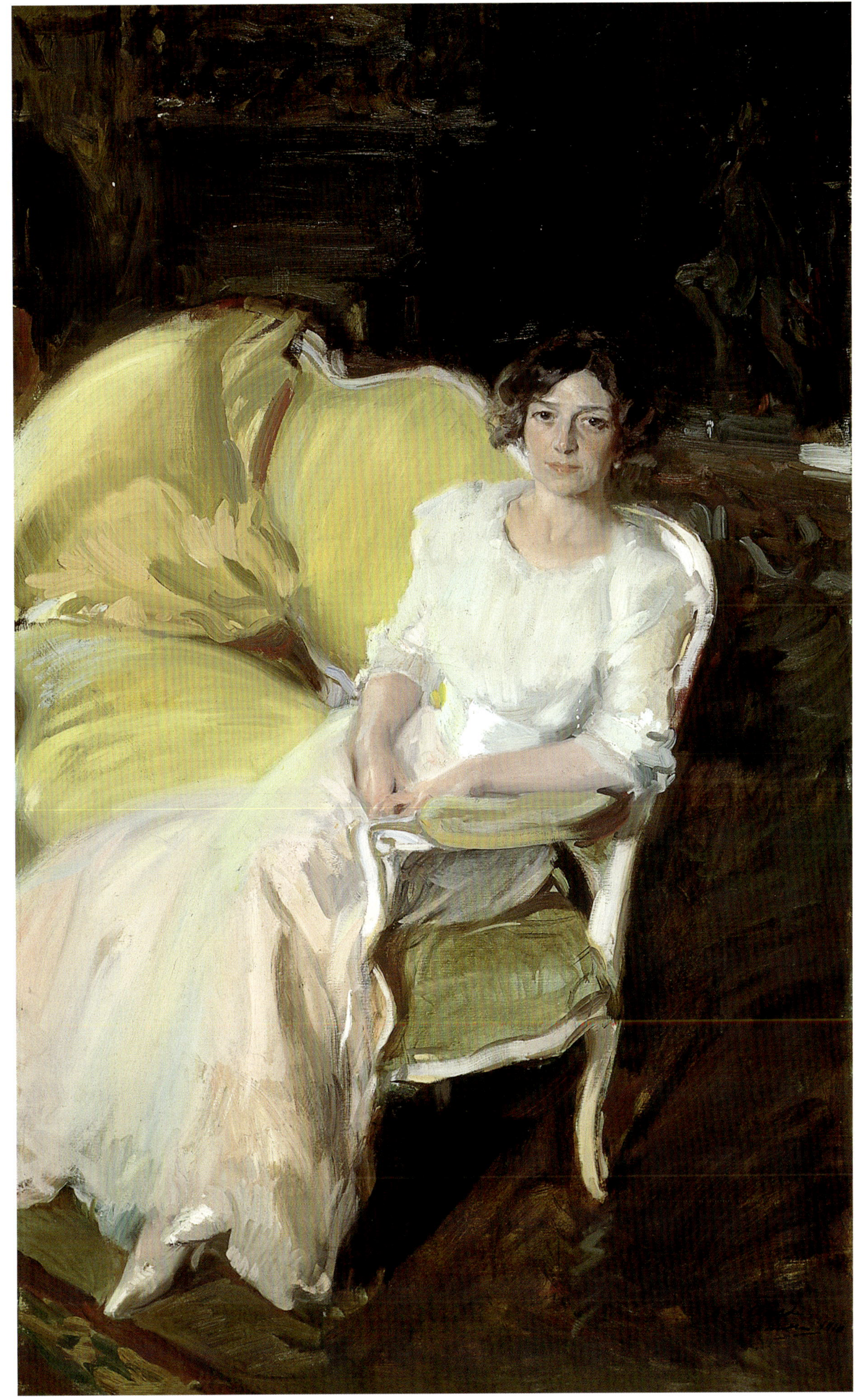

78 *Clotilde Seated on a Sofa*

1910
Oil on canvas, 70¾ x 43¼ in.
Signed: "A mi Clotilde /
J. Sorolla 1910"
Madrid, Museo Sorolla [inv. 900]
(BPS 2590)

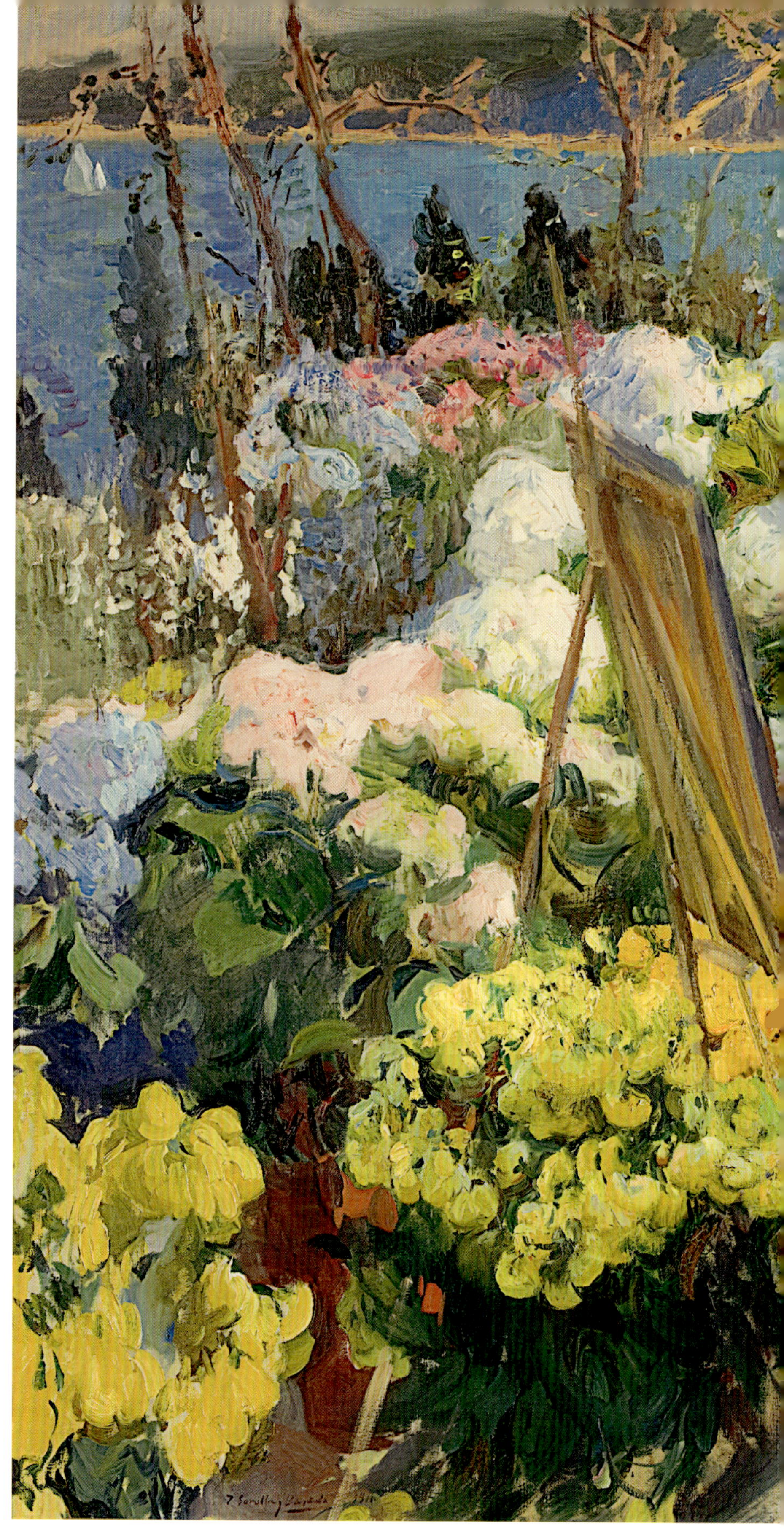

79 *Louis Comfort Tiffany*

1911
Oil on canvas, 59 x 88¾ in.
Signed: "J. Sorolla y Bastida 1911"
New York, The Hispanic Society
of America [inv. A 3182]
(BPS 2749)

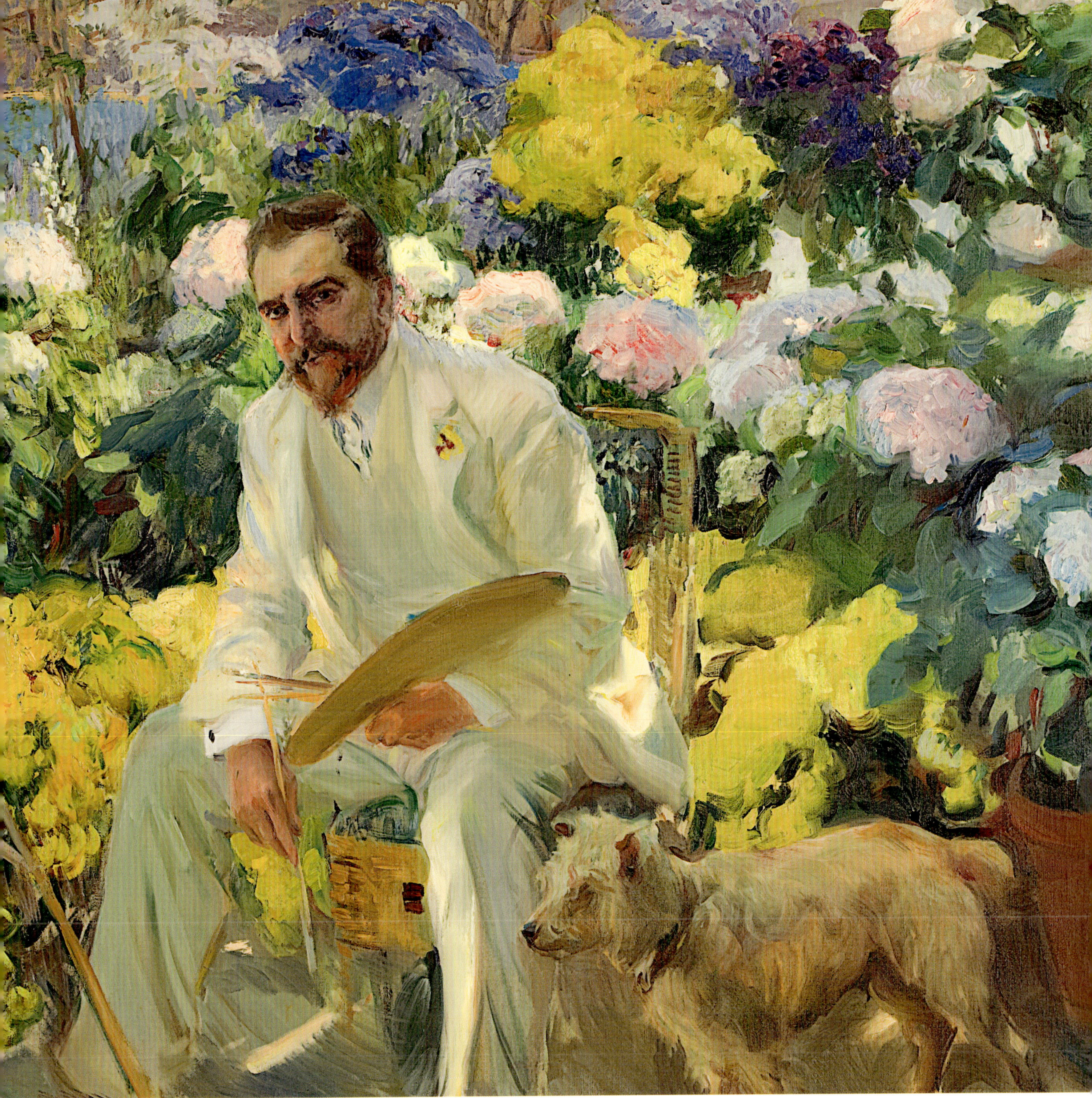

80 *The Nap*

1911
Oil on canvas, 78¾ x 79¼ in.
Signed: “J Sorolla B / 1912”
Madrid, Museo Sorolla [inv. 985]
(BPS 3157)

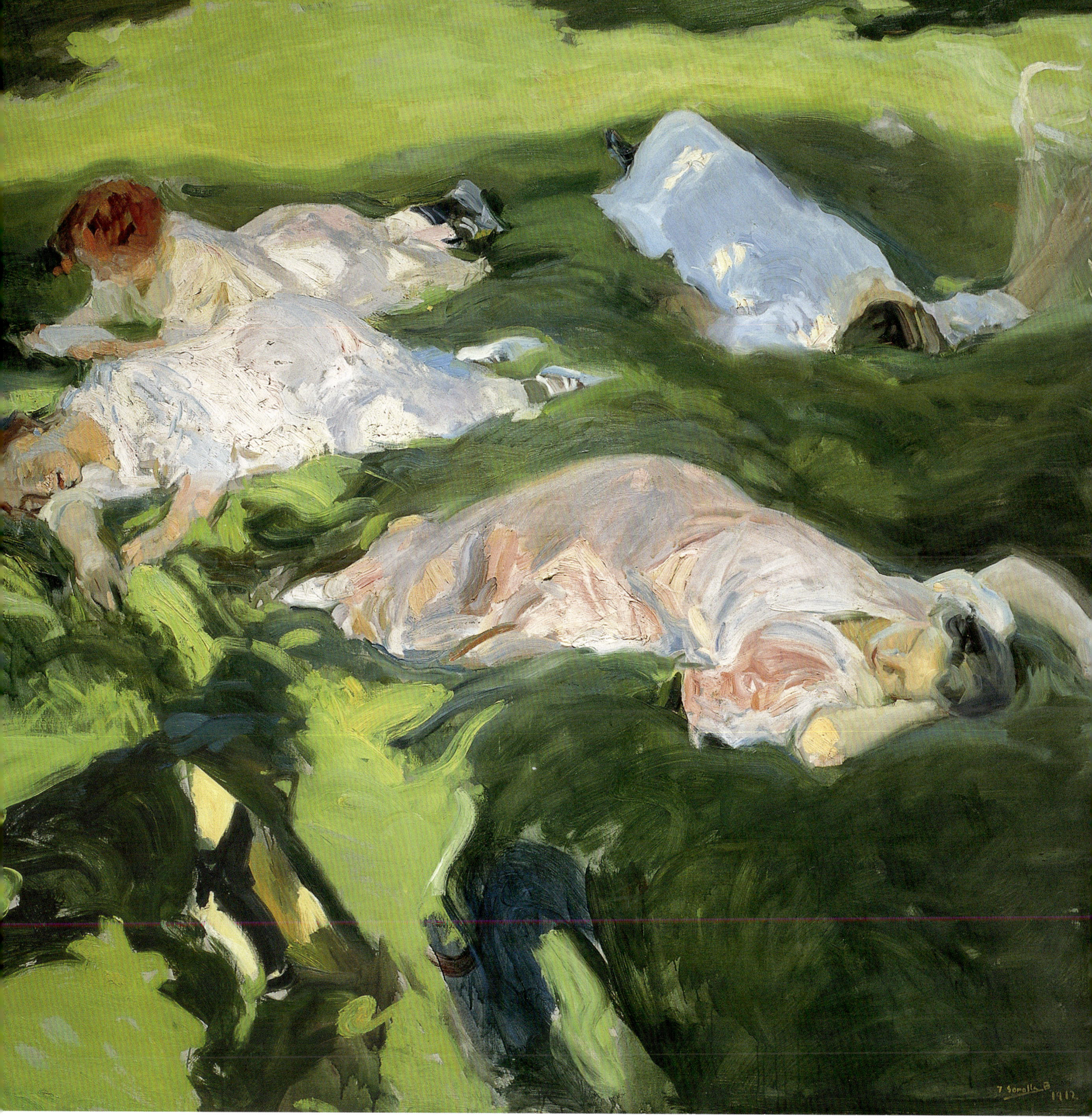

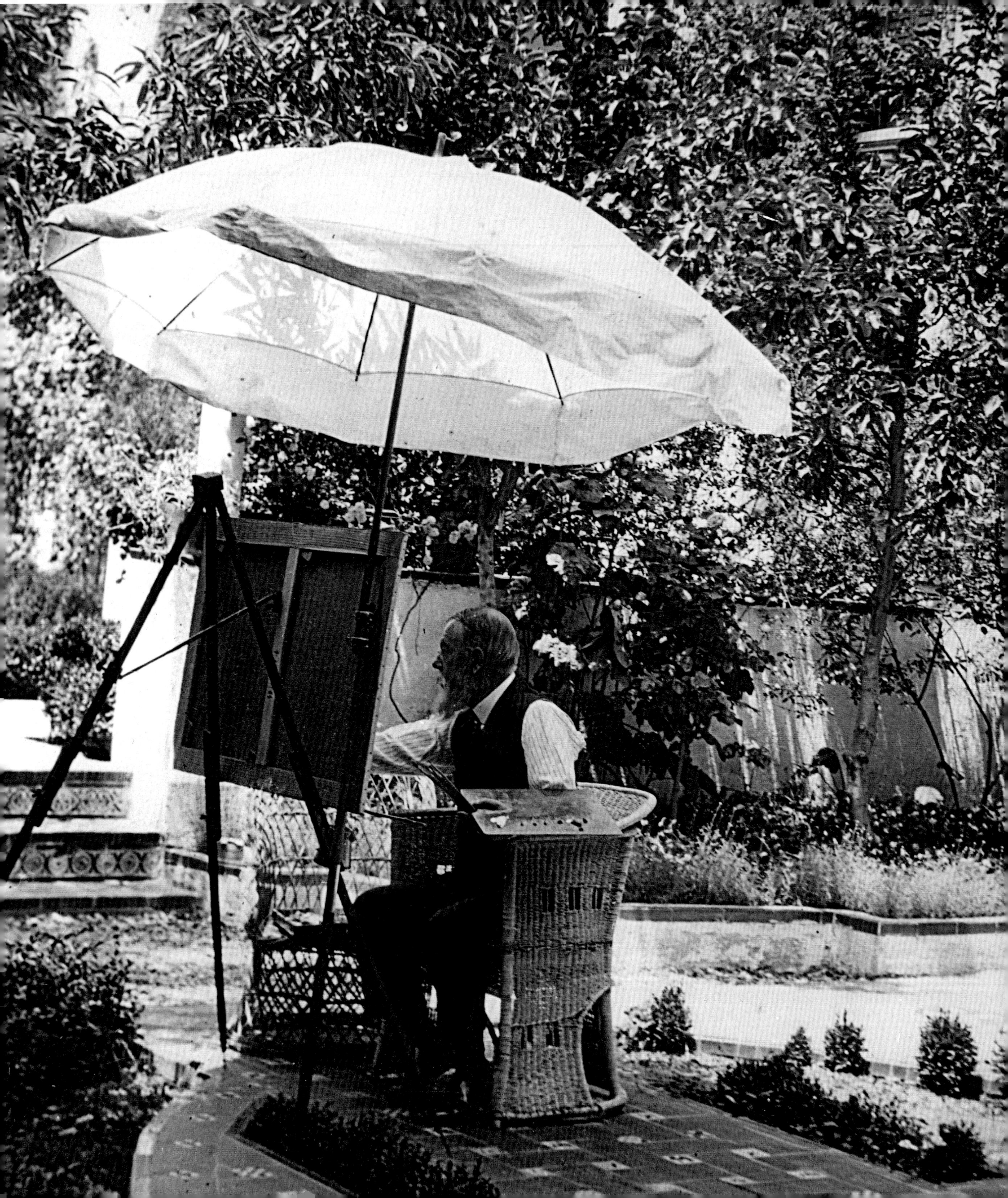

CREATIVE MATURITY (1912–20)

The third stage of Sorolla's artistic career, which takes place between the years 1912 and 1920, starts in the middle of his creative maturity and at the peak of his international popularity and reputation. He dedicated a good part of this time to carrying out the decoration of the library at the Hispanic Society of America in New York, a colossal project which Sorolla accepted for the challenge it presented, and which affected the artist greatly, for it obliged him to travel continuously in order to document the cultures, traditions, and costumes of the different regions in Spain, and to familiarize himself with the landscapes and the light in which they were to be depicted. This was what he called the "search for impressions," which were then transferred onto his enormous canvases. Sorolla put such courage and honor into this great artistic work that it taxed him physically and emotionally in such a way that it proved detrimental to his health. It was a period in which he kept growing as a man and as a painter, as he progressed to the limit of what he believed his painting ought to be: the reflection of his passionate and sensitive view of nature. During these years, he also repeatedly painted the gardens of his home and produced some of his greatest beach paintings, which are perhaps his most sensitive and skillful works, and which do not have any relation to the decoration at the Hispanic Society of America. Says Sorolla:

> My only wish ever since I entered the Academy of Fine Arts in Valencia was to create a frank painting, one in which nature was interpreted as it truly is, exactly how it should be seen…and I believe, eh?…that I have achieved what I aspired to do. It is now that my hand obeys my eye and my feelings completely.[1]

The decoration for the Hispanic Society kept him occupied from 1912 until 1919. During the first year, he traveled ceaselessly

Joaquín Sorolla painting in the garden of his house in Madrid, 1920. Photograph attributed to Arthur Byne. Madrid, Museo Sorolla [80.197]

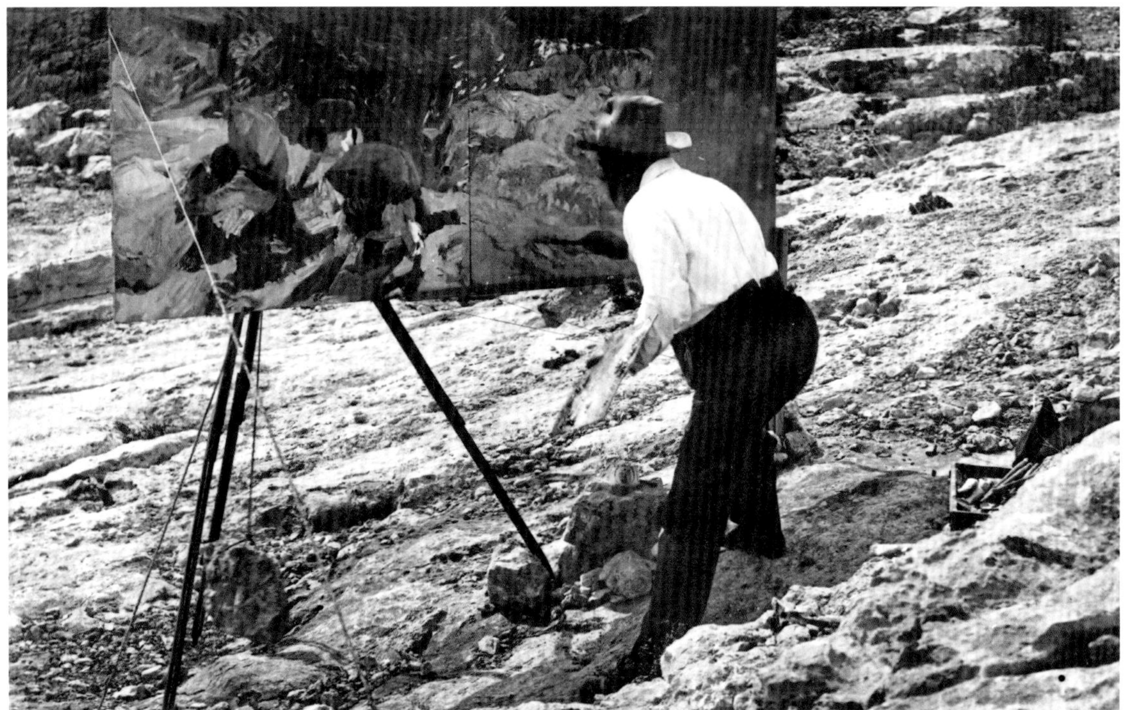

Joaquín Sorolla painting *The Smugglers* in Ibiza, 1919. Photograph by Narciso Puget Viñas. Madrid, Museo Sorolla [80.189]

around different Spanish regions to paint in situ, directly from nature, a number of large studies that would later help him to compose the definitive panels. During the next three years, he produced a total of eleven panels dedicated to Castile, Andalusia, Aragon, Navarre, Gipuzkoa, Galicia, and Catalonia. He traveled to each of the regions to paint the corresponding panel, and he always painted outdoors.

Sorolla's health began to deteriorate. In 1915, he starts to mention in his letters the tremors he suffers when he is moved emotionally while painting, tremors that last more than an hour: "My hand and my vision grow tired, but my desire to paint will never be satiated!"

He took four more years to paint the last four panels, those dedicated to Valencia, Alicante, Extremadura, and Ayamonte. During these years, he also painted portraits for the gallery of distinguished Spaniards for Huntington, such as *The Poet Juan Ramón Jiménez* [fig. 91], and portraits of his family and friends, including an outstanding one of his son, *Joaquín Sorolla García, Seated* [fig. 92]. In Seville and Granada, he painted views with a new intimacy, whether of the Sierra Nevada [fig. 94] or of his own garden—*Oleanders in the Courtyard of the Sorolla House* [fig. 93], *Wallflowers in the Garden of the Sorolla House* [fig. 100]. During his summers in San Sebastián, always accompanied by his family, he painted numerous views of its beach and breakwater, such as *The Breakwater at San Sebastián* [fig. 95].

Sorolla's great sensitivity, which brought him so much pleasure and suffering, is reflected in this letter written to his wife in 1916, when he was painting one of the panels dedicated to Valencia, *Riding in Croupe, Valencia*. The work was a very emotional undertaking, as the subject was his homeland:

The Yellow Rosebush of the Sorolla House [fig. 101], and *Garden of the Sorolla House* [fig. 102]. On June 20, 1920, in that garden, while he was working on a portrait for the wife of Ramón Pérez de Ayala,[7] Sorolla suffered a brain hemorrhage that ended his painting days.

There is no one better than Pérez de Ayala himself to describe Sorolla's last moments:

> One fine, warm morning in Madrid in June, in his garden, Sorolla was painting my wife's portrait while I observed. We three were alone, under an arbor. He stood once and headed toward his studio. As he ascended the steps, he fell. My wife and I came to his aid, thinking that he had tripped. We lifted him onto his feet, but he could not hold himself up. The left side of his face was tightened into a grimace, a childlike and sorrowful expression that prompted empathy, pity, tenderness. We realized the dramatic truth; the string that was pulled taut had snapped (Sorolla felt the terror and premonition of paralysis; years before he had suffered a mild case). Even in the state he was in, rebelling against the misfortune that had already seized him in its iron fist, Sorolla wanted to keep painting. We attempted to dissuade him, but in vain. He insisted in the irritated way a spoiled child does when he is denied something unexpectedly. The palette kept falling from his left hand; his right hand, with the paintbrush poorly held, barely obeyed him. He made four long and shaky brushstrokes, desperate strokes; four silent screams, already at a distance from his former life. Unforgettable pathetic brushstrokes!—"I can't," he murmured, with tears in his eyes. He was left hunched over himself, as if engrossed in the remaining light of his intelligence, almost extinguished, and, suddenly, with an absurd and invisible sigh, he said: "Let there be one more idiot, what does the world care?"[8]

His family's efforts to help him recover were in vain. He died in the month of August of 1923, while they were spending the summer in Cercedilla, at his daughter María's house.

Two years after Sorolla's death, his wife, Clotilde, made her will, and inspired by the love she felt for her husband and his work, and to preserve his memory, she donated all of his possessions to the Spanish State in order to found the Museum Sorolla.

NOTES

1. Rodolfo Gil, *Sorolla*, Madrid, Sáenz de Juberá-Hermanos (*Monografías de Arte Universal*, 7), 1913, pp. 25–30.
2. Sorolla (Valencia) to Clotilde (Madrid), February 3, 1916. *Epistolarios de Joaquín Sorolla, II. Correspondencia con Clotilde García del Castillo (1912–1919)*, eds. Víctor Lorente, Blanca Pons-Sorolla, and Marina Moya, Barcelona, Anthropos, 2008, letter no. 360, p. 270.
3. Sorolla (Alicante) to Clotilde (Madrid), November 30, 1918. *Epistolarios de Joaquín Sorolla II*, letter no. 475, pp. 351 and 352.
4. Sorolla (Alicante) to Clotilde (Madrid), December 22, 1918. *Epistolarios de Joaquín Sorolla II*, letter no. 499, pp. 369 and 370.
5. Sorolla (Ayamonte) to Clotilde (Madrid), June 21, 1919. *Epistolarios de Joaquín Sorolla II*, letter no. 579, pp. 429 and 430.
6. Sorolla (Ayamonte) to Clotilde (Madrid), June 29, 1919. *Epistolarios de Joaquín Sorolla II*, letter no. 587, p. 435.
7. *Portrait of the Señora de Pérez de Ayala*. Madrid, Museo Sorolla, inv. 1276 [BPS 3441].
8. Ramón Pérez de Ayala, "Sorolla," *La prensa*, Buenos Aires (October 7, 1923).

Joaquín Sorolla painting *The Galician Piper* and *Galicia, the Cattle Fair* in Villagarcía de Arosa, 1915. Madrid, Museo Sorolla [80.167]

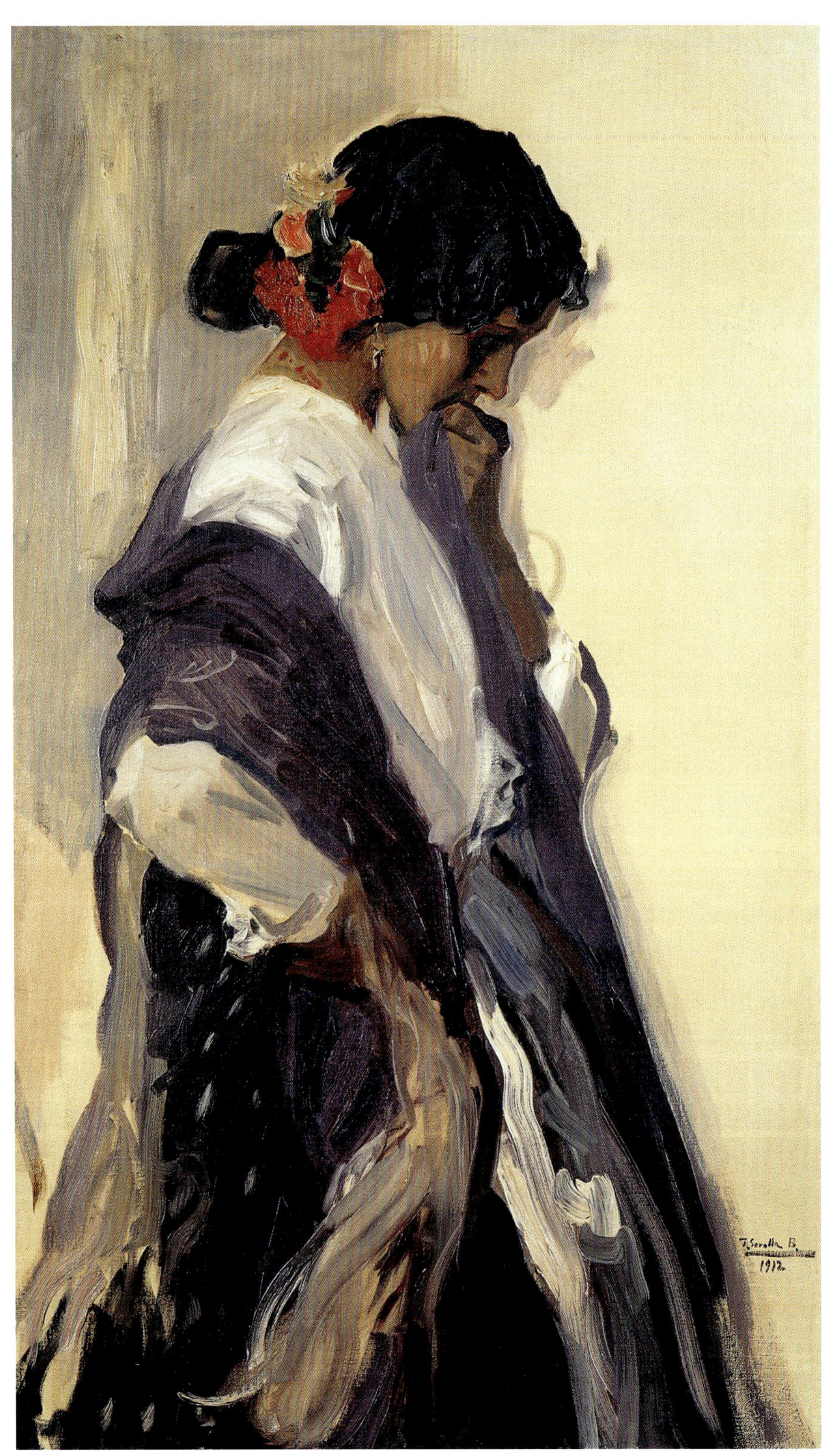

81 *A Gypsy Woman*

1912
Oil on canvas, 43½ x 25 in.
Signed: "J. Sorolla B. / 1912"
Private collection
(BPS 4713)

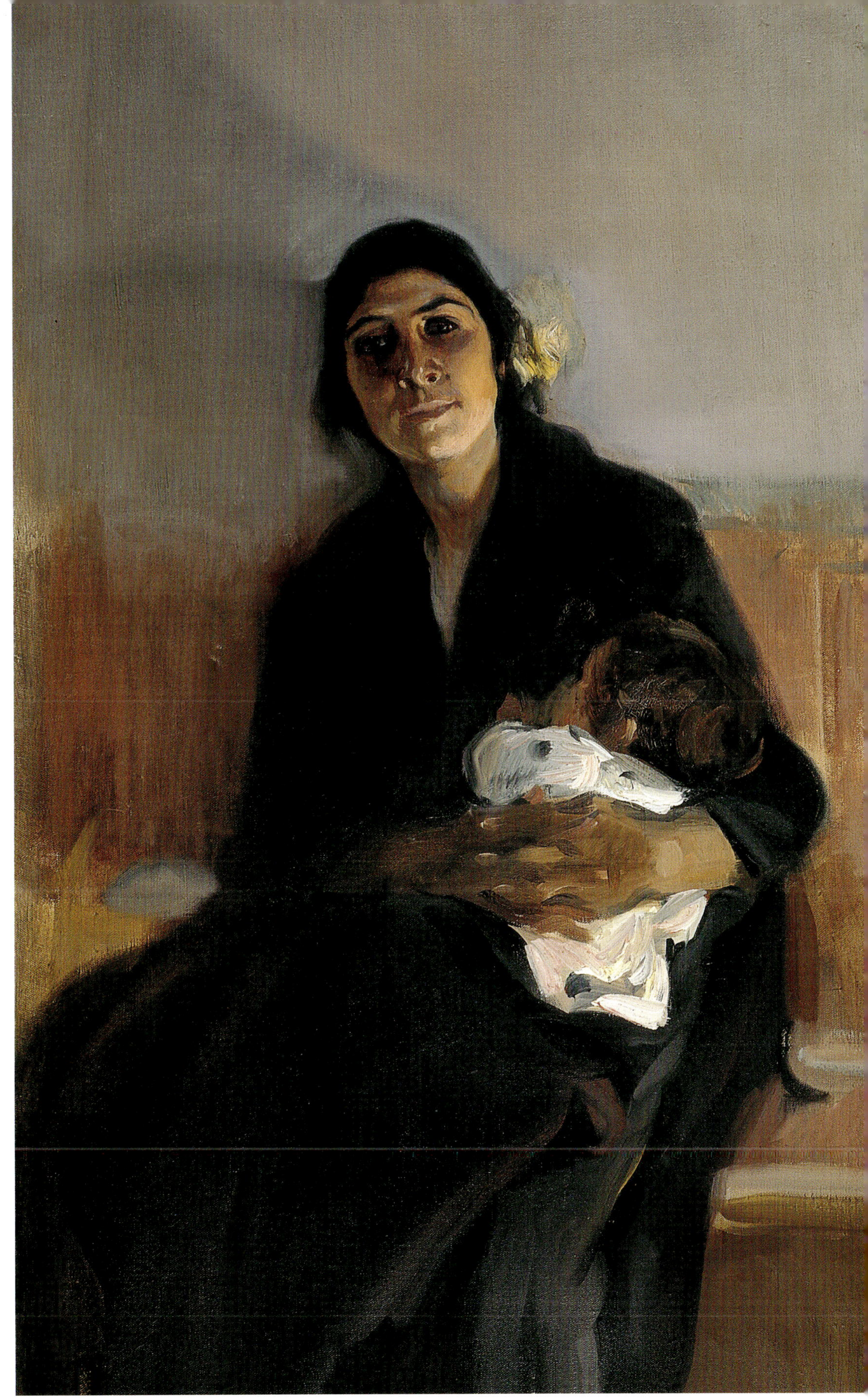

82 *Joaquina the Gypsy*

1914
Oil on canvas, 49½ x 32 in.
Madrid, Museo Sorolla [inv. 1042]
(BPS 3212)

83 *Regla Manjón, Countess of Lebrija*

1914
Oil on canvas, 29½ x 40½ in.
Signed: "A La Condesa de Lebrija su amigo / J Sorolla / 1914"
Private collection
(BPS 2940)

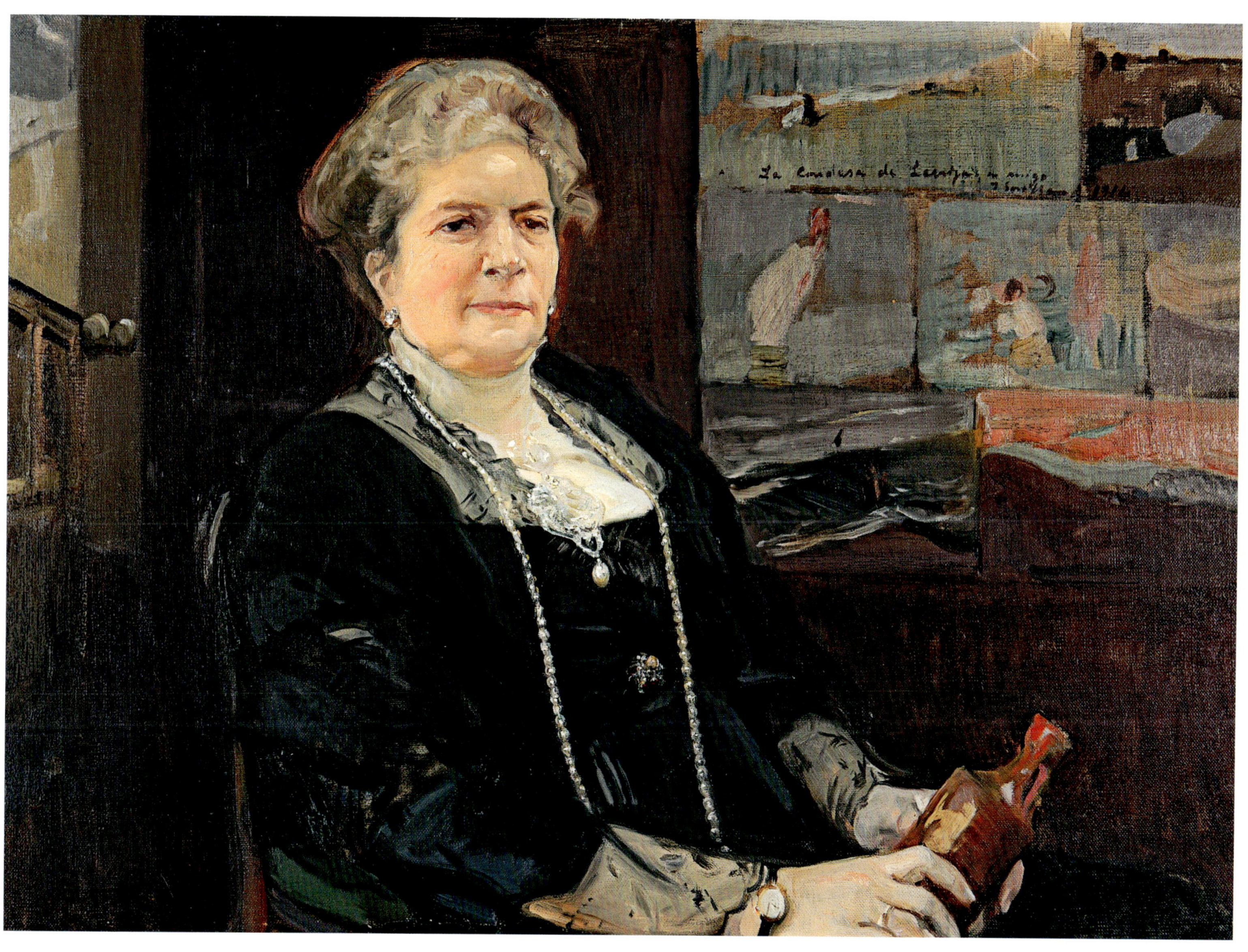

84 *Seville, Holy Week Penitents*

1914
Oil on canvas, 10 ft. 11¼ in. x 9 ft. 10¼ in.
New York, The Hispanic Society of America
[inv A. 1809]
(BPS 2806)

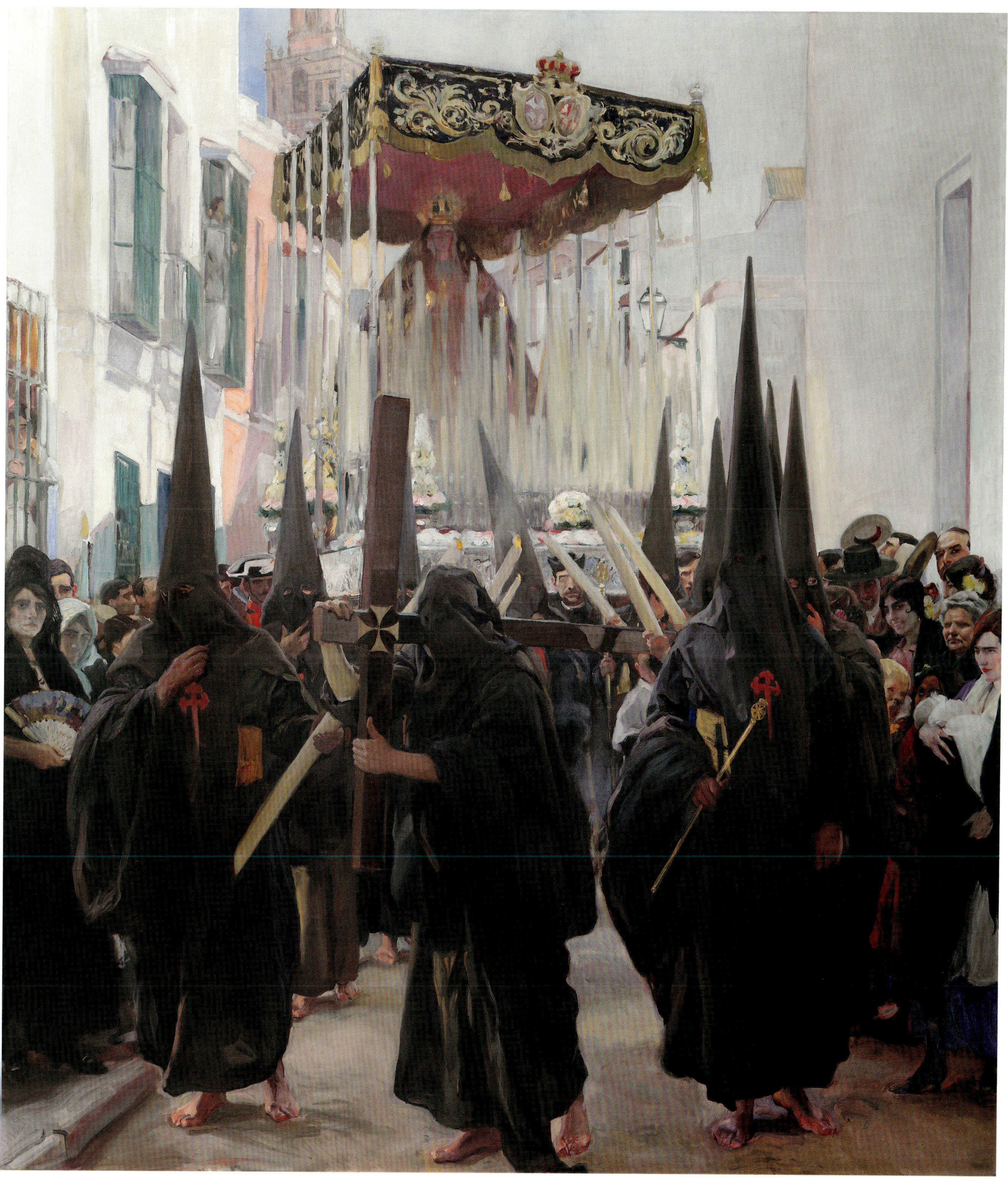

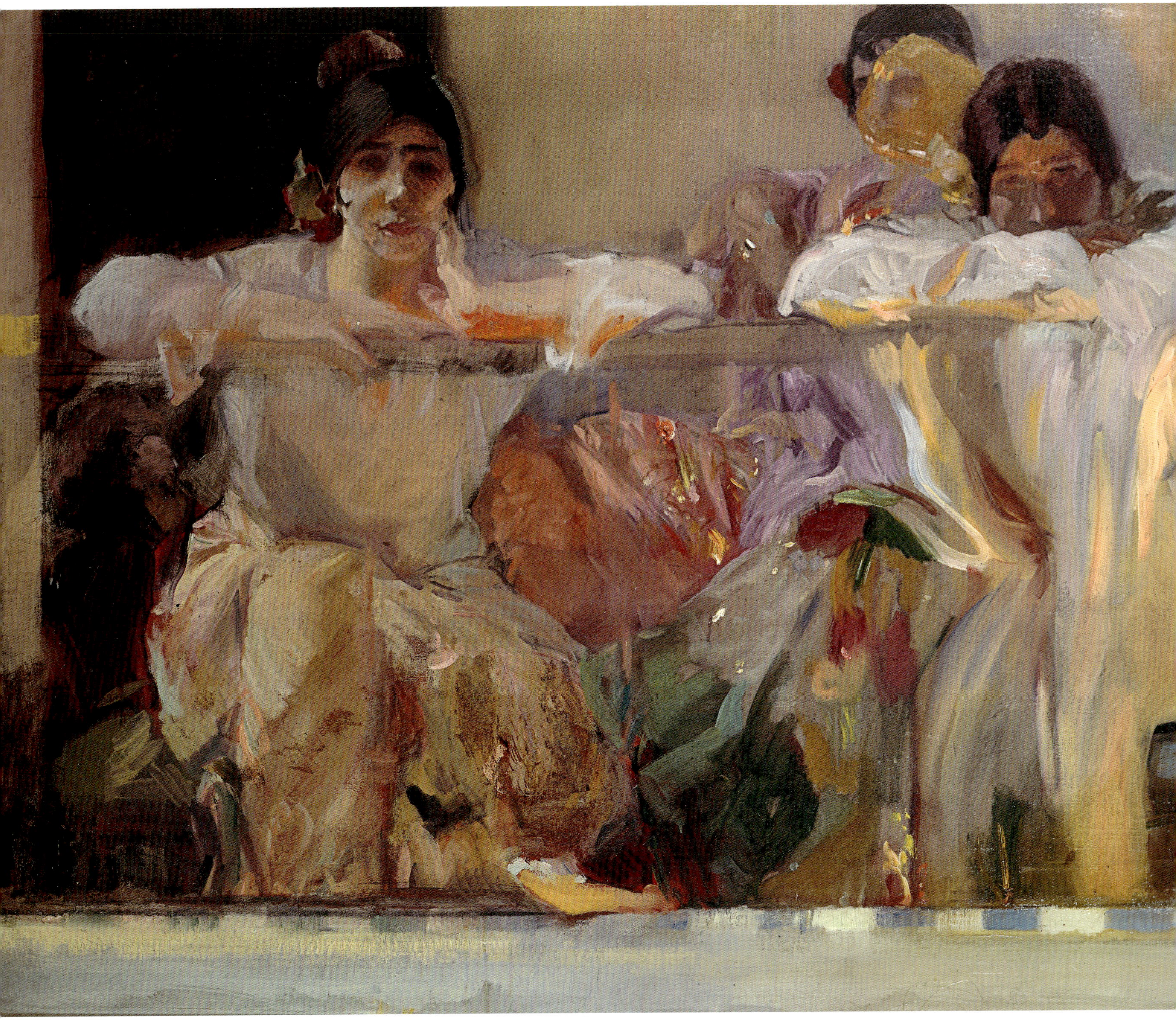

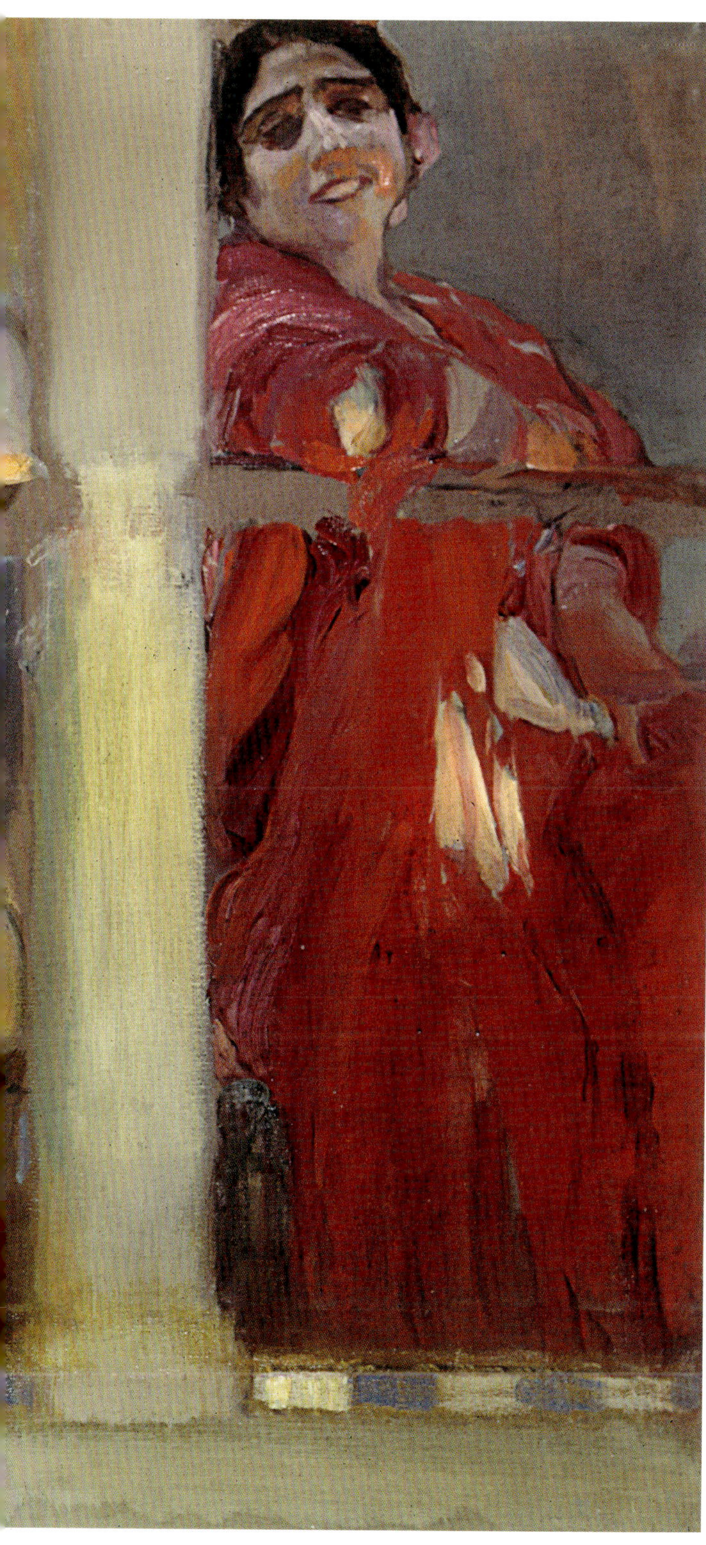

85 *Artists' Patio, Café Novedades, Seville*

1915
Oil on canvas, 49¼ x 82¾ in.
Private collection
(BPS 2671)

86 *Beached Boats, Valencia*

1915
Oil on canvas, 39¼ x 47¼ in.
Private collection
(BPS 2985)

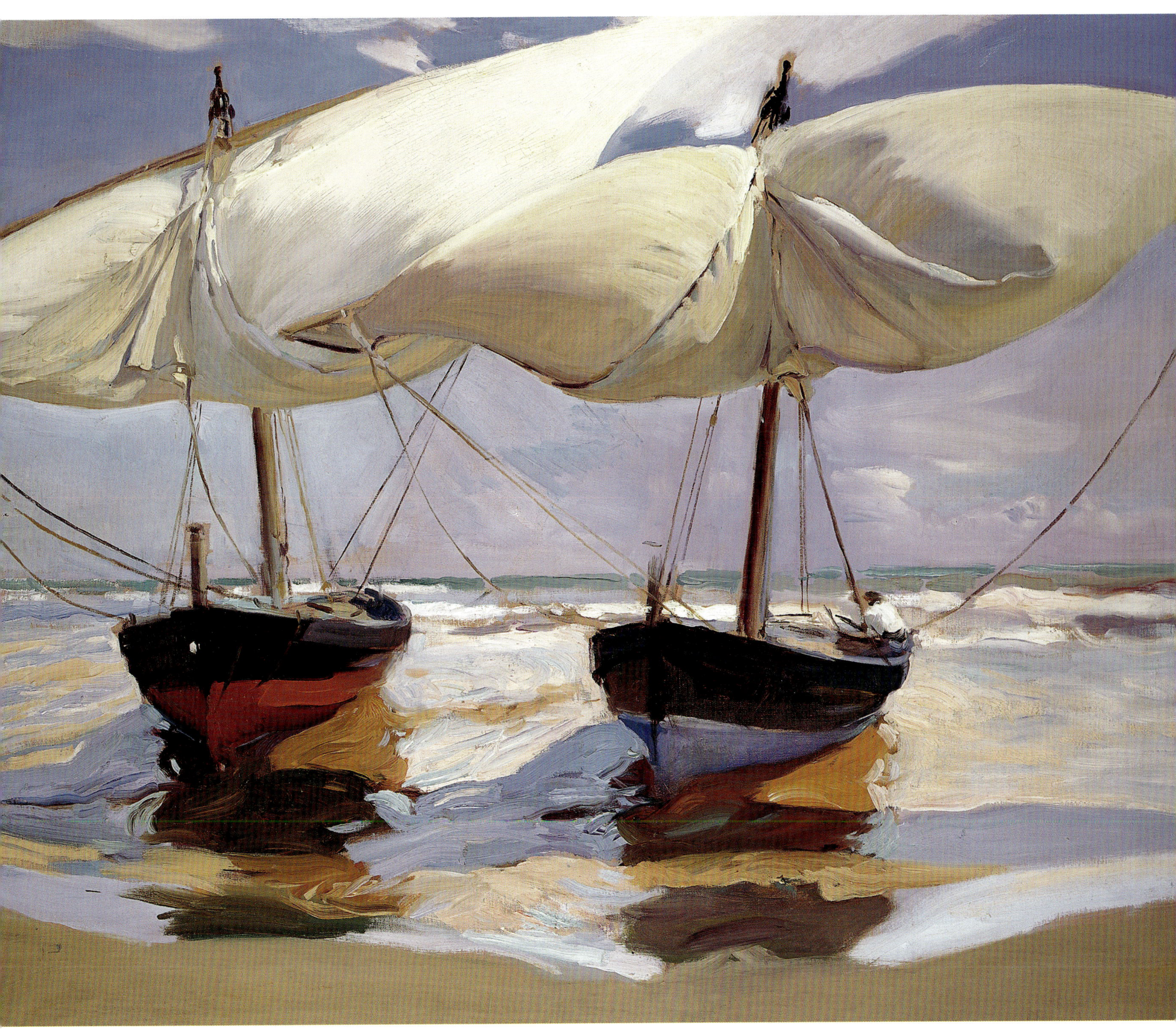

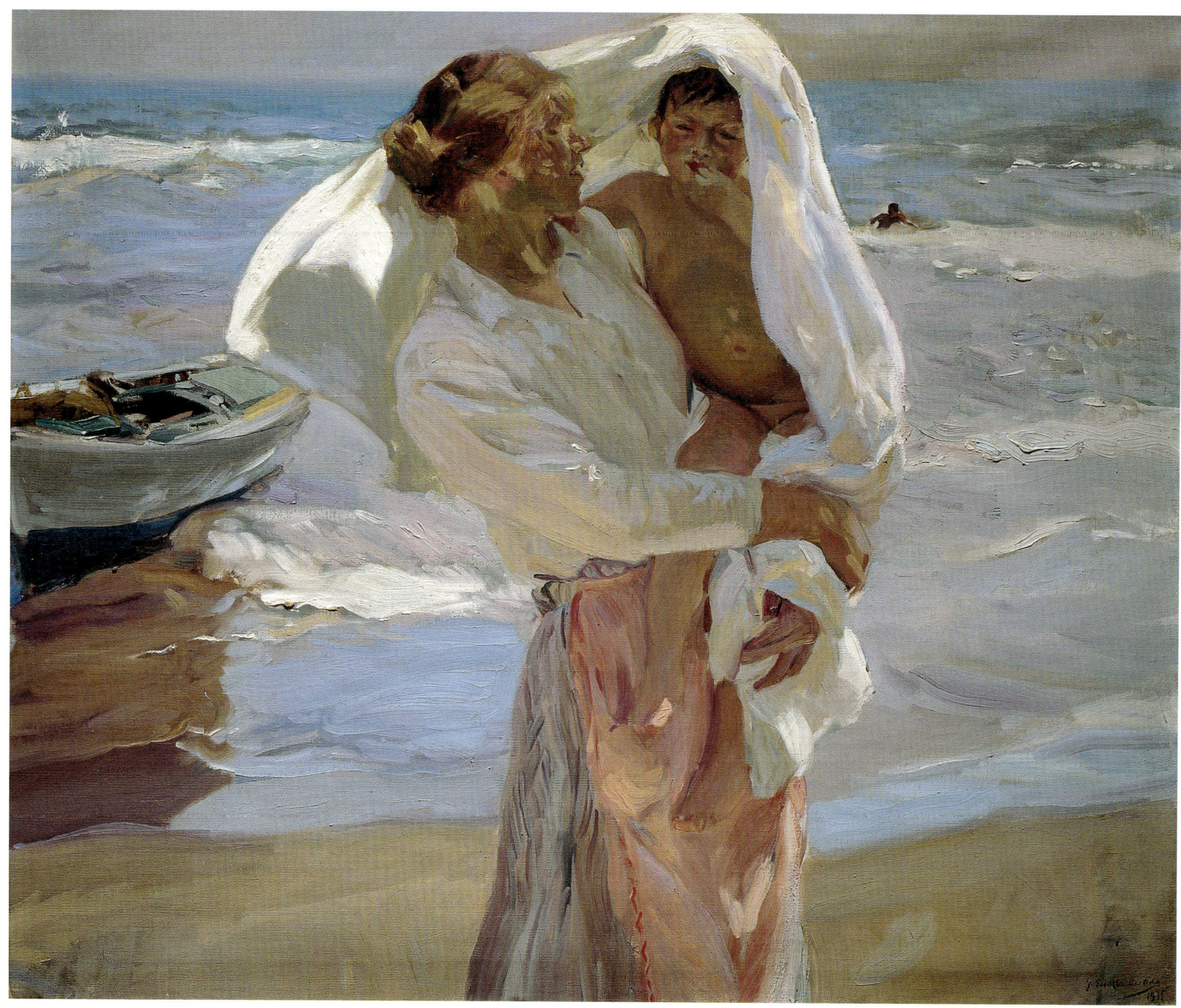

87 *After Bathing, Valencia*

1915
Oil on canvas, 51¼ x 59¼ in.
Signed: "J. Sorolla Bastida / 1915"
Madrid, Museo Sorolla [inv. 1115]
(BPS 3286)

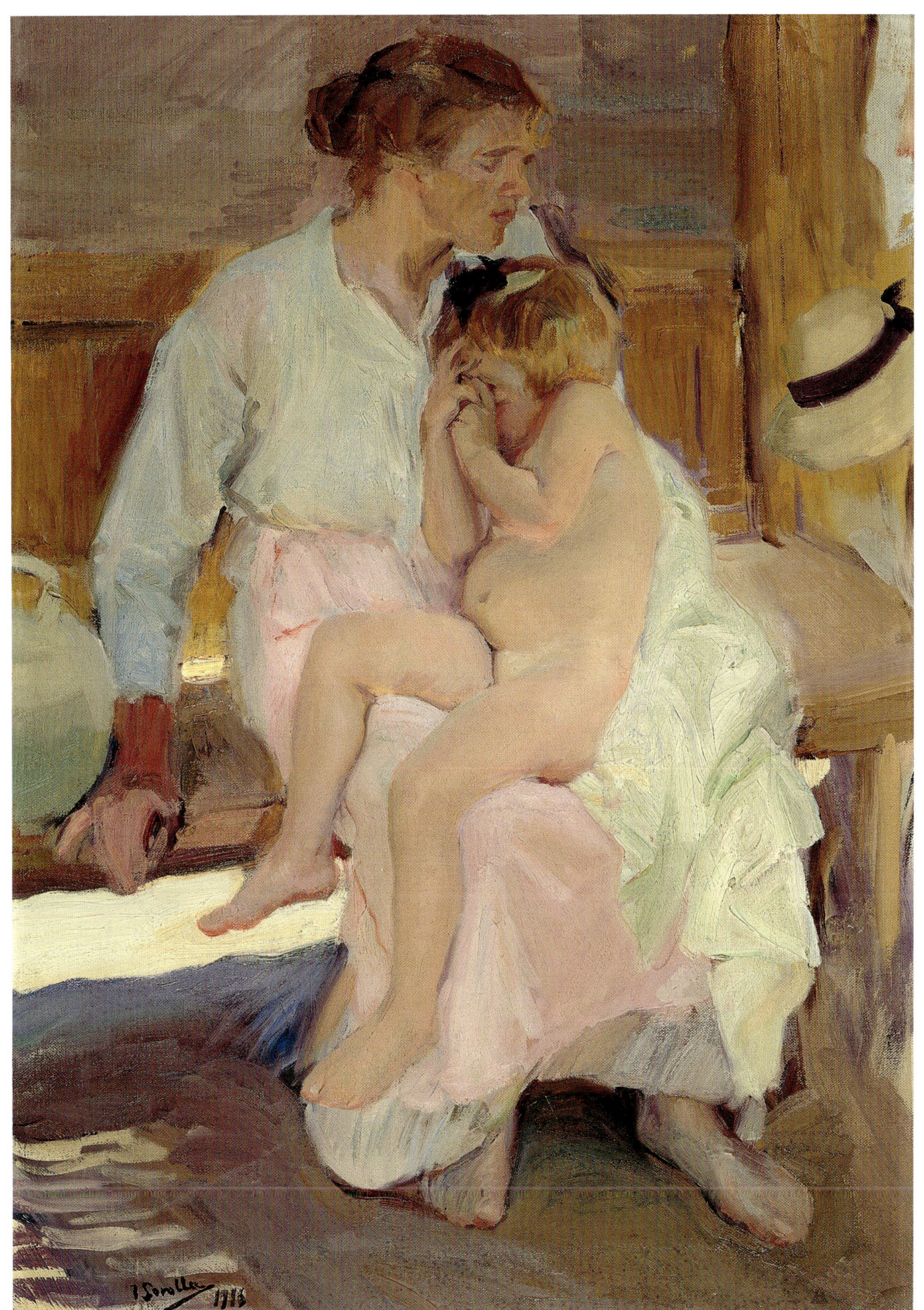

88 *Mother and Daughter, Valencia Beach*

1916
Oil on canvas, 39½ x 27½ in.
Signed: "J Sorolla / 1916"
Private collection
(BPS 3023)

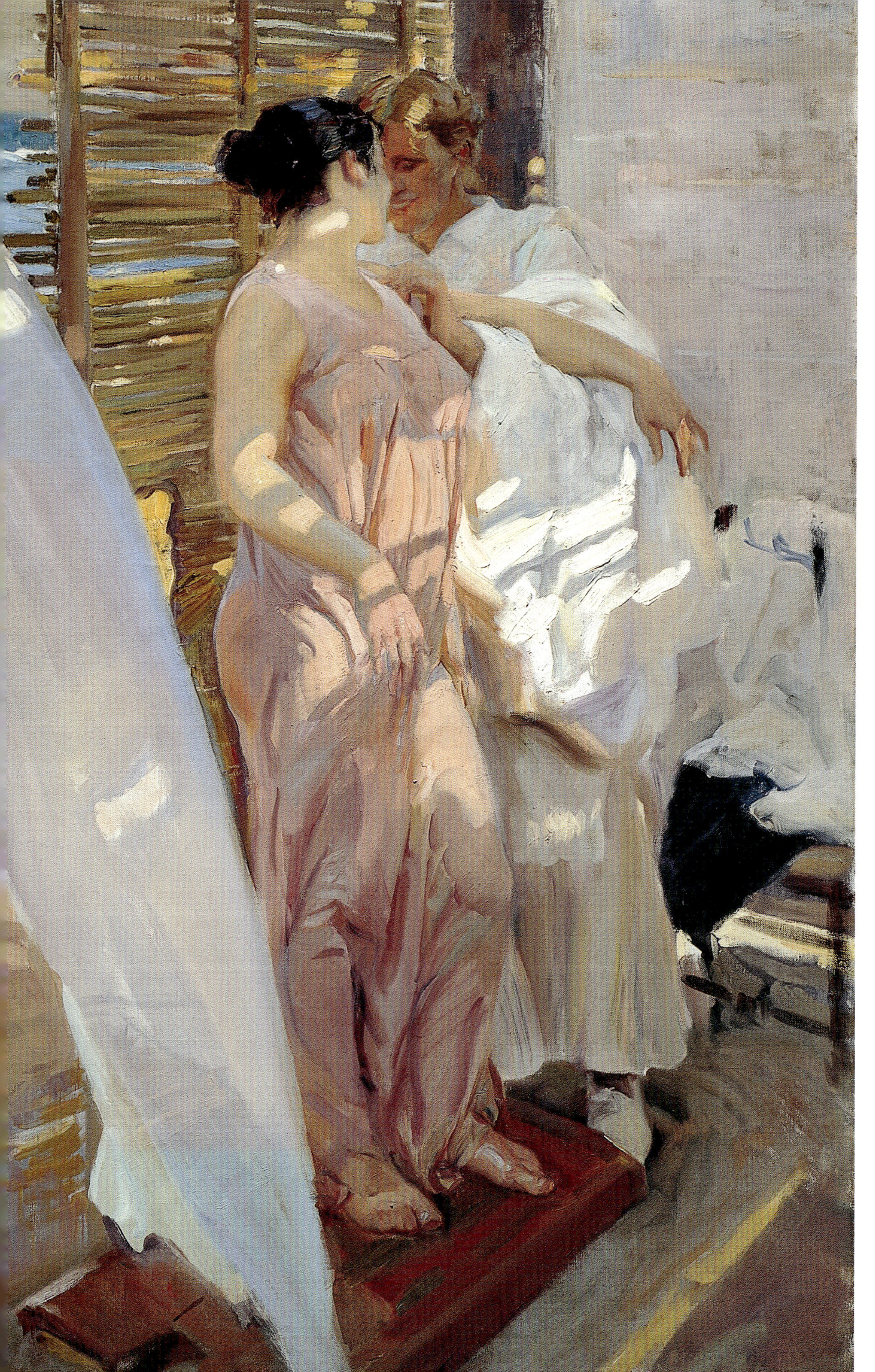

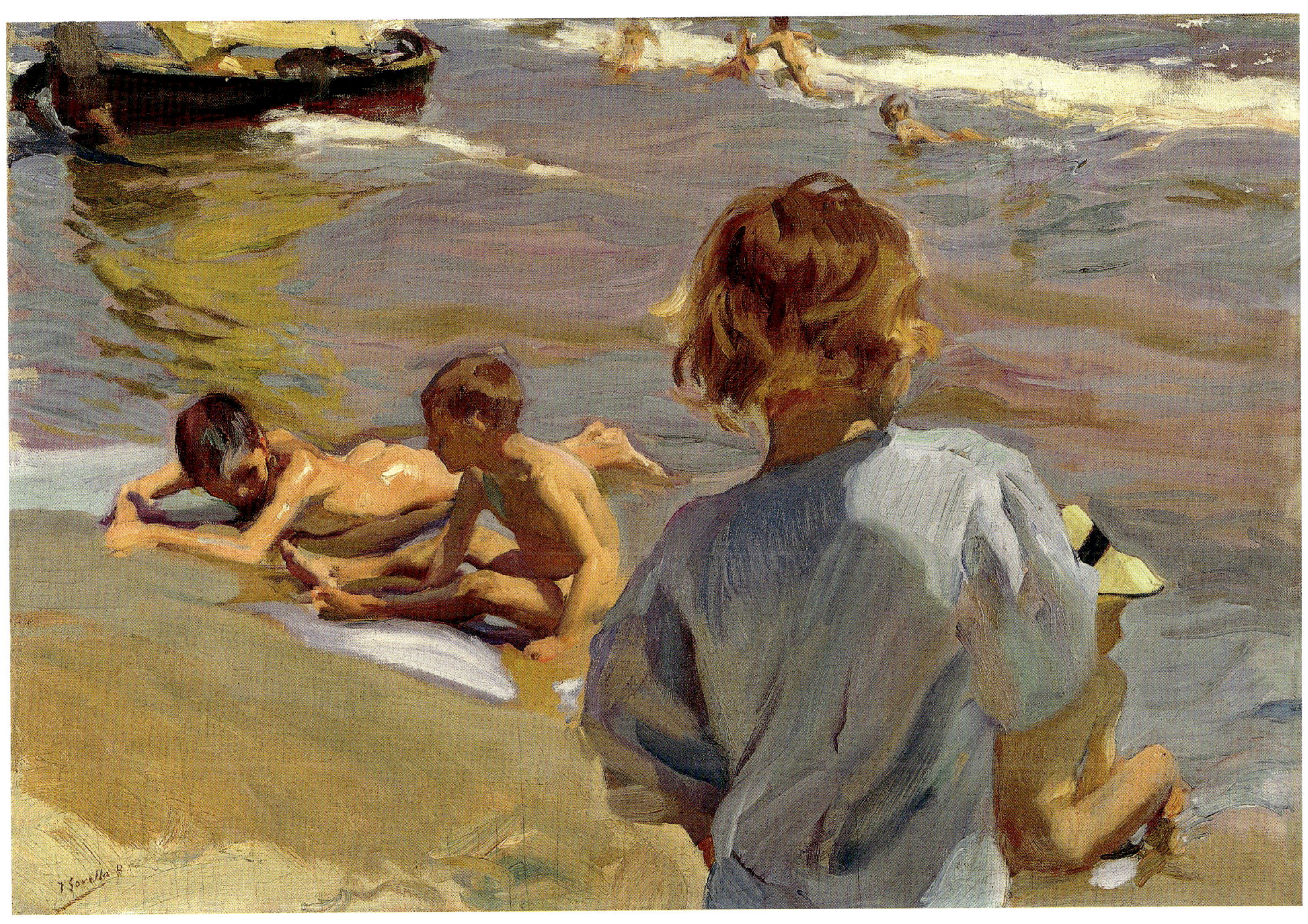

90 *Children on the Beach, Valencia*

1916
Oil on canvas, 27½ x 39½ in.
Signed: "J Sorolla B"
Private collection
(BPS 2895)

89 *After the Bath, the Pink Robe*

1916
Oil on canvas, 82 x 49¾ in.
Madrid, Museo Sorolla [inv. 1134]
(BPS 3305)

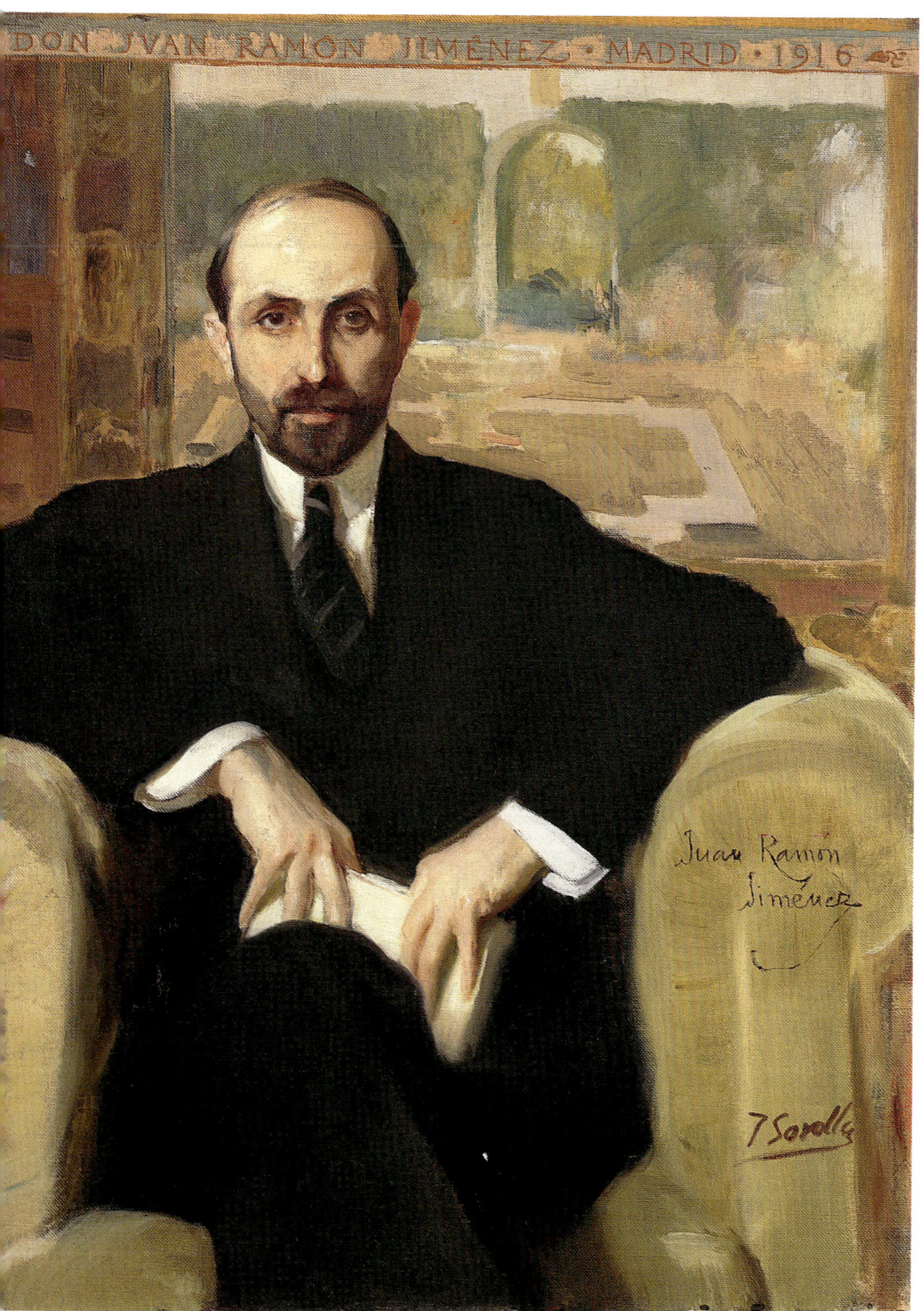

91 *The Poet Juan Ramón Jiménez*

1916
Oil on canvas, 46¾ x 32¾ in.
Signed: "J. Sorolla"
Signed by the sitter: "Juan Ramón y Jiménez"
Inscription: "DON JUAN RAMON JIMENEZ MADRID 1916"
New York, The Hispanic Society of America [inv. A 1932]
(BPS 2757)

92 *Joaquín Sorolla García, Seated*

1917
Oil on canvas, 49½ x 32 in.
Madrid, Museo Sorolla [inv. 1206]
(BPS 3369)

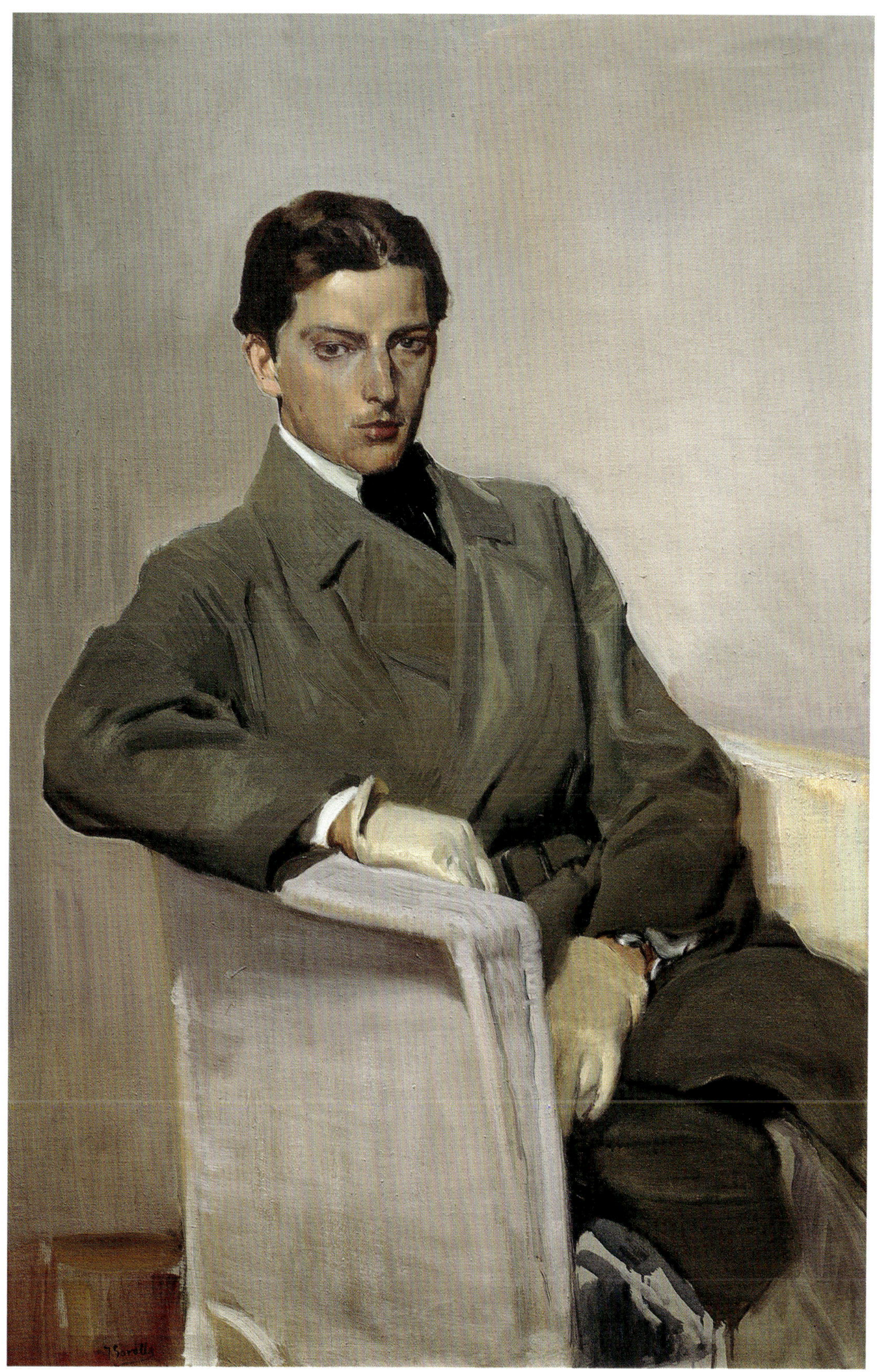

93 *Oleanders in the Courtyard of the Sorolla House*

c. 1918
Oil on canvas, 41¼ x 32¼ in.
Signed: "J. Sorolla B"
Private collection
(BPS 3032)

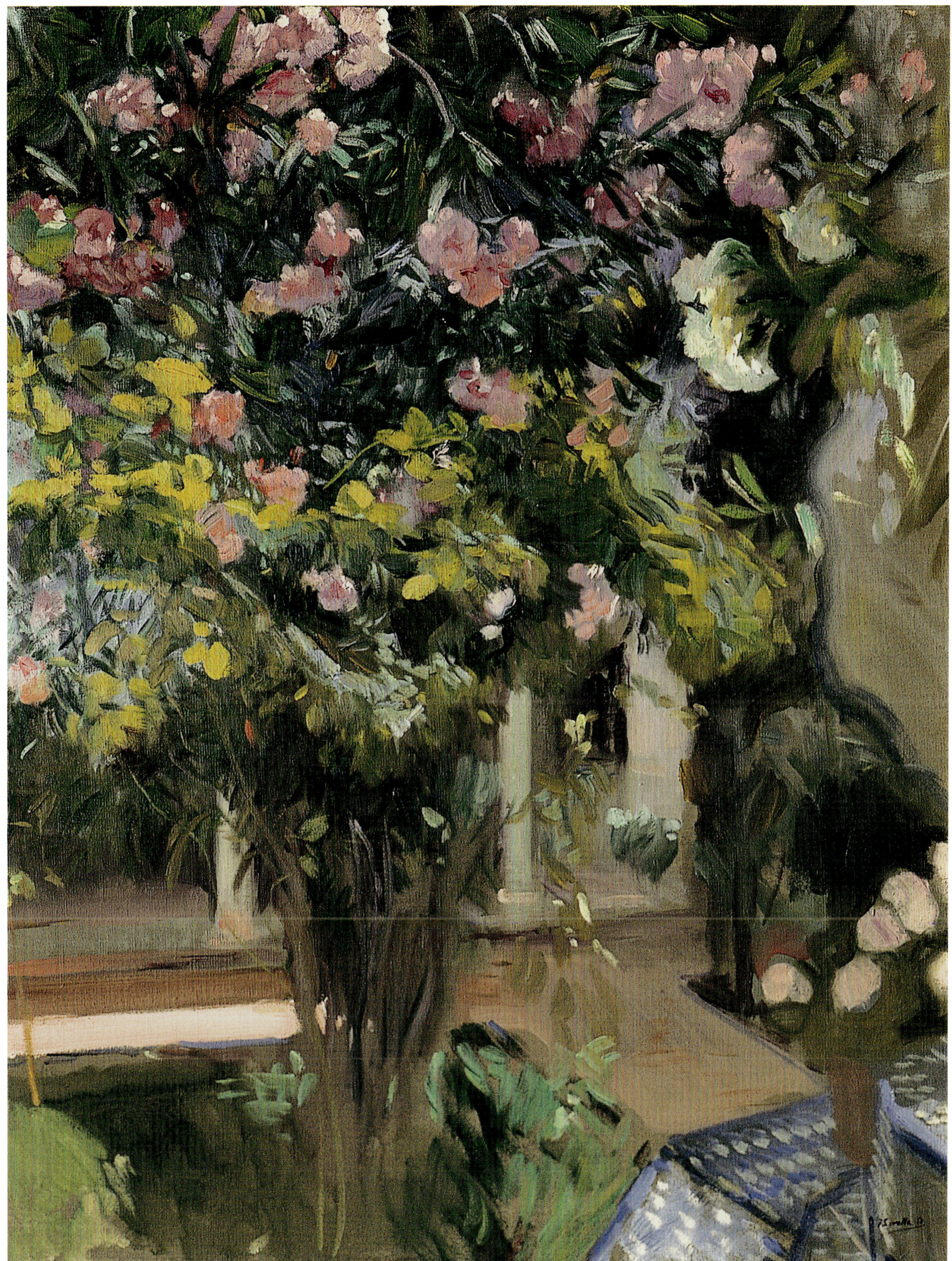

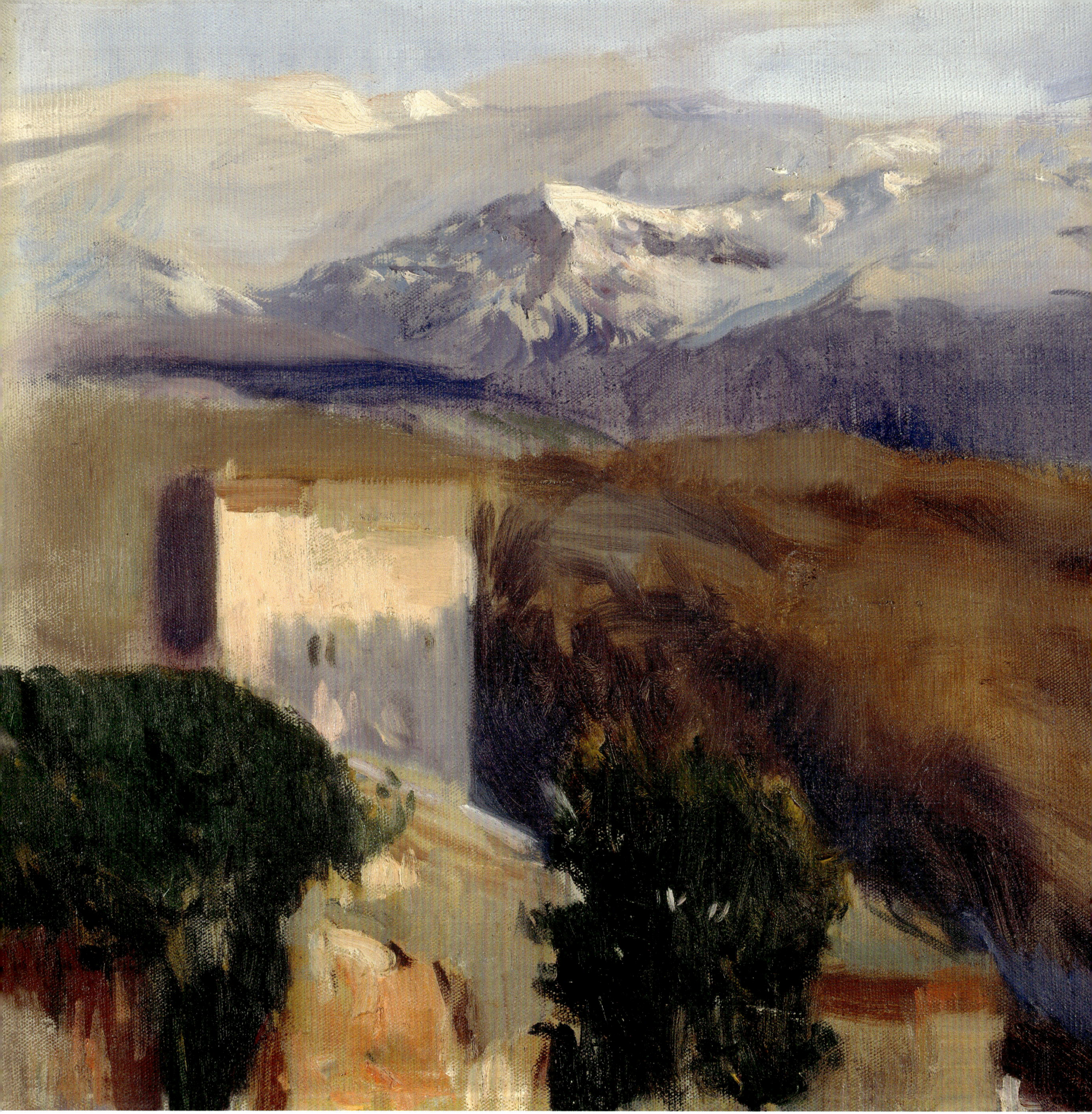

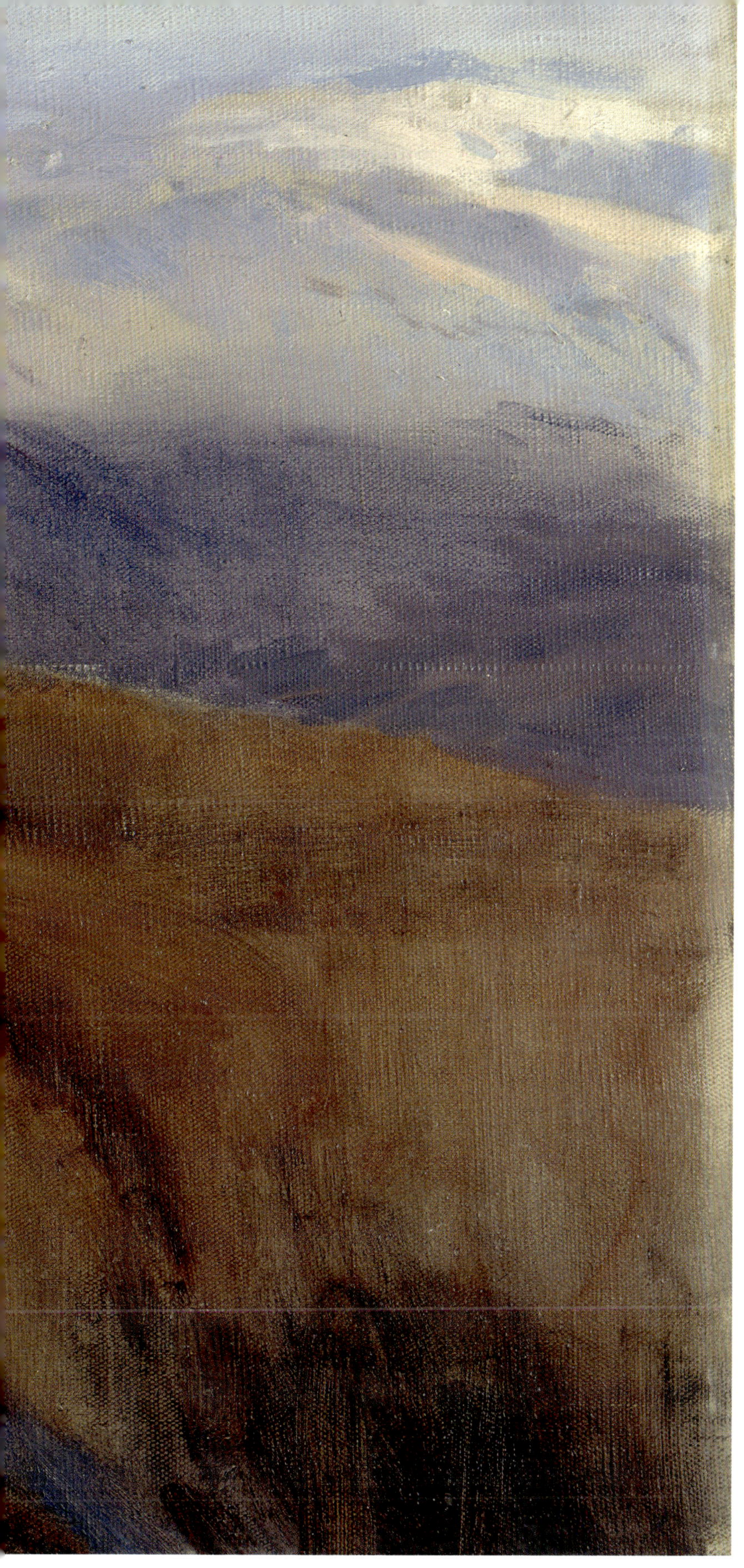

94 *Sierra Nevada, Granada*

1917
Oil on canvas, 25½ x 37½ in.
Private collection
(BPS 2167)

95 *The Breakwater at San Sebastián*

1918
Oil on canvas, 32 x 41¼ in.
Madrid, Museo Sorolla [inv. 1178]
(BPS 3348)

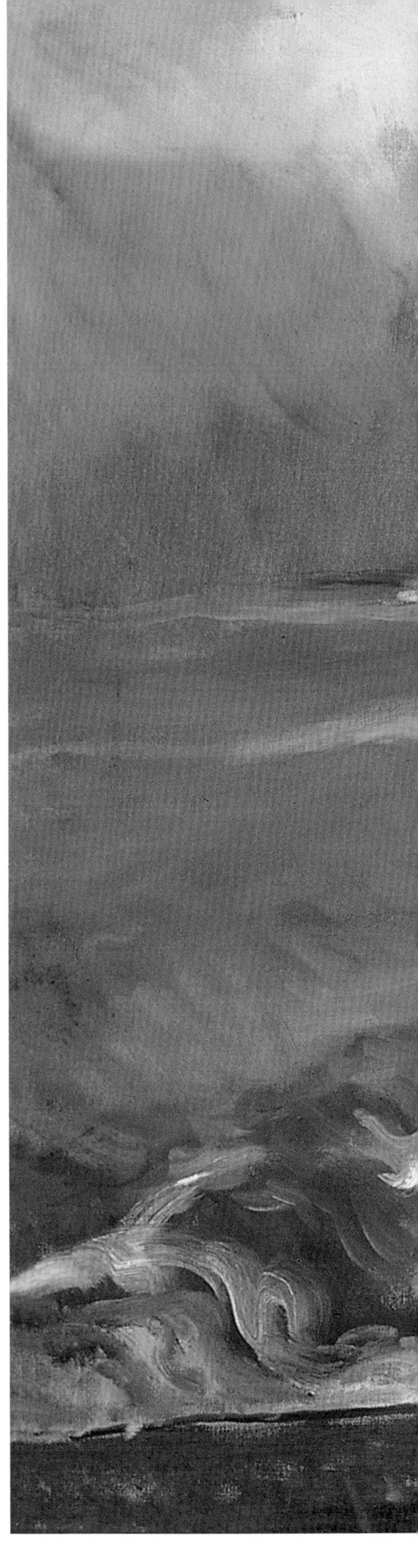

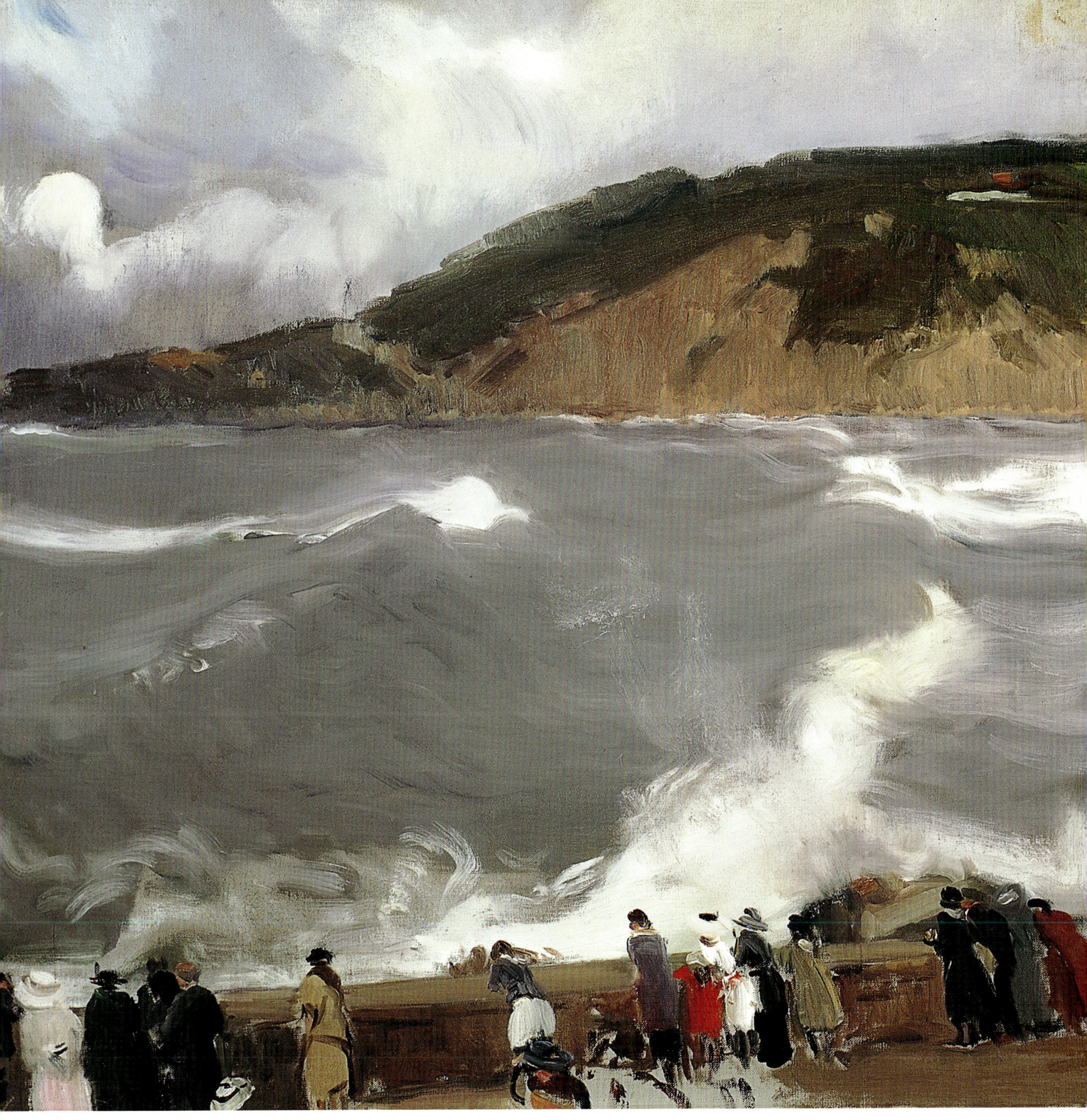

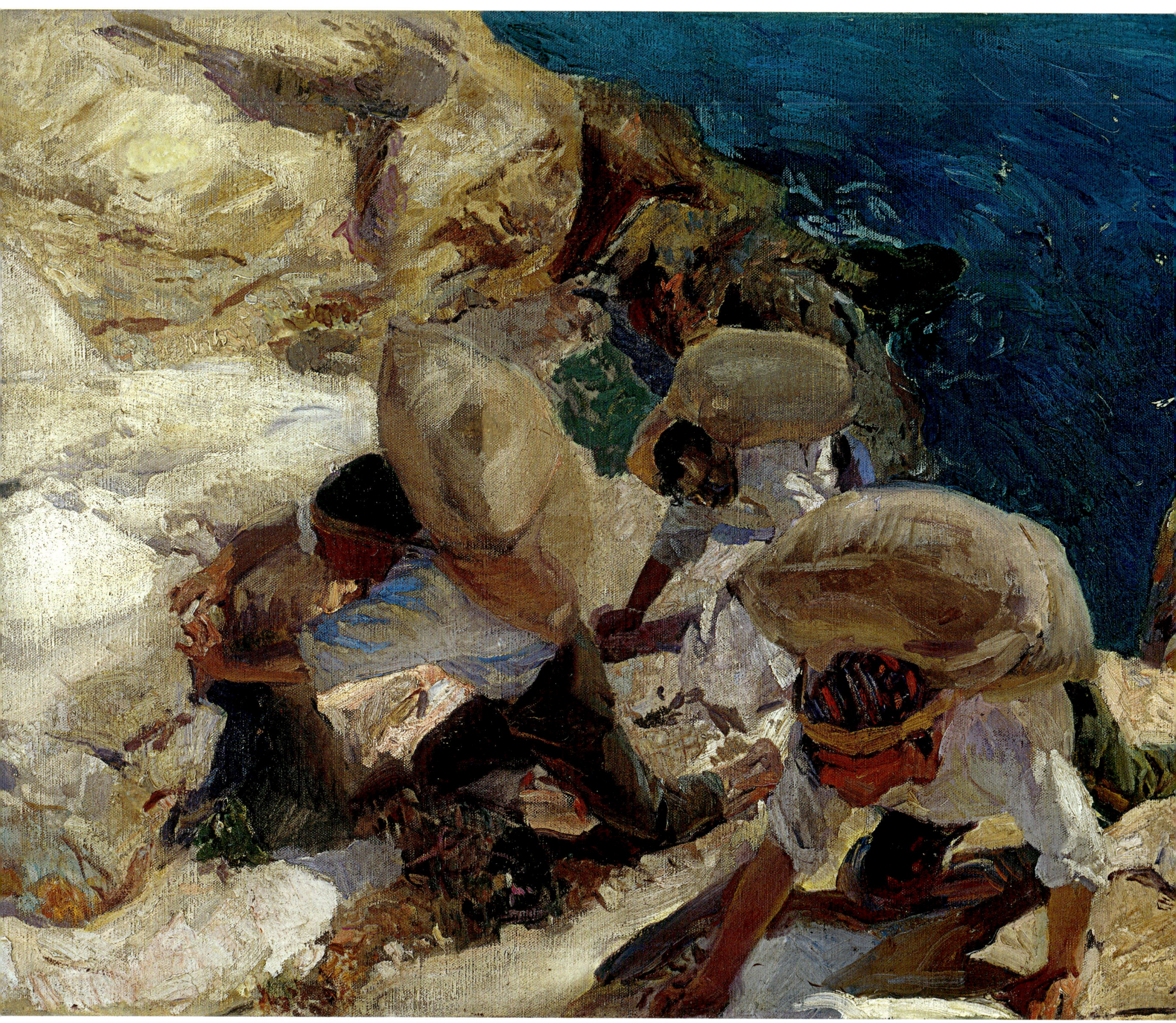

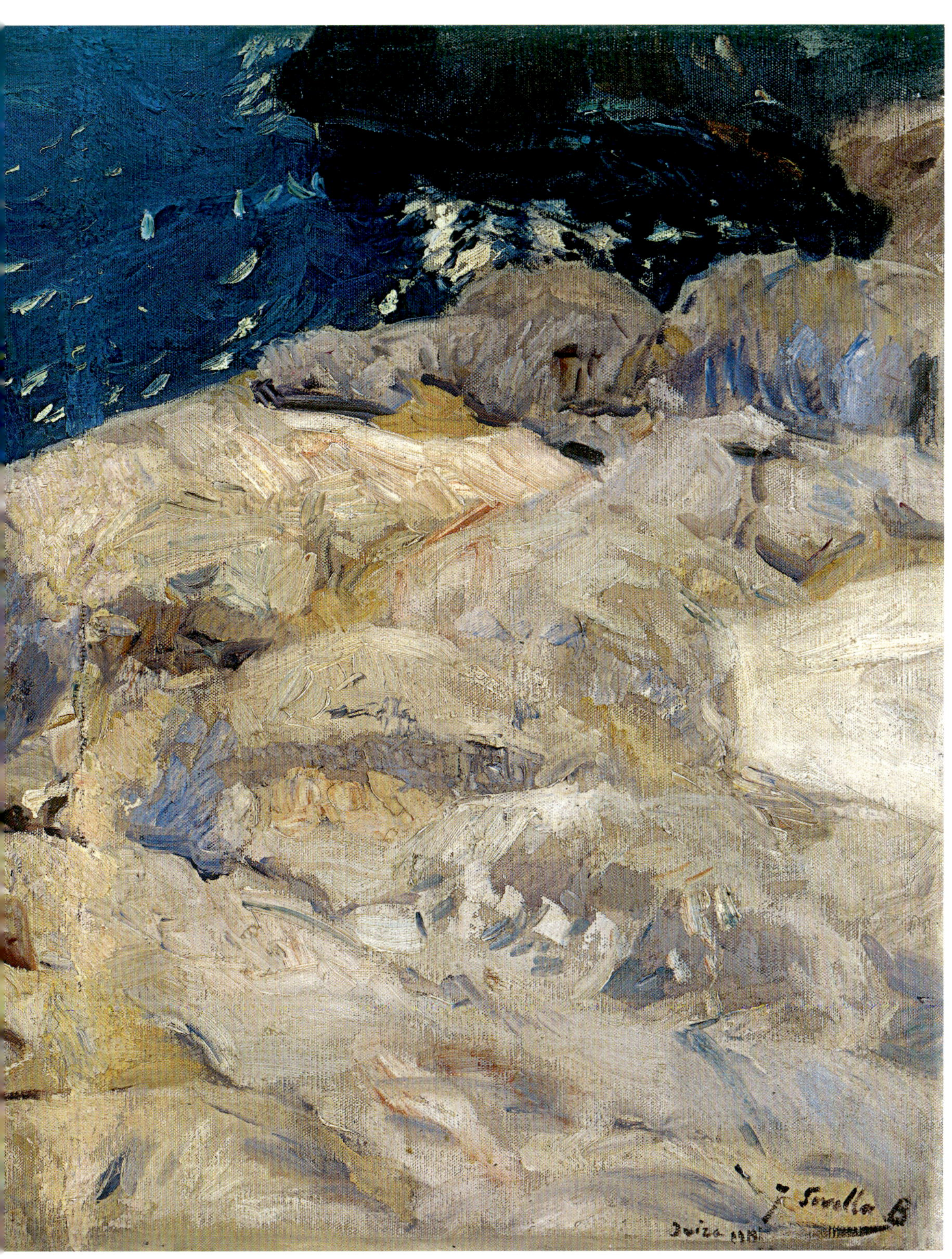

96 *The Smugglers*

1919
Oil on canvas, 33 x 65¾ in.
Signed: "J. Sorolla B / Iviza 1919"
Private collection
(BPS 2923)

97 *Ayamonte, the Tuna Catch*

1919
Oil on canvas, 11 ft. 5½ in. x 15 ft. 11 in.
New York, The Hispanic Society
of America [inv. A 1812]
(BPS 2818)

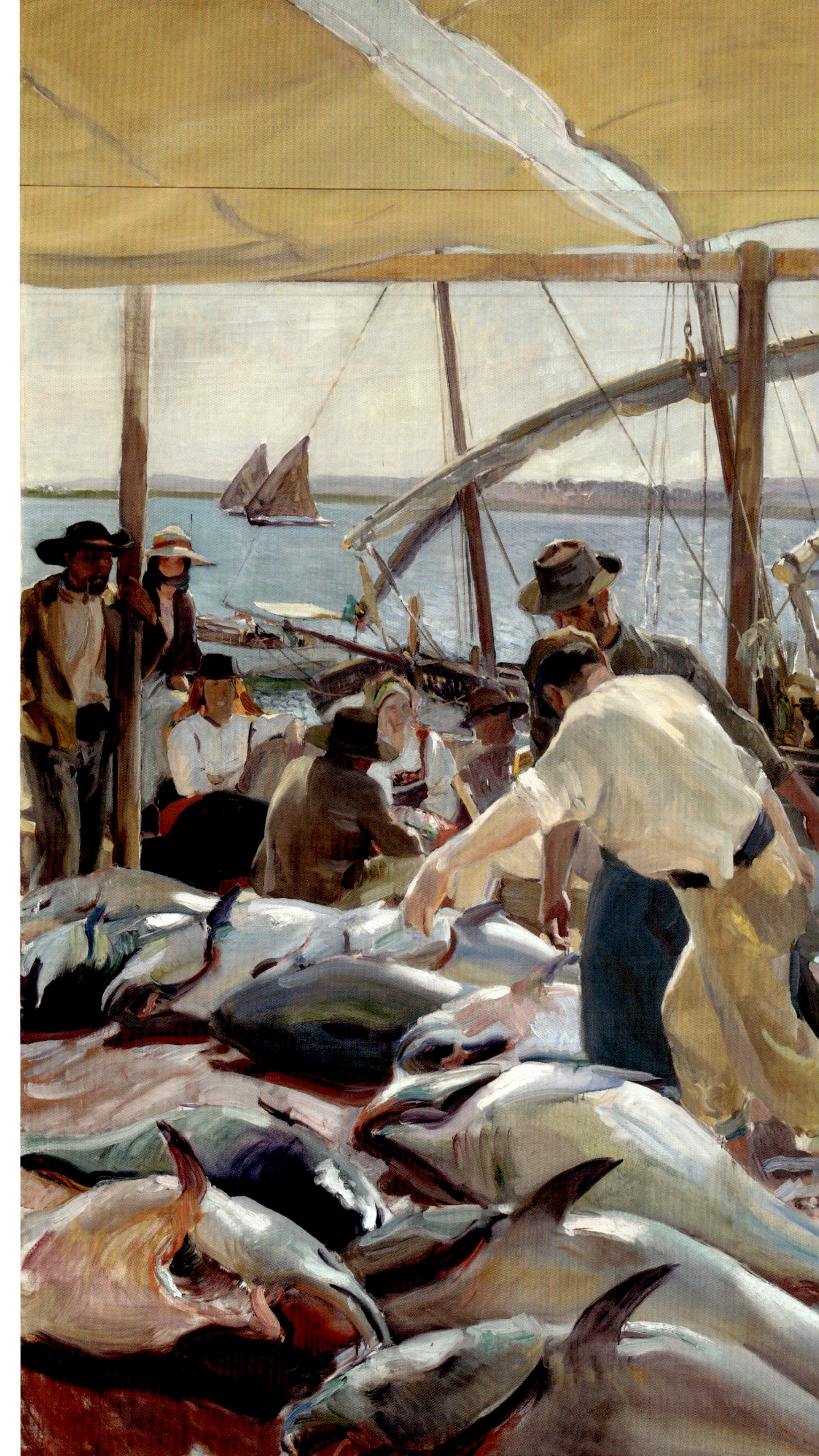

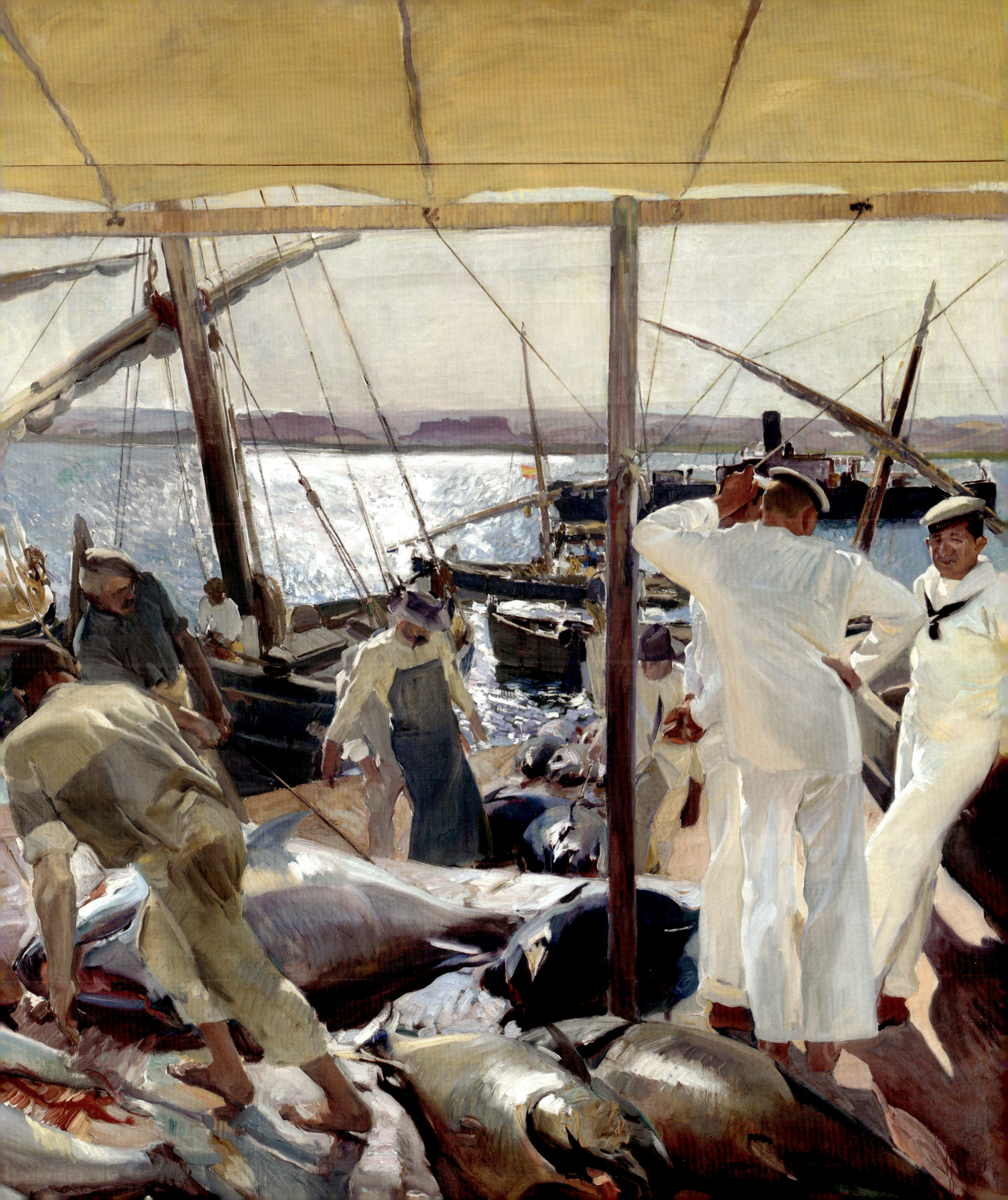

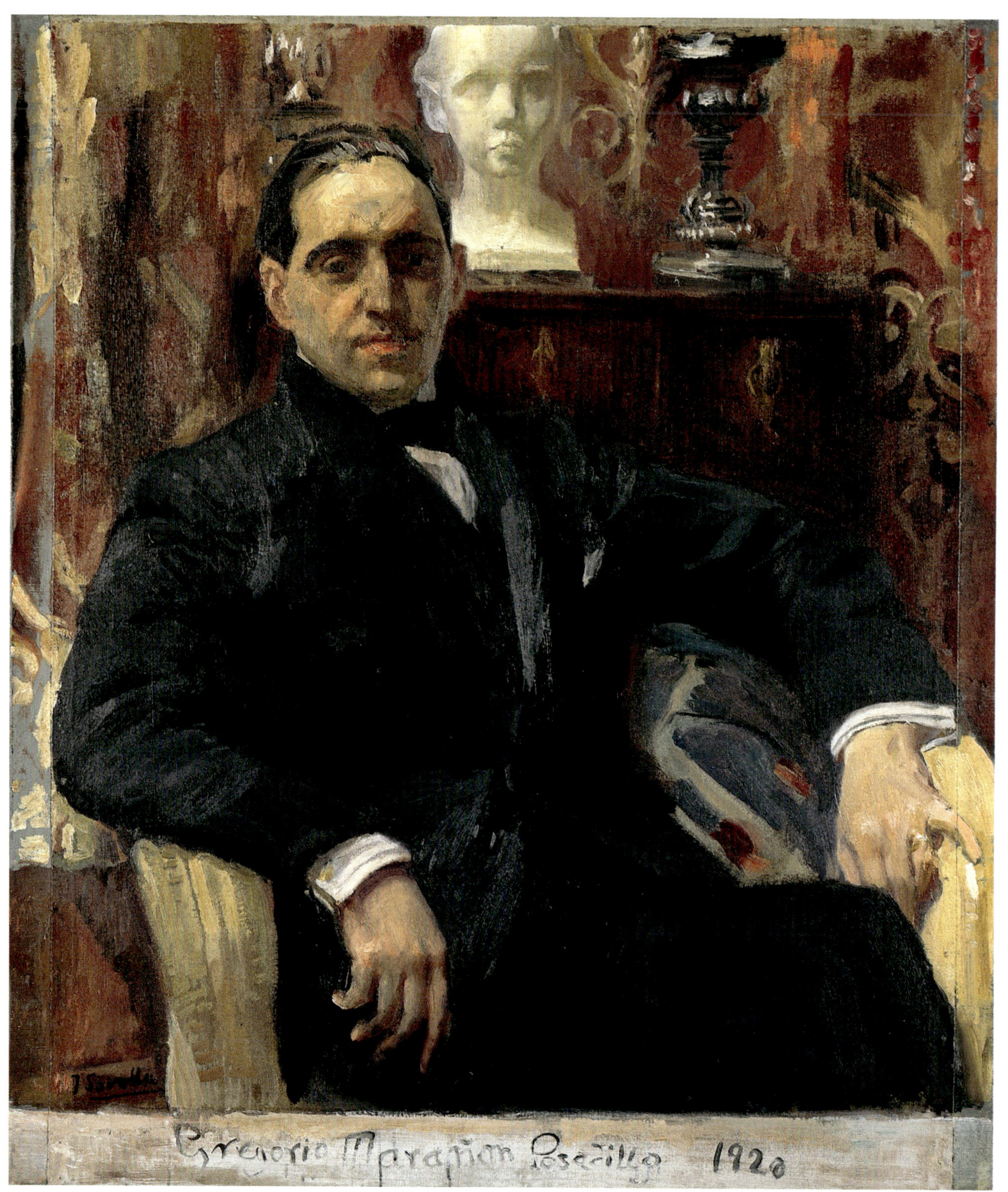
Gregorio Marañon Posadillo 1920

99 *White Roses from the Garden of My House*

1920
Oil on canvas, 37¾ x 25¼ in.
Signed: "J Sorolla Bastida"
Private collection
(BPS 3038)

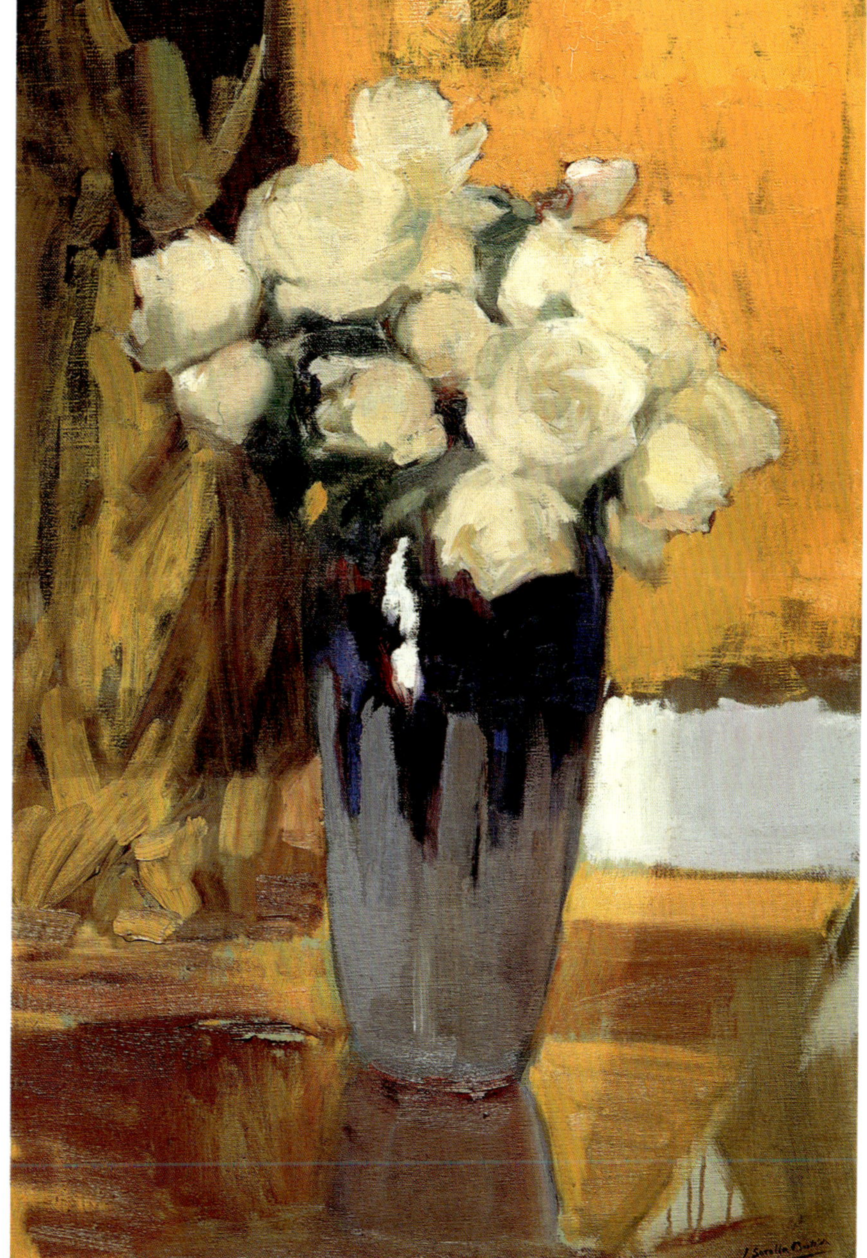

98 *Gregorio Marañón Posadillo*

1920
Oil on canvas, 41¾ x 35¼ in.
Signed: "J. Sorolla"
Signed by the sitter: "Gregorio Marañón Posadillo 1920"
New York, The Hispanic Society of America [inv. A 1935]
(BPS 2801)

100 *Wallflowers in the Garden of the Sorolla House*

c. 1920
Oil on canvas, 20½ x 28 in.
Signed: "J. Sorolla Bastida"
Private collection
(BPS 3033)

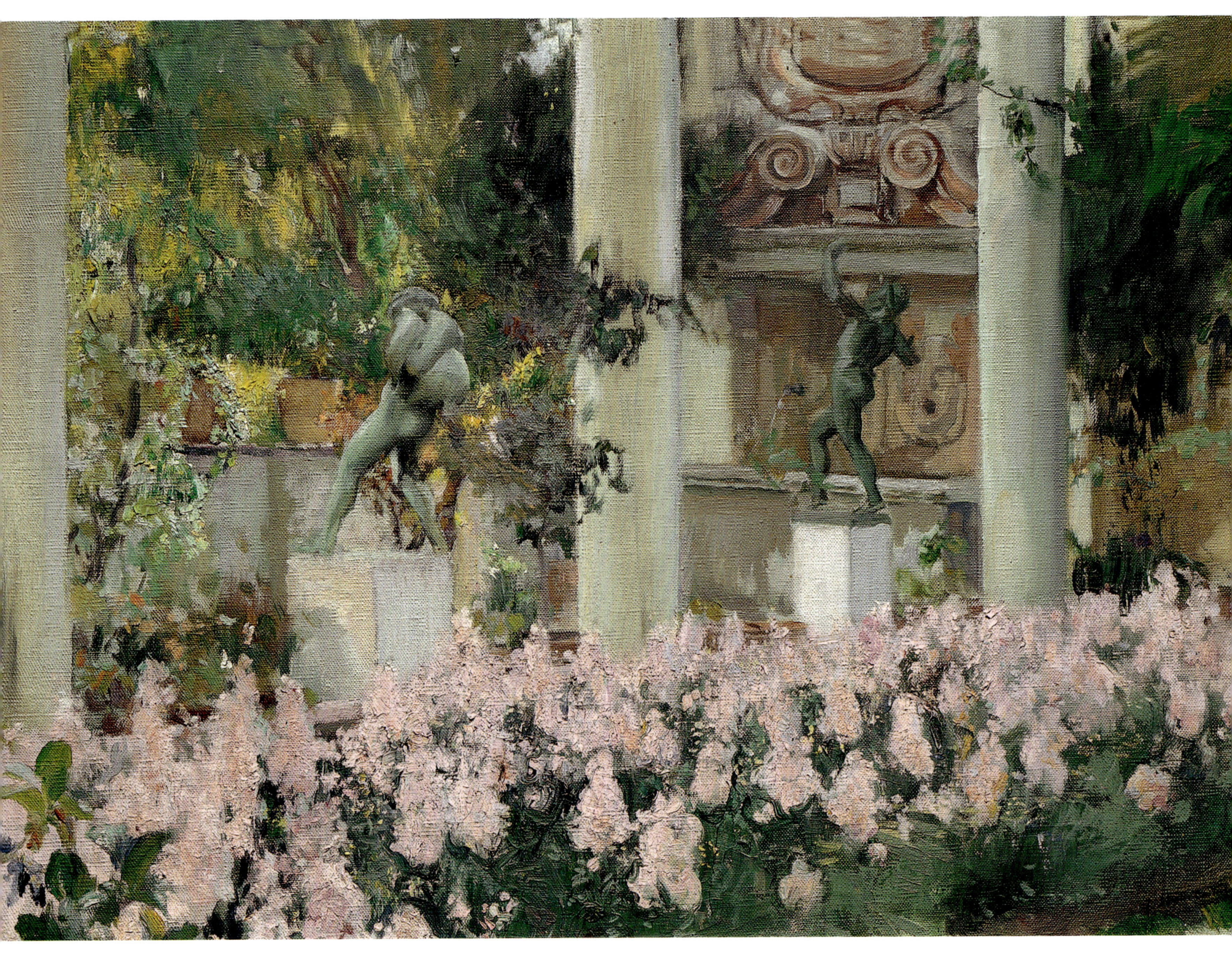

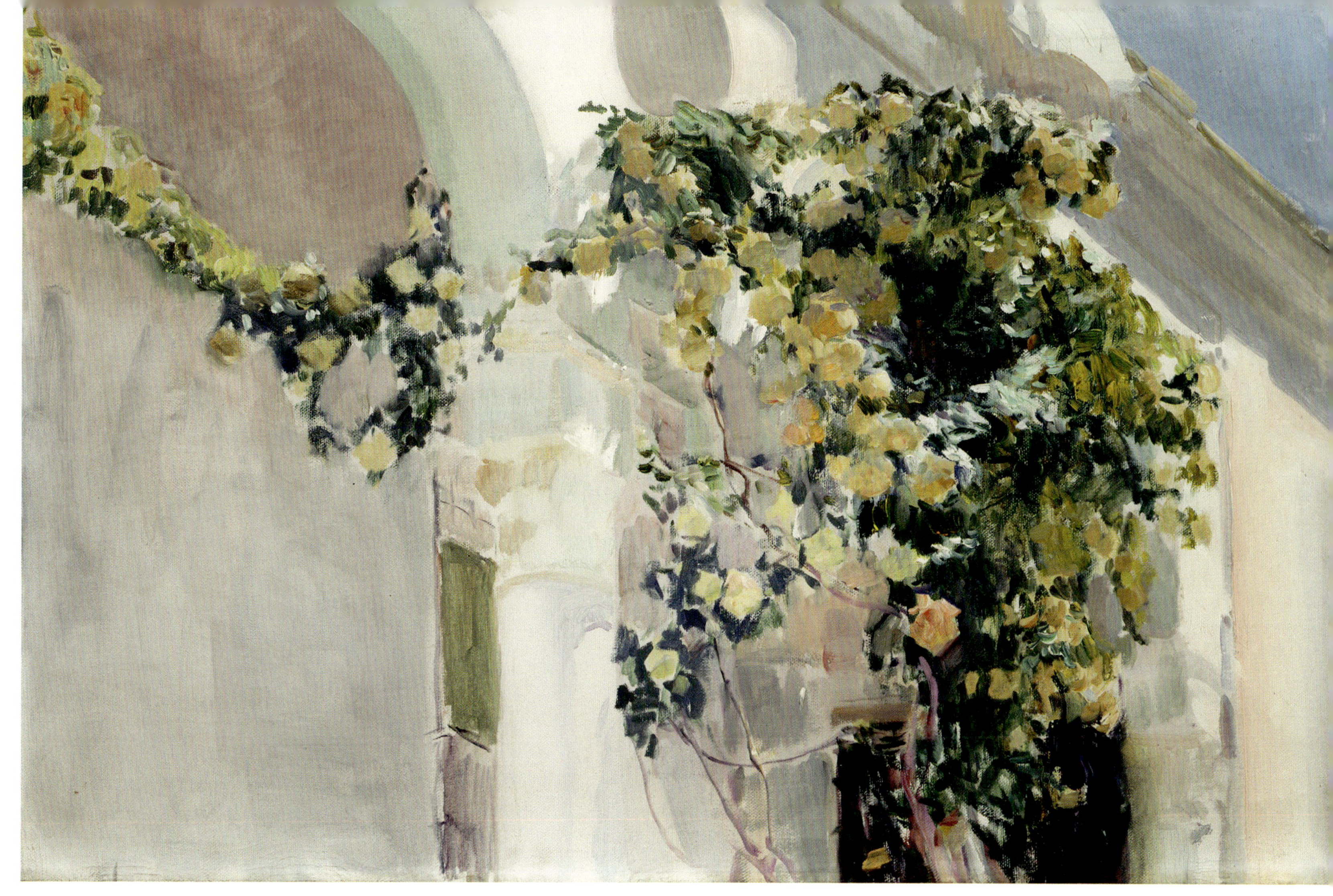

101 *The Yellow Rosebush of the Sorolla House*

c. 1920
Oil on canvas, 25¼ x 37½ in.
Madrid, Museo Sorolla [inv. 1240]
(BPS 3405)

102 *Garden of the Sorolla House*

1920
Oil on canvas, 41¼ x 35½ in.
Madrid, Museo Sorolla [inv. 1274]
(BPS 3439)

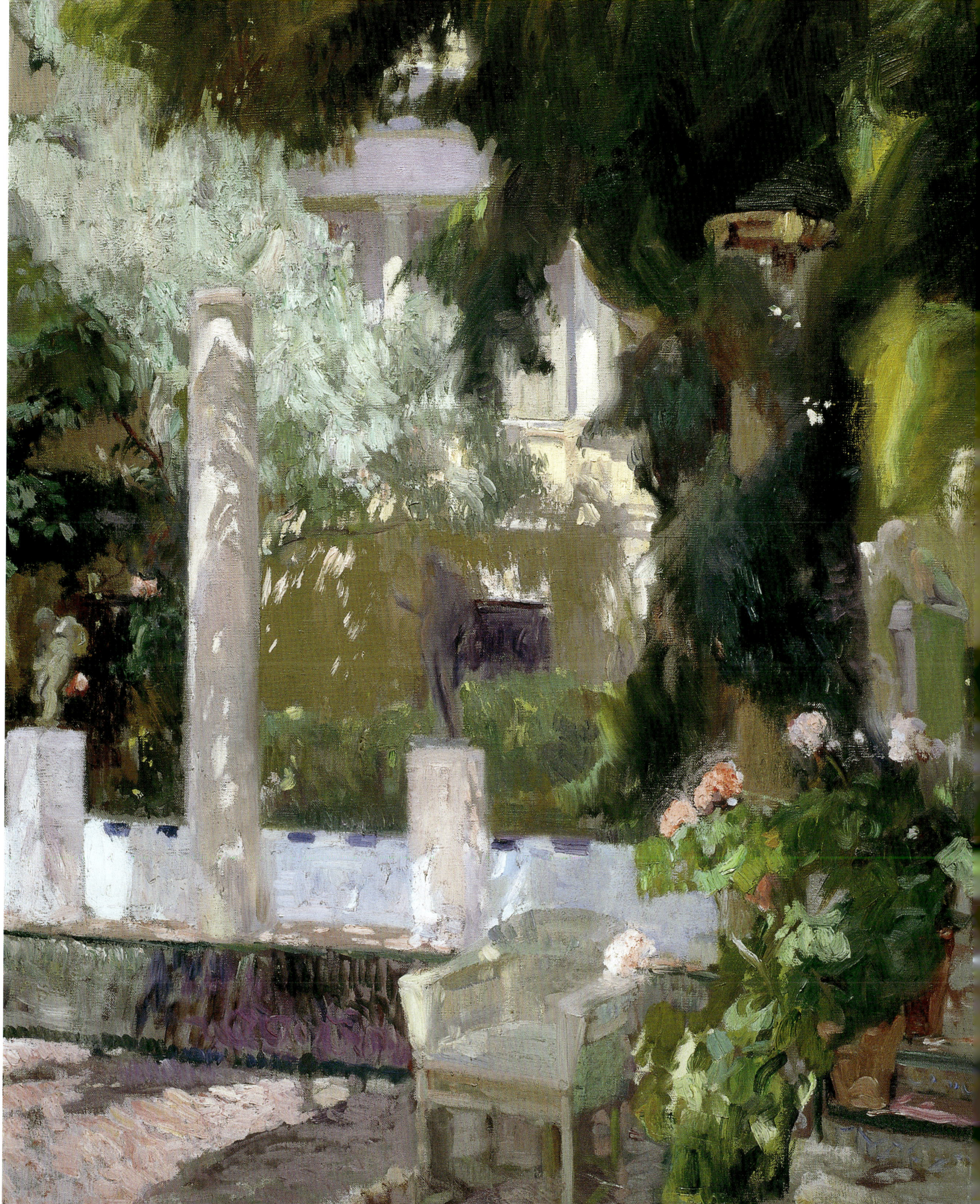

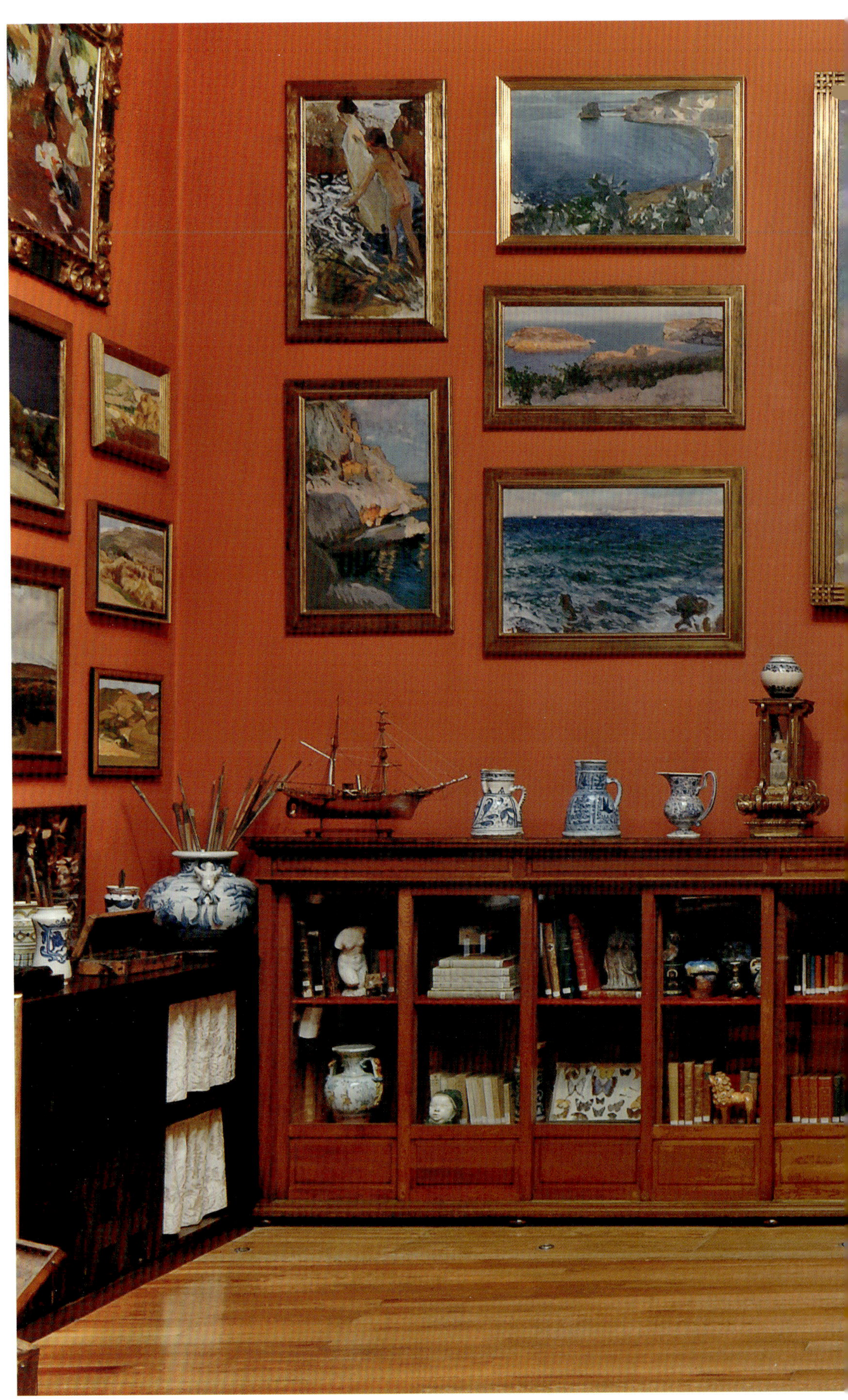

Interior of Room III at the Sorolla House (Museo Sorolla) in Madrid, formerly the artist's studio

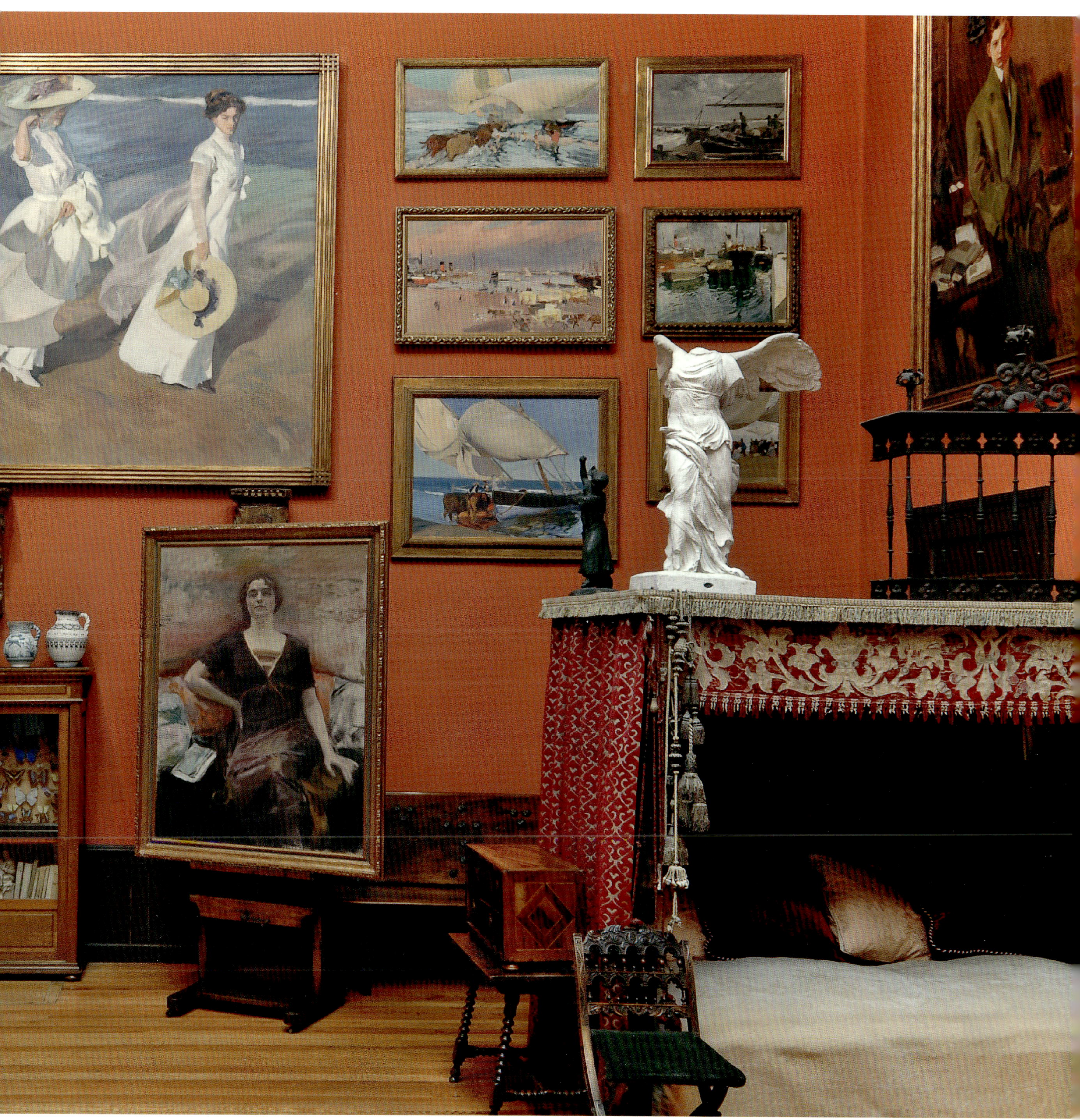

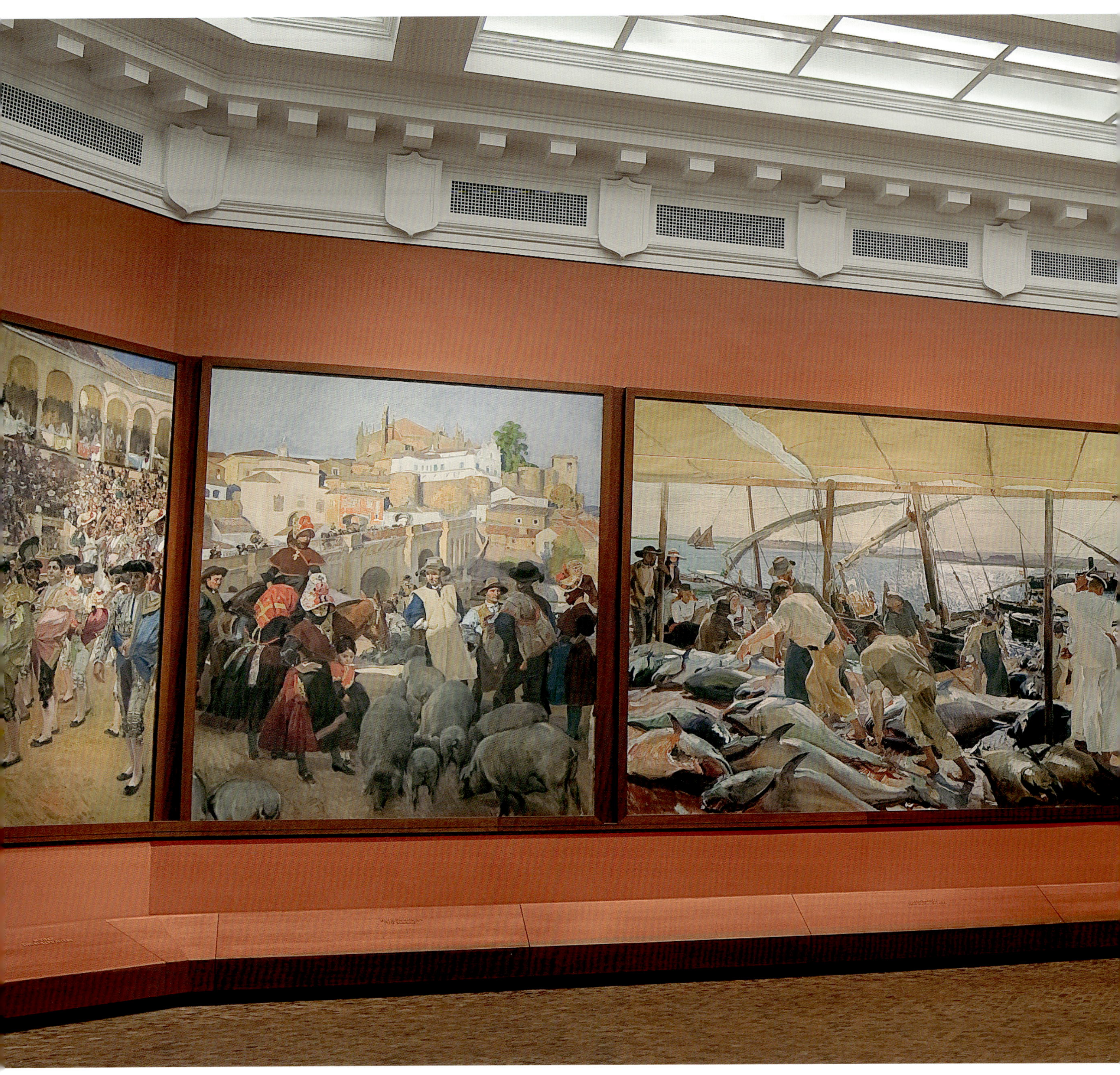

Vision of Spain as seen today at The Hispanic Society of America, New York

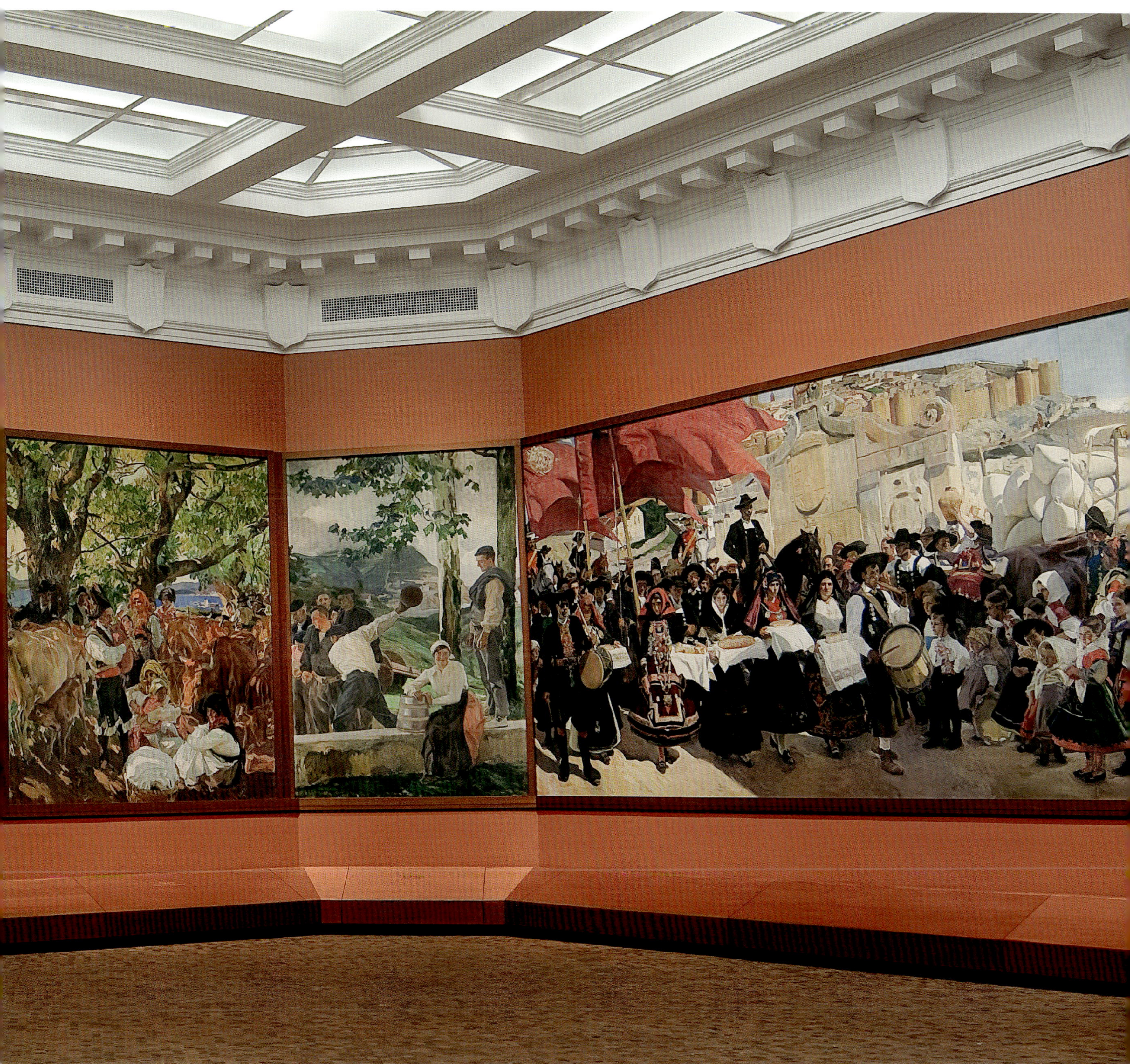

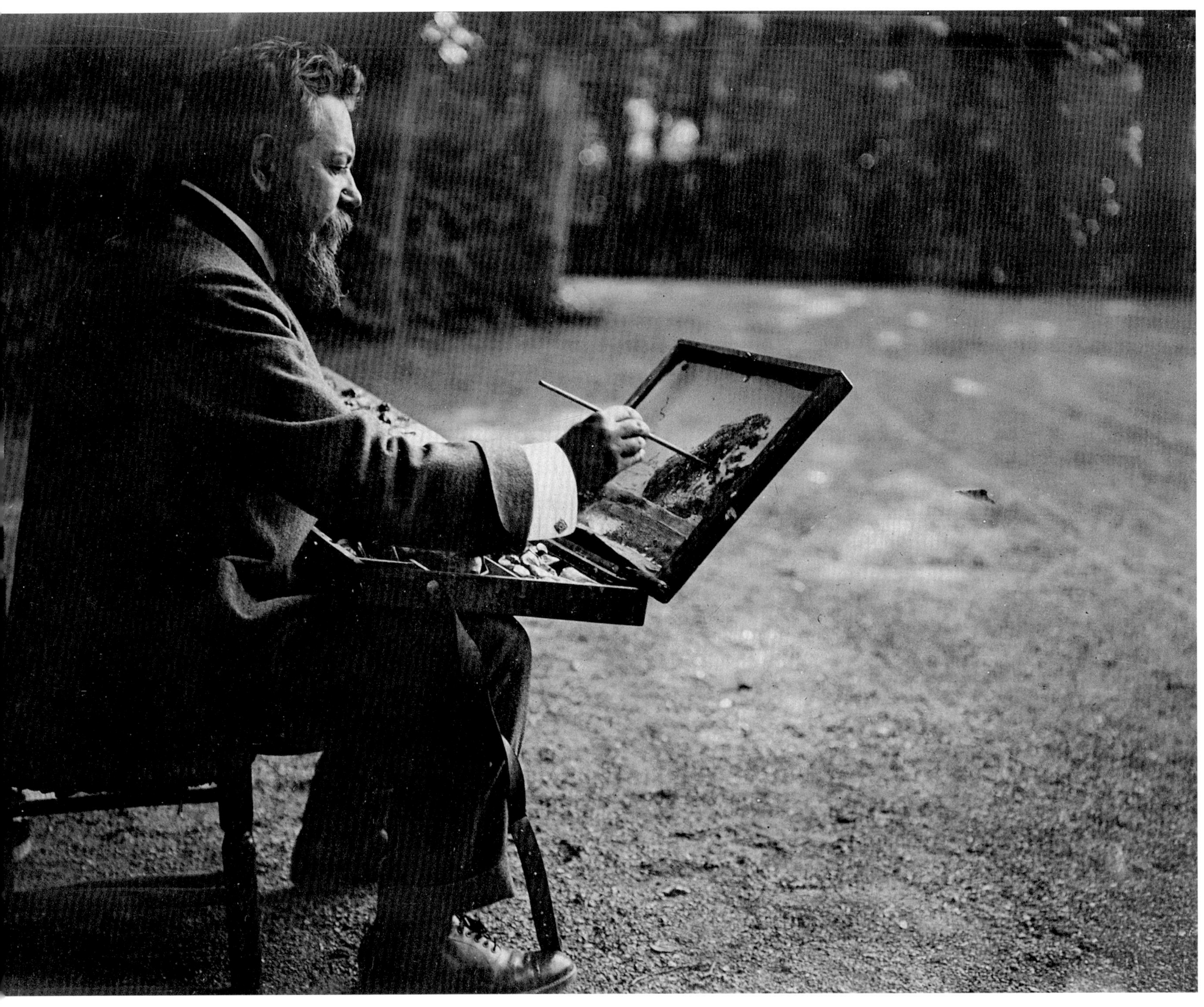

CHRONOLOGICAL BIOGRAPHY

Joaquín Sorolla painting
View of the Palace of La Granja, Segovia,
1907. Madrid, Museo Sorolla [80.078]

1863 Joaquín Sorolla y Bastida, Gascón, Prat, Bux, Tenas, Escorihuela i Sadurní was born at five o'clock in the morning on February 27 in the first-floor apartment of a house located on Calle Nueva 4 in Valencia.

He was the first son of Joaquín Sorolla Gascón, a native of Cantavieja (Teruel) and a resident of Valencia since 1853, and María Concepción Bastida Prat, a native of Valencia of Catalan origin. His parents—married on May 29, 1862 in Valencia—were modest textile merchants who owned a shop called Seis Dedos.

The day after his birth, Joaquín was baptized in the parish church of Santa Catalina in Valencia, the same place where his parents had been married the year before.

1864 On December 4, Joaquín's sister, Concha Sorolla, was born in Valencia.

1865 The local register of inhabitants reveals that aside from his parents and his sister, two shop assistants, one of them a nephew of the father, and two servants also lived in the house.

The Sorolla family moved to Calle Barcelona 6, where on August 25 Joaquín's father died at the age of thirty-two, only a few days after his mother had passed away at the age of twenty-seven, both from cholera.

The two orphaned children were adopted by an aunt on their mother's side, Isabel Bastida Prat, and her husband, José Piqueres Guillén, a master locksmith by profession. The couple had no children of their own. From that moment on, Joaquín, affectionately known as Chimet by his adoptive parents, lived in the ground-floor apartment of Calle Larga de la Sequiola 20, a street afterward called Don Juan de Austria.

1874 Shortly before turning twelve, Joaquín began attending the Escuela Normal Superior grammar school in Valencia, where his innate aptitude for drawing and painting soon became apparent.

1876 On the advice of the director of the school, Baltasar Perales, José Piqueres enrolled Joaquín in the evening drawing classes imparted by sculptor Cayetano Capuz at the School for Artisans in Valencia. This institution was located on the former Calle de las Barcas, today Calle del Pintor Sorolla. Joaquín's performance in geometric drawing and applied geometry in art won him many school prizes.

1878 Joaquín entered the School of Fine Arts in Valencia, run by the Royal Academy of San Carlos, whose director was the painter Salustiano Asenjo. Sorolla's professors included the engraver Ricardo Franch, the sculptor Felipe Farinós, and the landscape painter Gonzalo Salvá. Mariano Barbasán, Salvador Abril, Javier Juste, Constantino Gómez, and Cecilio Pla were some of his fellow students. Through Juan Antonio García del Castillo, one of the students in his drawing from the model class, Sorolla made the acquaintance of Juan Antonio's father, the Valencian photographer Antonio García Peris, who purchased a small painting of fruits—*Still Life*—to help Joaquín out, becoming Sorolla's patron during his initial years as a painter.

Upon finishing his studies at the School for Artisans, on September 28 Sorolla obtained the second prize awarded by the Valencian Board of Artisans Schools, which consisted of a diploma and a box of paints.

1879 Sorolla won the third-class medal at the Regional Exhibition in Valencia with *School Courtyard*.

Luis Santonja Crespo, Marquis of Villagracia and Sorolla's patron, who the previous year had helped Joaquín enter the School of Fine Arts, contributed to the so-called "redemption in cash" that exempted Sorolla from military service.

Sorolla used the upper floor of Antonio García's house on Plaza de San Francisco 10 as his first studio. There he also began to work as an illustrator, coloring photographs for García's studio.

1880 Sorolla received the silver medal at the exhibition organized by the recreational club Sociedad Recreativa "El Iris" of Valencia for the oil painting *A Moor Waiting to Take His Revenge*.

1881 After finishing his studies at the School of Fine Arts in Valencia, Sorolla traveled to Madrid and visited the Museo del Prado, where he was fired with enthusiasm for the work of Diego Velázquez.

At the National Fine Arts Exhibition in Madrid, which opened on May 18, he presented three oil paintings under the common title of *Seascape*, one of which was *Seascape, Boats in the Port*.

He moved to a studio in Calle San Martín 9 in Valencia.

1882 Sorolla traveled to Madrid a second time and copied works by Velázquez in the Prado. It is highly likely that this year he also visited Rome, as two portraits of Italian personalities signed by Sorolla exist in that city.

1883 Sorolla received the gold medal at the Regional Exhibition in Valencia, held between July and October, for his painting *Nun at Prayer*.

He moved to a studio on Calle de la Corona in Valencia.

1884 In May, Sorolla traveled for the third time to Madrid to compete in the National Fine Arts Exhibition that opened on May 24, to which he submitted his first large-format painting executed out of doors in the arena of the Valencia bullring and with a history subject, *The Second of May 1808*. The work, which earned him a second-class medal, was purchased by the Spanish State for the office of the cabinet for 3,000 pesetas.

Sorolla again copied works by Velázquez in the Prado, such as *Queen Marianne of Austria (Copy of Velázquez)*.

In June, he applied for a travel grant from Valencia's Provincial Council to continue his studies in Rome, and he was admitted to the examination after being previously tested by the jury in the subject of theory and history of the fine arts, which he had not yet finished. The three examinations were held in the autumn, and Sorolla received the grant by unanimous vote with his *The Palleter Declaring War on Napoleon*. The grant consisted of an annual allowance of 3,000 pesetas during three years.

At this time, he was already engaged to Clotilde García del Castillo, the third of Antonio García Peris and Clotilde del Castillo Jareño's five children. Clotilde had been born on October 22, 1864. It is possible that this relationship had its beginnings three or four years earlier, when both were very young.

1885 On January 3, Sorolla arrives in Rome to take up his grant, presenting himself to the director of the Spanish Academy in Rome on the following day. His professors were Francisco Pradilla, José Villegas, and Emilio Sala.

In Rome he met Pedro Gil Moreno de Mora, who became one of his closest friends. Invited and accompanied by him, Sorolla traveled to Paris in April, where he remained until the early autumn, painting in museums and visiting exhibitions, among them the Salon organized by the Society of French Artists. He expressed particular interest in the exhibitions of the naturalist painters Jules Bastien-Lepage and Adolf von Menzel and was impressed by their preference for *plein air* painting and rural scenes.

In October he returned to Rome, where he spent the last two months of the year finishing the first shipment of canvases he had to prepare as a grantee of Valencia's Provincial Council.

1886 Sorolla sent six drawings and two oil paintings to Valencia, *Female Nude* and *The Crucified*, which Antonio García submitted to the Provincial Council in compliance with the grant's regulations.

He then traveled to the Italian cities of Pisa, Florence, Venice, and Naples, where he painted oils and watercolors, many of which were acquired by local dealers.

He made at least ten works featuring female peasants from Assisi, the drawing *Italian Girl* being a study for one of them.

1887 After recovering from a bout of malaria, Sorolla returned to Spain in May to take part in the National Fine Arts Exhibition held in Madrid, to which he submitted the large-format canvas *The Burial of Christ* and the drawing *Nude Study*. The former only received an honorary mention, which the artist apparently refused. Disillusioned in spite

Sorolla and his wife, 1888. Photograph by Antonio García Peris

Clotilde García del Castillo, *c.* 1889–90. Photograph by Antonio García Peris

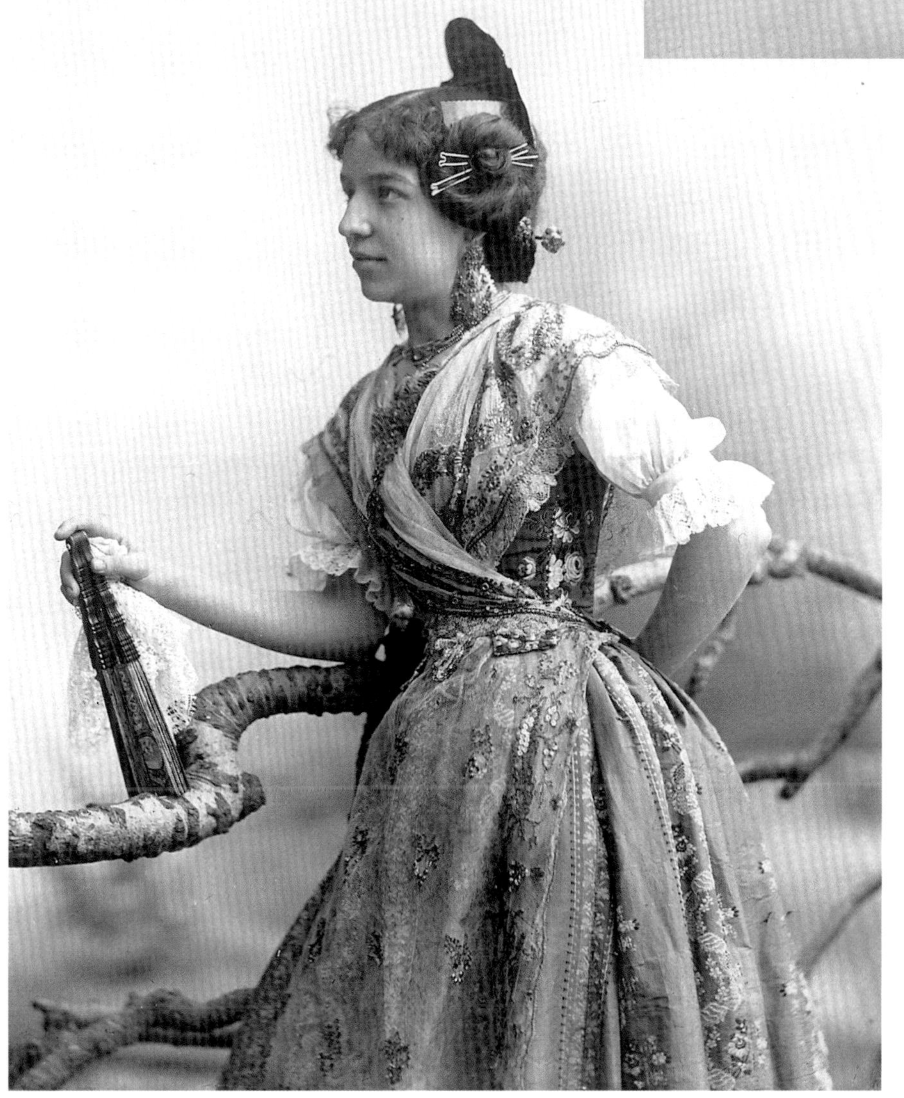

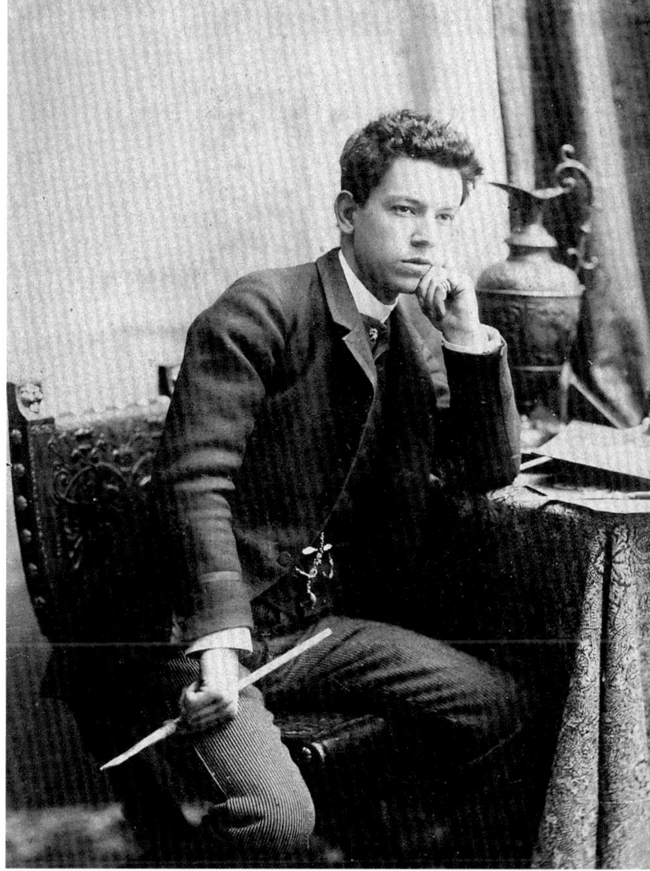

Joaquín Sorolla, *c.* 1881

of his teacher Francisco Pradilla's congratulations, he returned to Italy. After a brief stay in Rome, he moved to the city of Assisi, where his friend José Benlliure y Gil was living with his family, in order to escape from an epidemic as well as to find peace and quiet.

In Assisi, he finished the painting *Father Jofré Protecting a Madman*, which he dispatched to the Provincial Council of Valencia on December 10 in compliance with his grant. At the same time, he sent *Resting Bacchante* as a gift to his patron, Antonio García, and the watercolor *Bacchanalian Dance* to his friend and future brother-in-law, Juan Antonio García del Castillo, as a wedding gift.

1888 After Sorolla's application for a one-year extension of his grant in Rome was accepted on May 11, the artist returned to Valencia and married Clotilde García del Castillo on September 8. The couple then set off on their journey to Rome. After a brief stay in the Italian capital, they decided to settle in Assisi, where Sorolla began to paint genre scenes to cover their economic needs.

His principal client at the time was the Valencian dealer and painter Francisco Jover, who lived in Rome and purchased eight works, principally watercolors, from him for a total of 1,450 pesetas.

Among other works, this year he painted *Praying Saint*.

1889 After his grant ran out in December 1888, Sorolla dedicated himself completely to the execution of works to sell. In 1889, the dealer Francisco Jover bought five pictures from him, paying a total of 1,750 pesetas for them.

The couple returned permanently to Spain via France, where they stayed at the home of their friends Pedro and María Gil and visited the World Fair in Paris.

Back in Spain, they stayed for a short time in San Sebastián, where Sorolla made a series of sketches of the port.

In June, they established themselves temporarily in Valencia at the house of Clotilde's parents and in El Campet, the Garcías' home in the agricultural region near Valencia called La Huerta. There Sorolla painted *Valencian Dance in the Orange Grove*.

After deliberating, the couple decided to establish their permanent residence in Madrid, moving to the capital in the winter.

Sorolla took part in the Tenth Exhibition of Watercolors and Drawings organized in Madrid, an event that opened on May 11 in the gallery of the Society of Watercolor Artists.

1890 In Madrid, Joaquín and Clotilde rented a house and studio on Plaza del Progreso, where their daughter María Clotilde was born on April 13.

The painter Francisco Jover died in February, and in accordance with his express instructions, Sorolla was chosen to complete his *The Queen Regent María Cristina Taking Her Constitutional Vows*, a work commissioned from Jover by the Senate.

Sorolla participated in the National Fine Arts Exhibition that opened in Madrid on May 5, where he received a second-class medal for *Paris Boulevard*, an oil canvas he painted in Madrid based on sketches he had made in Paris in 1885 and 1889. He also exhibited *Valencian Customs*.

Afterward, he took part in the Exhibition of Pastels and Watercolors organized by the Círculo de Bellas Artes club in Madrid with the works *The First Child*, *Seller of Religious Images*, *Moorish Serenade*, *The Caulker*, *Premature Autumn*, the gouache *Fuenterrabía*, and two pastel studies.

The couple spent Christmas in Valencia.

1891 On January 19, Sorolla returned to Madrid alone, as his daughter María had fallen ill in Valencia.

There he finished painting *Beach Rascal* and dispatched it to the International Art Exhibition in Berlin, for which he was a member of the jury for the selection of works representing Spain.

At the end of February he traveled to Valencia to collect his wife and daughter, returning immediately to Madrid.

The Biennial Exhibition of the Círculo de Bellas Artes club in Madrid, inaugurated on May 11, featured *He's Going to Eat You Alive!*, *The Jealous Boyfriend*, *The Reserve*, *Doctor Rafael Cervera*, and *Female Bust* by Sorolla.

After a short trip to Paris in June, Sorolla spent August and September with his family in Valencia and in Buñol (Valencia), whose climate favored the delicate health of his daughter María. That summer, he painted *Peeling Potatoes*.

After the summer he returned to Madrid, where he worked in his studio for the rest of the year.

1892 At the International Art Exhibition in Munich, Sorolla won the second-class gold medal for his oil painting titled *Rogation in Burgos in the 16th Century*.

Sorolla spent the summer with his family on the beaches of Valencia, traveling from October 7 to 12 to Buñol on his own, since his wife was eight months pregnant and not fit enough to accompany him.

In October, at the International Fine Arts Exhibition in Madrid, he won another award: a first-class medal for *Another Marguerite!*, *After the Bath*, *Ex Voto*, *The Night Watchman*, *The Flower-Sellers*, *Beach Rascal*, *The Happy Day*, and the portraits of Agustín Otermín, Eduardo García, and Doctor Rafael Cervera were also displayed at this event.

He then returned to Madrid to take part in the exhibition of the Círculo de Bellas Artes club, to which he submitted two oil paintings, both titled *Peasant Woman*.

In December, he took part in the exhibition organized at the Salón Amaré in Madrid, where he displayed his *Scene of the Port at Valencia*, *Female Nude*, *After the Bath*, *The Mayor*, *Beach Rascal*, *Sea Study, Jávea*, *Sea Study*, *The Calf*, *Asturian Landscape*, and three other works.

At the Christmas contest conducted by the magazine *Blanco y Negro*, Sorolla was chosen the most admired painter by the public with 14,201 votes, followed by Francisco Pradilla with 6,844 votes.

Sorolla traveled with his family to Valencia for the Christmas holidays and painted ten studies of orange trees in the fertile farming area of Alcira. On this occasion, their stay was prolonged until the beginning of February 1903.

Family scene at El Cabañal, Valencia, *c.* 1904. Photograph by Antonio García Peris. Madrid, Museo Sorolla [80.250]

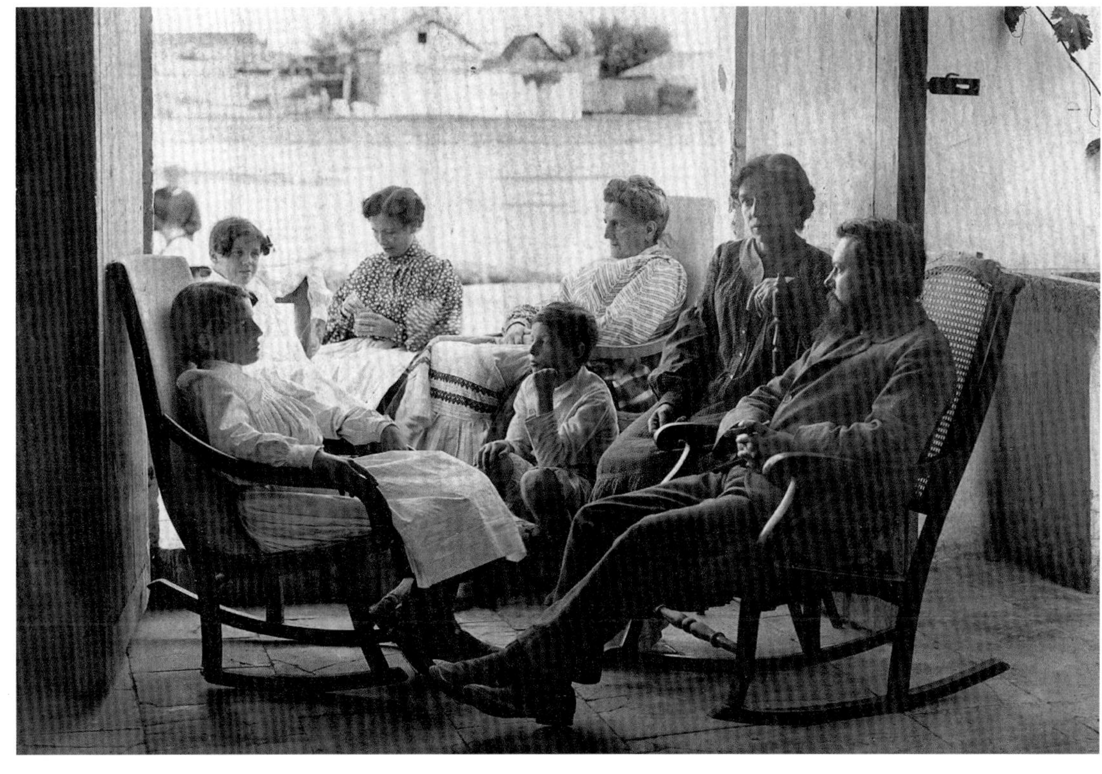

1903 In the spring, Sorolla journeyed with his family to León, where he painted a series of market scenes before moving on to San Esteban de Pravia, Asturias, where he worked on *Field in Asturias*, *San Esteban de Pravia*, *Sea and Rocks in San Esteban, Asturias*, and *Asturian Reaper*.

He was named president of the jury for the National Exhibition of Painting.

Toward the end of June he traveled with his wife to Paris, where he displayed *After the Bath* and *Preparing Raisins, Jávea* at the Salon. From there, on June 27 they set off on a short tour of Belgium and Holland. He then presented *Fisherman's Wife* at the International Art Exhibition in Berlin.

On their way back to Spain, they must have passed through Biarritz, where Sorolla dedicated a painting to Artal's wife.

Back in Paris, Sorolla exhibited the oil paintings *My Children* and *Female Nude* at the International Society of Painting and Sculpture.

From Paris, Sorolla and his wife journeyed via Barcelona to Valencia, where they spent the rest of the summer with their children in the fertile farming area of Alcira and on the beach at El Cabañal. There Sorolla painted *Afternoon Sun* as well as a series of studies for this work and *Bulls in the Sea*.

Sorolla dispatched *The Cape of San Antonio, Jávea* and *Effect of the Sun on the Sea* to the Fifth International Exhibition of Art in Venice, and *After the Bath* to the International Art Exhibition in Berlin.

The Royal Academy of Fine Arts of Lisbon elected him academician of merit by acclamation, and on November 13, he was unanimously voted corresponding academician in Madrid by the Royal Academy of Fine Arts of San Carlos in Valencia.

1904 Sorolla spent the winter painting in his studio in Madrid, producing among other works his self-portrait, a likeness of José Ramón Mélida, and the group portrait *My Children*.

At the National Exhibition of Fine Arts and Artistic Industries in Madrid held in May, where he presided over the jury, he presented *My Children*, *Morning Sun*, *After the Bath*, and the portraits of Clotilde, José Ramón Mélida, Asterio Mañanós, the photographer Christian Franzen, the painter Aureliano de Beruete, and Aureliano de Beruete y Moret, the son of Beruete.

He sent *Afternoon Sun*, *Valencian Fisherwomen*, *The Three Sails*, and two studies titled *Orange Trees* to the International Art Exhibition in Berlin. To the Salon in Paris, he dispatched *Children at the Seashore* and *Family of Fishermen*. The former was acquired by the American artist Alexander Harrison, who donated it some years later to the Philadelphia Museum of Art.

Bath-Time was shown at the Fourteenth Exhibition organized by José Artal at the Salón Witcomb in Buenos Aires between June and July.

Sorolla spent the first part of the summer with his family in Asturias, where he painted new works such as *The Nalón River, Asturias.* After a short stay in Pasajes de San Juan, Guipúzcoa, and San Sebastián, he traveled to Alcira and the beach of El Cabañal in Valencia, where he painted numerous works, among them *Summer, Midday at Valencia Beach,* and *Sewing the Sail.*

In October, the Spanish government made him a member of the organizing committee for the Spanish participation at the International Art Exhibition in Munich.

At the end of the year, after having produced approximately 250 works in twelve months, Sorolla moved to a new house and studio in Calle de Miguel Ángel 9 in Madrid.

1905 Sorolla spent the first months of the year in Madrid, where he painted mostly portraits, including *José Echegaray* and *The Family of Rafael Errázuriz.*

In June, he traveled to Paris with his wife and his daughter María after having sent *Afternoon Sun* and *Summer* to the Salon that opened in May. They remained twenty days in Paris, where he painted a portrait of the wife of Pedro Gil and together with his friend planned his one-man show scheduled

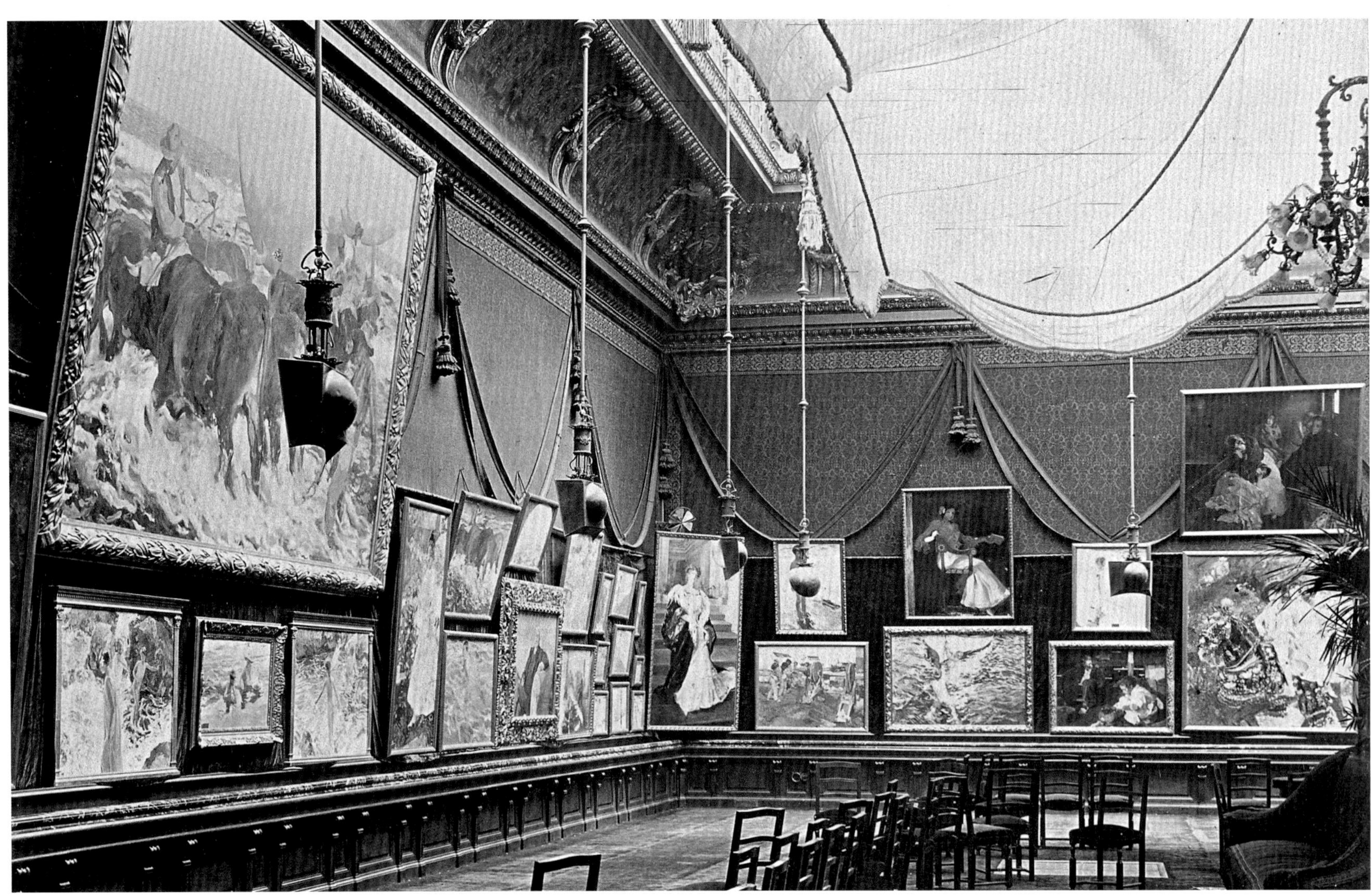

Exhibition of Joaquín Sorolla's work
at the Galerie Georges Petit in Paris, 1906

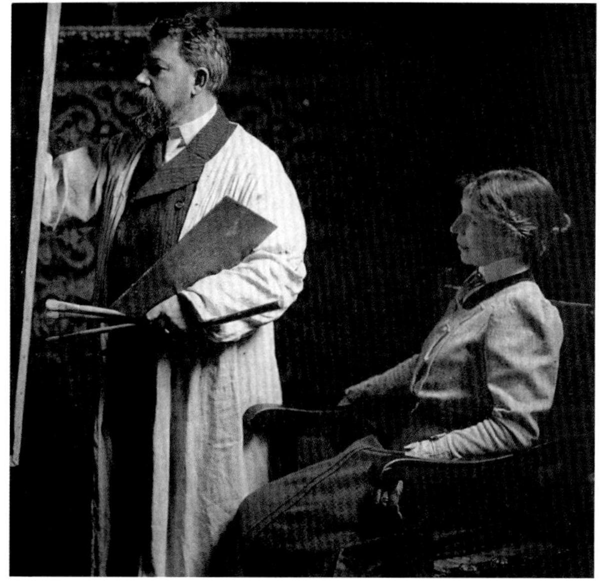

Joaquín Sorolla and his wife, *c.* 1906. Photograph by Christian Franzen y Nissen. Madrid, Museo Sorolla [80.031]

Joaquín Sorolla painting on the beach at Biarritz, 1906. Madrid, Museo Sorolla [80.060]

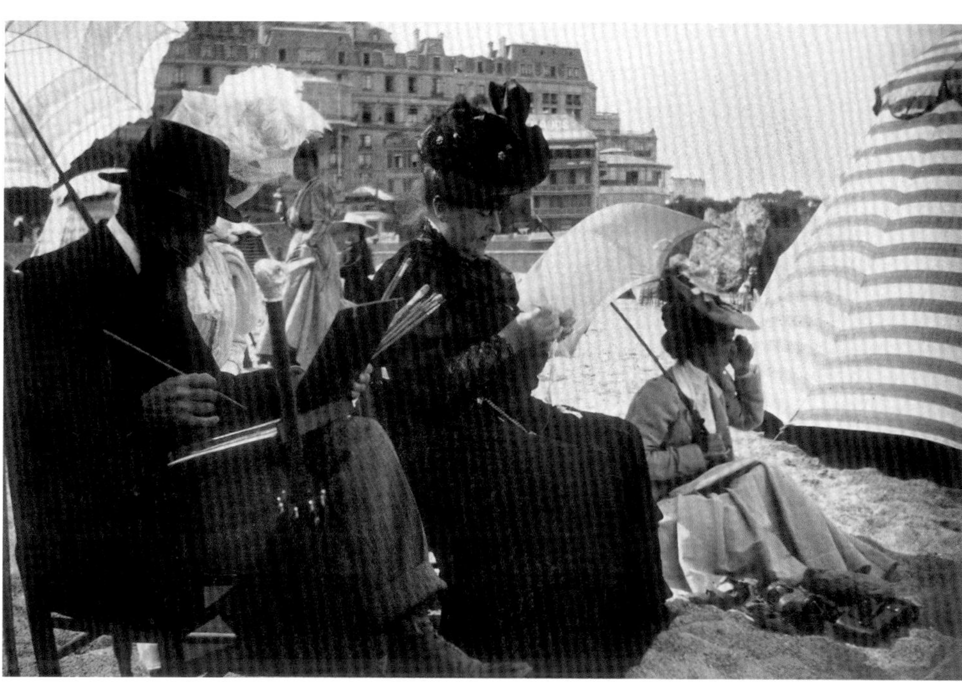

for the following year. The family returned to Spain at the end of July.

Sorolla was made an honorary corresponding member of the Society of French Artists.

In June, he participated in the Sixth International Biennial in Venice with *Sewing the Sail,* which was purchased by the Galleria d'Arte Moderna di Ca'Pesaro in Venice.

During the exhibition organized in London by the Society of Painters, Sculptors, and Engravers, he displayed *The Grandfather.*

Together with his family, he spent the first part of the summer in Valencia, painting at the beach of La Malvarrosa, and from July 10 onward in Jávea, Alicante, where he went in the company of the physician Luis Simarro. There he made a series of scenes featuring the sea, rocks, and children swimming, including *The Cape of San Antonio, Jávea; The White Boat, Jávea; Clotilde and Elena on the Rocks, Jávea; Rocks and White Boat, Jávea; Swimmers, Jávea; On the Rocks, Jávea;* and *The Bath, Jávea,* for many of which his wife and children posed as models.

During the first days of autumn, probably back in Valencia, he painted the portrait of his parents-in-law, *My Children's Grandparents.* The rest of the year he spent in Madrid preparing his first solo exhibition scheduled for 1906. The number of portraits he produced that year reached thirty.

He was appointed chairman of the visual arts section for the 1905–6 course at the Ateneo science and literary club in Madrid, a position he retained until 1910–11.

On November 17, he purchased a plot of land from the Duchess of Marchena on Paseo del Obelisco (now Paseo General Martínez Campos), today a part of the site of the Museo Sorolla.

1906 During the first months of the year, Sorolla painted seventeen portraits of family and friends, including *The Benlliure Arana Family,* or *Lucrecia Arana with Her Son, Señora de Sorolla in Black, The Actress María Guerrero as Lady Nitwit, Santiago Ramón y Cajal,* and a *plein air* portrait of his daughter, *María Dressed as a Valencian Farmworker.* He also painted *Riding en Croupe,* using his daughters as models.

He participated in the Paris Salon with *Valencian Fisherwomen* and in the International Art Exhibition in Munich with *An Investigation.*

From June 11 to July 10 his first one-man show, entitled Exposition Sorolla y Bastida, was held in Paris with resounding public, critical, and economic success. Of the 450 works he displayed at the Galerie Georges Petit, sixty-five were sold for a total sum of 230,650 francs. As a sign of gratitude, he donated *Preparing Raisins, Jávea* to the Musée du Luxembourg, and it is now in the Musée des Beaux Arts de Pau.

During Sorolla's stay in Paris, where he was accompanied by his wife, he painted, among other works, the plein air portraits of the painter Raimundo de Madrazo, Pedro Gil Moreno de Mora, María Planas de Gil, and the French actor Coquelin Cadet.

In June, he was appointed chairman of the visual arts section of the Ateneo in Madrid, and on July 17, he was made an Officer of the Legion of Honor in France.

In the summer he moved with his family to Biarritz, where he executed numerous coastal and beach scenes, such as *Lighthouse Walk at Biarritz*, *Low Tide, Elena in Biarritz*, and *Beach at Biarritz*. During his stay, Sorolla underwent prostate surgery; in gratitude for services rendered, Sorolla painted Dr. Albarrán's portrait.

Before returning to Madrid, the Sorolla family spent a few days in San Sebastián, where they visited Dr. Madinaveitia when María fell ill.

From October 9 to 14, while painting in Segovia, Sorolla visited the nearby gardens of La Granja de San Ildefonso, which left a strong impression on him. Due to the cold, however, he only painted one canvas in this magnificent setting.

From October 21 until probably the beginning of November, he made twenty paintings of the city of Toledo, such as *The Blind Man of Toledo*, and of Toledo's surroundings, including *The Shadow of Alcántara Bridge*. On this brief stay, he was accompanied by Aureliano de Beruete and Beruete's wife, with Clotilde and his daughters only visiting him during the last few days he was painting there.

When the health of María worsened and she was diagnosed with tuberculosis, Sorolla decided to accept the generous offer of his friend Carlos Urcola and move the family to the country estate of La Angorilla, located in the mountains of El Pardo in the outskirts of Madrid. This he did in January of the following year.

1907 On January 14, Sorolla moved with his family to La Angorilla, where he painted *María Convalescing in El Pardo* once she had begun to recover from her illness. From February on, he also worked in his studio in Madrid.

For this reason, he did not attend his exhibitions in Germany organized by Eduard Schulte in Berlin, Düsseldorf, and Cologne. In the three galleries he displayed 280 works. Although well received by the public, these shows were neither economically nor critically a success. In Berlin, his paintings were exhibited in two large rooms at the Schulte Gallery between February 3 and March 1. The other rooms showed works by Friedrich Kallmorgen (1856–1924), Richard Friese (1854–1918), Heinrich Sperling (1844–1924), Norbert Pfretzschner (1850–1927), Hans Bohrdt (1857–1945), Alfred von Pflugl (1863–1929), Emil Richard Weiss (1875–1942), and Gustav Schönleber (1851–1917), among other artists.

In June, he was named corresponding member of the Association of Italian Artists of Florence and honorary president of the Valencian Club of Buenos Aires, together with Teodoro Llorente, Vicente Blasco Ibáñez, Mariano Benlliure, and Salvador Giner.

In July and August, he participated in the Exhibition of Fine Arts in Cádiz with one work.

Once his daughter María had recovered, he spent the summer with his family in La Granja de San Ildefonso, Segovia, painting diverse versions of the palace gardens there and the portrait *King Alfonso XIII in Hussar's Uniform*. He also portrayed his wife in the same surroundings in *Clotilde Strolling in the Gardens of La Granja* and his daughter in *María at La Granja*.

Back in Madrid, during the autumn he painted *Leonese Peasants* using sketches he had made in León and Astorga.

On November 16, he traveled with his pupil Tomás Murillo to Valencia, where he executed a substantial number of paintings in the port and on the beach of La Malvarrosa, such as *The Arrival of the Boats*.

On December 17, his wife and children joined him in Valencia, and they celebrated Christmas together in the home of Sorolla's parents-in-law.

1908 Sorolla began the year painting in the port and on the beaches of Valencia until he returned with his family to Madrid on January 17.

On February 1, he journeyed to Seville to paint the portrait *Queen Victoria Eugenia in an Ermine Cloak*, which presided over his next exhibition in London. The queen's obligations meant that she often had to cancel the short daily session she granted Sorolla, who used the free time to paint various panoramas of the city and sixteen vistas of the gardens of the Reales Alcázares palace, such as *Reflections in a Fountain*. Toward the middle of the month, taking advantage of the queen's absence, he made a brief trip to paint in Córdoba, returning immediately to Seville to continue working on the portrait. Once this was finished, he repaired to Madrid on February 28.

On March 5, he was made corresponding foreign member of the Royal Society of Fine Arts of Brussels.

Accompanied by his friend Benigno de la Vega-Inclán, on April 19 Sorolla traveled to London, where from May 4 to July 4 he put 278 works on show (according to the catalog, which had a prologue by the art critic Leonard Williams) at the *Exhibition of Paintings by Señor Sorolla y Bastida* at the Grafton Galleries. The show was inaugurated by the Spanish ambassador in representation of Their Majesties the King and Queen of Spain.

Although sales in the amount of £2,690 amounted to only half of those made in Paris, this exhibition was marked by a very important event: the visit of the American Hispanist Archer Milton Huntington, founder of the Hispanic Society of America in New York, inaugurated in 1904. Huntington not only purchased several works by Sorolla, he also offered to take his work to New York.

In London, Sorolla saw his friends the painters John Singer Sargent and Anders Zorn.

Before the exhibition ended, Sorolla traveled to Paris on May 30, where his family awaited him, and they returned together to Madrid on June 7.

In May, he was made a member of the Hispanic Society of America in New York.

That summer in Valencia, he painted feverishly at the beach of La Malvarrosa, producing among other works *Going for a Bath, Valencia*, *Sea Idyll*, *After the Bath*, and *Valencian Boats*. At the end of September, back in Madrid, he executed a series of portraits in his studio, such as *The Photographer Antonio García in His Laboratory* and *Manuel Bartolomé Cossío*, and he also prepared the works he would take to the United States at the beginning of the following year.

This period in Madrid was only interrupted by a brief trip to Saragossa, taken alone, between October 20 and 26.

Sorolla and his family spent Christmas at his in-laws' home in Valencia.

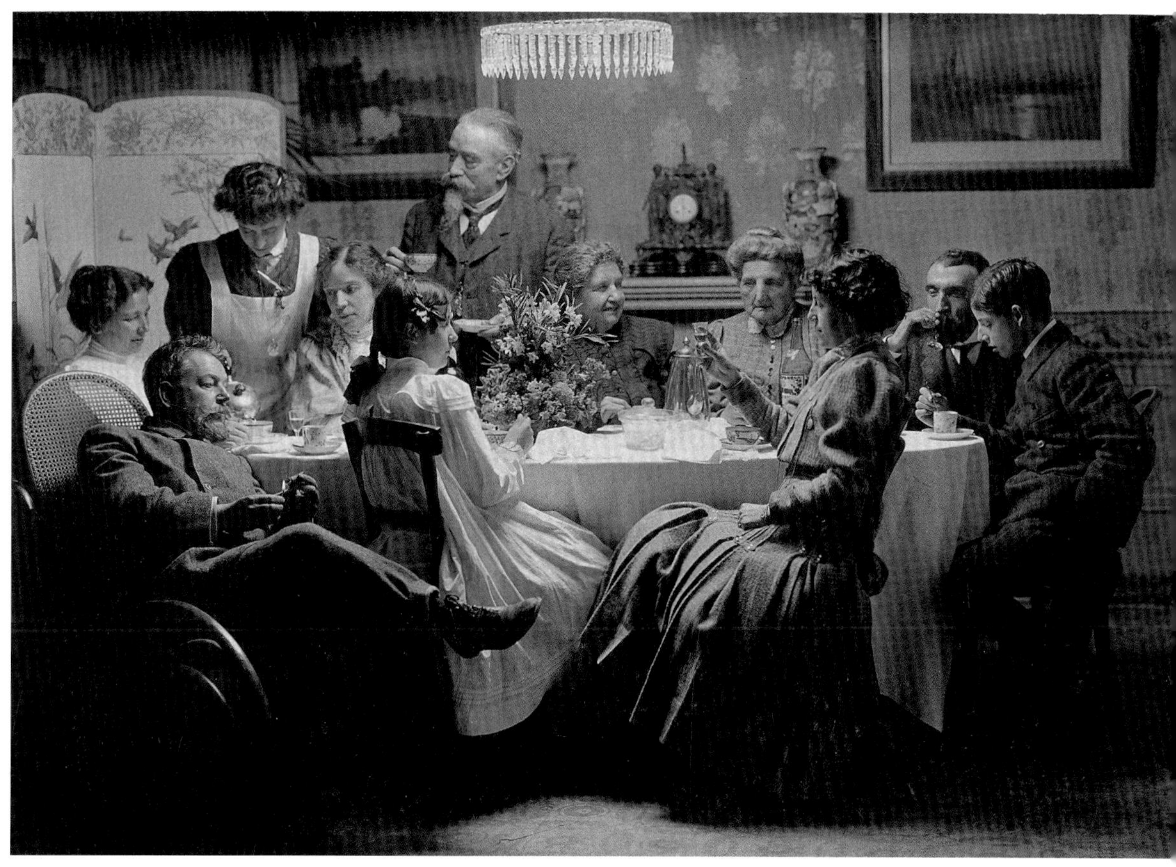

Joaquín Sorolla and his family at his in-laws' house, Christmas 1907

1909 On January 24, Sorolla, his wife, his daughter María, and his son Joaquín embarked from the port of Le Havre for New York on the ocean liner *Lorraine*.

Shortly thereafter, on February 4, the artist attended the inauguration of his one-man exhibition in New York, *Joaquín Sorolla y Bastida at the Hispanic Society of America*. He presented a total of 356 works at this show, which was visited by approximately 160,000 people. The 20,000 catalogs printed for the occasion completely sold out. By the end of the first stage of his American tour on March 8, he had sold almost 150 works. Apart from the economic success this represented, Sorolla was also well received by the New York critics.

The exhibition, reduced to 201 works, continued at the Fine Arts Academy in Buffalo from March 19 to April 10 and at the Copley Society in Boston from April 20 to May 11.

The number of works sold in all three cities added up to 195, for a total $181,760. The Hispanic Society was the major buyer with twenty-six paintings, including *Afternoon Sun*, *Leonese Peasants*, *Sea Idyll*, and *After the Bath*. In honor of this exhibition, the Hispanic Society of America published the book *Eight Essays on Joaquín Sorolla*, with contributions by Aureliano de Beruete, Leonard Williams, and six other critics.

In May, Sorolla traveled to Washington to paint the portraits of the President of the United States, William Howard Taft, and his wife at the White House. All together, he produced more than twenty portraits during his stay in that country.

The Hispanic Society of America unanimously conferred upon him the institution's medal.

On the voyage back to Spain, Sorolla and his wife stopped for a few days in Paris, arriving in Madrid toward the end of June. They immediately set off for Valencia, where they were reunited with the rest of the family. There, Sorolla painted on the beach until the end of September, producing such important works as *The Horse's Bath*, *Antonio García on the Beach*, *Strolling Along the Seashore*, *The Little Sailing Boat* and *Boys on the Beach*.

Sorolla submitted his *Afternoon Sun* to the Salon of the Society of French Artists.

The Regional Exhibition in Valencia dedicated the Room of Honor (no. 12) to Sorolla, displaying eleven of his paintings there, among them *Valencia Beach* and the portraits *The Painter Aureliano de Beruete*, *Manuel Bartolomé Cossío*, *Eulalia de Urcola*, and *Doctor Simarro*.

Sorolla traveled to Paris for the second time that year between October 19 and 26 to paint the portrait of Thomas Fortune Ryan, who also commissioned a major painting on Christopher Columbus. With a view to researching the subject, Sorolla journeyed through Andalusia, setting off from Seville. From November 17 to 19, he visited La Rábida and Palos de Moguer, and upon not finding what he wanted, he continued to Granada, where between November 21 and December 1 he painted for the first time the gardens

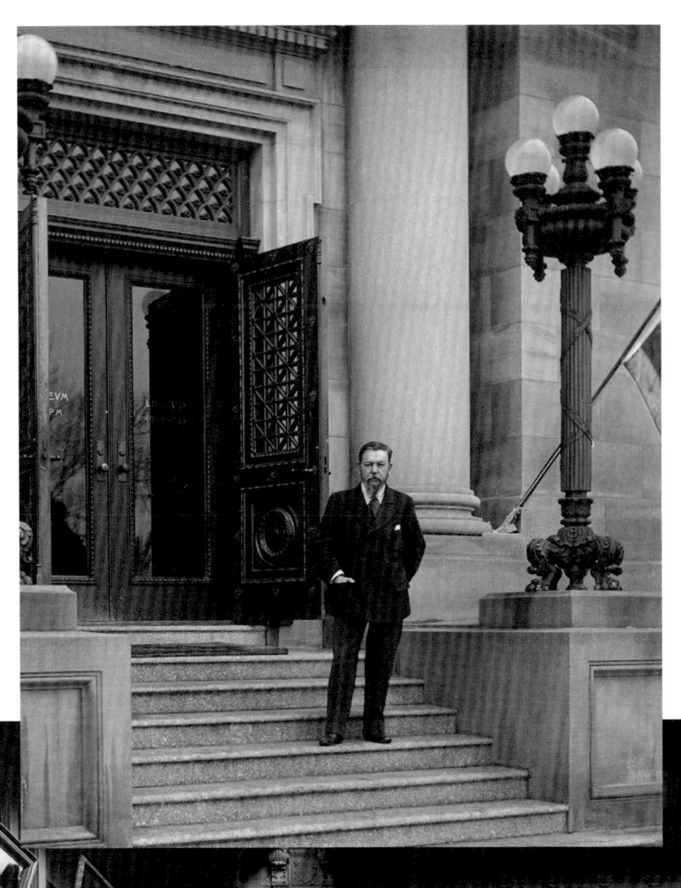

Joaquín Sorolla on the stairs of the Hispanic Society of America, New York, 1909. Photograph by Sebastián Cruset. Madrid, Museo Sorolla [80.100]

Hispanic Society of America, New York, 1909. Photograph by Sebastián Cruset

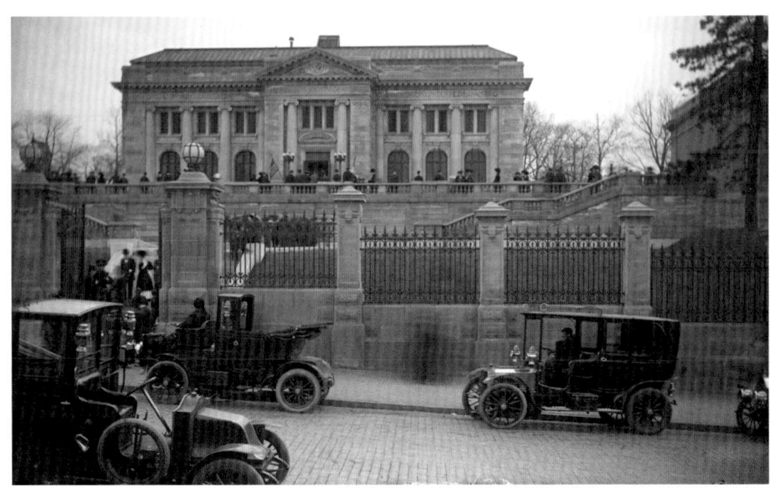

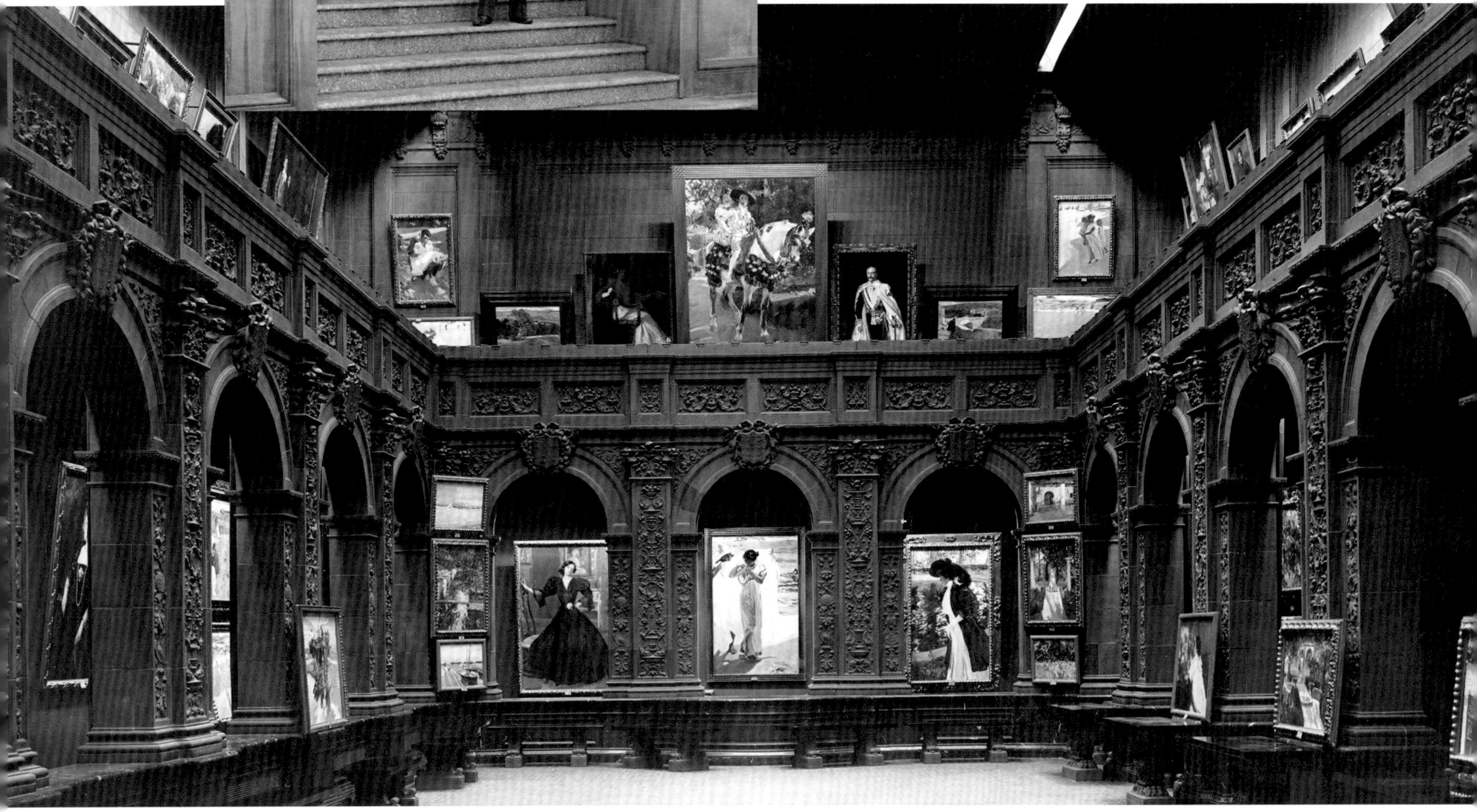

Sorolla's exhibition at the Hispanic Society of America in New York, 1909. Madrid, Museo Sorolla [81.317]

of the Alhambra and the Generalife, vistas of the city, and views of its nearby Sierra Nevada mountains.

On his return to Madrid, he commissioned the project of his future house and studio from the architect Enrique María de Repullés y Vargas.

1910 In late January, Sorolla traveled again to Andalusia, this time with his family. From January 25 to February 12, he painted numerous garden scenes and landscapes in Seville, including *Sunny Afternoon in the Alcázar of Seville*. The Sorollas then visited Granada from February 13 to 24, Málaga from February 25 to March 2, Ronda from March 15 to 17, and Córdoba from March 18 to 20, from where they returned to Madrid.

From March 25 to 28, Sorolla visited Avila, and from March 29 to April 2 Burgos, where he was surprised by a snowstorm he reproduced in some of his pictures.

In the spring, he worked on the preparatory studies and the final painting commissioned by Thomas Fortune Ryan, *The Departure of Christopher Columbus from the Port of Palos*. He also made magnificent portraits of his family, among them a group portrait painted out of doors, *My Wife and Daughters in the Garden*.

He participated in the Exhibition of Ancient and Modern Portraits and Drawings organized by the City Council of Barcelona, showing the portraits of the Prince of Asturias, the Infanta Isabel of Bourbon, Carlos Vázquez, and the Countess of Muguiro, as well as *María Convalescing in El Pardo*, *Elena and María in Old Valencian Costumes*, *My Family*, and *Self-Portrait*.

In his studio, he then painted the portraits of King Alfonso XIII of Spain, José Echegaray, and José Gestoso on commission from the Hispanic Society of America for its portrait gallery.

He sent *Valencian Fishermen* and *Setting Sun* to the International Fine Arts Exhibition in Santiago de Chile and *White Slave Trade*, *Mending the Nets*, *Valencian Fisherwoman*, *After the Bath*, *Valencian Peasant Woman*, *Boy with Grapes*, and *Valencian Boat* to the Spanish Exhibition of Art and Decorative Industries in Mexico City.

The portraits of President William Howard Taft and *Clotilde Strolling in the Gardens of La Granja* were shown during the spring at the International Exhibition of Contemporary Painters organized by the Carnegie Institute in Pittsburgh, Pennsylvania.

On April 27, he was appointed, by royal order, board member of the Casa del Greco in Toledo.

In May he purchased a new plot of land, adjacent to the one he already owned, from his friend Aureliano Beruete, and in early July work began on his new house, today the site of the Museo Sorolla.

In the summer he traveled to Zarautz with his family, staying at the Hotel Perla. There he painted numerous scenes of the interiors of taverns and of his family on the beach, including the canvases *Under the Awning, Zarautz* and *Under the Awning, Beach at Zarautz*.

On September 17, he traveled to Valencia with his pupils Teodoro Andreu and Tomás Murillo, and he painted several scenes of El Cabañal beach.

From October 1 on, he produced some of his best portraits of his family in Madrid. At the National

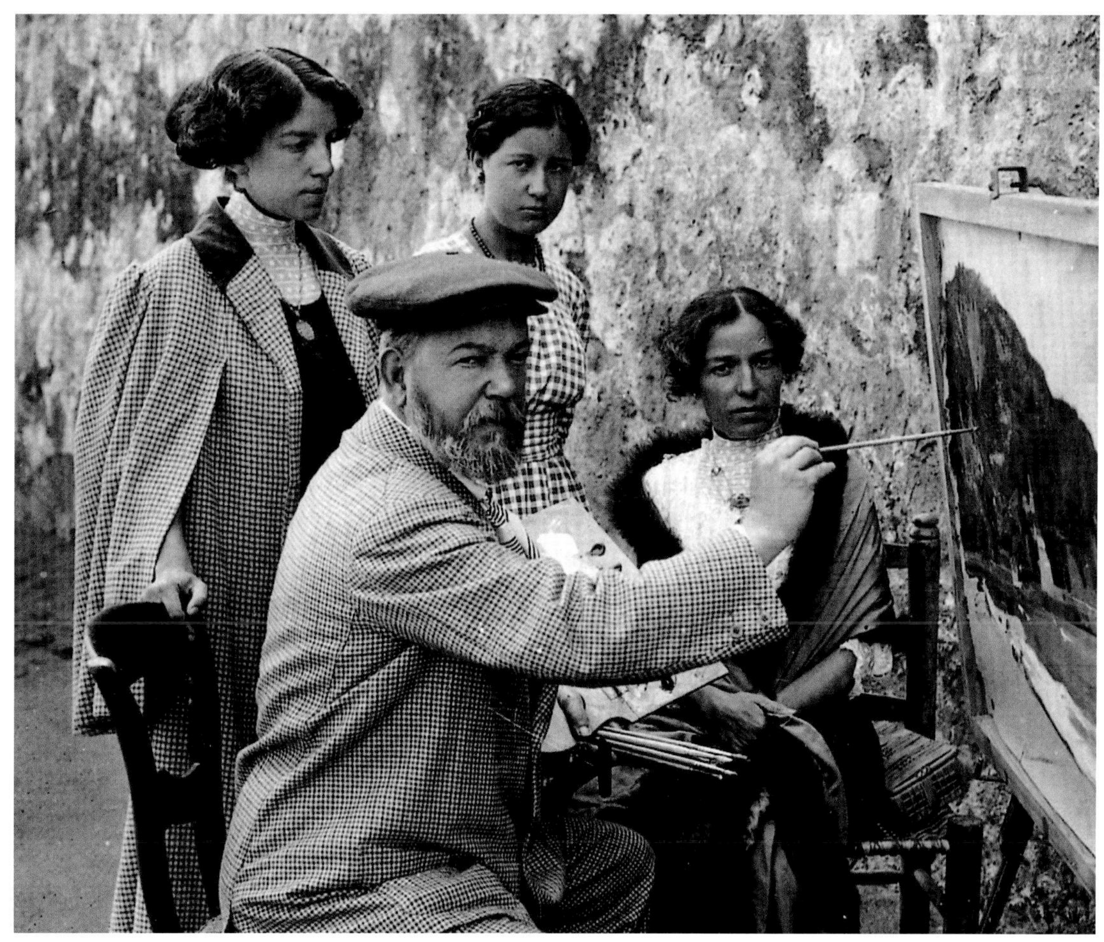

Joaquín Sorolla, with his wife and daughters, painting *María on the Beach at Zarautz*, 1910. Madrid, Museo Sorolla [80.116]

The second studio
at the Sorolla House,
Madrid, 1911

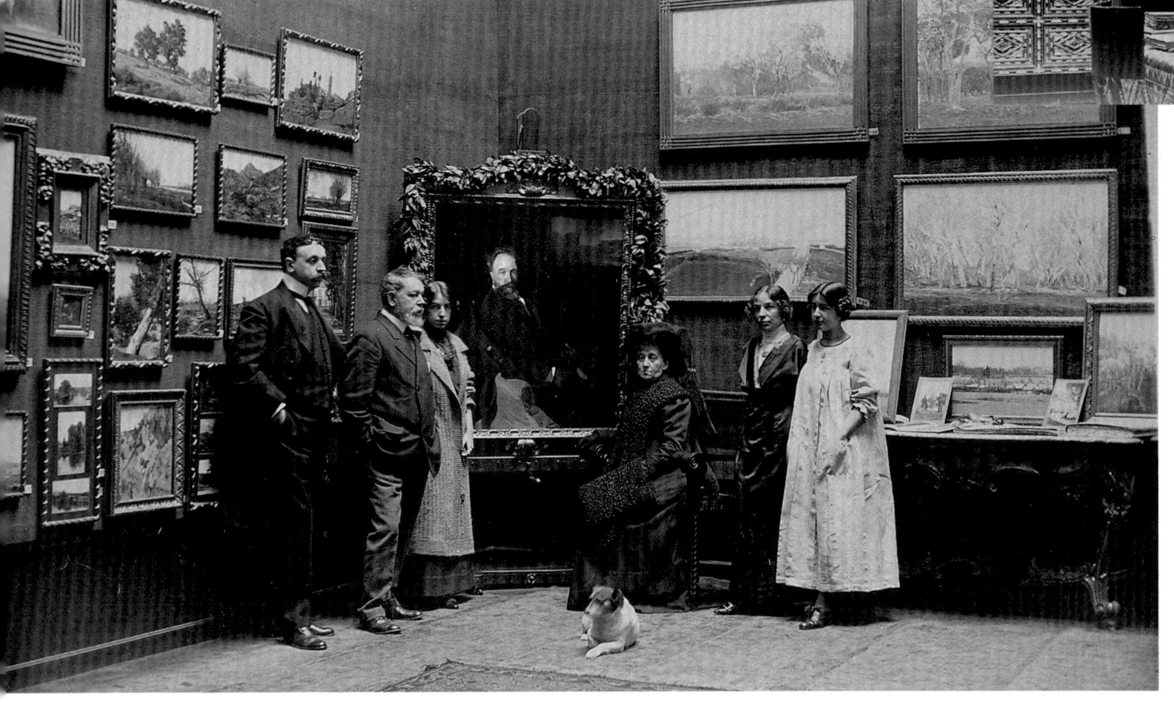

Exhibition in homage to Aureliano de Beruete at the Sorolla House, Madrid, 1912. Photograph by Mariano Moreno García

Exhibition of Painting, Sculpture, and Architecture in Madrid, held in the Palacio del Retiro pavilion, he showed *María Convalescing in El Pardo*.

Between October 20 and November 4, he visited Paris to personally present Thomas Fortune Ryan with the painting *The Departure of Christopher Columbus from the Port of Palos*. He also met up with Archer Milton Huntington to fix the dates for his next trip to the United States. In addition, he painted several portraits, among them *Loubat*, *Troubetzkoy*, and *Mrs Townsend*.

Sorolla spent the rest of the year in Madrid, except for a five-day trip to Galicia and Salamanca from November 15 to 20.

The writer Rafael Doménech published the first biographical and critical study on the artist under the title *Sorolla. Su vida y su arte* (*Sorolla: His Life and His Art*).

1911 On January 21, Sorolla set off on a new trip to the United States accompanied by his wife. They traveled from Madrid to Paris and from there to England, leaving their son Joaquín there to study. This time they sailed on the *Lusitania* and arrived in New York on January 28.

Upon arriving in New York, Sorolla presented some of his new works at the Hispanic Society of America. Then he traveled to Chicago, where on February 14 the exhibition *Joaquín Sorolla y Bastida*, featuring 161 works, opened at the Art Institute of Chicago under the auspices of the Hispanic Society of America. By the time the exhibition closed on March 12, it had been visited by more than 100,000 people. During the course of the exhibition, Sorolla painted various portraits and gave a series of master classes at the Art Institute.

The same exhibition traveled to St. Louis, Missouri, where it was presented at the City Art Museum from March 20 to April 20. Income from sales at these exhibitions surpassed $80,000.

Back in New York, Sorolla continued to paint portraits, including one of Louis Comfort Tiffany in the gardens of his home in Long Island, as well as some beautiful gouaches with views of the city made from his hotel room, such as *Marathon, New York*.

On May 24, the Sorollas boarded the ocean liner *Mauretania* and arrived in London on the 29th, where they visited their son Joaquín for a few days.

Sorolla then spent a month in Paris making portraits. Upon returning to Spain at the beginning of July, he and his wife collected their daughters in Valencia and spent the summer together in San Sebastián, where the artist painted one of his emblematic works, *The Nap*.

Toward the end of September, work on Sorolla's new house in Madrid was completed.

In the autumn he painted portraits such as *Clotilde in Evening Dress* in Madrid. He also traveled once again to Paris where, on November 26, he signed a contract with Archer Milton Huntington for $150,000 to create a series of representative panels of regions of Spain and Portugal titled *Vision of Spain* for the library of the Hispanic Society as a frieze 70 meters long and three and a half meters high (230 feet long and 12 feet high). The maximum period set for the realization of this major undertaking was five years.

From Paris, Sorolla traveled to Barcelona and, after a short stay there, he returned to Madrid.

He participated *hors-concours* (out of competition) in the International Fine Arts Exhibition in Rome with eighty-five works that were put on show in the hall of honor of the Spanish Pavilion.

On December 2, he was named corresponding foreign member of the Academy of Fine Arts of France, succeeding the Dutch painter Jozef Israëls.

The Literary and Artistic Society of Catalonia unanimously elected him an honorary member.

From December 15 to January 4, his work *Drawing on the Sand* was exhibited at the Milwaukee Art Society.

Shortly before Christmas, Sorolla moved with his family to the new house and studio on Paseo del Obelisco (currently the Museo Sorolla).

1912 On April 17, in the studio of his new house, Sorolla inaugurated an exhibition in homage to his friend, the recently deceased Aureliano Beruete. The event was presided over by Sorolla's superb portrait *The Painter Aureliano de Beruete*.

Sorolla made numerous studies of the composition and installation of the panels that would cover the walls of the library of the Hispanic Society of America. He decided to travel around Spain to make firsthand studies of the different regional types he would later use in the final paintings for this decoration, painting them life-size.

From March 22 to 29, he visited the towns of Oropesa, Lagartera, and Talavera de la Reina in the province of Toledo. He must also have made a brief trip to Segovia, of which we only know through two studies he made of Segovian types. From May 11 to 19 he was in Avila, from May 30 to June 1 in Salamanca, and from there he went to Candelario, Salamanca. On June 2 he traveled to Villar de los Álamos and from there to La Alberca, Salamanca,

Joaquín Sorolla painting *Rider of Salamanca*, 1912

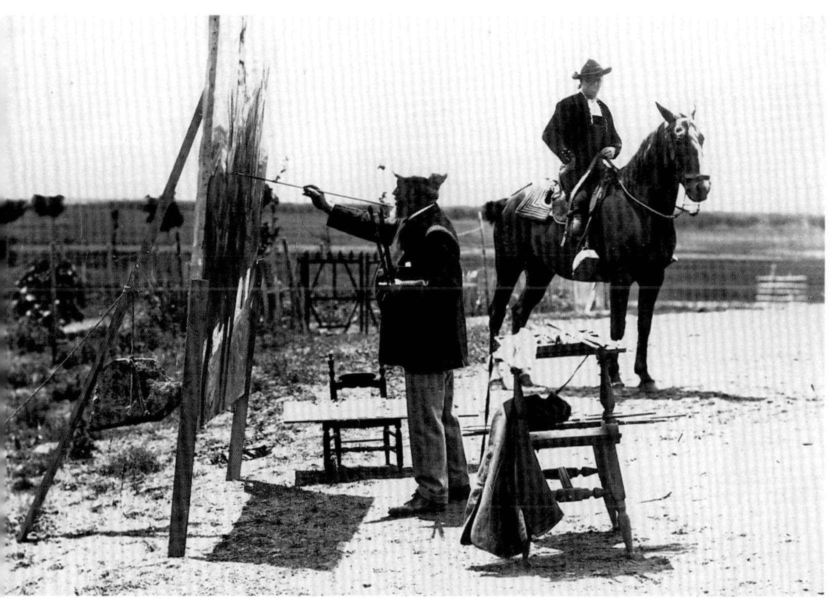

Joaquín Sorolla painting *Types of Soria*, 1912. Madrid, Museo Sorolla [80.144]

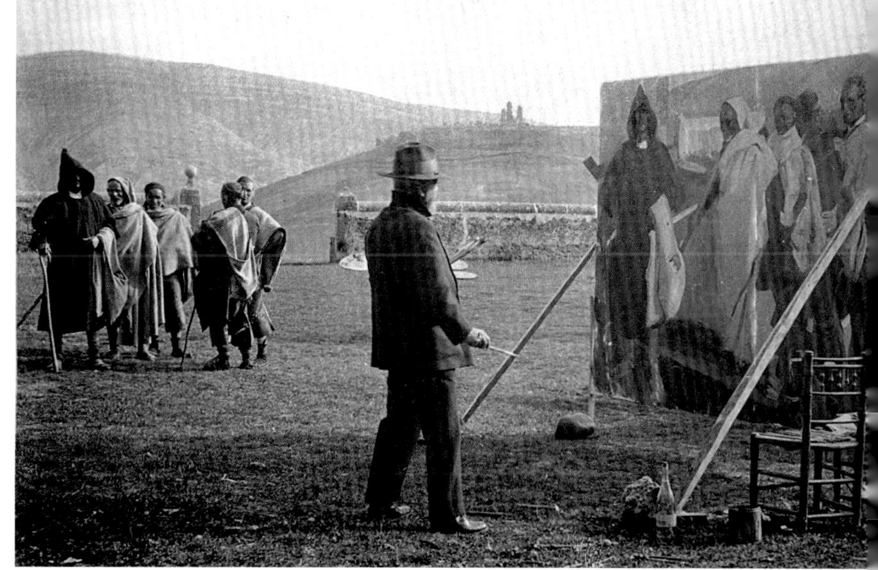

on June 10. After having produced seventeen large-format studies, he returned to Madrid on June 18.

On June 9, he was unanimously elected president of the Association of Painters and Sculptors of Madrid.

The Royal Academy of Fine Arts in Milan named him honorary member.

Sorolla received a gold medal at the International Exhibition of Modern Art held in Amsterdam for *The Female Bathers*.

He spent the first fortnight of July in Biarritz with his son Joaquín and painted, among other works, the portraits of Archer Milton Huntington and of his wife Helen Huntington. From his base in San Sebastián, the rest of the summer he continued to travel to paint in situ studies from the life of regional cultures from Roncal, Navarre, between August 22 and 28, as well as from Isaba and Ansó, Huesca, between August 29 and 31. During this period, he only painted three large studies in El Roncal.

He returned to San Sebastián via Roncesvalles and Biarritz, and from September 9 to 14 he painted four large studies of fishermen and of several mountain peasant women who had just arrived from Santander in Lequeitio, Biscay. In San Sebastián he painted *Preparing and Dragging Tuna,* which in some way would inspire his last panel.

On September 20, he returned with his family to Madrid and, ten days later, on September 30, he traveled alone to Jadraque, Guadalajara, and Numancia, Soria, where he produced a large study. Subsequently, he went to Soria from October 1 to 9, where he executed two large-format studies. Sorolla returned to Madrid only to set out once again to visit Alcázar de San Juan on October 25 and 26, Campo de Criptana, Ciudad Real, from October 27 to November 2, where he painted two studies, and Toledo between November 3 and 7, where he made five studies with views of the city.

The last months of the year he remained in Madrid painting. His work was shown in Boston in an exhibition at the Copley Society of Art.

1913 Sorolla spent the first months of the year in Madrid with his daughter María, who was recovering from a relapse in her illness. During this time, he painted in the surroundings of Madrid.

His wife and daughter Elena traveled to London to look after his son Joaquín, who was hospitalized due to a motorcycle accident.

In April, Sorolla moved with his daughter María to a house in Cuesta de las Perdices on the outskirts of Madrid, a place on higher ground with views of the mountains and fresh air. There he installed his outdoor studio and began to paint the 14-meter-long panel (46 feet) dedicated to Castile and León: *Castile, the Bread Festival*. By the time he traveled to San Sebastián in mid-September for an audience with King Alfonso XIII, the panel dedicated to Castile and León was almost finished, including the more than one hundred figures portrayed in it.

From San Sebastián he journeyed to Paris with his pupil Francisco Pons Arnau to paint new portraits commissioned by Thomas Fortune Ryan and to meet Archer Milton Huntington, who agreed to extend the deadline for the decoration of the Hispanic Society of America and accepted the exclusion of Portugal from the program.

In Paris, Sorolla met Auguste Rodin.

Sorolla returned to Madrid on October 27, from where he made short trips to Avila and Toledo to make a series of sketches to finish the panel. The last few months of the year were dedicated to completing the panel of Castile.

Sorolla displayed works in two American exhibitions: at the *Exhibition of Paintings by Contemporary Spanish Artists* organized at the Art Institute of Chicago, he presented *María Convalescing in El Pardo*; while at the exhibition *A Collection of Paintings by Contemporary Spanish Artists,* which opened on November 23 at the City Art Museum in St. Louis, Missouri, he showed *The Two Sisters*.

1914 After spending the first two months of the year in Madrid making numerous portraits, on March 3 Sorolla traveled to Seville to work on the next *Vision of Spain* panel. From March 16 to April 29 he painted *Seville, Holy Week Penitents* in the monastery of San Clemente. He also produced three studies of processions and seven paintings of Andalusian women. In all this time, he only took a brief rest from March 28 to April 3 to visit his family in Madrid. He remained in Seville until May 3.

On March 16 he was unanimously voted a full member of the Royal Academy of Fine Arts of San Fernando in Madrid, occupying the place left vacant by the recently deceased painter Salvador Martínez Cubells.

Back in Madrid, he sent fourteen works to the Eleventh International Biennial in Venice, including *Sewing the Sail, The Nap, San Martin Bridge*, and various landscapes.

Between May and August, he showed *Basque Drinker* at the *Exhibition of Modern Spanish Art* in Brighton, a show that also traveled to London, where it was displayed between October and December at the Grafton Galleries.

He also participated in the exhibition at the Memorial Art Gallery in Rochester, New York.

In the summer he traveled with his family to San Sebastián and from there to Jaca, Huesca, to paint the panels dedicated to Navarre and Aragon. There they celebrated the wedding of his daughter María with his pupil Francisco Pons Arnau on September 7. After completing the panels *Aragon, the Jota* and *Navarre, the Town Council of Roncal*, as well as five studies of regional types and landscapes, the Sorollas returned to San Sebastián. There, in early October, the artist finished the only painting in the series dedicated to the Basque Country, *Guipúzcoa, the Game of Skittles*. He also made two landscape studies and numerous sketches of the beach.

He returned to Madrid on October 6 and the following day, with the next painting in mind, he made his way to Seville and from there to Jerez de la Frontera, Cádiz, where he stayed until October

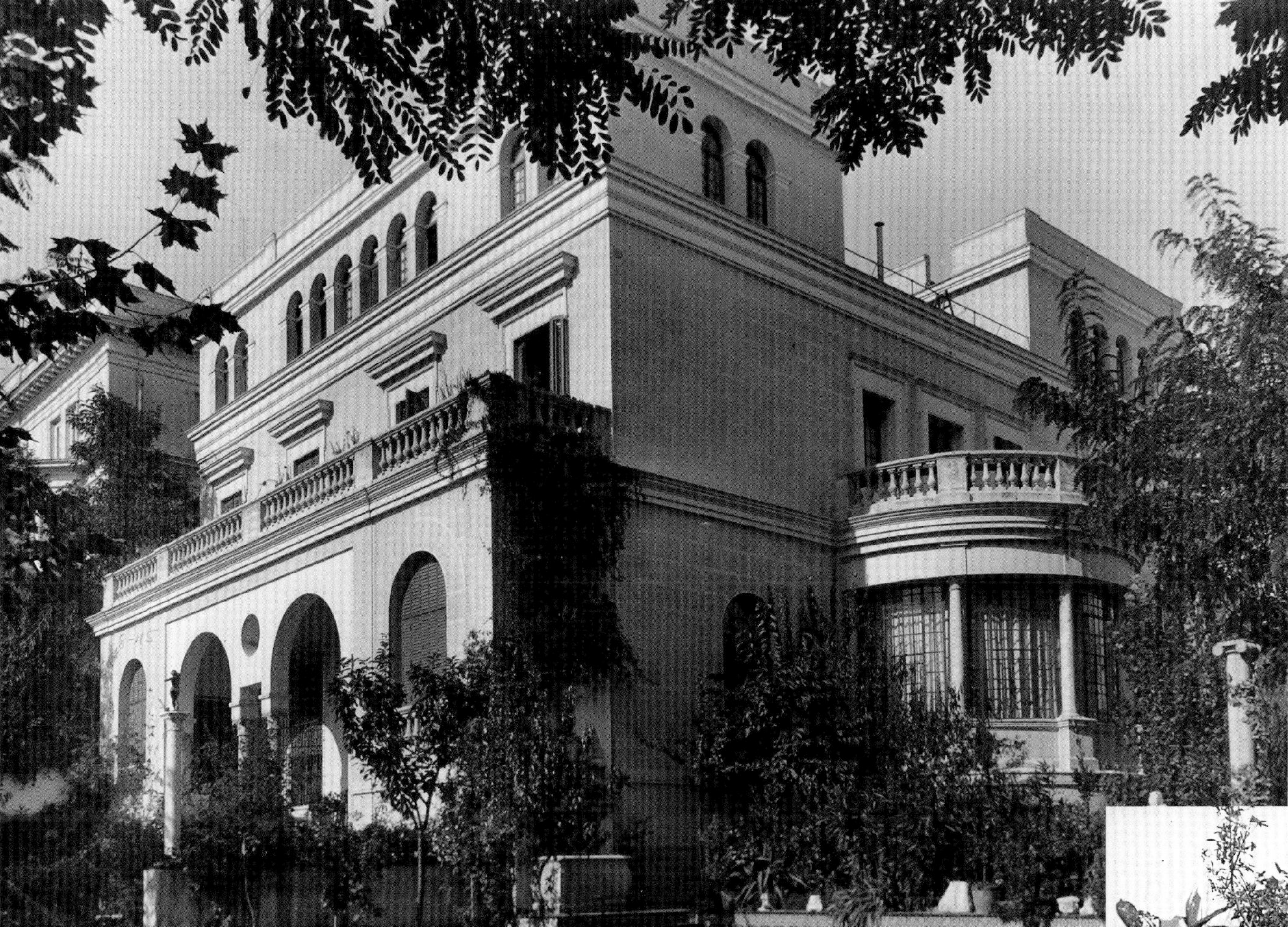

Sorolla's house, 1915. Photograph by Anna Christian. New York, The Hispanic Society of America [14649]

Joaquín Sorolla in the garden of his house, 1915. Madrid, Museo Sorolla [80.125]

15 at the country estate of his friend Pedro González, 'El Cuco,' and made ten studies of the grape harvest.

Back in Seville, he decided to paint a new panel called *Andalusia, the Round-Up* at La Tabladilla, a country house on the outskirts of the city, executing it between November 6 and December 12. In addition, he made numerous studies of agaves, prickly pears, and fields of olive trees, as well as seven studies of bull herders with spears.

Upon receiving news of his mother-in-law's demise, he made a brief trip to Valencia, returning with his wife to Seville, where they spent Christmas with their children Joaquín and Elena.

1915 Between January 7 and February 7, his oil painting entitled *The Two Sisters* was exhibited at the Minneapolis Institute of Arts.

In the first days of the year, Sorolla traveled to Madrid to stay with his daughter María, returning on January 15 to Seville, where he continued to work on the

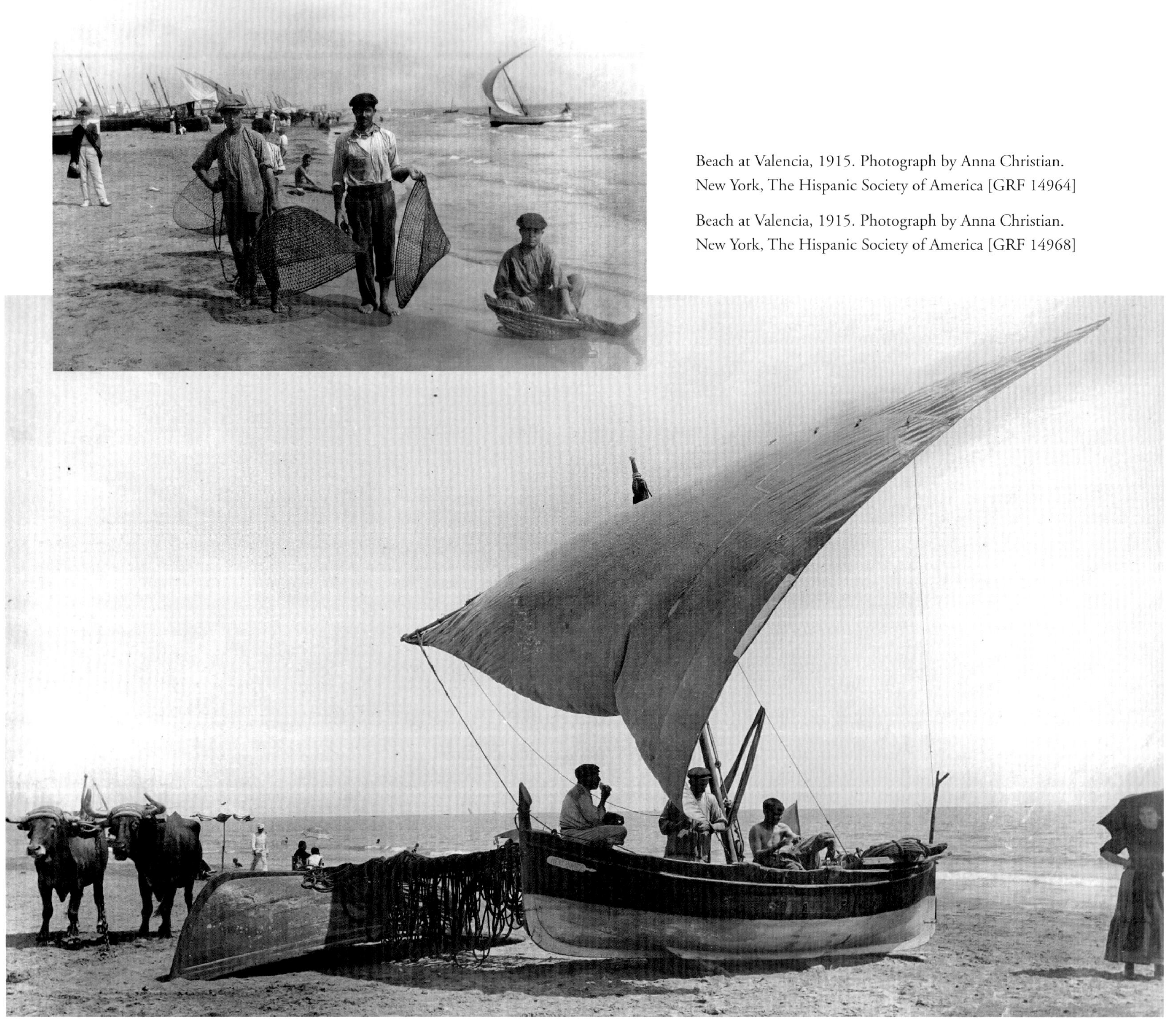

Beach at Valencia, 1915. Photograph by Anna Christian.
New York, The Hispanic Society of America [GRF 14964]

Beach at Valencia, 1915. Photograph by Anna Christian.
New York, The Hispanic Society of America [GRF 14968]

last two panels dedicated to Andalusia. He completed *Seville, the Dance*—for which only a few sketches and one study are known—in February and *Seville, the Bullfighters* in April. He also painted five studies of patios and four paintings of groups of Andalusian women.

After completing these works, he repaired to Madrid and rested there for a fortnight before traveling on May 19 with his son to Valencia and Barcelona in search of the subject of his next panel. There he met Antonio Gaudí, with whom he visited the works of La Sagrada Familia. He sketched out the first studies for the panel dedicated to Catalonia.

Sorolla and his son returned to Madrid on May 27, whereupon he decided to spend a month and a half of the summer with his family in Valencia and to paint beach scenes, such as *Beached Boats, Valencia*, not connected to the commission from the Hispanic Society of America.

At the Fine Arts Exhibition held in Valencia's Palacio Municipal exhibition hall between July and August he presented, *hors concours* (out of competition), his canvas *Joaquina the Gypsy*.

On July 15, once again with his family, he traveled to Galicia and stayed at the Castillo de Vista Alegre in Villagarcía de Arosa, where between July and September he painted the panel entitled *Galicia, the Cattle Fair* with the river in the background, as well as two large-format studies.

On September 8 he returned to Madrid, and toward the middle of the next month he traveled to Barcelona, ready to begin work on the next panel. With the help of the painters Carlos Vázquez, Hermen Anglada Camarasa, and Santiago Rusiñol, he visited different places along the coast, and on the beach of Santa Cristina in Lloret de Mar, Girona, he discovered the background for his next painting, for which he made two studies.

In order to paint the new panel *Catalonia, the Fish*, he installed himself on the beach of La Barceloneta in an inn called Baños Orientales. Except for a rest of two weeks in Madrid motivated by health problems—these were the first signs of the illness that would force him to take a long rest at the beginning of the following year—he painted the work in La Barceloneta between October 7 and December 12.

In Barcelona, he was visited by Giovanni Boldini.

1916 After resting during the first two weeks of the year in Madrid, Sorolla left for Valencia on January 15 accompanied by his pupil Teodoro Andreu. There he found and decided on the subject of his next panel. He set up his studio in the country house of his father-in-law, Antonio García, and began work on the panel *Valencia, Riding en Croupe*, which he realized between January 31 and March 15. From February 25 on, he was joined by his wife and daughter Elena.

He returned to Madrid and worked from April to June in his studio, where he made the portrait *Juan Ramón Jiménez* for the Hispanic Society of America and painted in the gardens of his house.

On June 20, he traveled to Valencia and organized the First Exhibition of Young Valencian Artists, in which his daughters, María and Elena, as well as his son-in-law, Francisco Pons Arnau, participated. Elena won a medal for her sculpture. Sorolla also rented a house on the beach of El Cabañal and had it fixed up in order to spend a long summer there with his family, painting.

From July to October he stopped working on the Huntington commission and painted some of his best works of the beach, among which *After the Bath, the Pink Robe* stands out.

In the autumn he went on a pleasure trip with his wife and daughter Elena through Andalusia and on to Tetuán, only painting one canvas in the gardens of the Reales Alcázares in Seville.

During the last six months of the year, he stopped working on anything related to the decoration of the Hispanic Society of America in New York. He spent Christmas with his family in Madrid.

1917 On January 5 he traveled in the company of his pupil Santiago Martínez to Seville, and from there to Mérida, Cáceres, and Plasencia, where he arrived on January 9, precisely on the day of the market, where inhabitants from Montehermoso turned up in their picturesque hats. Having found the subject for the panel dedicated to Extremadura, he decided not to paint it then, however, due to the intense cold, and he returned to Madrid on January 11.

At the invitation of King Alfonso XIII, he went to Lachar, Granada, on January 26 to take part in a hunt at the country estate of the Count of Benalúa and to make sketches for a portrait of the king out hunting. The hunt was cancelled due to bad weather, and on February 1 the rest of the guests set off on an eventful excursion to the region of Las Alpujarras, which Sorolla quickly abandoned and returned to Granada. There he painted his last nine visions of the Alhambra, the Generalife and the Sierra Nevada, among them *Sierra Nevada, Granada*. Sorolla repaired to Madrid on February 13, four days before his daughter María gave birth to his first grandchild, Francisco Pons Sorolla.

He was appointed to the committee for the organization of the National Fine Arts Exhibition in Madrid, which was held at the Palacio del Retiro pavilion in May and in which he took part with one work.

In the spring and autumn, he painted seventeen portraits in his studio in Madrid, nine of them for the Hispanic Society of America, notably *Mariano Benlliure* and one of his son entitled *Joaquín Sorolla García, Seated*. He also produced numerous paintings of the gardens of his house.

In July he showed *Sewing the Sail* at the Second Exhibition of Painting, Sculpture, and Decorative Arts organized by the Association of Young Artists in Valencia.

He spent the summer with his family in Villa Sorolla, situated on the slopes of Monte Igueldo, in San Sebastián, where he continued to paint numerous studies, landscapes, and views of the breakwater.

On his return to Madrid, he sent a canvas to the Exhibition of the Artistic and Literary Society of Catalonia in Barcelona.

On October 20, together with his pupil Santiago Martínez, he traveled once more to Plasencia to make *Extremadura, the Market*. He painted it between October 25 and November 4 in the courtyard of the house of his friend Fernando Sánchez Ocaña, using people from Montehermoso as his models. This panel was the only one he did not complete on site, but rather finished it in his studio in Madrid after returning there on November 7. He also made two studies and a painting.

Sorolla spent the last months of the year and Christmas with his family.

1918 On January 1, Archer Milton Huntington visited Sorolla in his house and was entirely satisfied with the progress of the work for the Hispanic Society of America.

During the first months of the year, Sorolla worked in his studio in Madrid, where he made the portraits of José Ortega y Gasset, Antonio Machado, José Benlliure, and Miguel Blay for the portrait gallery of the Hispanic Society of America.

On January 10, he was made a full member of the board of trustees of the Museo de Arte Moderno in Madrid. On February 23, he was made honorary chairman of the executive committee for the First Spanish Congress of Fine Arts organized by the Association of Painters and Sculptors in Madrid.

During Easter he traveled without his wife to Seville, painting between March 24 and April 2 his last twelve studies of the gardens of the Alcázar. On his return to Madrid, he continued painting portraits and views of the gardens of his house.

He sent *Mother and Daughter*, *Rainy Day*, and *To the Water* to the Exhibition of Valencian Art held at the Palacio de Bellas Artes in Barcelona during the spring.

On July 1 his father-in-law, Antonio García, died in Valencia. Sorolla attended the funeral with his family and spent a fortnight in Valencia, returning to Madrid on July 16.

Sorolla took part in the Third Exhibition of Art at the Universidad Literaria in Valencia organized by the Association of Young Artists in Valencia with *Mother and Daughter*, *The Novice*, *To the Water*, *Rainy Day*, *View of Seville*, and *Patio with a Small Fountain*.

The artist spent the summer with his family in San Sebastián, painting new landscapes and scenes of the beach and the breakwater. During the preceding months he had not painted anything related to the decoration of the library of the Hispanic Society of America in New York.

At the end of September, on the 28th, he traveled to Alicante with his son, Joaquín, from where he planned to visit the famous palm grove in Elche. This he did on October 1, but due to his son's delicate state of health, a flu epidemic in Elche, and the fact that the dates had not yet matured and acquired the color he desired, he returned to Madrid on October 12 without having begun the panel.

Back in Alicante on November 22, this time accompanied by his pupils Alfredo Carreras and Emilio Varela, he decided not to paint the canvas in Elche, installing himself more comfortably on the outskirts of Alicante in Juan Soler's country estate Huerta del Carmen. There he began the panel entitled *Elche, the Palm Grove* on November 27, only making sketches of an oven and some palm trees in Elche proper.

On December 8 he made a short trip to Murcia in the company of his friend, Dr. José López Campello. At the end of December, not having finished the panel, he decided to spend Christmas in Alicante without his family. There he celebrated Christmas Eve at the house of his friend and fellow student Heliodoro Guillén.

1919 Sorolla finished the Elche panel on January 9, and while it was drying, he traveled first to Murcia and then from January 12 to 14 to Benidorm, Denia, Jávea, Gata, and Calpe, Alicante, where he recalled happy times spent there in the past. He then returned to Alicante and, after a brief trip to Orihuela, Alicante, on the 16th, he left for Madrid on January 19. The next three months were spent painting portraits and scenes of the gardens of his house.

The painter sent *After the Bath*, *Valencian Fisherwomen*, *Mother and Daughter*, *Young Andalusian Girl*, *Children on the Beach*, *Portrait of Madame Dequis*, and *Fountain in the Patio of the Sorolla House* to the Goya et l'Art Espagnol exhibition held in Paris in April and May, and at the Musée des Beaux-Arts in Bordeaux in June and July.

On May 10, accompanied by Santiago Martínez, he left for Seville and traveled along the Andalusian coast, looking for the subject of his last panel. He stopped first in Huelva and then in Ayamonte, Huelva, a village on the border with Portugal, where he found what he was searching for. After installing himself at the Hotel Márquez, on May 18 he began to paint his last panel entitled *Ayamonte, the Tuna Catch*.

After more than a month of intense work during which his health started to visibly deteriorate, he finished the panel on June 29, thus completing his *Vision of Spain* mural cycle. In Ayamonte, he received the congratulations of His Majesty the King of Spain.

Sorolla waited for the canvas to dry before repairing to Madrid on July 8.

On June 27 he was appointed professor of Color and Composition at the School of Fine Arts of San Fernando in Madrid, and on July 8 director

Joaquín Sorolla and his wife in Ibiza, 1919

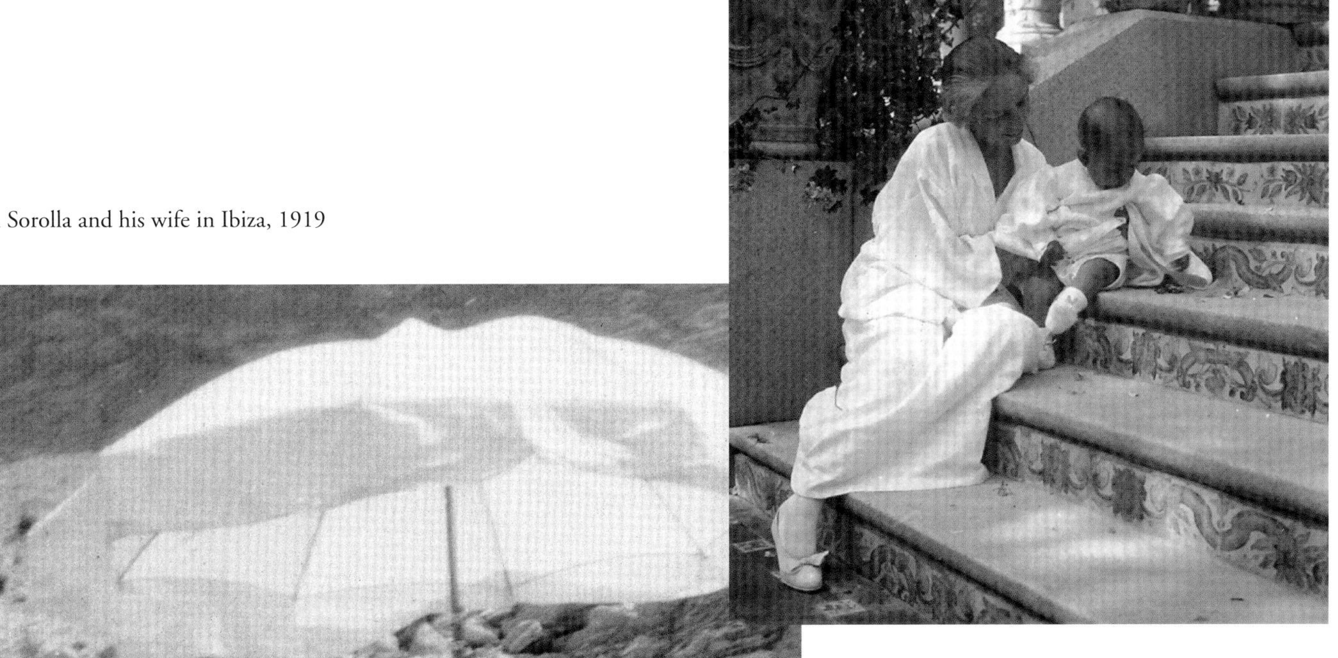

Clotilde with her grandson Francisco at Sorolla House, Madrid

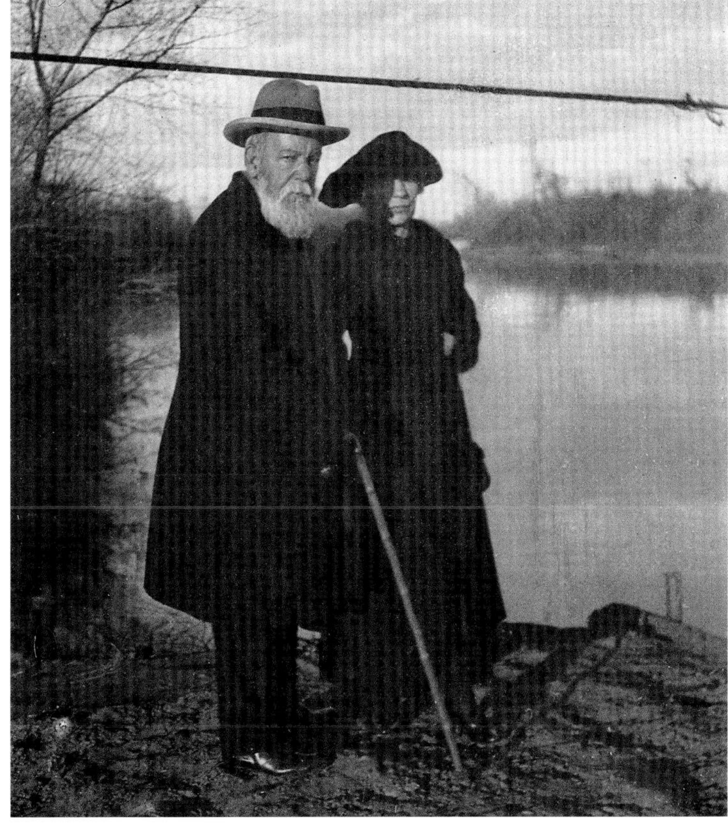

Joaquín Sorolla and his wife, *c.* 1920. Madrid, Museo Sorolla [80.349]

of the Residence for Landscape Artists established at the Monastery of El Paular.

The Academy of Fine Arts in Philadelphia put *The Two Sisters* on show in June. A couple of months later, in August, *The Novice* was displayed at the Exhibition of Fine Arts in Santander.

On July 26 he traveled to Valencia, where he was joined a few days later by his wife, his daughter Elena, and Dr. Sandoval. Afterward, they all traveled together to Majorca, where Sorolla painted numerous works, including the *Elena in the Cala de San Vicente*.

From there they went to Ibiza, where Sorolla painted *The Smugglers* on the cliffs there, a commission from Thomas Fortune Ryan. He also made *Looking for Shellfish*. In Ibiza, they were accompanied by his pupil Santiago Martínez and the painter Ernst Ziess.

On September 25, after being seen off with numerous honors, they sailed on the *Jaime III* to Valencia, where they spent a few days before repairing to Madrid at the beginning of October.

Sorolla spent the last few months of the year giving classes at the School of Fine Arts of San Fernando and painting portraits and scenes of the gardens of his house.

1920 During the first six months of the year, Sorolla alternated teaching at the School of Fine Arts of San Fernando with painting. He worked in his studio, producing among other works the portraits *Gregorio Marañón* and *Manuel Benedito* for the Hispanic Society of America.

In the spring he painted numerous views of the gardens of his house, including the *Garden of the Sorolla House*, as well as portraits of friends and members of the family.

On June 17, in this same garden, he suffered a brain hemorrhage while working on the portrait *Señora Pérez de Ayala*. This stroke prevented him from ever painting again.

The portraits *María Moscardó* and *María Dalhander de Pastor* were displayed at the Exhibition of Painting, Sculpture, and Decorative Arts organized by the city of Valencia in July.

During the summer, Sorolla was taken by his family to Villa Sorolla in San Sebastián.

On October 26, Sorolla was taken in a wheelchair by his students to impart his class in color at the School of San Fernando for the last time.

His oil paintings *Portrait of the Marquise of Villaviciosa* and *After the Bath, Valencia* were sent to the *Exhibition of Spanish Paintings* held at the Royal Academy in London between November 20, 1920, and January 1921.

1921 Sorolla's condition worsened irreversibly.

His family took him to spend the summer at Villa Sorolla, on the road to the lighthouse, in San Sebastián.

1922 Sorolla was named corresponding member of the Academy of Fine Arts in Berlin.

Sorolla's wife purchased two watercolors (today at the Museo Sorolla) at the exhibition and auction of Sorolla paintings that had belonged to his friend Dr. Simarro organized at the Ateneo in Madrid.

On June 8, Sorolla's daughter Elena married Victoriano Lorente in Madrid.

As the artist's condition continued to worsen, he was taken to spend the summer in Valencia, where he stayed in the Casa Blanca, a small mansion with a garden on the beach of La Malvarrosa.

1923 On January 11, Sorolla's aunt and adoptive mother, Isabel Bastida, died at the age of eighty-five. His second grandchild, José María Lorente Sorolla, was born to his daughter Elena.

The exhibitions *Manifestación de Arte Valenciano* in Madrid and the International Exhibition organized at the Art Club of Philadelphia showed works by Sorolla.

The artist spent the last month of his life in Cercedilla, Madrid, at the home of his daughter María, where he died on August 10 at 10:30 p.m. At the time of his death, he was accompanied by his wife, his children María and Joaquín, his son-in-law Francisco Pons Arnau, and his pupil Fernando Viscaí. He was attended to by Drs. Sanchiz and Barús, who were substituting for his usual physicians Drs. Marañón and Lafora, who were on holiday.

His close friend Mariano Benlliure was immediately notified and made a mold of Sorolla's face for a death mask and another of his right hand with the help of his pupils, Luis Darmini and Mariano Rubio.

Sorolla's remains were taken to his house in Madrid, where a funeral chapel was erected.

The funeral procession in Madrid, led by Mariano Benlliure in representation of His Majesty the King, the Minister of Public Instruction in representation of the Spanish State, and Sorolla's son-in-law Francisco Pons Arnau, accompanied his remains to the Estación del Mediodía train station for the journey to Valencia, where he was buried with the honors of a field marshal. In Valencia, the funeral procession was again led by Mariano Benlliure in representation of His Majesty King Alfonso XIII, by the Lord Mayor of Valencia, and by the field marshal of the region. It proceeded along various streets, stopping at the Círculo de Bellas Artes club, opposite the chapel of La Virgen de los Desamparados, in front of the town hall and at the Plaza de San Agustín, where the troops marched past before the coffin. His remains were buried in the family vault in the cemetery of Valencia.

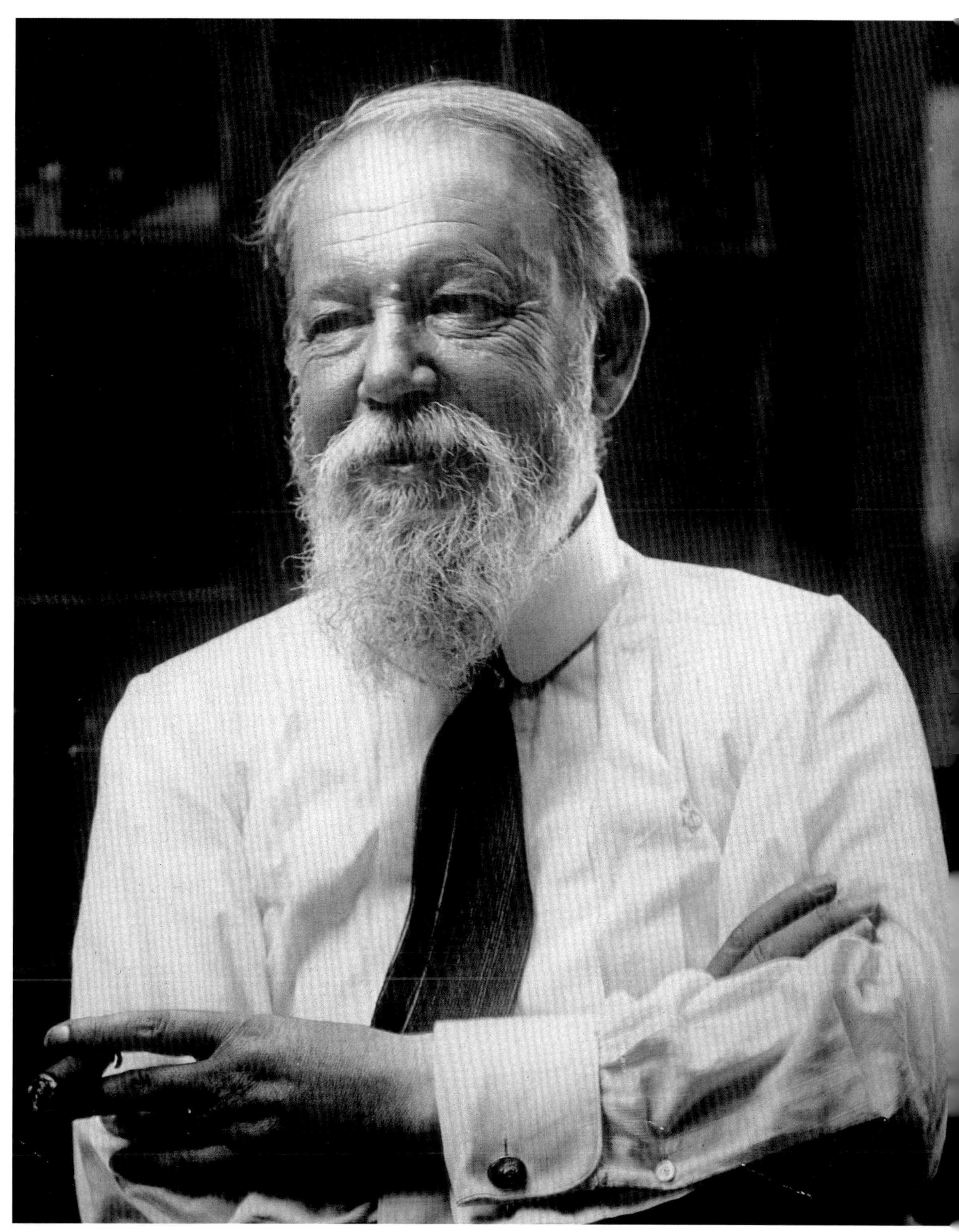

Joaquín Sorolla, 1920

JACKET *Strolling along the Seashore*, 1909. Madrid, Fundación Museo Sorolla (detail of fig. 64)

P. 2 *After the Bath*, 1908. New York, The Hispanic Society of America (detail of fig. 55)

P. 3 *María Dressed as a Valencian Farmworker*, 1906. Private collection (detail of fig. 38)

P. 4 *Boys on the Beach*, 1910. Madrid, Museo Nacional del Prado (detail of fig. 62)

P. 5 *Afternoon Sun, Beaching the Boat*, 1903. New York, The Hispanic Society of America (detail of fig. 25)

P. 6 *Garden of the Sorolla House*, 1920. Madrid, Museo Sorolla (detail of fig. 102)

P. 7 *Under the Awning, Beach at Zarautz*, 1910. St. Louis, Missouri, Saint Louis Art Museum (detail of fig. 65)

P. 8 *Self-Portrait*, 1904. Madrid, Museo Sorolla (detail of fig. 26)

The publisher wishes to express its gratitude
for the invaluable help, advice and support provided
by the Museo Sorolla and the Fundación Sorolla
throughout the production of this volume.

EDITED BY Rizzoli Electa
PRODUCED BY Ediciones El Viso
COORDINATION Lucía Varela
TRANSLATIONS Leyre Bastyr
COPY EDITING Philip Sutton
DESIGN Subiela Bernat
PREPRESS Lucam
PRINTING AND BINDING Printer Trento S.r.l., Trento

First published in the United States of America in 2012 by

Rizzoli Electa, a Division of
Rizzoli International Publications, Inc.
49 West 27th Street
New York, NY 10001
rizzoliusa.com

For Rizzoli Electa:
Charles Miers, Publisher
Margaret Rennolds Chace, Associate Publisher
Giulia Di Filippo, Editor

Library of Congress Control Number: 2012940162
ISBN: 978-0-8478-3933-9 (hardcover)

Seventeenth printing, 2026
2026 2027 2028 / 20 19 18 17
Printed in Italy

The authorized representative in the EU for product safety and compliance is Mondadori Libri S.p.A.,
via Gian Battista Vico 42, Milan, Italy, 20123, mondadori.it

Visit us online:
Instagram.com/RizzoliBooks
Facebook.com/RizzoliNewYork
Youtube.com/user/RizzoliNY

PHOTOGRAPH CREDITS

Boston, Massachusetts, © 2012 Museum of Fine Arts, Boston. All rights reserved / Scala, Florence, fig. 41
BPS Archive, pp. 23, 24-25, 68-69, 199, 201, 204, 206, 209, 212, 213 (left), 219, 221; figs. 1, 5, 6, 8, 10, 12, 15, 18, 20, 23, 30, 31, 35, 38, 39, 42, 44, 45, 50, 52, 53, 75, 81, 83, 85, 86, 88, 90, 93, 94, 96, 99, 100
Chicago, Illinois, Photograph © The Art Institute of Chicago, fig. 60
Dallas, Meadows Museum, fig. 43
Havana, Museo Nacional de Bellas Artes de Cuba, figs. 28, 48, 68
Los Angeles, California, The J. Paul Getty Museum, fig. 69
Madrid, Courtesy Banco de España, fig. 34
Madrid, Courtesy Arango Collection, fig. 29
Madrid, Cuauhtli Gutiérrez, cover, pp. 192-193, 224; fig. 58
Madrid, Museo de la Real Academia de Bellas Artes de San Fernando, fig. 13
Madrid, Museo Nacional del Prado, figs. 3, 22
Madrid, Museo Sorolla, pp. 11, 19, 21, 65, 66, 70, 71, 152, 153, 154, 158, 196, 205, 207, 210, 211, 213 (right), 215 (down); figs. 11, 26, 27, 40, 51, 57, 59, 61, 62, 63, 64, 66, 67, 70, 71, 74, 77, 78, 80, 82, 87, 89, 92, 95, 101, 102
Madrid, Patrimonio Nacional, fig. 46
México D.F., Museo Nacional de San Carlos Collection, CONACULTA-INBA, reproduction authorized by Instituto Nacional de Bellas Artes y Literarura, 2012 (Jorge Vértiz ©, CENCROPAM/INBA), fig. 16
Mexico, Courtesy Pérez Simón Collection, fig. 17
New York, © 2012. Image copyright The Metropolitan Museum of Art / Art Resource / Scala, Florence, figs. 32, 36
New York, Brooklyn Museum, fig. 21
New York, Courtesy The Hispanic Society of America, pp. 156, 157, 194-195, 215 (up), 216; figs. 25, 37, 55, 56, 73, 76, 79, 84, 91, 97, 98
Oviedo, Masaveu Collection (©2012 Gonzalo de la Serna), figs. 33, 72
Oviedo, Museo de Bellas Artes de Asturias, figs. 14, 54
Paris, Agence photographique de la Réunion des musées nationaux,
© RMN-Grand Palais (Musée d'Orsay) / Gérard Blot / Hervé Lewandowski, fig. 4
Philadelphia, Pennsylvania, Philadelphia Museum of Art / The Bridgeman Art Library, London, fig. 24
Saint Louis, Missouri, Saint Louis Art Museum, fig. 65
San Diego, California, San Diego Museum of Art, fig. 47
Udine, Civici Musei e Gallerie di Storia e Arte, fig. 2
Valencia, Museo de Bellas Artes de Valencia (Paco Alcántara), figs. 9, 49
Valencia, Museo de la Ciudad. Ayuntamiento, fig. 19
Venice, Fondazione Musei Civici Venezia, fig. 7

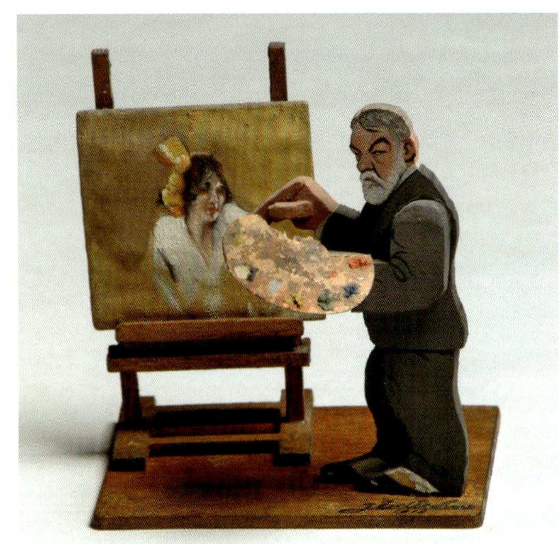

"I have never wanted to be nor do I want to be,
nor will I ever want to be anything but a painter."